T0337412

'As a Minister of Power, I had initiated path-breaking reforms in all segments: generation, transmission, and distribution and at that time had first-hand experience of the political economy of the power sector. This book is one of the few to deal with this important subject and what it means for the future of the sector. It would be of great interest to a wide range of people, including students of state politics, and power sector policymakers and regulators.'

—Suresh Prabhu, Minister of Commerce & Industry, and Civil Aviation and former Minister of Power

'Over the past quarter of a century, India has tried to reform its power sector to expand the supply of electricity, make it more accessible, reliable, and affordable. Success has been mixed because this reform is as much political as it is technocratic. What lessons do we learn from experience so far? How do we move forward now, when the new imperative of making electricity generation more environmentally sustainable is also thrown in? This anthology is the first systematic and analytical assessment of what has been accomplished and what now needs to be done. It is of value not just to academics and scholars but also to industry players themselves as well as to the policy community, politicians included.'

—Jairam Ramesh, Member of Parliament and former Union Minister

'All anecdotal evidence suggests that politics and electricity are inseparable. The systematic study in this important book provides a framework for analysis that can facilitate improvement in electricity governance in India.'

—Pramod Deo, former chairman, Central Electricity Regulatory Commission, Government of India

'*Mapping Power* is a pioneering effort to systematically understand the interaction between politics and electricity in India. The case studies of electricity reform in fifteen Indian states vividly demonstrate that if politics is about power, then power—in the form of electricity—is about politics. The book makes a compelling case that an efficient and financially resilient electricity sector can only emerge if it is also an engine of equitable development and the path to both lies in a more creative politics and not the artifice of depoliticization.'

— Devesh Kapur, Starr Foundation Professor of South Asia Studies at Paul H. Nitze School of Advanced International Studies (SAIS), Johns Hopkins University, USA

Mapping Power

Mapping Power
The Political Economy of Electricity in India's States

edited by
Navroz K. Dubash
Sunila S. Kale
Ranjit Bharvirkar

OXFORD
UNIVERSITY PRESS

OXFORD
UNIVERSITY PRESS

Oxford University Press is a department of the University of Oxford.
It furthers the University's objective of excellence in research, scholarship,
and education by publishing worldwide. Oxford is a registered trademark of
Oxford University Press in the UK and in certain other countries.

Published in India by
Oxford University Press
2/11 Ground Floor, Ansari Road, Daryaganj, New Delhi 110 002, India

ISBN-13 (print edition): 978-0-19-948782-0
ISBN-10 (print edition): 0-19-948782-0

ISBN-13 (eBook): 978-0-19-909374-8
ISBN-10 (eBook): 0-19-909374-1

Typeset in Dante MT Std 10.5/13
by The Graphics Solution, New Delhi 110 092
Printed in India by Rakmo Press, New Delhi 110 020

Contents

Preface

The power sector has proved to be a particularly sticky and pernicious problem plaguing India's political economy. For those of us tracking the sector over time, there is a repeated sense of déjà vu. At the heart of this persistence is a distribution sector that remains stubbornly resistant to a series of technical treatments over the years. Central bailout schemes are announced with fanfare, yet have to be periodically renewed, re-invented, and re-launched. Loss levels, largely due to theft, remain stubbornly high despite efforts at unbundling, regulation, and other forms of reform. Moreover, the distribution sector is periodically saddled with bad generation planning, leading to either too much high-cost power, or too little supply. For the most part, India's businesses and citizens, and among the latter particularly the poorest, cannot count on dependable electricity.

However, this experience is not uniform; some states have tried to reform and failed, some have not tried at all, and a few have tried and succeeded. Yet, in this comparative story across states lies a mystery: given the importance of electricity to livelihoods and quality of life, surely improving electricity is a sure-fire path to political success? If so, why is it not taken more often and more successfully?

The editors of this volume have individually, over the years, grappled with this question in our writings in various ways. Navroz K. Dubash has, in a series of articles in the *Economic and Political Weekly* and elsewhere, looked at the record of state efforts at distribution reform, at introduction of competition and choice, and in an earlier book co-authored with Narasimha Rao, at the experience with state electricity regulators—*The Practice and Politics of Regulation*. Sunila S. Kale has authored the first serious historically rooted comparative analysis of state electricity politics—*Electrifying India*. Ranjit Bharvirkar has worked with government institutions, regulators, civil society groups, and NGOs in various states examining state-specific reform and has also looked at state experiences with emergent renewable energy for the erstwhile Planning Commission.

This volume emerged from our collective conviction arising out of our past work that to improve Indian electricity, we need a better understanding of the political economy of the sector. Technical solutions that dominate the discourse—how to introduce open access, how to fix bidding arrangements, how to improve regulation—are all necessary. However, they rest on the political willingness and ability to make and execute necessary decisions. If there is a single message of this book it is this: the path forward for Indian electricity lies through finding ways to generate more political pay-offs from improving electricity, and to do so requires understanding the political economy of the sector. In the introduction to this book, we lay out our framework for doing so, the 15 state-cases that follow put that framework to use, and the conclusion draws out the lessons from comparative experience.

It is our hope that this volume will help provide a bridge, so that those interested in state politics understand and engage the importance of electricity to state politics, and those focused on electricity appreciate the relevance of the larger political context within which they operate. We also hope that the volume induces more substantive engagement with the different realities of each state, rather than examining electricity predominantly through a central government lens.

In an effort to understand state-specific experiences, this volume is built around research conducted by an exceptional group of young scholars—the authors—each of whom spent time in one or more states conducting interviews, gathering information, and drawing the material into a compelling state specific narrative. One of the authors, Ashwini K. Swain, contributed greatly by also compiling quantitative data across the various state chapters. The authors all contributed to shaping the substance of the volume through discussion and feedback on drafts. The simple fact that so many high-level young scholars now see the electricity sector as an exciting area for the study of politics is a hopeful sign. The authors had considerable opportunity for interaction with the editors, both in person and virtually, in order to forge a cogent volume. We are grateful that they have chosen to participate and give their time and effort to this project.

We are also deeply grateful to the many government representatives, utility officials, regulatory officials, civil society, and media representatives who granted the authors time, and shared their wisdom and insight. While the final papers represent the views of chapter author(s), and the interviewees cannot be held responsible for the conclusions reported here, this work would not have been possible without their expert assistance.

Two senior colleagues, Pramod Deo, former Chair of Central Electricity Regulatory Commission (CERC), and Shantanu Dixit of the Prayas Energy Group, attended a preliminary workshop and shared their wisdom on interview approaches and techniques with the authors, for which we are very grateful. Daljit Singh read and commented on various outputs from this project, and also contributed a background paper. Vishnu Rao contributed greatly to the background understanding of the Tamil Nadu study. Two research assistants, Jonathan James Guy and Nikhil Mandalaparthy, ably assisted with editing, referencing, and fact-checking.

At the Centre for Policy Research, Ankit Bharadwaj and Madhura Joshi helped with research and administrative assistance, and Richa Bansal and Dhruv Arora managed communication and outreach. Navroz K. Dubash's contribution to this project was supported through a grant for energy and climate work at the Centre for Policy Research from the Oak Foundation, USA.

At the Regulatory Assistance Project, Robert Lieberman provided invaluable support and assistance in conceiving this project and brainstorming at various points during the analysis phase including review of the document.

Part of Sunila S. Kale's time in India in 2016 was supported by a Fulbright-Nehru Academic and Professional Excellence Award. At the University of Washington, thanks for research assistance to Vinnu Komanapalli, and for generous leave to colleagues at the Jackson School of International Studies and its director, Resat Kasaba.

We are also grateful to two anonymous referees for their comments, which were incisive and helped us sharpen the final product. Finally, we are thankful for the able stewardship of this project by the team at Oxford University Press.

Navroz K. Dubash
Sunila S. Kale
Ranjit Bharvirkar

Tables and Figures

Tables

Figures

Abbreviations

AAP	Aam Aadmi Party
ACS	Average Cost of Supply
ADB	Asian Development Bank
APDP	Accelerated Power Development Programme
APDRP	Accelerated Power Development and Reform Programme
APTEL	Appellate Tribunal for Electricity
ARR	Average Revenue Realized
AT&C	Aggregate Technical & Commercial
BJP	Bharatiya Janata Party
BPL	Below poverty line
CAG	Comptroller and Auditor General of India
CAGR	Compounded annual growth rate
CAPEX	Capital expenditure
CEA	Central Electricity Authority
CERC	Central Electricity Regulatory Commission
CM	Chief Minister
CPI(M)	Communist Party of India (Marxist)
CPP	Captive Power Plant
CSO	Civil society organization
DDUGJY	Deendayal Upadhyaya Gram Jyoti Yojana
discom	Distribution company
DSM	Demand-Side measures/management
EHT	Extra high-tension
FDI	Foreign direct investment
GoI	Government of India
GSDP	Gross State Domestic Product
GST	Goods and Service Tax
GSVA	Gross State Value Added

HT	High-tension
IAS	Indian Administrative Service
INC	Indian National Congress
IPP	Independent power producer
JD	Janata Dal
JGY	Jyotigram Yojana
LT	Low tension
MNRE	Ministry of New and Renewable Energy
MoU	Memorandum of understanding
MSP	Minimum support price
MW	Megawatt
NDA	National Democratic Alliance
NHPC	National Hydro Power Corporation
NSVA	Net state value added
NTPC	National Thermal Power Corporation
O&M	Operations and maintenance
OA	Open access
OBC	Other backward classes
OPEX	Operating expenditure
PAC	Public Accounts Committee
PFC	Power Finance Corporation
PPA	Power Purchase Agreement
PSE	Public sector enterprise
PwC	PricewaterhouseCoopers
R&M	Renovation and modernization
RA	Regulatory Assets
R-APDRP	Restructured-Accelerated Power Development and Reforms Programme
RE	Renewable energy
REC	Rural Electrification Corporation
RGGVY	Rajiv Gandhi Grameen Vidyutikaran Yojana
RPO	Renewable Purchase Obligation
RRF	Rural Revenue Franchisees
RWA	Resident Welfare Association
SAC	State Advisory Committee
SAIL	Steel Authority of India
SC	Scheduled caste
SEB	State Electricity Board

SERC	State Electricity Regulatory Commission
SPSE	State public sector enterprise
SPV	Special Purpose Vehicle
SS	Shiv Sena
ST	Scheduled tribe
T&D	Transmission and distribution
Transco	Transmission Company
UDAY	Ujwal Discom Assurance Yojana
WB	World Bank

SUNILA S. KALE

NAVROZ K. DUBASH

RANJIT BHARVIRKAR

Introduction

A Framework for Mapping Power

Twenty-five years after 'power sector reform' was enshrined as a key component of India's larger process of economic liberalization, the key facts in the sector remain depressingly familiar. State electric utilities continue to face high levels of both losses and debts, the latter serving as a continued drag on state exchequers (Figure I.1).[1] Even more significantly, there remains a sizeable portion of the population without access to electricity and an even larger share without high-quality access (Figure I.2). A cycle of electricity shortages has been replaced by a glut of overpriced power in some states, exacerbating problems at the distribution end of the sector. Further, as a new twist on old problems, during 2016–17, India witnessed the simultaneous coexistence of surplus power capacity and hundreds of millions without power.[2]

This persistence of problems—albeit often in new forms—comes despite several generations of reform efforts, beginning in the early 1990s. These include, opening doors and providing incentives to new private generation; a spate of distribution-company and regulatory reforms, often but not always stimulated by international financial agencies; an omnibus federal Electricity Act in 2003 intended to nudge the

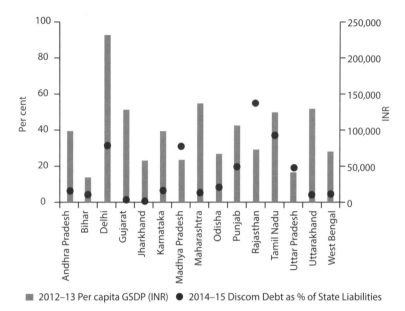

FIGURE I.1   State Economic Metrics
Source: Power Finance Corporation Limited (PFC). 2011, 2013, 2015, 2016. *Reports on Performance of State Power Utilities.* New Delhi. (We have given data only for the 15 states included in this volume.)

sector towards a competitive market structure; and successive efforts by the central government to bail out and restructure distribution company finances. As this list should prove, the problems in the sector have not persisted for want of effort at solutions. But their persistence speaks to a common, and underlying, flaw in the approach taken thus far.

A signal thesis of this volume is that the catalogue of past efforts to reform the power sector fundamentally has failed to engage with the sector's embeddedness in the broader politics of power in India's states. Most of the aforementioned reforms emanated from government agencies in New Delhi, but their implementation—like most implementation in the power sector—has taken place in the country's scattered provincial capitals, by state-level bureaucrats, politicians, and engineers. By 'mapping power', we refer to the need to understand the power sector's role in both shaping and being shaped by electoral politics, the extent to which efforts at reform work with or against existing political currents, and, ultimately, whether reform can result in a

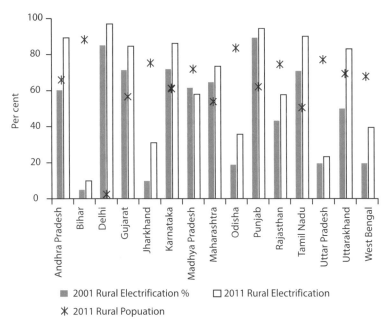

■ 2001 Rural Electrification % □ 2011 Rural Electrification

✳ 2011 Rural Popuation

FIGURE I.2   State Rural Electrification
Source: Central Statistics Office (CSO). 2010, 2012, 2014, and 2016. *Energy Statistics.*
New Delhi: Ministry of Statistics and Programme Implementation, Government
of India. (We have given data only for the 15 states included in this volume.)

sustainable virtuous cycle in which providing better power also brings
more political rewards. A common thread running through past reform
measures is the impulse to bypass or insulate the sector from politics.
This impulse, we argue, is misplaced. Electricity reform will succeed
only if it provides greater political payoffs from change than from maintaining a flawed status quo, and this is how it should be in a democratic
polity.

Understanding how to build a virtuous political cycle in the power
sector requires starting at the state level, although certainly supple-
mented by an understanding of central and international effects, and
technology drivers. It also means taking seriously the diversity of state
politics and state power sectors, even while recognizing patterns in that
diversity. Finally, it requires exploring politics beyond the power sector
alone, including party politics, the politics of regionalism within states,

and patterns of economic development. For all these reasons, this volume is organized around state case studies.

By focusing on the specificities of states and patterns among them, we hope this volume moves beyond asserting that politics matters to electricity outcomes, to proposing ways of understanding how it matters. Furthermore, how it matters inevitably varies with state context; there is no single uniform prescription for change. In this introductory chapter, we propose a framework for analysing state politics, including party politics; key power sector variables like subsidies and the cost of supply; and an attention to the real and imagined gains from the distribution reforms of the late 1990s. This framework is put to work in the fifteen state case-study chapters that follow. The resultant mapping of power, in both senses of the term, we argue is a necessary first step to designing democratically sustainable electricity reforms.

Even as India's power sector is seized with twentieth century problems, however, the emergent challenges of the new century loom large. Larger global forces are driving down costs in renewable energy, making coal fired power plants less attractive to invest in, and making possible new forms of grid and demand management. All of these suggest the potential, perhaps even the necessity, of entirely rethinking the organization of electricity.[3] How will Indian states, grappling with mundane problems of theft, inefficiency, debt, and high cost, fast forward into this new electricity era? Understanding the problems of the past is essential to addressing the challenges of the future. Drawing on the state case studies, we raise a set of questions around whether and how the new direction of electricity will exacerbate existing problems, provide unexpected solutions, or even render redundant the old problems.

In the remainder of this introduction, we examine and critique current diagnoses for India's problematic power sector and make a case for why a political economy focus paired with an institutional lens provides a useful approach. Following this, we provide a short historical review of the Indian power sector, outline our analytic framework and methods, and finally, provide a set of state 'snapshots' that anticipate the volume's empirical chapters.

Flawed Diagnoses and Incomplete Solutions

Debates over the diagnoses of problems in the Indian power sector and possible solutions have been shaped by a variety of global ideas. A key literature to tap in analysing the power sector focuses on the effectiveness of state-owned enterprises, including public utilities. One view that has been dominant over the last several decades avers that state-owned firms are beset with inefficiencies, corruption, and poor performance compared to private firms.[4] Drawing on global examples, some have argued that the pathology of public ownership plays out through principal-agent problems, soft-budget constraints, and the lack of penalty for poor management.[5] Others point to excessive state intervention leading to rent seeking and corruption, with the ancillary effect of limiting growth and development.[6] The associated policy prescriptions, then, advocate following a global model of reform and restructuring[7] in order to limit the role of the state and public sector firms, whether through outright privatization of state assets or through the growth of private actors alongside publicly owned utilities;[8] mechanisms to enable greater competition;[9] and independent regulators to limit the influence and pressures of politics.[10]

At another point on the spectrum are critics of centralized approaches to energy, many of whom are motivated by the failure of the grid to provide universal and adequate power, particularly for rural, poor, and dispersed citizens. Often these types of arguments rest on an implicit and occasionally explicit argument that decentralization of all types—whether in governance, public services, or electricity supply—is better able to address local needs. Advocates of decentralized energy provision emphasize technology-driven solutions like small-scale generation, micro-grids, and distributed renewables.[11]

In our view, both categories of analysis ignore the potential political implications of their proposed solutions. Despite two decades of effort, reorganizing the sector around open access to spur competition, privatization, and carriage and content separation have failed to substantially change the sector. The failure is largely explained by the fact that these solutions pose political risks that few state-level political actors, who both want to provide public services to their constituencies and get re-elected, would want to hazard.[12] The bureaucrats, engineers, and politicians are neither all venal nor all incapable of seeing clearly the problems in the energy sector; rather the solutions on offer suggest following the impossible route of 'depoliticizing' what is inherently a political set of calculations and choices. The second category of analysis is equally problematic. Decentralized supply poses a risk to the very public nature of the grid; like all public spaces, the grid reinforces the idea of society as a collective, bound together through mutual obligations and responsibilities. Further, and more pragmatically, consumers consigned to what is now, at least, unstable, low quality, and potentially higher cost electricity may well organize politically to demand better options.[13]

In short, both of these categories of analyses fail to take seriously the political consequences of power provision in a state's political economy, and in turn, how the weight of the broader political economy exerts pressures and constraints on the kinds of options that are available to state actors. As the fifteen state-level chapters of this volume propose, those state governments that have improved their power sector's performance have done so by pursuing reforms that take cognizance of political realities. A better starting point for any analysis of the power sector, we suggest, is the recognition that the sector and its challenges are inherently political problems, and only by understanding them as such and devising solutions that take political dynamics into account can progress be made in terms of building an inclusive, equitable, and financially durable electricity sector. The research from this project suggests that policies that are designed solely to insulate the sector from politics or to 'depoliticize' the sector, as have been attempted for the last several decades in India, will yield few benefits. Instead, reform programmes that have explicitly engaged the political challenges of the sector have a better chance at being implemented in ways that are attuned to state-level needs.

Beyond pointing to vague categories like 'political will' or 'corruption', we propose that a more useful framework to understand India's power sector is rooted in a political economy analysis of the sector as it is embedded in the larger state political economy. Our approach is also informed by an attention to how institutions (or the 'rules of the game') shape trajectories (including path dependence, the 'stickiness of rules', and how new rules often become layered atop older ones rather than replacing them)[14] and structure how actors in the sector understand the constraints and opportunities that face them.

Indian Power over Seventy Years

From Colonial Inheritance to Layered Deadlock

In 1947, Independent India inherited an electric system that was concentrated in the cities, uneven across provinces, and with far lower per capita consumption than in the advanced industrial economies to which Indian planners and engineers anxiously compared themselves.[15]

At independence, with few exceptions, India's planners, politicians, and nationalists were all convinced of the need to electrify the country as a whole in order to confront the vast economic and social challenges facing them. In an instance of institutional 'stickiness', the 1948 Electricity Act, produced in parallel to the drafting of the constitution, kept intact key features of energy sector governance that had prevailed under the British, namely that electricity remained on the concurrent list of the constitution. However, in a stark departure from British policy, each newly created state was mandated to set up a publicly owned, vertically integrated utility, a State Electricity Board (SEB). In part, such a moment of institutional change was possible because global standards for the sector were also pointing in this direction; most newly sovereign countries in Asia, Africa, and Latin America were following similar routes of building state-owned monopoly utilities.

Retaining electricity under joint control of central government and states soon produced problems. In a foreshadowing of the future inability of the central government to enforce action, many states delayed setting up SEBs, in some cases by a decade and a half. State governments made immense progress in building their grids outwards from provincial capitals. However, they also often succumbed to rivalry with adjacent states over shared natural resources such as coal and waterways, and also failed to make most effective use of scarce capital and natural resources.

From the 1960s to the 1980s the costs of supply came to outstrip the revenues generated in the sector. In some states, this was the result of an eager focus on rural electrification and ancillary efforts to make rural access more widespread by lowering tariffs, with the aim of transforming rural development.[16] In states that became the key sources of food staples—rice, wheat, sugarcane—the provision of rural electricity transformed rain-fed agriculture by enabling groundwater pumping. In other states, technical inefficiencies in distribution and transmission were joined by increasing levels of thefts. Furthermore, the shift from meters to flat-rate tariffs for agricultural users, a policy that began in Punjab in 1968 and continued to diffuse across states over the next several decades, distorted SEB bookkeeping with the effect that good data in the sector became extremely scarce.

Flat-rate tariffs have persisted even as their negative effects became more widely understood.

With declining levels of investment available for transmission and distribution, the overall technical efficiency of state utilities suffered, leading to shortages and increasingly creaky wires. Most states offset losses on account of non-remunerative agricultural consumption as well as technical and financial inefficiencies by cross-subsidizing the better-paying segments of the load: industry, commercial establishments, and in some cases urban domestic consumers.

In response to these problems, the central government expanded its own presence in the sector through successive efforts at layering new actors and rules on top of existing ones, each tasked with responding to a perceived deficiency in the sector. The process began with the Rural Electrification Corporation in 1969 (to finance rural projects), the formation of the National Thermal Power Corporation (NTPC) and National Hydro Power Corporation (NHPC) in 1975 (to enable larger-scale generation), the Power Finance Corporation in 1986 and the Power Grid Corporation in 1989 (to build out the country's high-voltage transmission system). As piecemeal solutions, each of these central government attempts was effective at tackling particular aspects of the sector's governance; for example, the total generating capacity benefitted substantially due to the growth NTPC and NHPC.

Taken collectively, however, the central government's efforts failed to provide a comprehensive solution to the most intractable problems facing the sector. In some cases, a solution in one arena had the perverse effect of making another problem more acute. For example, while NTPC provided much-needed capacity additions, its health and robustness has seemingly gone hand-in-hand with the financial weakening of state utilities, in the process exacerbating many of the challenges facing state governments today. By the early 1990s, many distribution sectors faced a series of endemic problems (high loss levels, incomplete electrification, power shortages, underinvestment in transmission and distribution), some of which were the result of the initial institutional framework that made coordination along the lines of a national grid difficult, and others of which were the unintended consequences of piecemeal or 'layered' changes over the four decades after the 1948 legislation was enacted.

The Reform Era

A new era for energy governance began in the 1990s as part of the overall shift in Indian economic policy away from the Nehruvian order of public ownership and government control. This turn within India corresponded to global ideological changes in energy sector governance that were underway since the late 1970s, which sought to create more spaces where private companies could operate in a sector that was once firmly understood to be the prerogative of the state.[17] Some of the events of the reform era preceded the Electricity Act 2003 (hereafter EA03) and others have followed from it. In many instances, a few states had already experimented with reforms that were later copied and reinforced by the central legislation.

The Indian power sector, with its problems of insufficient supply and financially troubled utilities, was in the direct cross hairs of reformers. From the 1990s, various layers of reform have been attempted by state governments and mandated by New Delhi, including a push to privatize generation, privatize distribution (with only marginal success), the organization of an independent regulatory system throughout the 1990s, and episodic experiments in financial and organizational restructuring supported by various multilateral lending agencies and by the central government.[18] The World Bank, in particular, had a considerable role shaping the agenda for reform, driven by its own 1993 policy laying out a vision for power sector lending to developing countries.[19]

Electricity generation became one of the first sections of the Indian economy to be opened up to private investment, beginning in 1991. Reformers believed that a rush of private money heralded by the hundreds of MOUs signed with private companies and entrepreneurs, would enable capacity additions and also wrest more efficiency and productivity from public utilities. Even though only a small number of the initial MOUs materialized as new power plants, the cumulative effect has been transformative. From a sector dominated by publicly owned capacity up until the early 1990s, privately owned generating capacity has grown rapidly over the last two decades. As of 2016, 42 per cent of generating assets are in the private sector, 33 per cent are owned by state-level utilities, and 25 per cent by the central government utilities that were established in 1975.[20]

Unlike privatization of the generation sector, however, distribution company (discom) privatization has had limited success and mixed results.[21] Only two states—Delhi and Odisha—fully privatized their distribution sectors in the early 2000s; by 2015, Odisha's four distribution utilities all had returned to government control after a decade and a half of desultory performance under private owners. Despite these experiences and the lack of interest from buyers, though, there continues to be talk about distribution privatization as a catchall solution.

Of all of the reform steps, it is perhaps the creation of independent regulators that promised to address what by the mid-1990s was identified as the core problem of the distribution sector—the intermixing of utility governance with political considerations. Although the first Electricity Regulatory Commissions were created by individual states authorized by state-level legislation, the central government quickly superseded these decentralized acts with a decree of its own, the Electricity Regulatory Commissions Act, 1998. As the literature suggests and the state-specific chapters in this volume confirm, the State Electricity Regulatory Commissions (SERCs) function quite differently across the country and with varied effectiveness.[22]

Finally, the central government has periodically led financial and organizational renovation and restructuring of state electricity sectors. The first of these attempts, the Accelerated Power Development Programme (APDP), in 1999 required establishment of regulatory commissions, unbundling of the integrated SEB, and 100 per cent metering in exchange for funds to renovate older power plants and strengthen their distribution and transmission networks. The programme was expanded, refurbished, and renamed twice; first in 2001 (as the Accelerated Power Development and Reform Programme [APDRP]) and then again in 2008 as the Restructured-APDRP (R-APDRP). More recently, in 2015, the central government announced a new initiative, Ujwal Discom Assurance Yojana (or UDAY). Like its predecessors, the goal of this programme is to improve the operational and financial efficiency of distribution utilities. The innovation of UDAY was in the financing mechanism; rather than issuing grants or loans, UDAY transfers the bulk of discom debt to the state government, allowing utilities to re-enter markets with sounder financial health. State governments and discoms can in turn raise cash to repay lenders by issuing bonds. As of June 2017, 27 states had signed up for UDAY and several of these have successfully issued UDAY bonds. As the state-level empirical papers that follow suggest, however, a number of state-level policymakers and bureaucrats view UDAY as falling in the long line of restructuring measures that came before, and are sceptical that it constitutes a permanent solution to the problems facing their states.

Twenty-First Century Challenges

The ongoing challenges of the past risk being exacerbated in the early part of the twenty-first century by two new challenges. The first relates to uncertainties and shifts in electricity demand. India has historically struggled to meet rapidly increasing electricity demand, fuelled by rapid economic growth; industrial and commercial activity has grown, and so has household demand as income growth has expanded appliance use. As a result, in the first decade and a half of this century thermal power plants were being constructed in India at a rapid clip, with 92 GW added in the Twelfth Five Year Plan from 2012–17, a remarkable 42 per cent of the total thermal capacity as of October 2017.[23] However, increasingly mining and transportation sectors have been unable to keep pace, such that India began importing coal for the first time in its history despite the country's substantial coal reserves, which in turn led to a substantial push to ramp up domestic coal production. More recently there are strong indications of an overshoot in demand growth projections. Decreased demand for Indian exports due to the global financial crisis, growing global protectionism, and weak competitiveness have muted industrial demand.[24] Unexpected success with energy efficiency programmes may be another factor.[25]

This has led to a curious phenomenon where India has rapidly shifted from a chronically scarce power situation to a 'surplus' power capacity country. This situation has an effect on the finances of the sector, as existing plants have to back down and run at uneconomically low rates.[26] The term 'surplus' is misleading, however, as excess capacity coincides with roughly 40 million households without access to power.[27] The coincidence of these two seemingly contradictory facts is due almost entirely to the unresolved political economy of the distribution companies. As loss-making entities, discoms would rather limit sales to low-tariff rural and poor consumers.

A second set of challenge arises from rapid technological changes in the sector. This has enabled the steep decline in the cost of renewable energy (RE) and electricity storage technologies rapidly in India and globally, driven by global forces.[28] As a result, RE is increasingly becoming the cheapest source of electricity globally, with implications both for existing generation assets and in how the electricity system is managed. Both renewable electricity and storage are highly modular and eminently scalable and can be deployed at both utility-scale (that is, hundreds of megawatts) and small-scale (that is, a few kilowatts), the latter making it suitable for end-users to generate electricity directly rather than procuring it from the grid.[29] By contrast, conventional sources of electricity—coal-fired, nuclear, hydroelectric, and gas-fired—are cost-effective only when deployed at utility scale. As a result of these technological changes, the well-understood historical nature of the power sector is starting to change rapidly; the growth of RE promises to turn consumers into active participants in the power sector, an unprecedented phenomenon.[30] While less widely discussed, an additional technological change is the growing scope for enhanced energy efficiency, in part enabled by information technology. Indian policymakers, or indeed policymakers anywhere, have limited experience to draw on in designing electricity systems that suit these new technologies.

Addressing past and ongoing problems of making realistic demand projections, improving financial performance, expanding quality and access, as well as future challenges of negotiating an RE transition have an important factor in common: they all are likely to be shaped and constrained by the historical legacy of power sector governance. The starting point, therefore, is to understand the path-dependent manner in which Indian states have either locked themselves into their current low levels of performance, or in more rare cases, set their state's power sectors on more positive trajectories. In order to provide such a historically informed investigation, we deploy a uniform analytical framework across this volume.

Analytic Framework

The state-level analyses are informed by a framework, which we arrived at inductively and iteratively updated based on early field reports, interview material, and preliminary analyses produced by the research team working in their individual field sites. This framework identifies key factors and variables and the dynamics through which state politics interacts with changes in the power sector.

A few key overarching themes inform the state-level research. First, power sector dynamics cannot be understood independent of broader political economy trends. Second, state-specific political economy considerations are key to understanding the political economy of the power sector. Third, sector governance reforms have often carried an implicit assumption that electricity governance should aim at *insulating* the sector from politics. This is likely misguided; our research suggests that it is better to understand the extent to which reforms are informed by and address the political context in each state. These dynamics are captured in Figure I.3, which helps identify key factors and variables to be explored through state-specific research, and which also informs the discussion in the concluding chapter.

A motivating question for this project is to ask why India's electric utilities have failed to achieve the minimal *outcomes* (represented on the right-hand side of Figure I.3) of universal electricity access, quality electric supply, financial stability, and environmental quality, which we understand to be the ultimate goals of any electricity sector. Answers to this question have typically focused on the *reforms* attempted over the last 20 years, with an almost unchecked assumption that tweaking the rules of the game (for example, by unbundling) or introducing new sets of rules and actors (like regulators and private actors) would help to achieve these minimum expectations. These include the global 'standard model' of reform: state-led internal reforms, financial restructuring, and emergent forms of outsourcing.

A key question that motivates our volume's state-level analyses is: to what extent has the design and application of reforms addressed the particular problems and the particular politics of each state's electricity sector? Based on our case studies, we identify four categories that are crucial for any understanding of the political economy of power: *demand for access and service quality, demand for subsidies, cost of supply,* and *available financial space.* Our particular focus is on how these technical parameters, which are certainly part of the literature and public debate, shape state politics as we explain below:

1. *Demand for access and service quality*: Are state leaders confronted by a mobilized demand for enhanced access to electricity, or for improved service quality?

2. *Demand for subsidies*: Do state leaders face a political demand for subsidies, whether explicit or implicit, where the failure to provide

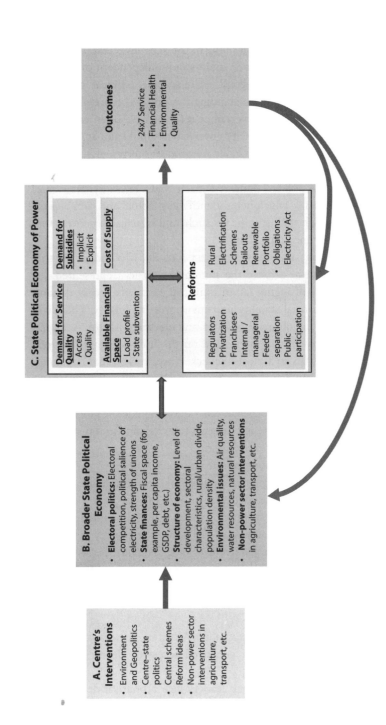

FIGURE I.3   Analytical Framework for Mapping Power
Source: Authors.

these subsidies (or the threat of their elimination) imposes political costs? By demand for explicit subsidies, we mean mobilization by various groups for subsidised tariffs, whereas demand for implicit subsidies includes direct theft and opportunities for graft where efforts to restrain these actions risk political costs.

3. *Cost of supply*: How high are the costs of supply in the state? This is a function of the nature of generating sources within the state, the quality of long-term contracts, and also the state's ability to access low cost power from wholesale markets.

4. *Financial space*: What is the balance of factors that enables a state to financially manage political demands while avoiding a cycle of declining quality and deteriorating finances? This category is an amalgam of: (a) the ability to cross-subsidize which depends on load profile (proportion of industrial users) and the extent of open access utilization and/or captive power use that limits that cross-subsidy; and (b) extent of potential transfers from non-electricity sector fiscal resources, from either state government or centre, that serve as a buffer for the power sector.

The first two—demand for access/quality and subsidies—represent political demands placed on the system, and the last two represent the extent of breathing room that enables states to manage those political demands. These four categories, combined with the reform process and the interaction between them, constitute a way to map the political economy of power in states (Figure I.3: C).

A key theme of this volume, however, is that the political economy of electricity in Indian states is not determined solely by factors internal to the electricity sector; instead electricity politics is shaped by and shapes the larger state political economy (Figure I.3: B). Electoral politics, in particular the presence or absence of competitive populism (free power to select groups, for example) drives subsidy demands. But it can also be salient to generation politics, as with controversial independent power producer (IPP) projects. Labour politics, another element in state political economy, can affect the prospects of attracting industry, and also be directly salient to electricity politics, by shaping the scope for distribution company reform. Load profile is also shaped by state politics, as in efforts to attract industry or the push for rural electrification, both of which significantly change the load profile. A characteristic of the volume is the effort to locate the political economy of electricity in *broader state political economy*.

An important caveat: though our focus in this volume is on state-level analyses, we recognize that an individual state's political economy is also shaped by *central government interventions* (Figure I.3: A), factors such as which government is in power, ideas about the power sector, and mandates for RE. Similarly, we also recognize how non-power interventions (Figure I.3: A), such as inter-sectoral linkages in the future between transport and power and the connection between water and power in the agricultural sector, could lead to transformative changes in the power sector and its politics. While we consider these issues in brief, they are not the focus of our theoretical framework or of the empirical chapters. This is because analytical depth requires some focus, and we have sought to shine the spotlight on the details of state politics, which, in our view, are the most understudied element of the electricity sector. We hope that our volume will help support and propel future studies that take up these very important issues in a similarly comparative framework.

Approach and Methods

The case studies that comprise this volume apply the analytical framework described above to fifteen states. Since our primary approach is inductive, we sought cases that could reasonably be expected to capture the range of state circumstances. The resultant choice of states meets this criterion, with the exception of representation from the Northeast, which is an unfortunate shortcoming.

Chapters are based on qualitative social research methods, primarily semi-structured interviews to harness the insights of key actors that populate the sector, buttressed by robust use of quantitative and other forms of data available from the government. During one month of field research, researchers carried out anywhere from twenty to forty interviews, largely on a not-for-attribution basis, in addition to gathering relevant data and reports and carrying out broader literature reviews. Interviewees included regulators (retired and active), energy secretaries (retired and former), managing directors or other senior managers of discoms, consultants, journalists who cover power sector issues, and civil society groups.

Each case study chapter has common elements. First, consistent with our historically attuned framework, individual chapters delineate the historical currents that have produced the contemporary outcomes in each state, with electricity policy and politics broken down into discreet historical periods in order to depict more clearly the forces that have unfolded over time in each state. Second, every state-level analysis contains a timeline depicting key moments in electricity policy and key political developments in the state, with the aim of enabling a sharper analysis of the political dimensions that have guided, constrained, or enabled electricity policy. Third, each chapter makes use of a common set of quantitative data accessed from the Power Finance Corporation in order to provide a larger numerical context for the accompanying narrative. While data discrepancies continue to be a problem in Indian power discussions, we have sought to minimize (but not eliminate) the resultant difficulty of comparison across states by confining ourselves to data from a single, reputable source.

The research approach also built in several procedures to enhance consistency of approach across the states, collaborative learning, and quality control. To ensure consistency and collaboration, the researchers were brought together with the editors at the inception of the project and midway through the research. Despite our efforts to normalize the research process and output, there remain important points of divergence across the state-level analyses contained in the following fifteen chapters. In part, this is due to the profoundly different conditions and contexts of each state, a fact that was an important intellectual motivation for us in carrying out this project. Given the varied social and political terrain of India, a proper analysis of the power sector in India must start as the sum of its various state-level parts.

Mapping Power: A Snapshot

To conclude this introduction, we provide a brief snapshot of each state case study. Each description outlines the dominant state narrative, and draws attention to specific explanatory factors that drive electricity politics in each state. As these brief descriptions suggest, the state cases represent considerable diversity. But as we discuss in the concluding chapter, they also enable the construction of an analytical framework through which to systematically examine the politics of electricity in

Indian states. We return to the larger questions that animate this volume in the final chapter.

Andhra Pradesh's (AP) electoral politics has frequently provided electricity a starring role, largely due to the way that electoral competition between the state's two main parties (the Telugu Desam Party [TDP] and Congress), first led to flat rate tariffs in 1982, contributing to financial losses, lack of investments, and deteriorating quality of supply. With World Bank support, the TDP (led by Naidu) embarked on reform and restructuring, with the prospect of future privatization. The accompanying steep tariff hike that led to mass protest, interpreted as an anti-reform backlash and a signal cause of the TDP's electoral loss in 2004. The reintroduction of free power to farmers by the Congress further entrenched subsidies. Under Congress rule from 2004–11, the sector experienced another bout of shortfalls, losses, and growing subsidy, until 2014, when under Naidu's TDP again, and post separation with Telangana, AP gained from a slightly enhanced industrial load share and decreased agricultural load share. Naidu has since embarked on a more stealthy reform effort, focused on new investments in supply, efforts at energy efficiency, as well as signing up for the UDAY scheme. AP illustrates the constraints on reform efforts compounded by inadequate attention to the challenges of political transition.

Bihar's electricity sector was in low-level equilibrium for many years. Rural electrification was limited, and therefore the state had little agricultural consumption. The seeds for change were sowed during the Lalu era of the 1990s. Although Bihar's power sector deteriorated, newly empowered lower castes demanded public service improvements, including in electricity. By the time Nitish Kumar emerged as chief minister in 2005, and even more so in his second term, he was able to capitalize on this demand and benefit politically by providing reliable and universal electricity. The conditions for reform were favourable: a combination of initially low political pressure and stress on the regulatory process because of low access, high political support for enhanced access, central funds for grid-extension, and the availability of low-cost market purchases enabled Bihar to take advantage of surplus power in other states. Consequently, Bihar was able to shift from low-level equilibrium to a virtuous cycle. To sustain this cycle, however,

Bihar will have to avoid future subsidy traps and potential future supply constraints.

Delhi's electricity sector represents a case of privatization in the face of electoral populism. There was strong initial electoral support for privatization-based reform introduced by the Congress government, which did indeed yield some service quality gains to customers and political advantage to the incumbent government. However, it also set in place the seeds of future discontent, by introducing tension between the credibility of the reform package and that of the regulator. Reforms became politically unpopular through mobilization of active political support around limiting tariff hikes and questioning the gains from reform. Moreover, financial pressures rose as a result of two forces: growing regulatory assets allowed by the regulator as a way of staving off tariff increases and increases in power purchase costs due to imprudent contract lock-in. A new Aam Aadmi Party (AAP) government sought to bring about consumer gains through transparency-focused reform along with targeted subsidies, but this fell afoul of Delhi's federal politics. Reform allowed Delhi to change the equation between politics and electricity, but not in a manner that was sustainable.

Gujarat's power sector in the 1990s followed a path similar to other relatively prosperous states. A high share of industrial consumption helped buoy the sector's finances, enabling populist measures to agriculturists, notably flat-rate tariffs and diminished accountability. This pattern shifted when a decade of competitive elections came to an end in 1998, replaced by a long period of BJP rule. Under conditions of electoral stability, that state not only undertook a gradual set of reforms that included establishing a regulator, unbundling, feeder separation to introduce transparency, but also struck a political deal with farmers to curtail, rationalize, and improve the quality of agricultural supply. Several conjunctural factors also helped: an unusually high state capacity, an effective regulatory commission that was able to challenge the reported Aggregate Technical & Commercial (AT&C) loss figures and the state's broader economic success enabled both continued cross-subsidies and direct fiscal support. Gujarat also became a leader in RE capacity, although that first-mover position has loaded the state with expensive RE contracts in a period of rapidly declining RE costs. The overarching story, however, is of Gujarat using its breathing space and favourable economic conditions to carve out a gradual reform process that provided political rewards for power sector improvements.

Jharkhand was carved out of Bihar, and at the time of separation received an endowment of cheap power, sources of cheap natural resources (for example, coal), and a large industrial customer base. However, the power sector has been treated as a source of rents through contracts rather than a source of political support, with successive unstable and short-term governments following an extractive rather than developmental approach. Moreover, the industrial customer base was tied to private utilities and the Damodar Valley Corporation (a Government of India undertaking) and therefore was not available as a source of cross-subsidy. The net effect is that Jharkhand has been trapped in a low level equilibrium of low access and low political demand for access.

Karnataka's successive governments have had to contend with regional imbalances in levels and modes of development; the state has struggled to provide resources for the less-developed, and agrarian northern districts that also play a key role in the competitive politics of the state. Until the 1980s, cheap hydro-power allowed the state to accommodate these rising demands, even as dynamic tertiary economies centred on Bengaluru were creating a new political and economic image for the state. Naidu's attempt at reforms in neighbouring Andhra Pradesh and the resulting political defeat was instructive for politicians in Karnataka, who took from the episode the lesson that any shift away from the provision of subsidized access to electricity for the northern districts would lead to a political backlash. Karnataka's reforms, therefore, rather than adopting strict economic principles in which cost-of-supply determines tariff and all regions are treated equally, evolved a strategy of bureaucratic negotiation that enables wealthier regions to offset some of the costs associated with ongoing public subsidies to the northern regions and farmers. This has led to a relatively stable equilibrium, although arguably one that is dependent on continued willingness of wealthier regions to sustain this arrangement.

Madhya Pradesh is in low-level equilibrium of low-quality supply, high loss levels, low collection efficiency, and growing subsidy. This outcome persists despite a reform effort, but one which only consolidated bureaucratic control and introduced a tariff shock without tangible gains to the population. The state has bet on electricity supply as a growth industry, increasing capacity five-fold since 2000; but the resultant overcapacity could further limit room to manoeuvre. The electricity sector continues to be perceived as a political risk, a perception shaped by a post-reform electoral loss for the reforming party, the INC, in 2003.

Maharashtra is locked into a fragile equilibrium of unsustainable subsidies and high-cost supply—a pattern initiated by the Enron project and repeated more recently. This situation is mitigated by the fact that the state achieved household electrification earlier than most others, is relatively wealthy and can afford direct subventions, and has plentiful industrial consumers for cross-subsidies. However, Maharashtra's equilibrium is threatened by the prospect of industrial flight from the grid; the state faces increasing pressure from open access on one hand, which will dilute the ability to cross subsidize, and high-cost power on the other. Reforms increased transparency in a way that has made public participation more active, but the state has failed to make the kinds of managerial and organizational changes that would have improved the overall performance of the sector.

Odisha in the mid-1990s was a poor state with limited rural electrification but vast reserves of coal and ample hydro supply. There was a cross party consensus around mineral based development with enhanced generation capacity as the route for the state to emerge as the 'powerhouse of India'. Odisha became the first to sign up for a large World Bank package to design and implement reforms, including distribution sector privatization. The state-owned GRIDCO did indeed profit from selling the state's cheap hydropower to neighbouring states, but the effect of reforms on Odisha's citizen–consumers was negative: tariffs for existing consumers increased and rural electrification all but stopped under private discom ownership. This low-level equilibrium was sustained throughout the decade of the 2000s until a conjuncture of new factors made sector finances precarious again: centrally funded grid expansion led to an increase of rural, costly-to-serve consumers even as increasing demand forced a turn to higher cost thermal power, and in the face of higher costs, industrial customers shifted to captive power. The failure of reform is underscored by cancellation of the last three private licenses in 2015 throwing the problem back into the state's hands. Odisha risks tipping from low-level equilibrium to a vicious cycle.

Punjab is a high-income state with a predominantly agrarian economy, the first in India to achieve universal village electrification and household access. Promises of free power for farmers came at a time when electricity constituted a substantial input in farm costs. Now, even as the economic significance of the subsidy has fallen and free power yields few electoral gains, no party in the state can risk eliminating the subsidy. In addition to cross-subsidy from industrial consumers, paying consumers are also charged increasing levels of cess and duties to balance the high cost of subsidies. Populist inertia strains the ability of any one actor to break from the status quo. On the supply-side, high-cost, long-term contracts signed over the last five years with private generators have curtailed the potential benefits of demand-side management (since far from curbing demand, the utility needs to encourage it) and renewable energy (because with a supply glut, no one has an appetite for new sources of energy, however virtuous they may be).

Rajasthan went from very low levels of electrification and limited capacity to high levels of electricity consumption, greater access, and greater generating capacity over the last two decades. An important factor is that although geographic variations within the state lead to very different cost-to-serve conditions, a single tariff is levied across the state. Both major parties—INC and BJP—have taken turns offering greater power subsidies, focused on short-term thinking about the potential electoral benefits of power rather than long-term planning for the overall financial and technical health of the sector. Despite reform efforts, loss levels have not been staunched, financial health continues to decline, and the situation is exacerbated by unwise high-cost supply choices, leading to a declining spiral.

Tamil Nadu, one of the wealthiest states in India, has achieved almost universal electrification, and has the highest renewable energy capacity—both wind and solar—in the country. Over the last three decades, two regional parties—the Dravida Munnetra Kazhagam (DMK) and the All India Anna Dravida Munnetra Kazhagam (AIADMK)—have alternatively governed the state and are locked into a pattern of competitive populism in which electricity subsidies play a big role. Early on, subsidies were well targeted and were also financially covered through cross-subsidies from other consumers and direct support from the government. By the 1980s, concern for financial discipline of the utility was abandoned, power for irrigation was made free, flat-rate meters were introduced, and growing theft was concealed under the carpet of agricultural subsidies, all leading to the deteriorated quality of supply and even more cross subsidies. Reform efforts did little to change the situation, with the state government controlling the electricity regulatory commission to prevent the ailing utility from reforming itself and protecting it from any competition. Ironically, Tamil Nadu is considered to be a power surplus state now due to falling industrial demand. There are few signs of Tamil Nadu climbing out of this spiral.

Uttar Pradesh (UP)—one of the largest states in India in terms of population and political influence—is also one of the poorest states with a very large rural population that has very low levels of access to electricity. UP has seen a highly competitive political environment over the last couple of decades with intense jockeying for power occurring among three major parties—Samajwadi Party (SP), Bahujan Samaj Party (BSP), and Bharatiya Janata Party (BJP). The bifurcation of the state leading to the creation of Uttarakhand led to UP losing access to a significant amount of cheap hydropower thereby raising its overall cost of power procurement over the last decade. The relatively high share of domestic, rural, and agricultural consumption coupled with high level of poverty has made it politically extremely hard to implement any kinds of sustained reforms (for example, privatization has been attempted several times and failed on each occasion, efforts to reduce AT&C losses, improving bill recovery, raising tariffs, etc.) in the UP power sector. With high levels of political competition, successive UP governments have been unable to incur the political costs of reducing rampant theft and electricity misgovernance; this also makes it challenging to credibly offer enhanced electricity access as a political strategy, locking the state into a vicious cycle at low levels of electricity access.

Uttarakhand was created out of UP and endowed with a substantial benefit: sole access to cheap hydropower. Low-cost power allowed the state to attract industry by cutting tariffs, providing a stable financial base, and enabling a well-functioning sector. With low tariffs, the power sector has not become an arena for populist policies despite frequent electoral shifts. However, this comfortable situation also limited the pressure to use the breathing room created by low cost power coupled with high share of industrial consumption to address long-standing loss levels in other parts of the state. As the limits of low-cost power are reached, the threat to Uttarakhand's high-level equilibrium comes from having to turn to high-cost thermal power and stagnating industrial consumption.

West Bengal had been in a low-level equilibrium characterized by low access levels but also, therefore, limited demands for subsidies. Nonetheless, declining finances prompted the long-standing Communist Party of India (Marxist) (CPM) government to undertake reforms, but these were focused in internal restructuring, including successful negotiations with labour unions, with positive outcomes for loss levels and discom finances. However, the 2011 elections brought a change in government in part due to larger state politics around industrial policy, and the winning Trinamool Congress (TMC) initially returned to a more populist tack. The effect of blocking additional tariff hikes, and expanding rural electricity access led to worsened discom finances. There are signs that the TMC may slowly come to believe in the electoral benefits of a long-term power sector view, one that limits the temptation for populist policies. If so, the turn towards a vicious cycle between electoral and power politics may be avoided.

Notes and References

1. The Reserve Bank of India estimates that states' Gross Fiscal Deficit as percentage of state GDP due to the central government's most recent effort at financial restructuring (called UDAY) increased from 2.9 per cent to 3.6 per cent for the year 2015–16 and is projected to increase from 2.3 per cent to 3.0 per cent in 2016–17. Reserve Bank of India, 'State Finances: A Study of Budgets of 2016–17', May 2017, available https://rbidocs.rbi.org.in/rdocs/Publications/PDFs/0SF2016_12051728F3E926CFFB4520A027AC753ACF469A.PDF (accessed on 1 April 2018).

2. Prayas (Energy Group), 'The Price of Plenty: Insights from "Surplus" Power in Indian States', June 2017, available http://www.prayaspune.org/

peg/publications/item/335-the-price-of-plenty-insights-from-surplus-power-in-indian-states.html (accessed on 1 April 2018).

3. Bharath Jairaj, Sarah Martin, Josh Ryor et al., 'The Future Electricity Grid: Key Questions and Considerations for Developing Countries', World Resource Institute, May 2016, available https://www.wri.org/sites/default/files/The_Future_Electricity_Grid.pdf (accessed on 1 April 2016).

4. The World Bank, *Bureaucrats in Business: The Economics and Politics of Government Ownership* (Oxford: Oxford University Press, 1995).

5. See, for example, John Waterbury, *Exposed to Innumerable Delusions: Public Enterprise and State Power in Egypt, India, Mexico, and Turkey* (New York: Cambridge University Press, 1993).

6. For an early example of this critique leveled at the Indian case, see Jagdish N. Bhagwati and Padma Desai, *India, Planning for Industrialization: Industrialization and Trade Policies since 1951* (London: Oxford University Press, 1970).

7. Xu Yi-chong, 'Models, Templates, and Currents: The World Bank and Electricity Reform', *Review of International Political Economy* 12(4) (2005): 647–73.

8. Gajendra Haldea, *Report of the Sub-group on Public Private Partnership in the Distribution of Electricity* (New Delhi: Planning Commission, 2012).

9. V. Ranganathan, 'Electricity Act 2003: Moving to a Competitive Environment', *Economic and Political Weekly* 39(20) (May 15–21, 2004): 2001–5.

10. Frank A. Wolak, 'Reforming the Indian Electricity Supply Industry', in *Sustaining India's Growth Miracle*, ed. Jagdish N. Bhagwati and Charles W. Calomiris (New York: Columbia University Press, 2008), 115–65.

11. For a recent summary, review, and meta-analysis of this literature, see Stefano Mandelli, Jacopo Barbieri, Riccardo Mereu, and Emanuela Colombo, 'Off-grid Systems for Rural Electrification in Developing Countries: Definitions, Classification and a Comprehensive Literature Review', *Renewable and Sustainable Energy Reviews* 58 (2016): 1621–46.

12. See Navroz K. Dubash and Daljit Singh, 'Of Rocks and Hard Places: A Critical Review of Recent Global Experience with Electricity Restructuring', *Economic and Political Weekly* 40 (50) (2005, 10–16 December): 5249–59.

13. Giridhar Jha, 'Bihar Village Clamours for Real Electricity', *India Today*, 6 August 2014, available http://indiatoday.intoday.in/story/bihar-village-dharnai-nitish-kumar-clamours-for-real-electricity/1/375733.html (accessed on 1 April 2018).

14. For a discussion of two main schools (historical institutionalism and rational choice institutionalism), see Kathleen Thelen, 'Historical Institutionalism in Comparative Politics', *Annual Review of Political Science* 2(1) (1999): 369–404.

15. One of those to express concern was planner and engineer, M. Visvesvaraya. See Sunila S. Kale, *Electrifying India: Regional Political Economies of Development* (Palo Alto, CA: Stanford University Press, 2014).

16. The idea of subsidizing electricity was in keeping with global trends. Across the developing and industrialized world, making energy affordable was one important tool for states that sought to foster economic growth and confront poverty, particularly for rural citizens.

17. Sunila S. Kale, 'Current Reforms: The Politics of Policy Change in India's Electricity Sector', *Pacific Affairs* 77(3) (2004): 467–91.

18. Scholarly treatments of this period include S.L. Rao, ed., *Powering India: A Decade of Policies and Regulation* (New Delhi: Academic Foundation, 2011); Alok Kumar and Sushanta K. Chatterjee, *Electricity Sector in India: Policy and Regulation* (New Delhi: Oxford University Press, 2012); Joël Ruet, *Privatising Power Cuts: Ownership and Reform of State Electricity Boards in India* (New Delhi: Academic Foundation, 2005); Joël Ruet, ed., *Against the Current: Organizational Restructuring of State Electricity Boards* (New Delhi: Manohar Publishing, 2003); and Navroz K. Dubash and Sudhir Chella Rajan, 'Power Politics: Process of Power Sector Reform in India', *Economic and Political Weekly* 36(35) (September 2001): 3367–90; Rahul Tongia, 'The Political Economy of Indian Power Sector Reforms', in David G. Victor and Thomas C. Heller eds, *The Political Economy of Power Sector Reform: The Experiences of Five Major Developing Countries*, (Cambridge and New York: Cambridge University Press, 2007), 109–74.

19. The World Bank, *The World Bank's Role in the Power Sector* (Washington DC: World Bank, 1993).

20. Government of India, Central Electricity Authority, 'Power Sector', October 2016, availale http://cea.nic.in/reports/monthly/executivesummary/2016/exe_summary-10.pdf (accessed on 1 April 2018).

21. For reviews, see S.L. Rao, *Governing Power: A New Institution of Governance, the Experience with Independent Regulation of Electricity* (New Delhi: TERI, 2004); Prayas (Energy Group), *Many Sparks but Little Light: The Rhetoric and Practice of Electricity Sector Reforms in India* (Pune: Prayas, 2017); and Dubash and Rajan, 'Power Politics'.

22. See Prayas (Energy Group), *A Good Beginning but Challenges Galore* (Pune: Prayas, 2003); and Navroz K. Dubash and Narasimha Rao, *The Practice and Politics of Regulation: Regulatory Governance in Indian Electricity* (New Delhi: Macmillan, 2007).

23. Central Electricity Authority of India, 'Executive Summary', October 2017, available http://www.cea.nic.in/reports/monthly/executivesummary/2017/exe_summary-10.pdf (accessed on 1 April 2018).

24. Government of India, Ministry of Finance, Department of Economic Affairs, Economics Division, 'Economic Survey 2016–17', January 2017, available https://www.indiabudget.gov.in/es2016-17/echapter.pdf (accessed on 1 April 2018).

25. Dashboard for real-time updates available at: www.ujala.gov.in/ (accessed on 1 April 2018).

26. Prayas (Energy Group), *The Price of Plenty: Insights from 'Surplus' Power in Indian States* (Pune: Prayas, 2017).

27. Ministry of Power, 'Shri R.K. Singh launches "Saubhagya" Web-Portal—a Platform for Monitoring Universal Household Electrification Ministry of Power', Press Information Bureau, Government of India, Ministry of Power, November 2017, available http://pib.nic.in/newsite/PrintRelease.aspx?relid=173548 (accessed on 1 April 2018).

28. Bloomberg New Energy Finance, 'Accelerating India's Clean Energy Transition', November 2017, available https://about.bnef.com/blog/accelerating-indias-clean-energy-transition/ (accessed on 1 April 2018). Also see https://www.lazard.com/perspective/levelized-cost-of-energy-analysis-100/ (accessed on 1 April 2018).

29. R. Deshmukh, R. Bharvirkar, A. Gambhir et al., 'Changing Sunshine: Analyzing the Dynamics of Solar Electricity Policies in the Global Context', *Renewable and Sustainable Energy Reviews* 16(7) (September 2012): 5188–98.

30. Jairaj et al., 'The Future Electricity Grid'.

1

ASHWINI K. SWAIN

Transforming Reforms

Hype, Hostility, and Placation in Andhra Pradesh's Power Sector Reforms

A ndhra Pradesh's (AP) experience with electricity reforms and their political ramifications has not only been fascinating a case for political analysts, but also have influenced reform approaches in other states. The relatively underdeveloped state, lacking much institutional lock-in (similar to Odisha and Haryana), emerged as one of the pioneers of the global model of electricity reforms, endorsed by the World Bank. While other states and the central government chose to pursue reforms by stealth, AP consciously selected an explicit reform strategy for the power sector as well as the wider economy. Between 1995 and 2004, a pragmatic and reform-oriented state government initiated a departure from welfaristic populism that was limiting the state's fiscal manoeuvrability. Despite continued pro-poor spending and some economic gains, the reform agenda was faced with mass hostility, and is alleged to have resulted in a political debacle for the incumbent state government. During both the populism and pragmatism eras of state politics, electricity service and pricing emerged as key political instruments. Subsequently, the much-hyped reform agenda was halted, giving way for the resurgence of populism. Following the state's bifurcation in 2014, AP restored the reform champion to the position of chief minister

(CM). In quest of an ambitious transformation, the state now follows a stealthy reform approach, seeking to balance reform with welfare, both within the power sector and the wider economy.

In this backdrop, this chapter explores the political economy of AP's electricity sector transitions over four periods, with the objective to explain the drivers of policy choices and their outcomes. Drawing on the findings, it discusses the transformations in electricity reform strategy over two phases of reforms and analyses the implications of past experiences for ongoing reforms in the sector.

After undergoing three reorganizations,[1] the southern state of AP is the seventh largest Indian state by size, and is the tenth largest by population. Politics in the state has been shaped over the past six decades, with significant shifts in electoral politics and public policy. Following three decades of Indian National Congress (Congress) hegemony, the state experienced bi-party competition in the 1983 elections, with the emergence of the Telugu Desam Party (TDP). The arrival of Telangana Rashtra Samithi (TRS) in 2004 and Praja Rajyam Party (PRP) in 2009 unleashed multiparty electoral competition in the state. The participation of the Yuvajana Sramika Rythu Congress Party (YSR Congress) in the 2014 state elections has not only the limited presence of national parties in state politics, but has also inaugurated a new era of electoral competition between two regional parties. During the era of Congress dominance, the state's public policy was largely aligned with and dictated by the central government. Subsequently, there was some resentment and mobilization among the rural peasantry, who were seeking state-sponsored welfare benefits. However, this did not convert into any political organization. The TDP was successful as a political alternative, building on N.T. Ramarao's (NTR) charisma and populist promise to deliver subsidized welfare goods, catering to demands of organized communities. The TDP's N. Chandrababu Naidu, after taking over power in 1995, attempted to depart from populism in favour of pragmatism, through market-centric reforms and the retreat of the state, while continuing vital pro-poor spending. Political backlash in the 2004 state assembly elections led to Congress's victory over TDP and was perceived to be a condemnation of the reform agenda; Congress halted the reforms and brought back competitive populism. The following decade under Congress rule saw a return to the status quo in economic policy, a gradual embrace of populism by Naidu, and a greater thrust on statehood for the underdeveloped region of Telangana.[2] In his current stint as chief minister, the reform champion Naidu seems to be vigilant and cautious of the political conditions. While he continues to champion ambitious and transformative reform plans, seeking a balance between reform and welfare, areas with direct impacts on the voters are spared from any sweeping change.[3]

Throughout its different incarnations, AP has been an agricultural economy. The state's 62 per cent population depend on agriculture and allied activities for their livelihoods, which is significantly higher than national average of 48 per cent.[4] In 2016–17, agriculture contributed 32 per cent of Gross State Value Added (GSVA), much above the national average of 17 per cent, while industry and service sectors contributed 22 per cent and 46 per cent, respectively.[5] Despite its high dependency on agriculture, in 2014–15 AP recorded the seventh highest GSVA among all states and recorded the tenth highest per capita income among the major states, slightly higher than the national average.[6] During the economic reforms period, the undivided state recorded a higher-than-national-average growth rate in per capita income,[7] despite a marginally lower-than-national-average growth in Gross State Domestic Product (GSDP).[8] While agriculture's share in GSDP has been consistently dropping, the share of the population dependent on agriculture has remained stagnant. Faster growth in non-farm sectors, especially service sectors concentrated in cities, has widened regional income disparities.[9] The newly-bifurcated AP now hopes to carry out a 'structural shift' from agricultural dependency to thriving industry, and foresees a decline in the agricultural workforce and a corresponding boom in the industrial workforce. The state aims to be 'a happy, inclusive, responsible, globally competitive, and innovation-driven society through structural transformation and by sustaining inclusive double-digit economic growth, to become one amongst the three best states in India by 2022, to achieve the status of a developed state by 2029, and a leading global investment destination by 2050'.[10]

Notwithstanding its economic status, AP's electricity sector is ahead of many states. The state has the fifth largest generation capacity among states, with 22,069 megawatt (MW), mostly under private ownership. Keeping with its welfarist approach, the state has already achieved universal access to electricity service.[11] Additionally, it has 1.6 million irrigation pumps running on electricity.[12] While agricultural consumers receive 7–8 hours of supply on rotation, the rest of the consumers are free from any scheduled load shedding. Power demand in the state is well balanced between cross-subsidized and cross-subsidizing consumers, while a major portion of the revenue comes from industrial consumers (Figure 1.1). Agricultural and domestic consumers account for 26 per cent and 24 per cent of power demand respectively, while high-paying industrial and other consumers account for 35 per cent and 15 per cent respectively.[13] However, the state recorded a per capita consumption of 987 kilowatt hour (kWh) in 2015–16, lower than the national per capita consumption of 1,075 kWh.[14]

Two electricity distribution companies (discoms) in the state have shown substantive operational efficiency. State level aggregate technical and commercial (AT&C) loss has not exceeded 20 per cent during the past decade, and shows a declining trend (Figure 1.2). Eastern Power Distribution Company of Andhra Pradesh Limited (APEPDCL) has

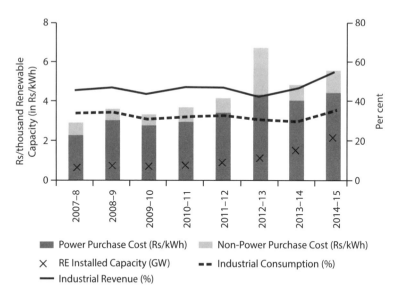

FIGURE 1.1   Physical and Financial Profile: Andhra Pradesh
Source: CSO, *Energy Statistics* (New Delhi: Central Statistics Office, Ministry of Statistics and Programme Implementation, Government of India, 2010, 2012, 2014, and 2016); PFC, *Reports on Performance of State Power Utilities* (New Delhi: Power Finance Corporation Limited, 2011, 2013, 2015, and 2016).

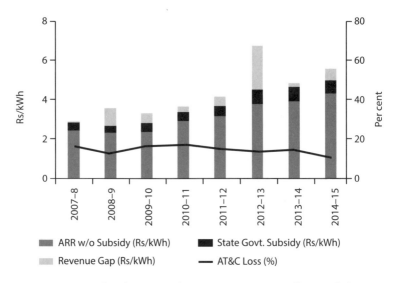

FIGURE 1.2   Supply-side Costs and Revenue Recovery: Andhra Pradesh
Source: PFC, *Reports on Performance of State Power Utilities* (New Delhi: Power Finance Corporation Limited, 2011, 2013, 2015, and 2016).

been able to reduce AT&C losses to 5.5 per cent, the lowest among all discoms in India, while Southern Power Distribution Company of Andhra Pradesh Limited (APSPDCL) faced a loss of 11.5 per cent in 2015–16.[15] The state level revenue gap per/kWh has been fluctuating (Figure 1.2); in the first quarter of 2017–18, it was estimated to be Rs 0.49, slightly higher than the national average of Rs 0.43.[16] State government subvention has been increasing consistently; in 2014–15, Government of Andhra Pradesh (GoAP) provided Rs 30 billion subsidy in lieu of free power supply to agriculture, which amounted to 15 per cent of discoms' total revenue from sales. In 2014–15, both discoms recorded combined commercial losses of Rs 25 billion after subsidies were received,[17] which made up a little more than 8 per cent of gross fiscal deficit of AP in that year.[18] As of 30 September 2015, both discoms had accumulated an outstanding debt of Rs 147 billion,[19] about half of their annual revenue requirements, and amounting to 12 per cent of state's outstanding liabilities.[20] In the Fifth Integrated Rating for State Power Distribution Utilities, APEPDCL and APSPDCL received A and B+ grades[21] respectively, which is a grade higher than the previous year.[22]

The Fall of Andhra Pradesh State Electricity Board (1982–95)

The AP State Electricity Board (APSEB) made a modest start in 1959, with 200 MW of installed capacity,[23] 686 MkWh generation and 0.27 million service connections.[24] By 1995, the generation capacity increased 25-fold to 5,111 MW, and actual generation increased thirty-fold to 20,529 MkWh.[25] During this period, the Board achieved substantive progress in physical infrastructure development, but failed to maintain managerial and operation efficiencies due to political interference. By the mid-1980s, most of the state's towns, villages, and hamlets were connected to the electricity grid. Following the introduction of the Green Revolution in the state in the late 1960s and subsequent increases in agricultural demand, pump energization was expedited. Between 1967 and 1985, agricultural connections increased by ten times and crossed 0.6 million connections.[26]

Although organized rural communities had been demanding electricity access for some time, the central government's push for expedited rural electrification and pump energization, supported with finance from the Rural Electrification Corporation, acted as a major driver for electrification in AP. Congress dominance in the state facilitated the execution of central policy signals.[27] The Board's tariff structure maintained a careful balance between economic rationality and welfare goals until the mid-1970s. Until 1976, agricultural and domestic consumers paid higher tariffs than industrial consumers, while commercial consumers paid the highest tariffs. Beginning in the mid-1970s, the state's political economy emerged as an important driver of sectoral decision-making. By this time, rural communities were mobilizing, led by the landed elites, expressing resentment against the government and demanding state-sponsored welfare goods, including subsidized electricity supply. The Congress government in AP obliged these demands by marginally reducing the agricultural electricity tariff and keeping the domestic tariff stagnant, while industrial and commercial tariffs increased as usual.[28]

A major shift took place in 1982, when TDP was founded and gained public support as a viable alternative to the Congress Party. TDP formed its election agenda by adopting demands from organized rural communities, including the demand for subsidized agricultural electricity supply.[29] De-metering and a flat-rate tariff were not yet in the public discourse. The state government was already contemplating these options, drawing on precedents in other agricultural states, but was met with resistance from the Board.[30] On the other hand, during the last phase of Congress dominance in AP, the party underwent a leadership crisis; between 1978 and 1983, the party appointed five CMs. Vijaya Bhaskara Reddy, taking charge of the CM position just three months ahead of the next elections, introduced a flat-rate tariff for agriculture based on pump capacity on 1 November 1982. This desperate move by the Congress Party failed, and TDP won the 1983 state assembly elections with a huge majority. Agricultural revenue dropped by 62 per cent and kept on decreasing, though it was compensated through aggressive increases in industrial tariff.[31] Though NTR did not intend to bring in a flat-rate tariff,[32] he not only continued it but also kept the tariff stagnant.

However, APSEB was financially comfortable till the early 1990s, with extensive use of cross-subsidization. In 1992–3, the Board recorded a small commercial loss of Rs 40 million, which increased to Rs 10 billion in 1994–5. By 1995, the Board had already energized 1.6 million irrigation pumps, resulting in a subsidy burden of Rs 14 billion,[33] accounting for more than 2 per cent of the state's GSDP.[34] Consequently, the unmetered share of the Board's power supply (agricultural supply and transmission and distribution [T&D] losses) surpassed metered supply. While one-third of the Board's income from sales was going to meet interest payments, it was unable to raise additional finances for the required investments.[35] While APSEB's non-remunerative load was increasing, the Board experienced a flight of some high-paying industrial load in early 1990s, pushing it into bankruptcy.[36] Owing to the emergent financial crisis, the Board could not add adequate generation capacity corresponding to the demand increases, which resulted in frequent load shedding for all categories of consumers. The seasonal peak demand from agriculture was met by load shedding industrial consumers.

In the background of the deteriorating situation in the sector and the Centre's opening up of the sector to private participation, GoAP contemplated various reform options. In 1995, a high-level committee was set up to prepare a reform plan for the sector. The committee suggested a functional restructuring of the Board, pragmatic resource planning, the creation of an independent regulatory body, and the implementation of a cost-reflective tariff process. Though it advised against outright privatization and asked the state to retain licensing and key regulatory functions, hinting at a much softer approach to reforms, the state government was still unsure about implementing the commit-tee's suggestions.[37] Although TDP regained power in 1994 based on populist campaign promises, the party found it politically difficult to tamper with its welfarist approach and populist electoral base.

Hyped Reforms, Social Resistance, and Political Backlash (1996–2004)

A major shift in AP's public policy came after Naidu seized power from NTR, through a 'palace coup'-like situation in 1995. Unlike his father-in-law, Naidu considered welfaristic populism to be outdated and believed in a development paradigm based on the centrality of market forces and gradual withdrawal of the state. He was explicit in his criticism of NTR's approach to welfare and development as well as his intent to reform the economy. With the objective to initiate a public discourse, he released a series of white papers explaining the non-feasibility of government subsidies, the need for reduction in expenditure on welfare schemes, the need to limit state control, dismantling public sector and opening doors for foreign private capital. Subsequently, within a few months of taking power, Naidu reneged on the very three planks on which TDP came to power in 1994: he raised the price of rice supplied through the public distribution systems, relaxed the prohibition on liquor, and raised the agricultural electricity price.[38]

The rise in the agricultural electricity tariff prompted mass protests and opposition from farmers' groups, to which the government was forced to respond with a direct subsidy to the Board so that the low tariff could be continued. However, this resistance at an early stage could not put a dent in Naidu's reform intentions. Instead, GoAP approached the World Bank for a structural adjustment loan to tide over its fiscal crisis. In response, the World Bank brought out a comprehensive economic reform plan for the state in 1997, covering the power sector. Going beyond the recom-mendations of the Hiten Bhaiya Committee, the World Bank suggested the corporatization and privatization of power utilities, an independent and transparent regulatory system, a comprehensive reform legislation, and cost-reflective tariff revision, including for the agricultural consump-tion.[39] An Adaptable Programme Loan amounting US$ 4,460 million was planned for an AP Power Sector Restructuring Programme, with a larger share from the World Bank and other international lenders.[40]

Within six months from the World Bank's recommendations, GoAP published a policy statement on power sector restructuring in June 1997 and later enacted the Electricity Reform Act of 1998. In February 1999, APSEB was unbundled into two entities: Andhra Pradesh Power Generation Corporation Limited (APGENCO) to oversee generation, and Transmission Corporation of Andhra Pradesh Limited to oversee transmission and distribution. The AP Electricity Regulatory Commission was also established in the same year. In April 2000, APTRANSCO was further unbundled into a transmission-only company with the same name and four discoms: AP Central Power Distribution Company Limited (APCPDCL), AP Northern Power Distribution Company Limited (APNPDCL), Eastern Power Distribution Company of Andhra Pradesh Limited (APEPDCL), and Southern Power Distribution Company of Andhra Pradesh Limited (APSPDCL).

While Naidu pursued institutional reforms swiftly, owing to the precedents of protests in 1995 and upcoming assembly elections in 1999, he was cautious on tariff revisions and waited till the Andhra Pradesh Electricity Regulatory Commission (APERC) became functional. The first tariff order from the commission raised tariffs for all categories of consumers, with domestic consumers facing the steepest increases of around 50 per cent. While the commission justified the tariff hike on grounds of rising costs and the necessity to reduce cross-subsidization from industrial and commercial consumers, the government excused itself by claiming that it was statutorily removed from the process. The government offered to reduce the effect on consumers by providing a direct subsidy to the utilities and thereby protecting domestic consumers from about 50 per cent of the tariff hike.[41]

Substantive transformations in the sector at this stage were facilitated by a consensus between a reform-oriented state government, a proactive regulator, and skilled upper management in the utilities. While the government pushed through institutional restructuring and carved out multiple institutions from a monolithic Board, the institutions carried forward the reform mandate. The well-staffed, well-trained, and well-supported APERC emerged as a proactive and pragmatic regulator. Top management in APTRANSCO and the discoms were instrumental in overcoming entrenched resistance to change and pursuing management reforms. These measures included incentive-based operational reforms, increased emphasis on improving industrial supply, optimization of agricultural demand, reduction of field-level corruption, and an improved consumer experience. With an oversight on implementation of reforms at the discom level, APTRANSCO held monthly meetings with employees' unions to review progress.[42] While the impetus for these management reforms seem to have come from utilities, state government facilitated it by recruiting the right people in upper management.[43] Simultaneously, Naidu took a keen interest in the progress by participating in some of the review meetings as well as engaging with the employees' unions separately.

However, Naidu was aware that taking the tariff to the level of cost of supply would be a Herculean task, especially for agricultural consumers, and would not be politically feasible. Along with institutional reforms and tariff revisions, he focused on demand-side measures to reduce the agricultural load. This included rural feeder segregation so that the agricultural supply could be easily rationed, as well as the upgrading of pumping infrastructure.[44] Along with the demand-side measures, GoAP also prioritized supply-side augmentation. Private sector investment in generation was already initiated through APGPC in 1991. Although 95 MoUs were signed by 1995, only two private-owned plants could materialize by the time institutional reforms were introduced.[45] With new generation capacity addition, energy deficit in the state was brought down from 22 per cent in 1996–7[46] to 1.5 per cent by 2003–4, when the all-India deficit stood at 7 per cent.[47]

Despite transparency and public engagement by the state government, the reform agenda faced with massive resistance from all blocks, including employees' unions, agricultural and domestic consumers, opposition political parties, and even from within the TDP.[48] Some of these agitations turned violent, requiring intervention from police and the judiciary. Resistance from left-wing parties was based on ideological grounds, opposing privatization, while the Congress Party presented political resistance and criticism. Consumer groups and employees' unions were opposed to privatization, as that would mean tariff hikes for the former and degradation of service conditions for the latter. Some of this resistance, especially from political parties and from employees' unions, could be mitigated through engagement and dialogue, while other groups persisted. The media seem to have played a crucial role in fostering the resistance by highlighting criticisms and branding the reforms as 'anti-people'. However, management reforms by the utilities combined with demand-side and supply-side measures resulted in significant efficiency gains (see Table 1.1) and improvements in service quality, resulting in a period of virtuous cycle.

Unlike in other states, Naidu and TDP did not get any political reward for these reforms and efficiency and economic gains. Rather, TDP's defeat in 2004 state assembly elections is widely perceived as a 'vote against anti-people reforms', especially those reforms made in the power sector. This interpretation of the 2004 election results is questionable for several reasons. First, the defeat of the TDP could be a result of anti-incumbency after two terms of Naidu; even the charismatic and populist NTR was voted out of power after his first term and never allowed two successive terms. Second, except for leftist parties, no mainstream political party made the 2004 election a contest on reforms.[49] Third, the vote sharing in the 2004 election does not support the political punishment narrative. TDP's vote share fell from 43.9 per cent in 1999 to 37.5

TABLE 1.1   Operational Efficiency in Andhra Pradesh's Power Sector (1999–2005)

Performance Indicators	1999–2000	2000–1	2001–2	2002–3	2003–4	2004–5
T&D Loss (%)	37.1	34.8	30.2	26.5	23.3	23.7
Cost Recovery (%)	61	67	69	83	85	88
Tariff Increase (%)	–	14.5	0.76	0.71	–0.71	–1.5
Metered Sale (% of Input)	37.9	38.7	40.9	44.5	48.3	52
Commercial Loss w/o Subsidy (Rs Billion)	30.65	29.36	28.23	16.34	15.89	13.03
Government Subsidy (Rs Billion)	30.64	29.36	24.57	18.76	15.13	13.03
Subsidy as % of Revenue	–	20.7	20.1	19	16	14
HT1 Revenue as % of Total Revenue	–	27.8	27.2	32.9	35	33.2
Cross-Subsidy as % of Total Revenue	–	27.7	24.9	24.8	22.2	18.7

Source: N.K. Dubash and D.N. Rao, *The Practice and Politics of Regulation: Regulatory Governance in Indian Electricity* (Delhi: Macmillan India, 2007).

per cent in 2004, resulting in a reduction of 133 seats in the assembly.[50] This drop in TDP's vote share could be explained by the political faction in the party, emergence of Telangana Rashtra Party (TRP) in state politics. The TRP, a party based on a Telugu identity similar to TDP, but additionally demanding separate statehood for Telangana, bagged 6.8 per cent of the vote share and 26 state assembly seats in 2004.[51] Congress' victory in the election could be explained by its alliance with the TRP. Moreover, Naidu was elected back to power with an absolute majority in 1999, despite a tariff hike in 1995, the reform agenda was made public through a policy statement in 1997 and reform act in 1998, and the support of World Bank was already concretized. Similarly, after the major tariff hike of 2000, TDP rather gained more vote share in the 2001 Panchayat elections, though it lost some seats. As compared to 43.83 per cent votes in the 1999 state assembly elections, it received 44.09 per cent votes in the 2001 Panchayat elections.[52] Both the election results show public resistance to electricity tariff led reforms did not really translate into political discontent against TDP.

Consolidation of Competitive Populism (2005–13)

After coming back to power following a decade of TDP rule, the Congress immediately introduced free power for agricultural consumers, with the aim of consolidating its vote bank in peasantry. Naidu, who was explicit about his opposition to welfaristic populism during his tenure, became apologetic about the reforms, especially the tariff rationalization. In the subsequent elections in 2009 and 2014, Naidu joined the bandwagon of competitive populism by offering free power to farmers, hoping to regain their support. Other political parties, including the TRS, PRP, and YRS Congress, were also in support of sustaining the free power policy. However, the state government failed to meet its commitment for subsidy reimbursement to the discoms. Until 2011–12, there was a significant gap in subsidy booked by the discoms and disbursed by the state government.[53] Over a decade of competitive populism and ceased attention to efficiency, the sector was again pushed back into the vicious cycle, undoing the gains from past reforms.

Following 2004, both sectoral reforms and development reached a standstill. While part of productive upper management continued for few years, APTRANSCO's oversight on discom performance and underlying engagement between utility employees ceased. By 2013–14, industrial HT sale dropped to 26 per cent, while their share in revenue increased to 40 per cent, implying an increase in cross-subsidization to compensate for the revenue gap. Tariff revision for domestic consumers became intermittent and minimal, not in sync with the rising cost of utilities. Commercial loss increased to Rs 7,700 crore and the state government's subsidies increased to Rs 6,300 crore, amounting to 25 per cent and 20 per cent, respectively, of revenue from sales.[54] While the energy demand increased, there was not much capacity addition, resulting in an increasing power deficit that soared to 17.6 per cent by 2013.[55] While quality of supply and discoms' financial health deteriorated, the thin but substantive stakeholder engagement and transparency ushered by APERC also receded over the decade.[56]

However, owing to sustained populism, the deteriorating quality of supply did not lead to any major discontent. By 2009 state assembly election, all political parties were backing the free power policy. As the deterioration in quality of supply was not much evident by then, electricity service had a subtle role in the election and possibly Congress gained by pioneering the policy.

New State and a New Reform Agenda (2014–17)

In 2014, AP went through its third state reorganization, this time to carve out the 29th state of India, Telangana, from the northwest region of the erstwhile state. Unlike in other cases, the electricity sector's resource allocation between the two states was proportionate to both population and demand. In fact, the new AP gained by a slight reduction in some loss-making areas, marginally reducing the agricultural load and increasing the industrial load. In the 2014 state assembly elections, reform-champion Naidu was brought back to power. Given his apologetic attitude towards reforms during his decade out of power, would Naidu pursue the unfinished reform agenda? Did the political failures of 2004 make a dent in Naidu's reform aspirations?

Naidu accepts that he was 'ahead of times' in his earlier attempt at reforms, and now seeks to 'balance reforms and welfare, using the systems to help the common man'.[57] His legendary zeal for reforms and belief in market forces appear intact; however, he seems to be following a path of stealthy reform in the sector, without touching the sensitive tariff issue. Rather, in 2017, Naidu requested the energy department not to raise the electricity tariff.[58] In a vision document for the state, the state government has set out to ensure the delivery of 12 'non-negotiable' basic needs for all, including electricity service.[59] Naidu claims that the government's economic reforms are meant to help the poor: 'We are handholding the lowest sections of the society. I am confident that people will be satisfied and stay invested in the changes we are undertaking'.[60] While attracting private investment in the sector, Naidu seeks to reduce the power bills for the consumers. He has suggested a five-point strategy: (a) enhancing renewable energy through adequate storage and optimal utilization of conventional plants; (b) vigorous implementation of energy efficiency measures; (c) strengthening of transmission and distribution network and reducing loss; (d) adoption of information technology for better consumer services; and (e) effective financial management of various power projects.[61]

Keeping with this vision, AP became the first state to join the central government's 24×7 Power for All scheme in 2014, with the target to connect all households in the state by March 2017.[62] Unusually for the Indian electricity sector, this target has been achieved precisely on time.[63] In May 2017, GoAP received a US$ 400 million loan from the World Bank and the Asian Infrastructure Investment Bank to ensure round-the-clock supply to all consumers.[64] Simultaneously, within three years, the state has exited a grave power deficit by raising its generation capacity by 65 per cent, largely through private ownership and renewable energy technologies. For 2017–18, the state is projected to have 10.8 per cent energy surplus and 3 per cent peak surplus.[65] The new reform agenda has a strong focus on generation capacity addition in order to power planned industrial growth in the state, and also to gain from the sale of surplus power. At the same time, AP wishes to be a leader in renewable energy. While Naidu boasts about sharing 10 per cent of India's solar target, he hopes to host 50 per cent of national solar equipment manufacturing capacity—all through private, mostly foreign, investment.[66] To complement and optimize renewable energy capacity, the state has ambitious plans to construct storage facilities at different scales, and has already initiated pilot projects. Keeping with this vision, the new AP has revised various renewable energy policies and regulations (Table 1.2).

TABLE 1.2   Timeline of Key Events: Andhra Pradesh

State Politics	Year	Power Sector Events
• TDP wins state assembly election; NTR becomes CM	1994	
• Naidu seizes power from NTR and becomes CM	1995	• Hiten Bhaiya Committee Report
• *World Bank Agenda for Economic Reforms in AP*	1996	
	1997	• GoAP Policy Statement on Power Sector Reforms
	1998	• AP Electricity Reforms Act, 1998
• TDP wins state assembly elections; Naidu becomes CM	1999	• GoAP and World Bank sign agreement on power sector reforms • World Bank project appraisal document on AP Power Sector Reforms Programme • Establishment of APERC • Unbundling of APSEB into APGENCO and APTRANSCO
	2000	• APTRANSCO further split to carve out four discoms • APERC issues first tariff order with hike for all consumers, leading to mass agitation • High Court upholds APERC order on tariff hike • GoAP signs MoU with MoP, GoI to expedite reform • APERC Standards of Performance Regulation • APERC Consumer's Right to Information Regulation
	2001	• Regular license issued to the discoms
	2002	• Financial autonomy granted for the discoms • Employee division among the utilities

• Congress wins state assembly election	2004	• APERC Establishment of Forum and Vidyut Ombudsman Regulation
		• Free power to agricultural consumers
	2005	• Transfer of PPAs to discoms
		• Terms and Conditions of Open Access
• Congress wins state assembly election	2009	
	2012	• Solar Power Policy
		• APERC RPO Regulation
• **State reorganization**	2014	• APERC Reorganisation Regulation
• TDP state assembly election in new AP; Naidu becomes CM		• New AP becomes the first state to sign 24×7 Power for All scheme
	2015	• Solar Power Policy
		• Wind Power Policy
		• APERC Tariff Determination for Wind Projects Regulation
• *Sunrise Andhra Pradesh: Vision 2029*	2016	• Launch of two National Programmes for Smart Pumps for Farmers and Energy Efficient Fans, in Vijayawada, Andhra Pradesh
		• Establishment of AP State Energy Efficiency Development Corporation (APSEEDCO)
		• AP joins UDAY
		• APERC Amendment to Open Access Regulation
		• APERC Consumer Grievances Redressal Forum, Vidyut Ombudsman and Consumer Assistance Regulation
		• Wind-Solar Hybrid Power Policy (DRAFT)
	2017	• APERC RPO Regulation
		• APERC Power Evacuation from Captive Generation, Co-generation and RE Source Power Plant Regulation
		• GoAP receives a co-financed loan from World Bank and AIIB for 24×7 Power for All

Source: Author.

To pursue the energy efficiency plans, the state set up a dedicated agency in 2016, AP State Energy Efficiency Development Corporation, in which it plans to invest Rs 2,470 crore, leveraging central government schemes.[67] Symbolically, expressing the Centre's support of state initiatives, two national programmes for smart pumps and energy-efficient fans were launched from Vijayawada, AP by the central government's Power Minister and Naidu.[68]

Despite the good operational efficiency, the power utilities in AP are still facing commercial loss and carrying forward an inherited debt. The state has joined Ujwal Discom Assurance Yojana (UDAY) in 2016, seeking to turnaround discoms' finances. With a loss level about half of the national average and a small revenue gap, AP has been ranked as the second-best-performing state among the 27 states participating in the scheme.[69] Similarly, to the past, in this phase of reform, AP is trying to pursue a state-specific reform agenda that is aligned with the Centre's initiatives and aims to leverage central assistance and funding.

***

AP's experience with power sector reforms is a transformation story—a transformation in reform approach. Despite high-level political will, supportive and skilled institutions (regulators and utilities), and the backing of the central government, early attempts at tariff-based reform during 1999–2004 failed to sustain. The virtuous cycle of improving discoms' health through tariff rationalization and subsequent improvement in quality of supply did not receive public support. While the state government attempted to build a reform coalition by engaging with stakeholders, consumers, who were averse to tariff hikes, did not support it. A shift in political power in 2004 not only stalled the reforms, but also pulled the sector into entrenched problems, by undoing the reforms' outcomes over the following decade.

The return of the reform champion to power in 2014 has brought back the reform goals, but with a transformed agenda. Now, Naidu aims to put the consumers at the centre for reforms, by offering them quality service at affordable prices upfront. In the second stint of reforms, the state has the support of old allies, including the National Democratic Alliance (NDA)-run central government, the World Bank, and the same set of state-level institutions and willing private investors. Will the consumer welfare-centric approach to reform be sustained? Will the state be able to put together an inclusive reform coalition, with the proactive participation of consumers? Clearly, Naidu has a better strategy this time, with complementing tactics. Its success will depend on how far the government can recover the costs of service from consumers. Will consumers pay more for electricity service as its quality improves? Will the sector be able to use realized adequate revenue to compensate the private investments being made? On the other hand, crucial parts of the reform strategy, especially capacity addition, are dependent on the projected industrial load. Without rapid industrial growth and energy demand, the surplus capacity will pull back the ailing discoms. If AP succeeds in the current wave of reforms, it will create an alternative model of electricity reforms—home-grown and consumer welfare-centric. Given the size of private investments being planned and carried out, failure would be catastrophic for the sector and the state economy.

Notes and References

1. First, in 1953, Telugu-speaking regions of Madras State were reorganized as Andhra State, the first linguistic state of independent India; second, in 1956, a unified Andhra Pradesh was formed by merging Andhra State with Telugu-speaking parts of the erstwhile Hyderabad State; third, in 2014, the state was bifurcated into Andhra Pradesh and Telangana, the 29th state of India.

2. K.C. Suri, 'Andhra Pradesh: From Populism to Pragmatism, 1983–2003', *Journal of Indian School of Political Economy* 15(1&2) (2003): 45–77; K.C. Suri, 'From Dominance to Disarray: The Telugu Desam Party in Andhra Pradesh', in Sudha Pai (ed.), *Handbook of Politics in Indian States: Regions, Parties, and Economic Reforms* (New Delhi: Oxford University Press, 2013), 166–79.

3. Interview with two academics, 23 January 2017, Hyderabad.

4. Government of Andhra Pradesh (GoAP), *Primary Sector Development: Status, Strategy and Action Plan*. Submitted to NITI Aayog (Hyderabad: Government of Andhra Pradesh and ICRISAT, 2015).

5. GoAP, *Socio Economic Survey 2016–17* (Hyderabad: Government of Andhra Pradesh, 2017).

6. RBI, *Handbook of Statistics on Indian Economy* (Reserve Bank of India, 2016).

7. U. Kumar and A. Subramanian, 'Growth in India's States in the First Decade of the 21st Century: Four Facts', *Economic & Political Weekly* 47(3) (2012): 48–57.

8. M.S. Ahluwalia, 'State Level Performance under Economic Reforms in India', in A.O. Krueger (ed.), *Economic Policy, Reforms and the Indian Economy* (New Delhi: Oxford University Press, 2002), 91–122; Planning Commission, *Data-Book Compiled for Use of Planning Commission* (New Delhi: Planning Commission, Government of India, 2014).

9. A.M. Reddy and M.C.S. Bantilan, 'Regional Disparities in Andhra Pradesh, India', *Local Economy* 28(1) (2013): 123–35.

10. GoAP, *Sunrise Andhra Pradesh: Vision 2029* (Hyderabad: Government of Andhra Pradesh, 2016).

11. GARV Portal, available https://garv.gov.in, (accessed on 12 August 2017).

12. CEA, *Energisation of Pumpsets*, May (New Delhi: Central Electricity Authority, 2017).

13. PFC, *Report on Performance of State Power Utilities* (New Delhi: Power Finance Corporation Limited, 2016).

14. GoAP, *Socio Economic Survey*.

15. Ministry of Power, *Tripartite Memorandum of Understanding amongst Ministry of Power, Government of India and Government of Andhra Pradesh and APEPDCL and APSPDCL (UDAY)*. 4 March (Ministry of Power, 2016).

16. UDAY Portal, available www.uday.gov.in, (accessed on 4 September 2017).

17. PFC, *State Power Utilities*.

18. RBI, *Handbook of Statistics on Indian States* (Reserve Bank of India, 2017).

19. MoP, *Tripartite Memorandum of Understanding amongst Ministry of Power*.

20. RBI, *Statistics on Indian States*.

21. 'A' grade implies high operational and financial performance capability and 'B+' grade implies moderate operational and financial performance capability.

22. MoP, *Fifth Annual Integrated Ratings of State Power Distribution Utilities* (New Delhi: Ministry of Power, 2017).

23. In 1961, AP's generation capacity was 213 MW, accounting for 4.7 per cent of the national capacity.

24. A.K. Swain, *Political Economy of Public Policy Making in the Indian Electricity Sector: A Study of Orissa and Andhra Pradesh* (MPhil dissertation, New Delhi: Jawaharlal Nehru University, 2006).

25. T.L. Sankar, 'Power Sector: Rise, Fall and Reform', *Economic and Political Weekly* 38(12–13) (2003): 1171–8.

26. Swain, *Public Policy Making in the Indian Electricity Sector*.

27. Interview with two ex-Chairmen of APSEB, on 23 and 24 January 2017, Hyderabad.

28. Swain, *Public Policy Making in the Indian Electricity Sector*.

29. Suri, 'Andhra Pradesh'.

30. S.S. Kale, *Electrifying India: Regional Political Economies of Development* (Stanford: Stanford University Press, 2014).

31. Swain, *Public Policy Making in the Indian Electricity Sector*.
32. Then Chairman of APSEB, N. Tata Rao, pointed out that NTR wanted to further reduce the agricultural tariff, while continuing with metered supply. After taking his oath of office, NTR had his first meeting with Rao and expressed concerns about 'economic implications of continuing flat-rate-tariff and political ramifications of reverting it.... Keeping with the political interest, N.T.R. decided to carry forward the economic blunder'. Interview with N. Tata Rao, ex-Chairman of APSEB, 17 May 2006, Hyderabad.
33. Planning Commission, *Annual Report on the Working of State Electricity Boards & Electricity Departments* (New Delhi: Planning Commission, Government of India, 2002).
34. RBI, *Statistics on Indian States*.
35. Sankar, 'Power Sector'.
36. In 1991, AP Gas Power Corporation (APGPC) was established as a joint venture of APSEB and 22 industries, marking the private sector's entry in AP's power generation. The industries had 85 per cent share of 100 MW commenced in 1991 and 75 per cent of 172 MW commenced in 1997. Although the plant was originally permitted only to generate, it was latter allowed to operate as a captive plant for the participating industries. Thereby, the Board lost some important sources of cross-subsidy. Swain, *Public Policy Making in the Indian Electricity Sector*; B.S. Pani, N. Sreekumar, and M.T. Reddy, 'Power Sector Reforms in Andhra Pradesh: Their Impact and Policy Gaps', *GAPS Series Working Paper 11* (Hyderabad: Governance and Policy Spaces Project, Centre for Economics and Social Studies, 2007).
37. Interview with two of the members of this high-level committee, on 24 and 25 January 2017, Hyderabad.
38. Suri, 'Andhra Pradesh'.
39. World Bank, *Andhra Pradesh: Agenda for Economic Reforms* (Washington DC: The World Bank, 1997).
40. Pani et al., 'Power Sector Reforms'.
41. Kale, *Electrifying India*.
42. N.K. Dubash and D.N. Rao, *The Practice and Politics of Regulation: Regulatory Governance in Indian Electricity* (Delhi: Macmillan India, 2007).
43. Early success of the utilities is credited to the first two Chairman and Managing Directors (CMDs) of the APTRANSCO. Anil Kumar Kutty, who was the last Chairman of APSEB and continued as first CMD of APTRANSCO, was instrumental in facilitating the institutional transition. Rachel Chatterjee, who took over as CMD of APTRANSCO in 2001, played an important role in implementing the management reforms in the discoms.

44. A.K. Swain and O. Charnoz, 'In Pursuit of Energy Efficiency in India's Agriculture: Fighting "Free Power" or Working with It?', *AFD Working Paper 126* (Paris: Agence Française de Développement, 2012).

45. Pani et al., 'Power Sector Reforms'.

46. PC, *Working of State Electricity Boards*.

47. MoP, *Power for All: Andhra Pradesh* (Ministry of Power, Government of India and Government of Andhra Pradesh, 2014).

48. Kale, *Electrifying India*.

49. K. Srinivasulu, 'Political Articulation and Policy Discourse in the 2004 Election in Andhra Pradesh', *GAPS Working Paper 1* (Hyderabad: Governance and Policy Spaces Project, Centre for Economic and Social Studies, 2004).

50. Interestingly, the vote share of the winner, the Congress Party, also dropped from 40.6 per cent to 38.5 per cent, though it gained ninety-four assembly seats.

51. Suri, 'Dominance to Disarray'.

52. K.C. Suri, 'Andhra Pradesh: Set Back for TDP in Panchayat Elections'. *Economic and Political Weekly* 36(41) (13 October 2001): 3892–5.

53. PFC, *State Power Utilities*.

54. PFC, *State Power Utilities*.

55. MoP, *Power for All*.

56. Interview with an NGO representative, 25 January 2017, Hyderabad.

57. A. Padmanabhan, 'Inside Chandrababu Naidu's Plan to Make Andhra Pradesh a Sunrise State', *Mint*, 7 July 2017, available http://www.livemint.com/Politics/ZzAXntmInHn4zblKOIR0nN/Inside-Chandrababu-Naidus-plan-to-make-Andhra-Pradesh-a-sun.html (accessed on 15 September 2017).

58. The Hindu, 'Naidu Asks Energy Deptartment not to Increase Power Tariff.' *The Hindu*, 9 August 2017, available http://www.thehindu.com/news/cities/Vijayawada/naidu-asks-energy-dept-not-to-increase-power-tariff/article19453503.ece (accessed on 15 September 2017).

59. GoAP, *Sunrise Andhra Pradesh*, 2016.

60. Padmanabhan, 'Inside Chandrababu Naidu's Plan'.

61. S. Akbar, 'Andhra Pradesh Embarks on Mission to Reduce Power Bills', *The Times of India*, 18 June 2017, available http://timesofindia.indiatimes.com/city/amaravati/andhra-pradesh-embarks-on-mission-to-reduce-power-bills/articleshow/59204744.cms (accessed on 15 September 2017).

62. MoP, *Power for All*.

63. GARV Portal, available https://garv.gov.in (accessed on 12 August 2017).

64. The project, to be implemented over five years, supports power transmission system strengthening, smart grid development in urban areas,

distribution strengthening in rural areas and technical assistance for institutional development and capacity building. The World Bank, 2017. 'New Project to Support 24×7 Power for All in Andhra Pradesh, India', available www.worldbank.org/en/news/press-release/2017/05/26/new-project-support-24×7-power-all-andhra-pradesh-india (accessed on 4 September 2017).

65. CEA, *Load Generation Balance Report 2017–18* (New Delhi: Central Electricity Authority, 2017).

66. Y. Mallikarjun, 'China's Longi to Set up Solar Cell Manufacturing Plant in A.P.', *The Hindu*, 24 September 2015, Hyderabad.

67. Business Standard, 'EESL to Invest Rs 24,700 cr for Energy Conservation in AP' *Business Standard*, 28 January 2017, available http://www.business-standard.com/article/news-ians/eesl-to-invest-rs-24-700-crore-for-energy-conservation-in-andhra-117012800782_1.html (accessed on 15 September 2017).

68. In addition, Naidu has prioritized a 40-year-old dormant irrigation project, that is, the Polavaram Project, and seeks to complete it by 2019 (Padmanabhan, 'Inside Chandrababu Naidu's Plan'). When completed, this project will cater to significant part of agricultural water need in the state and thus, expected to result in reduced agricultural electricity demand.

69. As of first quarter of 2017–18, UDAY Portal, available www.uday.gov.in (accessed on 4 September 2017).

2

MD ZAKARIA SIDDIQUI

Disempowerment of Incumbent Elite and Governance

A Case of Bihar's Electricity Sector

Despite Bihar's legacy of spearheading key political movements in modern Indian history, its government has long enjoyed what can be termed as an 'accountability holiday'. As a result of this holiday, access to most basic services like education, health, and basic energy needs have remained at low levels in comparison to other states. A recent study ranked Bihar among the worst performing states in case of infrastructure, social service, and law and order delivery.[1] Among major countries, India's per capita modern energy consumption is lowest and Bihar's is the lowest in India. It is only after 2005 that one begins to see some significant progress in governance and service. To make sense of changes in Bihar's electricity sector, a brief description of the state's overarching political context is given here.

Three Phases of Political History in Post-Independence Bihar

The history of post-independence Bihar can be divided in three periods, in which Lalu Prasad Yadav's fifteen-year rule (1990–2004) features centrally. First, prior to the 1990s, upper castes dominated the political landscape of Bihar, pervading the State Assembly, judiciary, police, and bureaucracy even in face of dwindling economic development. Bihar ranked lowest among Indian states in every reported social and economic indicator.[2] The 'system' of state-directed development strategy without a clear accountability mechanism allowed upper castes to plunder state resources for personal gain with impunity. In addition to the state machinery, upper castes also dominated the media. Even after a sustained disappointing performance by the Bihar government, the media rarely covered endemic issues of corruption. This dominance of upper castes in every sphere of power and influence was the legacy of the colonial era's system of revenue collection, the zamindari system. Due to half-hearted efforts to implement land reforms, upper castes remained in possession of their lands even in the post-independence era. The only option for the illiterate poor masses to get a share in state-directed development funds was to negotiate it with the help of their local zamindar, creating an entrenched system of clientelism where dominant land owners acted as exploitative middlemen between the poor and the state. The upper caste dominated the exploitative network that siphoned state-directed development resources was an integrated system. The zamindari system provided them the crucial advantage that helped them to gain dominance not only at local level but also at every other level of governance and influence such as bureaucracy, judiciary, and police. Such an integrated network allowed upper castes to unduly appropriate state power and resources for many decades.

The anti-emergency movement of 1975, led by Jayprakash Narayan and dubbed as a 'total revolution', was a watershed event in the history of modern Bihar. From this movement, a class of new political actors belonging to the lower castes emerged. Eventually, this paved the way for the second period of Bihar's political history; the fifteen-year regime of Lalu Prasad Yadav that began in 1990 and also saw a massive rise in the share of seats held by lower-caste candidates in the state assembly, crossing the 50 per cent mark.

In India, the period between the 1990s and the early 2000s are usually remembered as a period of progress and massive alterations in economic life. In Bihar, however, this period symbolizes deterioration and chaos, the economy stagnated and state infrastructure regressed. Lalu Prasad Yadav saw no prospect in reforming the corrupt bureaucracy and law-and-order system which was the key driver of the state-directed model of development. He had good reasons to doubt the system's ability to empower and deliver resources to the socially disadvantaged, as it had failed to do so for 40 years. Calculating that any effort to work through existing public institutions would further entrench the power of the upper castes in the 'system' instead of empowering lower castes, Lalu Prasad Yadav began to deliberately work towards weakening state capacity and development activities in order to prevent the flow of state resources to the former.[3]

Implementation of Other Backward Classes (OBC) reservation by the central government in August 1990 further heightened the conflict between Bihar's state bureaucracy and the lower-caste ruling party. Lending aggressive support to the central commission's recommendation to extend job and education quotas to OBCs, Lalu provided a formidable counter-slogan to Indira Gandhi's famous *Garibi hatao* (eradicate poverty) with *Bhurabal hatao* (remove upper castes, upper castes being—Bhumihars, Rajputs, Brahmins, and Lalas) and *Vikas nahin samman chahiye* (not development, we want dignity). To weaken the grip of the upper caste on bureaucracy, Lalu Prasad Yadav resorted to frequently transferring high-level bureaucrats, out-of-turn posting of lower-caste bureaucrats to significant positions; and refusing to fill vacant positions with new appointments. Lalu Prasad Yadav likewise remained unfriendly to corporate interests; for example, he initiated various charges of corruption against Tata Industries and did not extend their mining lease.[4] Thanks to Lalu Prasad Yadav's strategy of 'state incapacity by design', Bihar's electricity sector also deteriorated.[5]

While Bihar's overall economy stagnated during Lalu Prasad Yadav's tenure, there was also a sharp decline in poverty. From 1993 to 2005, the poverty ratio of Bihar (and Jharkhand) combined declined by 14 per cent (from 54.5 per cent to 41.5 per cent), compared to a less than 8 per cent decline nationally and a less than 2 per cent decline in Odisha.[6] Thus, the empowerment of backward castes during the Lalu Prasad Yadav era had real distributional consequences, notably the raised political aspirations of lower castes posed challenges for any future government.

The final blow to the legitimacy of state machinery was delivered when news of a 'fodder scam' surfaced in 1997. Bureaucratic activity came to a standstill as officers hesitated to sign any approval for fiscal expenditure, due to fear of being investigated for corruption. Faced with corruption charges, Lalu Prasad Yadav resigned, but not before ensuring his wife Rabri Devi was appointed interim chief minister, acting per his directions. In fact, the situation was so appalling that the government of a state with unending need of development expenditure was running a revenue surplus.[7]

The February 2005 election yielded a hung assembly with no clear winner, resulting in the invocation of President's Rule until the next election in November 2005. By this time, ongoing corruption charges overshadowed Lalu Prasad Yadav's anti-upper-caste narrative as the primary feature of his party's reputation. This shift especially occurred among many smaller lower-caste groups who did not benefit much from Lalu Prasad Yadav's regime; he tried to consolidate support among castes and groups that were more numerous—that is, the Yadavs and Muslims.[8]

After 15 years of being out of power and surviving Lalu Prasad Yadav's anti-upper caste rhetoric, the upper castes forged a coalition with yet another group of disempowered castes whose interests Lalu Prasad Yadav did not address. A new party named Janata Dal United (JDU)—representing the left-behind disempowered castes and led by Nitish Kumar—was swept into power with the help of the upper-caste Bharatiya Janata Party (BJP). This was the first instance in Bihar when a party solely representing upper castes had accepted a subsidiary status in a power-sharing coalition.

Bihar's trajectory of economic performance changed significantly after Nitish Kumar took over as Chief Minister in 2005, posting double-digit growth rates for most of the intervening years to the present. Serious crime rates began to fall significantly.[9] These trends were applauded by the media as result of Nitish Kumar's philosophy of *shushashan* (good governance) as opposed to the *jungle-raj* (literally, law of the jungle) of Lalu Prasad Yadav. The praise of Kumar's regime could partly be attributed to the willingness of upper-caste-dominated media to support Nitish Kumar's upper-caste-backed regime if it meant avoiding Lalu-style anti-upper-caste populism. Yet, the political mobilization of lower castes made it impossible for Nitish Kumar's government and bureaucracy to survive without addressing issues that the masses faced. In response, Kumar's government focused on reviving schools and building roads and bridges. However, not all results were positive, as crime against women and Dalits rose with little state response.[10] Nitish Kumar's government also neglected the electricity sector until widespread protests across the state in 2011 demanded its attention.

Electricity Sector and Political Context

Bihar's political turmoil and the performance of its electricity sector are intimately linked. Forty-four years post-independence, a meagre 12.5 per cent of households in Bihar were electrified, compared to a national average of 42 per cent.[11] In the case of rural household electrification, Bihar stood at 5.5 per cent against a national average of 30.5 per cent. In short, access to electricity remained limited to a privileged few in the state.

During the last decade of the twentieth century, when most states unbundled their monolithic electricity boards and introduced independent regulation, Bihar's electricity sector went from stagnation to new levels of deterioration. The secession of Jharkhand from Bihar in 2000 was an additional blow to the latter's already stagnant economy, as strategic natural resources and manufacturing hubs were located in the area that became Jharkhand. Hardship was also experienced by the Bihar's electricity sector because most of its generating plants and revenue-yielding industrial consumers were located in the ceded territory.[12] The continued deterioration of law and order and an almost non-functional bureaucracy during Lalu's period also affected the electricity sector adversely. Mass theft of distribution wires and transformers in particular led to the de-electrification of many villages. Lalu prevented upper-caste-dominated police forces from taking action against theft, as he thought they systematically discriminated against lower castes. According to one former employee of the Bihar State Electricity Board (BSEB), stealing wires almost became a profession. On one occasion this ex-officer, while on duty during the night, suspected that an observed disturbance in the system was due to the activities of wire thieves. He instructed the system operator to immediately switch the system back on in certain areas. The next morning, authorities found wire thieves dead adjacent to power lines, apparently due to electrocution.[13]

De-electrification of at least some villages was also the result of political rivalry. In some cases, village electrification was delayed due to caste rivalries between political representatives and bureaucrats. In such cases politicians encouraged people from their constituency to de-electrify villages already connected to the grid, in order to put pressure on BSEB.[14] From within, BSEB was turning into a battleground of factions which were based on caste groupings.[15] Non-technical staff handling finances and human resources often harassed engineers over issues such as promotions, pensions, and other benefits. Non-technical staff were also able to influence transfer decisions of engineers. In fact, during this period BSEB saw an influx of higher level officials from non-technical backgrounds, due to an inflow of Bihar Public Services Commission (BPSC) officials: for example, the secretary of BSEB was often a former BPSC officer. Owing to these factors, after a decade of Lalu's rule, household electrification declined from 12 per cent in 1991 to 10 per cent in 2001 in Bihar, while the national average went up to 94 per cent from 42 per cent during the same period.[16]

The disappointing performance of the state's electricity sector spurred an array of informal sector innovations catering to the accelerating demand for modern energy thanks to overall liberalization of the Indian economy.[17] Pump sets of smaller capacities powered by diesel/kerosene began to emerge.[18] Micro-grids powered by diesel generators serving small neighbourhoods and commercial centres became common. Many households in rural areas installed small battery-backed solar photovoltaic panels for their lighting requirements. To serve this demand, retail shops for solar panels have mushroomed in almost every district town since 2000. In fact, solar panels have become an important dowry/gift item for marriages.[19] However, the highly unregulated nature of this marketplace has often lured ill-informed consumers into buying cheap Chinese-made panels without any service or product warranty/guarantee, often becoming non-functional after a few months.[20]

A select few villages had shopkeepers rent out battery-based lamps to villagers at dusk, which were charged during the day using solar photovoltaic panels installed by shopkeepers. Such alternative models of accessing modern energy services were largely geared towards home lighting, neglecting the provision of high voltage electricity required for irrigation, cooking, and the rural industry. Additionally, these initiatives remained quantitatively insignificant in proportion to the scale of need.[21]

Thanks to the actions taken under President's Rule in the state, in 2005 the Bihar Electricity Regulatory Commission (BERC) was established. President's Rule unleashed the purview of the bureaucracy, allowing it to function after a considerable period of restraint during Lalu's period.[22] However, the BSEB continued to operate as a monolithic body even under Kumar's government. It was only after popular protests around the state in 2011 and 2012 that Nitish Kumar was compelled to give the electricity sector its due attention. Press reports from March 2011 indicate that mobs of people blocked roads and ransacked electricity board offices and power substations throughout the state. For example, in the Bhagalpur district, people were so enraged that the District Magistrate and Superintendent of Police narrowly managed to escape from being lynched by a mob.[23] In Bhagalpur, a group of more than 300 women laid siege to the BSEB General Manager's office. Such protests were a common scene in almost every district town. The severity of the crisis can be gauged by the fact that Bhagalpur was generating only 1–7 megawatts (MWs) of electricity during March 2011 against a demand requirement of about 60 MW. Silk workers became particularly militant in Bhagalpur, a result of the fact that the textile industry—a major source of employment for the district—has been one of the power crisis's worst victims.[24] Notably, all these protests were mostly spontaneous, occurring absent any declared political affiliations.

The unrest soon impacted the debate taking place in the state assembly. Stakeholders across the ideological spectrum urged the government to take drastic action towards improving the state's generation capacity. The crisis symbolically came to a head when the infamous 30 July 2012 impacted the Independence Day speech of Chief Minister Kumar, who publicly touted his commitment to improving the supply of power while making a plea for re-election. The timeline of key political events in the history of Bihar's power sector is given in Table 2.1.

Post-2012 Period: An Era of Reforms

Unbundling

As a first step towards addressing protests stemming from problems in the power sector, BSEB assets were unbundled into generation, transmission, and two distribution companies (servicing the northern and southern regions of Bihar respectively) in November 2012, each comprising a subsidiary of the newly formed Bihar State Power

TABLE 2.1   Timeline of Key Events: Bihar

State Politics		Power Sector Events
• Upper castes dominated all public institutions. • Zamindari system in villages and upper caste domination in every field of governance ensured accountability holiday for state government.	Prior to 1990	• Electricity sector barely survived. Only 12 per cent of households could have access to electricity by the end of this period.
• Increased political representation of lower castes in Assembly but bureaucracy, judiciary, and police was still upper caste dominated. • Lalu followed the policy of 'state incapacity of design' to dislodge upper castes from positions and influence. • A state with endless need of development expenditure was running budget surplus because bureaucracy came to a complete halt. • Due to this, several social and economic services became worse than the situation of 1990 while other states of India saw massive economic transformation after liberalization initiated in 1991. • However, due to empowerment of lower castes poverty decline during this period accelerated.	Post-1990 Phase 2: Lalu's Rule in Bihar 1990 to 2004	• In most states independent electricity regulatory body was established by this time, however continued to operate under monolithic Electricity board model without any pressure from independent regulator. • Performance of electricity sector probably even worse than the situation in 1990. • Percentage of household electrified declined to 10 per cent in 2001 from 12 per cent in 1990. • Thanks to lawlessness that prevailed due to policy of 'state incapacity design' theft of electricity distribution wires and transformers became rampant.

(Cont'd)

TABLE 2.1 (*Cont'd*)

State Politics		Power Sector Events
	2005 Phase 3: Post-Lalu Era	• Independent regulatory body for electricity was established in this era. • However, there was no perceptible change in the way the electricity board functioned.
• 'Fodder scam' and other governance failures eventually paved the way for New coalition under the leadership Nitish Kumar to take the seat of power in the state.		
• Thanks to the political empowerment of masses and lower castes, state government eventually became responsive; intuitions of social and economic infrastructure began to improve and economic growth rates generally crossed double digit.	2012 and after Phase 3: Elbow effect in electricity sector	• Due to continued ignorance of electricity sector state wide protests of common people erupted and in many cases turning violent. • Chief minister realizing the demand for improving electricity gave exclusive attention to the electricity sector. • A coincidence of simultaneous availability of funds for strengthening transmission and rural electrification really offered the opportunity for the government to increase access and the reliability of power. • Even with little of its own generation capacity Bihar has been able meet its demand at relatively lower cost due lower prices of prevailing national level short-term market for electricity. • With the period of four years access to electricity from mere 20 lakh households to 90 lakh households. Such a rapid progress in electrification was unprecedented in the history of the state.

Source: Author.

Holding Company (BSPHC). Interestingly, all of these subsidiaries are still located on different floors of the Bidyut Bhavan building in Patna where the erstwhile BSEB conducted business, raising the question of whether the unbundling was merely cosmetic in nature. Similarly, the Chairman-cum-Managing Director of BSPHC has the authority to transfer employees across subsidiaries. In many cases, contracts for each subsidiary are routed through the BSPHC. Thus, having separate entities increases the flow of information and information-related costs at disaggregated level due to regulatory requirements specifying that each company must file their own annual revenue requirement for tariff allowances. At the same time, these companies are able to share their capabilities due to the presence of a parent organization.

Improved Access

About 89 per cent of Bihar's 10.4 crore population still lives in rural areas.[25] The most recently available information (up to the year 2014–15) shows per day electricity consumption per household in rural Bihar is 1.4 kWh and for urban areas it is 4.3 kilowatt hour (kWh).[26] Village-level electrification has expanded rapidly since 2012: about 97 per cent of the villages were electrified by the end of May 2016. The growth in domestic consumers since 2005–6 has been phenomenal, from 1 lakh to 9 lakh in 2015–16. Bihar experienced a particularly sharp spike of new connections after unbundling in 2012, providing concrete evidence of successful reform. However, household electrification in rural Bihar still has a long way to go before universal access is achieved. Notwithstanding high levels of village electrification, about 87 per cent of the total 1.7 crore rural households in Bihar are yet to be electrified as of the end of May 2016.[27] Even in urban areas, census records show that 44 per cent of households have yet to use electricity as the main source of their lighting. Even more serious is the dearth of clean cooking facilities in Bihar: only 9 per cent had access to some kind of modern fuel (including kerosene) as recently as 2011.[28]

Improved Power Supply

While so many households have recently been electrified in Bihar, deficits in power supply have also been significantly reduced, both in terms of energy and capacity. The state has been able to procure enough power at a low cost even amid the fast-growing demand for power. The deficit in supply has remained particularly low since 2012. This increase in power demand was mainly due to rapid electrification and the addition of new domestic consumers. Meeting demand with little or no generation capacity of its own meant that Bihar was required to procure a significant amount of its power from external sources; for example, about 72 per cent of the power purchased by Bihar state in 2014–15 was sourced from central government-sector generators, that is, the National Thermal Power Corporation (NTPC) and the National Hydro Power Corporation (NHPC).[29] The state's own generating stations, meanwhile, contributed only a little more than four per cent, while the remaining 19 per cent of total power purchase came from short- and medium-term purchases available at much cheaper prices. Therefore, the increase in total power purchase costs as depicted in Figure 2.1 is accounted for

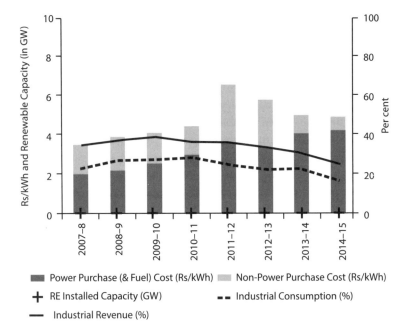

FIGURE 2.1 Physical and Financial Profile: Bihar

Source: CSO, *Energy Statistics* (New Delhi: Central Statistics Office, Ministry of Statistics and Programme Implementation, Government of India, 2010, 2012, 2014, and 2016); PFC, *Reports on Performance of State Power Utilities* (New Delhi: Power Finance Corporation Limited, 2011, 2013, 2015, and 2016).

by an increase in the volume of power purchased, rather than any real increase in the per-unit cost of power. On the other hand, Bihar's increasing dependence on short-term contracts for power provision has led to a significant decline in the overall cost per unit of power, which is entirely attributable to the reduced burden of fixed costs because Bihar does not need to maintain inefficient power plants (Figure 2.1).

A Saga of Subsidies

Obviously, this growth in the quantity of power consumption was largely made available through huge revenue subsidies from the state government. For example, in year 2014–15, revenue subsidy to the electricity sector—famously known as the 'resource gap grant'—totalled Rs 2,891 crore. A large part of these costs cannot be recovered through the BERC approved tariff scheme—even if billing and collection efficiency is 100 per cent—because approved distribution losses are smaller than the actual level. The government, through its massive revenue subsidy, is helping discoms to recover more than these losses so that retail tariffs for economically weaker consumer groups can be kept at lower levels than originally approved. Figure 2.2 depicts the turnaround in financial performance of discoms over time in per unit (KWh) terms. For example, in 2014–15, actual distribution loss was 38 per cent for the northern discom against its approved loss level of 21 per cent. This implied that the northern discom would not be able to recover Rs 519 crore of its cost because 17 per cent of its distribution loss was not considered to be part of the covered costs when BERC issued tariff regulations. However, the government's subsidy to the northern discom was more than enough to compensate for this revenue loss. In fact, the northern discom received close to Rs 700 crore in excess of its losses which allowed it to keep retail tariffs at lower levels than were specified by BERC. Figure 2.1 reflects this reality, as 2013–14 and 2014–15 show revenue surplus for discoms of Bihar in aggregate.

During various interviews, it was evident that any increases in tariffs were seen as unfeasible option because it might hinder the current momentum towards universalization of access to electricity. Once discoms are able to establish their credibility of reliable supply of power tariffs may rise in future. Therefore, discoms initial focus is on expanding the network and providing a hassle-free experience to new consumers.

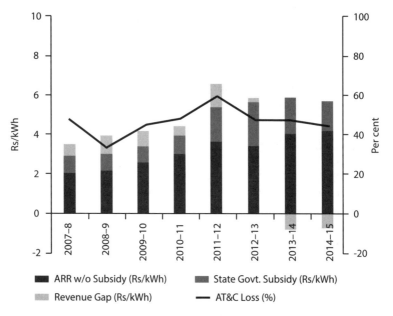

FIGURE 2.2   Supply-side Costs and Revenue Recovery: Bihar
Source: PFC, Reports on Performance of State Power Utilities (New Delhi: Power Finance Corporation Limited, 2011, 2013, 2015, and 2016).

Yet, for the latest tariff rates as of March 2017, the BERC approved a 55 per cent hike in electricity retail tariff to cover the costs of the discoms. Reacting to such a massive hike, the state government immediately announced subsidy of Rs 2,952 crore to limit the effective tariff increase to 20 per cent.

One problem that Bihar faces is a low demand for electricity connections, even in electrified villages. In order to deal with this situation, discoms are providing connections without any upfront installation charges; however, these are billed in later months to the consumers. There was clear emphasis among discom executives on increasing the efficiency of generation and transmission and billing the energy supplied.[30] Every new connection is metered, and there is lot of emphasis placed upon minimizing the gap between meter reading and billing. Both discoms have launched a pilot project of on-site billing using mobile devices. During field visits, it was promulgated that there are serious financial penalties and or imprisonment for the crime of stealing power. Upon hearing this, many people have chosen to become legal consumers. In the meantime, it appears that the government is willing to subsidize the electricity consumption of rural masses.

Regulatory Oversight

The role of BERC in improving the electricity sector's transparency can hardly be overstated. It is because of the BERC's continued effort that BSEB eventually began to file annual revenue requirements on time. BERC's role was crucial in ensuring the availability of information regarding cost of operations as well as formal recognition of electricity subsidies by the state. In sharp contrast to other states, in Bihar electricity tariffs are low not because regulators are forced by the government to avoid tariff increases, but instead because of the massive subsidy from the state budget discussed earlier. Thus, BERC has been successful in enforcing cost-reflective tariffs as mandated by Electricity Act, and has ensured explicit subsidy commitment from state finances. Unlike many other state electricity regulators, BERC has not become a victim of arm-twisting by state government, where regulators are forced to withhold due hikes in tariffs to reflect cost of supply often through informal means, for example, threat of punishment postings of regulators.

Availability of Financial Resources

Bihar has been able to improve the availability of electricity because of a political willingness to improve the sector among stakeholders was complemented by timely availability of financial resources for infrastructure capital investments. Funds from centrally sponsored programmes such as Accelerated Power Development and Reform Programme (APDRP) and its later avatars were used for improving urban network and meter installations while expansion of rural network was result of Rajiv Gandhi Grameen Vidyutikaran Yojana (RGGVY) and which later became Deendayal Upadhyaya Gram Jyoti Yojana (DDUGJY) after a change of government at the centre in 2014. These central resources were tied funds which could only be used in distribution sector.

However, simply improving and extending the distribution network would not have delivered power to end consumers if much-needed complementary investments in high voltage transmission capacity for transporting power from generation centres were not also available. Interestingly Bihar became a large beneficiary of the centrally administered Backward Regions Grant Fund (BRGF). A large part of this fund in case of Bihar was allocated for strengthening the transmission network, which played a key role in improving the availability of power.

In summary, the electricity sector has made great strides in improving physical performance due in no small part to federal funding.[31] Out of a total of Rs 12,000 crore that was awarded to Bihar under BRGF for the Twelfth Five-Year Plan period (2012–17), Rs 8,308.67 crore was earmarked for the electricity sector. It is also notable that Rs 6,395.19 crore is yet to be released by the central government according to information available till end of May 2016. During an interview, a senior bureaucrat working in the sector disclosed that the central Finance Minister has admitted the central government's inability to transfer the due amount in time. In anticipation of this obstacle, Bihar is planning to raise a loan against this expected amount in order to avoid time and cost overruns for the projects. Even before the Fifth Plan period, Bihar's electricity sector—especially its transmission sub-sector—received significant amounts of money under the Rashtriya Sam Vikas Yojana (RSVY) programme of central government, a previous avatar of BRGF, to help the backward districts of India. These grants for funding infrastructural expenditures are separate from and provided in addition to the aforementioned revenue subsidy from state government, known as the 'resource gap grant'.

Another factor critical to Bihar's success was the increased ability of Bihar's electricity bureaucracy to efficiently spend available fiscal resources. It has often been the case that Bihar could not utilize funds due to limited capacity to spend available financial resources. However, recent recruitment drives and the organizational restructuring of discoms, which are discussed at length later, have significantly enhanced the sector's capacity to spend available resources.[32] Thus, due to the availability of ample BRGF funding, all electricity sub-sectors of Bihar have been able to improve simultaneously. This rare coincidence of ample funding for improving the distribution and transmission sectors and low prices in the short-term power market has helped state government deliver widespread electricity access, even in rural areas.

Organizational Changes

Even with sufficient funding, however, some infrastructural projects have progressed very slowly because of a cumbersome contract-tendering process and limited human resources within the bureaucracy. Contracts for rural electrification projects were invited twice between January and June 2014, but both were cancelled due to lack of interest or unreasonably high bid amounts demanded by contractors. In one senior discom official's view, contracting is a process that should be handled by an independent agency of the state, rather than the engineers of the concerned electricity body, as is currently commonplace. The major reason for delay in tendering process historically has been officers' apprehension regarding corruption allegations. There is a fairly long history in Bihar of contracting processes resulting in legal disputes over suspected collusion and bribery.[33]

Perhaps a crucial factor in shaping the paranoid behaviour of bureaucrats was the infamous series of 'fodder scam' corruption cases that rocked Bihar government during Lalu's tenure. The then-newly appointed chairman-cum-managing director of the Bihar State Power Holding company decided to amend certain conditions for eligibility in the contracting process to increase bidder competition. Additionally, to ensure transparency, bids were opened within three days' time from announcement of the auction, while the entire process was conducted under video surveillance. After the award of rural electrification projects, contractors were monitored routinely by discom engineers. Thanks to these measures, no legal disputes arose after subsequent bidding processes, which was unheard of in the past.[34]

Another significant organizational change took place in workforce organization and augmentation. Prior to 2014, engineers dominated the electricity sector. In 2014, however, a recruitment drive by the discom brought in a significant number of non-engineers from other sectors. For recruiting engineering graduates, the Graduate Aptitude Test in Engineering score was used instead of additional examination, as was previously required. This measure reduced costs, increased selection transparency, and pre-empted any legal haggling on account of lack of fairness in examination.[35]

Additionally, the bureaucratic hierarchy was restructured on a functional basis. Previously, the hierarchy ran in the following descending rank without much attention to functional separation: chief engineer, executive engineer, assistant engineer, and finally junior engineer. Now this hierarchy operates according to well-identified functional areas, namely operation and maintenance, revenue, and projects. In the pre-2014 period, functional areas were not clearly identified, which made the delegation of responsibilities a problem. Due to increased staff strength and clarity in division of labour, bureaucratic capacity has increased significantly.[36]

Outsourcing Rural Revenue Collection

Bihar's rural revenue collection improved significantly after implementation of the Rural Revenue Franchisees (RRF) model in 2013, which deviates slightly from the standard model proposed by the central Ministry of Power. In Bihar's case, RRFs are paid for each collection as opposed to overall collection efficiency on the basis of billing at the distribution transformer level: Rs 4.50 for each meter reading, Rs 1.50 for each delivered bill, and three per cent of total revenue collection. The scope of RRF is limited to meter reading, bill distribution, and revenue collection; they have no role in managing the distribution network or undertaking capital expenditure. There are 3,500 RRFs currently active covering about 51 lakhs rural consumers in the state. In most states, RRFs are mostly non-functional, but in Bihar, RRF agencies comprise the backbone of rural revenue collection.[37]

Coordination between Political and Executive Leadership

The top two executives leading Bihar's electricity sector since mid-2014 are former Indian Administrative Service officers, known for their success in rehabilitating the state's road and bridge infrastructure.[38] When they were transferred to the electricity sector by the government, the intention was clear: the state government wanted to see similar improvements in electricity sector. The need for improvement was clear: despite electricity sector unbundling within two months of Nitish Kumar's Independence Day speech in 2012,[39] things did not change much on the ground until the aforementioned officials joined the electricity sector in mid-2014, given little more than one year's time to turn it around. One of the officers clearly identified rural electrification contract awarding and close monitoring of progress to be the top priorities of their team. This included replacing 35,000 non-functional distribution transformers in various parts of the state. The impetus to improve the electricity sector was sustained after Nitish Kumar won re-election in November 2014. Thus, successful coordination between the political and bureaucratic leadership has been a key aspect of positive changes in Bihar's electricity sector, a development which stands in marked contrast to Lalu's era.

***

Bihar's political churnings and the performance of its electricity sector are intimately linked. Performance of Bihar's electricity sector is embedded in three phases of political history. First, from independence until 1990, upper castes dominated every sphere of government and the media. State-directed development failed to deliver major social and physical infrastructure improvements, including electricity, due to appropriation of state resources by advantaged social groups.

Second, in the 1990s to mid-2000s, the era of chaotic lower-caste empowerment was led by Lalu Yadav. This period witnessed a significant rise in the political representation of lower castes in the state assembly and the national parliament. To stop the unabated flow of state-directed development funds to upper castes by way of corruption, Lalu deliberately clogged institutions of bureaucracy and police by ignoring paperwork, transferring staffers, and refusing to fill vacant positions. As result, Bihar faced the rare situation of economic stagnation and fiscal surplus, along with much-needed social change and poverty alleviation. However, after the 'fodder scam' of 1997 surfaced, corruption issues overshadowed Lalu's belligerent anti-upper-caste stance. Perhaps unsurprisingly, the experience of the electricity sector mirrored prevailing political and economic chaos in the state: general weakening of bureaucracy and law and order led to a decline in the number of electrified villages, due to mass-scale theft of electricity wires and transformers.

In the mid-2000s, newly elected Chief Minister Nitish Kumar rebuilt the institutions of bureaucracy and law enforcement, leading crime rates to decline. However, the situation in the electricity sector began to improve only after massive protests erupted against the dismal supply of and access to electricity in major district towns of Bihar. In response to the political urgency for rapid electrification these protests sparked, the untied central funds from BRGF provided much-needed infrastructural improvements of transmission sector that responded to peoples' demand for electricity services. The universalization of electricity access, occurring at a rapid pace in current times, contrasts sharply with the dismal performance of electricity sector prior to 2005. The bureaucracy in Bihar is still largely dominated by upper castes; however, thanks to new regulatory safeguards and lower caste mobilization, it is not possible for upper-caste bureaucrats to siphon resources away from the state and lower castes.

One additional factor that worked in Bihar's favour is that it had no obligation to purchase power from its own generating plants because they did not exist. Bihar purchases about 20 per cent of its required electricity from short-term market, where prices are considerably lower than standard long-term power purchase agreements. The vast sums of money that have been apportioned for the electricity sector demonstrates just how strong of a priority it has become for the Bihar government after the 2011 protests.

The focus of Bihar's overall policy strategy continues to be on extending the network and universalizing grid access, rather than the recovery of costs. Bihar has a historically low rate of household electrification, even in electrified villages, which suggests a problem on the demand side. Given the widespread poverty in the state, it is important to galvanize the economy with very high employment elasticity so that the poorest share the benefits of economic growth. Access to electricity can be very instrumental for promoting employment, especially the employment of women.[40]

Notes and References

1. Sudipto Mundle, Samik Chowdhury, and Satadru Sikdar, 'Governance Performance of Indian States', *Economic and Political Weekly* 51(36), 2016: 55–64.
2. Mundle et al., 'Governance Performance'.
3. Jeffrey Witsoe, *Democracy against Development: Lower-Caste Politics and Political Modernity in Postcolonial India* (Chicago: University of Chicago Press, 2013).

4. Sunila S. Kale and Nimah Mazaheri, 'Natural Resources, Development Strategies, and Lower Caste Empowerment in India's Mineral Belt: Bihar and Odisha during the 1990s', *Studies in Comparative International Development* 49(3), 2014: 343–69.

5. The term 'state incapacity by design' in the context of Bihar was coined by Santhosh Mathew and Mick Moore, 'State Incapacity by Design: Understanding the Bihar Story', *IDS Working Papers*, no. 366 (2011): 1–31.

6. S. Mahendra Dev and C. Ravi. 'Poverty and Inequality: All-India and States, 1983–2005', *Economic and Political Weekly* 42(6), February 2007: 509–21 (Table 8).

7. Rohan Mukherjee, 'Reviving the Administration: Bihar State, India 2005–2009', *Innovations for Successful Societies* (New Jersey: Princeton University, 2010), available https://successfulsocieties.princeton.edu/publications/reviving-administration-bihar-state-india-2005-2009 (accessed on 26 March 2018).

8. Jeffrey Witsoe, 'Lalu Yadav's Bihar: An Incomplete Revolution', in *Democracy against Development*, 51–78.

9. Arnab Mukherji and Anjan Mukherji, 'Bihar: What went Wrong? And What Changed?', *Working Paper No. 12/107* (New Delhi: National Institute of Public Finance). However, crimes against women were on the rise during this period.

10. Chirashree Das Gupta, 'Unravelling Bihar's Growth Miracle', *Economic and Political Weekly* 45(52), 2010: 50–62.

11. Government of India, *General Census of India* (New Delhi: Government of India, 2011).

12. Government of Bihar, 'Energy Sector, Important Indicators', Government of Bihar Energy Department, available http://energy.bih.nic.in/. (accessed on 26 March 2018).

13. Interview with senior ex-employee of Bihar State Electricity Board, Patna, 26 September 2016. All interviews for used in this research were conducted by the author on a not-for-attribution basis.

14. Interview with senior ex-employee of Bihar State Electricity Board, Patna, 26 September 2016.

15. Confirmed during several interviews but two interviews were particularly relevant. Interview with former junior executive in BSEB, Patna, 13 October 2016. Interview with midlevel executive currently working with one of the utilities in Bihar and was also working during BSEB days, Patna, 22 September 2016.

16. Government of India, *General Census*.

17. Based on extensive fieldwork done by the author in Jharkhand and Bihar in mid-2012.

18. Kalpana Wilson, 'Patterns of Accumulation and Struggles of Rural Labour: Some Aspects of Agrarian Change in Central Bihar', *The Journal of Peasant Studies* 26(2–3), 1999: 316–54.

19. Ankur Paliwal, 'Power-Starved Bihar Lights Up with Cheap Solar Panels', *Business Standard*, 16 September 2012, available http://www.business-standard.com/article/companies/power-starved-bihar-lights-up-with-cheap-solar-panels-112091602019_1.html (accessed on 26 March 2018).

20. Shreya Jai, 'Indian Solar Panel Makers Demand Anti-Dumping Duty against China', *Business Standard*, 9 June 2017, available http://www.business-standard.com/article/economy-policy/indian-solar-panel-makers-demand-anti-dumping-duty-against-china-117060600255_1.html (accessed on 26 March 2018).

21. Fieldwork done by the author in Jharkhand and Bihar in mid-2013.

22. Mukherji and Mukherji, 'Bihar'.

23. Gautam Sarkar, 'Residents on Warpath over Power Crisis', *The Telegraph*, 27 March 2011, available https://www.telegraphindia.com/1110327/jsp/bihar/story_13769279.jsp (accessed on 26 March 2018).

24. 'Parties Hit Streets for Power', *The Telegraph*, 31 May 2011, available https://www.telegraphindia.com/1110531/jsp/bihar/story_14048480.jsp (accessed on 26 March 2018); M.I. Khan, 'No Power to the People: Bihar Awaits *bijli rani*', *Rediff*, 1 June 2011, available http://www.rediff.com/news/slide-show/slide-show-1-no-power-to-the-people-bihar-awaits-bijli-rani/20110601.htm#1 (accessed on 26 March 2018); Raman Iyer, 'Protests Continue in Bihar Against Power Crisis', *TopNews*, 28 March 2011, available http://www.topnews.in/law/protests-continue-bihar-against-power-crisis-256643 (accessed on 26 March 2018).

25. Government of India, *General Census*.

26. Government of India Ministry of Power, '24×7 Power for All: A Joint Initiative of Government of India and Government of Bihar' (New Delhi: Ministry of Power, 2015), available http://powermin.nic.in/sites/default/files/uploads/BIHAR_PFA_REPORT_15.12.2015_With_Signature_II.pdf (accessed on 26 March 2018).

27. Government of India GARV Dashboard, 'Status of Rural Electrification in Bihar', 31 August 2017, available http://garv.gov.in/assets/uploads/reports/statesnaps/Bihar.pdf (accessed on 26 March 2018).

28. Government of India, *General Census*.

29. Calculated by author from power purchase information contained in tariff orders for discoms issued by BERC, 21 March 2015.

30. In the majority of interviews conducted with senior executives, emphasis on increasing the number of consumers was one observed trend.

31. Interview with senior bureaucrat who has worked in state and central electricity governance institutions, Patna, 18 October 2016.

32. Interview with senior executive who has portfolio across utilities in Bihar, Patna, 22 October 2016.

33. Interview with senior bureaucrat in state energy sector, Patna, 22 September 2016.

34. Interview with senior bureaucrat in state energy sector, Patna, 22 September 2016.

35. Interview with senior executive dealing with discom finances, Patna, 19 October 2016.

36. Interview with senior executive dealing with discom finances, Patna, 19 October 2016.

37. Interview with senior executive dealing with discom finances, Patna, 19 October 2016.

38. Nimah Mazaheri and Md Zakaria Siddiqui, 'Leadership and Institutional Change in the Public Provision of Transportation Infrastructure: An Analysis of India's Bihar', *The Journal of Development Studies* 49(1) 2013: 19–35.

39. Amit Chaturvedi and Manish Kumar, 'If Power Situation Doesn't Improve, I Will Not Seek Votes in 2015: Nitish Kumar', *NDTV*, 15 August 2012, available http://www.ndtv.com/india-news/if-power-situation-doesnt-improve-i-will-not-seek-votes-in-2015-nitish-kumar-496924 (accessed on 26 March 2018).

40. Taryn Dinkelman, 'The Effects of Rural Electrification on Employment: New Evidence from South Africa', *The American Economic Review* 101(7), 2011: 3078–108.

3

MEGHA KALADHARAN

Wielding Power in the Capital

The Case of the Delhi Electricity Distribution Sector

Delhi offers an interesting case study on the perils and rewards of a privatized distribution sector. In a sector which continues to be dominated by government players, Delhi is amongst the few states that have privatized their distribution sectors. The central government championed the cause of power sector reforms and the need to involve private sector participants throughout the 1990s, but in Delhi it was only under the Congress government's rule led by Sheila Dixit that it gained momentum and culminated in the privatization of the distribution sector in 2001.

In 1998, the newly elected Congress government paved the way for privatization to salvage an ailing distribution sector. The private distribution companies (discoms) brought in major technical and infrastructural overhauls and reduced aggregate technical and commercial (AT&C) losses from nearly 50 per cent in 1998[1] to under 15 per cent at present,[2] as set out in Figure 3.1. In the years that followed privatization, discoms closed the revenue gap early on and became profitable, but the absence of sustained tariff hikes led to the creation of staggering regulatory assets (RA), which continue to adversely impact their financial health despite being profitable on paper.

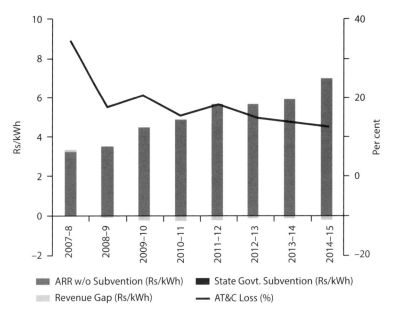

FIGURE 3.1   Physical and Financial Profile: Delhi
Sources: CSO, *Energy Statistics* (New Delhi: Central Statistics Office, Ministry of Statistics and Programme Implementation, Government of India, 2010, 2012, 2014, and 2016); PFC, *Reports on Performance of State Power Utilities* (New Delhi: Power Finance Corporation Limited, 2011, 2013, 2015, and 2016).

The regulator's inconsistent performance has also had a tangible impact on the distribution sector. The Delhi Electricity Regulatory Commission's (DERC) tariff determination function varied depending on the regulatory style of its chairperson at the time. This style transitioned from the first chairperson's need to establish its autonomy while also balancing the reform agenda to a period of stagnant tariff and regulatory uncertainty, followed by sustained and significant tariff hikes coupled with growing public outcry, especially by the Resident Welfare Associations (RWAs). From the discoms' perspective, while the tariff had been stagnant, the power purchase costs were going up considerably each year and formed the majority of its supply costs, as illustrated in Figure 3.2.

Consequently, the Aam Aadmi Party (AAP), an emerging political party under the leadership of Arvind Kejriwal, drew the battle lines for

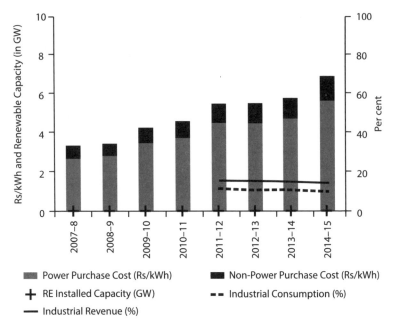

Figure 3.2   Supply-side Costs and Revenue Recovery: Delhi
Source: PFC, *Reports on Performance of State Power Utilities* (New Delhi: Power Finance Corporation Limited, 2011, 2013, 2015, and 2016)

the 2014 state election around tariff reduction and accountability of discoms. Since being elected, some of AAP's mandates—such as, ordering the CAG audit of discoms and imposition of penalties on discoms for unscheduled outages—may have gained the popular vote, but have faced constitutional roadblocks.

This chapter proposes to analyse the early sectoral issues of the need for privatization and the consistent underperformance of the state utility, the shifting of the debate to accountability of discoms, the modalities of regulating a private player providing a public good, the extent of government involvement in what should be an exclusively regulatory domain and, more recently, the impact of federal politics on the sector. The periodization of this chapter reflects the trajectory of the reform process, which closely mirrors the sub-national politics of each time period: the early years of Congress rule and Sheila Dixit's incumbency advantage that allowed her to implement reforms over the course of 15 years, the subsequent fomenting of a sectoral crisis arising from mounting RA and stagnant tariffs, the mercurial rise of AAP in an anti-incumbency wave, and the political impasse that brought the power sector to a standstill. Table 3.1 highlights key sectoral events in view of the political climate of the time.

TABLE 3.1   Timeline of Key Events: Delhi

Political Events	Year	Power Sector Events
• Congress wins Delhi Election	1998	• Pre-election riots break out over irregular power supply
	1999	• DERC established
	2001	• GNCTD issues transfer scheme rules; DVB unbundled into six entities: Transco, Genco, three private discoms—BRPL, BYPL, and TPDDL.
• Congress retains power in Delhi state elections	2003	
• Congress comes into power at the Centre	2004	• RA by DERC
	2007	• Commonwealth PPAs re-allocated to the three discoms, who protest on being forced to buy expensive power • MYT adopted by DERC
• Congress retains power in Delhi state elections	2008	• Significant reduction in AT&C loss levels achieved by discoms: 56 per cent in 2002–3 to 38 per cent in 2008–9
• Congress retains power at the Centre	2009	
	2010	• DERC Chairman, Mr Singh, drafts tariff order slashing tariff by 23 per cent; Order was challenged before court and held to be invalid.
• Aam Aadmi Party (AAP) formed under leadership of Arvind Kejriwal	2012	• 26 per cent tariff hike and 8 per cent surcharge ordered by DERC; Protests by BJP and AAP. • RPO Regulations issued by DERC

(Cont'd)

TABLE 3.1   (*Cont'd*)

Political Events	Year	Power Sector Events
• AAP forms minority government for 49 days	2013	
• BJP comes into power at the Centre • President's rule imposed in Delhi	2014	• AAP announces 50 per cent subsidy on consumption below 400 units • AAP orders CAG audit of discoms, which was challenged by discoms before Delhi High Court
• AAP wins Delhi state elections	2015	• Media leaks details of CAG report, which found discoms to have inflated RA by 8,000 crore. • Delhi High Court rules against CAG audit of discoms.
	2016	• AAP releases Delhi Solar Policy to promote rooftop solar projects—aims to install 1 GW by 2020 and 2 GW by 2025 • Delhi High Court invalidates various decisions taken by AAP without Lieutenant Governor's consent.

Source: Author.

1993–2005: The Impetus for Reform and the Privatization Experiment

The central government had championed the cause of power sector reforms and need to involve private sector participants throughout the 1990s, but in Delhi, it was only under the Congress government's rule from 1998 onwards that it gained momentum and culminated in the privatization of the distribution sector in 2002. The impetus for reform came from the mounting losses of the state utility, Delhi Vidyut Board (DVB), which were a drain on the public exchequer. Financial losses of DVB between FY 1995–6 and FY 1999–2000 rose from Rs 207 crore to Rs 1,103 crore. The DVB attributed the heavy financial losses to rampant theft, under-billing, poor collection practices, and a crumbling infrastructure. Therefore, it was not surprising that electricity became a key issue in the 1998 Delhi state elections. Bharatiya Janta Party (BJP) had held power in Delhi since 1993 but for the 1998 elections, the Congress built a successful campaign around the rise in the prices of essential commodities and the failure of the BJP government in Delhi to improve civic amenities in the capital.

Public protests arising from frequent power outages reached their crescendo during a particularly hot summer in 1998 and took a violent turn with rioting in the streets. This created the political space for the Congress to put forward a plank of reform of the power sector through privatization of the distribution segment. A few months later, the Sheila Dixit-led Congress' resounding victory, winning 52 out of the 70 seats, allowed the government to confidently pursue its reform agenda. This eventually led to unbundling of the DVB and privatization of the sector.

Within three months of assuming office, the Government of the National Capital Territory of Delhi (GNCTD) came up with the strategy paper on power sector reforms within the state. Delhi policymakers also had the benefit of learning from Odisha's experience, which had privatized its distribution sector in 1999 with problematic consequences.[3] Critics of privatization cited the Odisha example as a harbinger of what lay ahead, but the benefit of hindsight of the Odisha experience proved particularly useful for Delhi. As in Odisha, Delhi had negligible agricultural interests to look out for. The industrialist lobby and RWAs, which represented largely middle-class consumer interests, were powerful and in favour of privatization.[4] According to Jagdish Sagar, the last chairman of the DVB: 'We had Orissa [sic] in mind while determining the bid parameter. Orissa was partly unsuccessful due to inaccurate determination of T&D [transmission and distribution] losses and we wanted to avoid this. The consultants came up with the concept of AT&C losses, which is an aggregate of T&D loss and loss due to power theft, deficiencies in metering etc.[5]

Any threats of opposition by labour unions were proactively neutralized by allowing transfer of DVB employees to the new discoms with all benefits intact. Despite favourable conditions, the bureaucrats were under immense pressure to implement the reforms in a very limited time frame, perhaps to ensure that these measures would bear electoral gains.[6]

On launching the bid process, out of six pre-qualified bidders, only two bids were received on the date of bid opening: one from energy conglomerate Bombay Suburban Electricity Supply company (BSES), bidding for all three distribution companies and one from Tata Power, which bid only for north-northwest and southwest distribution companies. The bids from BSES and Tata Power Delhi Distribution Limited (TPDDL) were in the range of 13–14 per cent cumulative AT&C loss reductions, which were well below the 20 per cent criterion stipulated by the government. The GNCTD entered into negotiations with the parties and eventually, loss reduction target of 17 per cent over five years was agreed upon.[7] The GNCTD was criticized for setting unambitious loss reduction targets.

Eventually, in January 2001, less than one year after the launch of the strategy paper by the GNCTD, three private companies took over DVB's distribution function: BSES Rajdhani Power Limited (BRPL), BSES Yamuna Power Limited (BYPL)—together referred to as BSES—and TPDDL, previously North Delhi Power Limited (NDPL).[8]

In order to bolster investor confidence, the DERC was set up in 1999 as a first step towards sectoral reform. The early years of the DERC are particularly interesting, as the body walked a tightrope between establishing its regulatory autonomy and preventing the derailment of the government's reform agenda. The government, keen to keep a tight grip on the implementation phase, sought to curtail the DERC's regulatory autonomy through certain policy directions (Policy Directions), with far-reaching consequences.[9] The Policy Directions, among other things, (a) specified the mode of determination of AT&C losses; (b) directed the DERC to ensure that tariffs ensured a 16 per cent return on equity for the discoms; (c) specified that retail tariffs for all three discoms would be identical till 2006–7; and (d) required performance standards and tariff determined by DERC be consistent with the Policy Directions. While this appears prima facie to be a clear infringement of the DERC's autonomy, one of the key actors in the bureaucracy at the time argued, 'In India, regulatory risk is particularly relevant due to the prevailing populism. We had to beg investors to bid since no one was willing to take the risk. Therefore, we needed a pre-fixed package to attract investors and mitigate regulatory risk.'[10]

Further, a legal challenge to the privatization process was unsuccessful only because of the court's inability to turn 'the clock back' and 'undo all that has transpired in the intervening period', despite recognizing the legal infirmity of the entire process.[11]

In the foreground was also the performance of the discoms. In the first couple of years, the discoms achieved the targeted AT&C loss reduction levels (except BYPL in 2002–3), with NDPL bettering the target loss reduction levels by seven per cent in 2004–5. The loss reduction achieved by the three discoms cumulatively in the first three years resulted in savings equivalent to Rs 880 crore.[12] However, as compared to BSES, NDPL emerged as a more reliable operator, with the former already facing public ire over frequent power outages and large-scale billing errors. NDPL outperformed BSES by consistently overachieving its loss reduction targets and overall, brought the whole sector to a revenue surplus level by 2006–7. Improvement in billing and collection of past dues were among the major contributors of the financial turnaround of the discoms. In 2003, 64 per cent of the power cuts were attributed to BSES, while 19 per cent were attributed to Transco and 17 per cent to NDPL. It was not just the power cuts but also the large-scale billing errors by BSES that were a source of serious concern to the GNCTD. According to DERC's statistics, of the 8 lakh electricity bills generated by BSES between 1 February 2003 and 5 March 2003, as many as 2.4 lakh had billing errors.[13] Meanwhile, in 2003, BSES also underwent a management change and became part of the Reliance Group. This gap in achievement is partially attributable to the fact that AT&C losses at the time of privatization in Central/East Delhi under BSES where around 60 per cent, compared to NDPL's area where it was under 50 per cent; therefore, NDPL had a head start.

Despite these teething issues, the 2003 Delhi state elections delivered another landslide victory to the Congress. Delhi voters were taking notice of improvements in civic amenities, particularly in the power and water sector, pioneered by Dixit. In the absence of dramatic improvements at this stage, voters were willing to trust Dixit to continue her efforts by rewarding her with another term in office.[14] Internationally, the Delhi privatization model was beginning to gain recognition, as suggested by a World Bank paper in 2003, which states that early signs pointed to it being an 'impressive accomplishment' and commended the GNCTD's quick decision making to implement privatization.

Despite the strong electoral victory, sustaining political momentum for power sector reforms continued to be an uphill battle for the Congress in the face of tariff hikes and public patience wearing thin in awaiting noticeable improvements in quality of supply of power. The

DERC approved a 10 per cent tariff hike in 2005, which led to widespread protests against the tariff increase, a notion of fast-reading meters, and faulty billing. The protests, with political overtones, even resulted in calls for the chief minister to resign.[15] Buckling under pressure, the GNCTD sought to offset the 10 per cent tariff hike, through a combination of a government subsidy and adjustment by discoms of the amount already paid by the domestic and agriculture consumers towards the enhanced tariff.[16] Subsequently, while the resulting improvement in power quality became apparent to the public, the sustained tariff hikes started shifting public perception of the Congress' image from pro-development to anti-consumer and pro-discom, which proved to be a significant contributing factor to its eventual electoral loss in the 2013.

During this phase, two themes emerge: the long-term impacts of curbing regulatory autonomy by the government, and the initial improvements in quality of power supply, arising from the reduction in AT&C loss levels and improved collection and billing systems, that privatization brought in. The voters saw Dixit as a strong leader committed to improving civic amenities through quick and direct action, and in delivering the 2003 election victory to the Congress, the voters reaffirmed their belief in Dixit continuing to implement the development agenda that she had spearheaded in her first term. However, political gains came at a cost since the GNCTD's interference in the regulatory process somewhat undermined DERC's role. The DERC largely fell in line with the Policy Directions issued by the GNCTD, without offering much resistance. The DERC's failure to delineate its scope of functioning in the early years had an adverse impact on its image among consumers and the discoms. As forthcoming sections will illustrate, GNCTD's move to curb regulatory autonomy and dispense with procedural sanctity early on were inimical to sectoral governance in the long run.

2006–13: The Government and the Regulator—Seeds of Failure

The dissonance between the regulator and the government continued to widen in the early years with the appointment of the second DERC Chairman, Berjinder Singh in 2006. This period can be characterized as one of open hostility and conflict between the GNCTD and the regulator, which played a larger role in shaping the future of the sector, and perhaps set up the Congress for a future electoral loss.

Singh's appointment came in the aftermath of a damning 2005 report of the Public Accounts Committee (PAC) of the Delhi Legislative Assembly, which concluded that the DERC, instead of protecting consumer interest, had 'acted as a hidden hand of the government and distribution companies'.[17] The DERC was increasingly viewed as an anti-consumer organization, with RWAs staging protests and boycotting public hearings with allegations of not being given adequate opportunity to make their representations.[18] Following Berjinder Singh's appointment, there was no tariff hike in 2006–7, with the DERC citing favourable factors like refunds from central generating stations and arrears received from the Delhi Jal Board. This was to be a trend during Singh's term, with no tariff hikes between 2006 and 2010.[19] While the absence of tariff hikes during this period played well to the gallery, it resulted in creation of regulatory assets for discoms arising from non-cost reflective tariff.

Early in this period, in 2008, the Congress was re-elected with 42 seats, a relatively diminished performance compared to its 52 seat win in 1998. By this point, the performance of the discoms had noticeably improved with significant reduction in AT&C loss levels and fewer power outages. Moreover, the years immediately preceding the elections saw no tariff hikes. While by no means unambiguously popular, the electricity reforms in Delhi, at the minimum, appear to have had enough public support to avoid being a political liability, if not an obvious political positive.

However, the seeds of future problems were being sowed through growing conflict and cross purposes between the regulator and the GNCTD. Although the DERC's image among consumers was improving, the discoms were reeling from financial stress from being squeezed from two directions.

First, the mounting regulatory assets (RA), close to a staggering Rs 33 crore as of FY 2014–15 for the three discoms cumulatively,[20] negatively impacted, and continue to impact, the realized revenues of the discoms.[21] Although the Appellate Tribunal for Electricity (APTEL) ruled in 2011[22] that RA must be recovered over three years, the sheer magnitude of existing RA in Delhi meant this would have caused a major tariff shock. Revenue recovery was therefore scheduled over a longer period, with no relief to utility finances. Aggravating the problem were delays in 'truing up', where the DERC assigns lower power-purchase costs than used by discoms in their projected revenue requirements to keep starting tariffs low, thereby increasing the interest burden on cash-strapped discoms that have to borrow to purchase power increases. According to the discoms, the 8 per cent surcharge that the DERC subsequently introduced towards the recovery of RA was not enough to service even the interest on the principal.

Second, power purchase costs shot up due to high-cost power purchase agreements stimulated by perceived demand increases around the 2010 Commonwealth Games. Specifically the Delhi government, acting on behalf of Transco and projecting an 8–10 per cent increase in demand annually, entered into two power purchase agreements (PPAs) with National Thermal Power Corporation Limited (NTPC) and Tehri Hydro Development Corporation for 1,031 megawatt (MW) of power in addition to 490 MW previously contracted with Dadri Power Station.[23] These PPAs were reallocated in 2007, on the basis of each discom's average energy withdrawal for the period FY 2007–8 to 2011–12, leading to protests from BYPL in particular about the being forced to buy expensive power.[24] Delhi, unlike other states, receives the majority of its power supply from central public sector undertakings such as NTPC and National Hydro Power Corporation Limited. According to discom officials, these PPAs directly impacted tariff as they sell power at a higher rate than market rates and fuel accounts for 75 per cent of the cost (see Figure 3.2 for trajectory of increase in power purchase costs).[25] Since the long-term PPAs do not have an exit clause, discoms have no choice but to purchase power and can surrender power only if they can find an alternate buyer.

Another pressure point on supply was the central government's push towards mandatory procurement of renewable power by discoms. Towards this purpose, the DERC Renewable Purchase Obligation (RPO) and Renewable Energy Certificate Framework Implementation regulations were issued in 2012. The discoms were unable to meet their RPO and cited financial limitations in procuring more expensive green power while being saddled with massive RA.

Despite these growing financial pressures, the DERC under Berjinder Singh prepared to slash tariffs by nearly 23 per cent in 2010. However, Chief Minister Sheila Dixit intervened by issuing a policy direction to prevent the DERC from issuing the tariff order.[26] The tariff order was never formalized and became the subject of litigation.[27] During the course of this stalemate, Singh retired in September 2010, short by nearly five months of the full five-year term of chairperson. The absence of tariff hikes during his term resulted in increasing RA for discoms, and significant tariff shocks for consumers in subsequent years, which ranged from 22 per cent in 2011–12 to 26 per cent in 2012–13 and 5 per cent in 2013–14.

Predictably, there were large scale protests across the city, with BJP organizing sit-in protests and demonstrations across the city to force the Sheila Dikshit government to roll back the hike.[28] The protests were not without theatrics, with the BJP leader Vijay Goel storming into a public hearing that was under way at the DERC and holding the Chairman hostage. This move was perhaps to draw attention away from the *bijli-paani satyagraha* (electricity-water protest) launched by Arvind Kejriwal of the emergent AAP, who had been gaining much public and media attention.[29] Kejriwal was particularly vocal about the nexus between BSES and the Congress government and raised the issue of government interference in stopping the issuance of the 2010 tariff order.[30] Under Kejriwal's anti-corruption agenda, AAP started gaining momentum. Kejriwal's tactics, such as personally going to houses and reconnecting power supply which had been disconnected by discoms over non-payment of dues with a pair of pliers, albeit theatrical, were effective.

In 2013, reminiscent of the 1998 elections, battle lines were drawn around power sector reforms by the AAP. However, while the Congress in the 1998 elections had focused on the benefits of electricity distribution privatization, the AAP proceeded to tear down the projected success of the Delhi discoms with allegations of major financial irregularities by the discoms and collusion of discoms with the Congress government and DERC to keep tariffs high. The party also promised a Comptroller and Auditor General of India (CAG) audit of discoms, if elected. By this time AT&C losses were in the range of 8–15 per cent, and unscheduled outages were not frequent. Targets to reduce AT&C losses were replaced by demands for accountability and transparency in the functioning of the discoms. Despite the obvious improvements brought in by privatization, the tariff hikes from 2011 to 2013 seems to have weighed in more heavily with voters. While the Congress government attempted to distance itself from regulatory decision making, the voters swung in favour of Arvind Kejriwal's AAP and he assumed the office of chief minister in December 2013. Within a few days of Kejriwal's swearing-in DERC, perhaps to mark its territory early on, announced that there will be no tariff revision in the coming three months, and any proposal to revise tariff would need to follow procedure and take at least three months.[31]

2014–17: The AAP Regime and Winds of Change

The AAP government had pulled off an unpredictable victory and wanted to push for fulfilment of its various campaign promises, particularly in the power sector. From December 2013 to February 2014, AAP formed the minority government in Delhi for 49 days. Thereafter, Delhi came under President's Rule for a year under the BJP–NDA led Central Government, until AAP came back into power in the February 2015 elections. This section analyses how the interplay of federal politics, evidenced in the power struggle in Delhi between AAP, the central government, and the Lieutenant Governor (LG), has had a tangible impact on the distribution sector.

The year 2014 started out well for Delhi consumers, with the newly elected AAP government announcing a 50 per cent subsidy on power consumption below 400 units. However, in August 2014, the DERC announced a tariff hike of 8.3 per cent for domestic consumers. This time, during the President's Rule, the Union Government led by BJP–NDA stepped in to announce the allocation of Rs 260 crore for power subsidy.[32] Congress, now in the opposition, accused the central government of exercising pressure on DERC to hike the tariff and AAP of betraying the people.[33] Further, in November 2014, the DERC approved a fuel surcharge of 7 per cent for BYPL, 4.5 per cent for BRPL, and 2.5 per cent for TPDDL. However, within 24 hours, DERC rolled back its hike. Ironically, AAP, which had planned a citywide protest against the hike, alleged BJP's interference in DERC's functioning and highlighted the nexus between the government and regulator.[34] While consumers seem to be the obvious beneficiaries of large scale subsidies and tariff rollbacks, it is interesting that in the aftermath of AAP's victory, all political parties in Delhi seemed to have renewed their focus on electricity as a key election mandate, resulting in earlier undertones of the political economy undergirding the distribution sector becoming obvious overtones.

Eventually, AAP was re-elected to power after a resounding victory in the 2015 elections, following which it reintroduced the 50 per cent subsidy on consumption below 400 units.[35] In June 2015, DERC approved a surcharge of up to 6 per cent for BRPL and BYPL consumers and 4 per cent for TPDDL areas to adjust the power purchase costs incurred by the discoms in light of an APTEL directive to this effect. The Government wrote to the DERC to roll back its decision,[36] even though AAP had criticized similar interference in the regulator's functioning by Congress and BJP in the past. The DERC did not hike tariff in FY 2015–16, stating that the RA of the discoms had been covered to a large extent through tariff hikes starting from 2011. The DERC Chairperson also felt the need to clarify that the GNCTD had no role to play in the decision, though it was reported in the media that DERC had been under tremendous pressure from the AAP Government for 'favouring discoms'.[37] This did not prevent AAP from claiming credit for the stagnant tariff.[38] Further, reports emerged that the according to DERC's data, discoms were revenue surplus (see Figure 3.1).[39]

During its earlier term in 2014, the AAP also requested a CAG audit of the discoms, which was challenged in court by the latter. While the matter was sub judice, the CAG audit was already underway, and the media leaked details of the confidential report in August 2015. Media reports indicated that CAG found discoms to have inflated their RA by nearly 8,000 crore, bought costly power, suppressed revenue, dealt with other private companies without tenders and unduly favoured group companies.[40] However, in a serious setback to the AAP Government, the Delhi High Court declared all the work done by the CAG and contents of its report to be inoperative. In another case, the Delhi High Court declared the LG of Delhi as the administrative head of municipal government. The conflict arose when the AAP Government made a series of decisions without consulting LG Najeeb Jung, a Congress Government appointee. In the aftermath of the case, the LG held the appointment of the last DERC Chairperson, Krishna Saini, to be invalid and the post continues to lie vacant. AAP has challenged both the Delhi High Court decisions before the Supreme Court, where the matters are currently being heard.

As the matter is sub judice, as of 2017 the LG continues to wield considerable power in Delhi. The spillover of the conflict between the LG and the AAP government has paralyzed the distribution sector. As

Saini's appointment was invalidated, all decisions made by him since March 2016 were vitiated. There was no tariff order for FY 2016–17 and the FY 2017–18 tariff order did not allow a tariff hike, while the most recent tariff order for FY 2018–19 reduced tariff across all consumer categories, which has been problematic for the discoms, but the average consumers are unconcerned since they have been spared tariff hikes since 2015. However, this will contribute further to RA, which does not bode well for the discoms or consumers in the long run.

While political tensions continue to run high, certain developments in the renewable energy sphere and demand-side management (DSM) could hold the key to the sector's future. In addition to the renewable purchase obligation (RPO) fulfilment, solar energy has gained prominence with the AAP government's issuance of the Delhi Solar Policy in June 2016. The Solar Policy recognizes Delhi's low potential for wind and hydro-power and the need to shift to rooftop solar projects, pegging Delhi's solar potential at 2,500 MW. It further highlights that the solar energy tariff in Delhi has become cheaper than conventional energy tariffs for the government, commercial–industrial categories as well as the domestic consumers falling in the highest tariff slab, and is expected to achieve grid parity for domestic consumers falling in the low-medium tariff slab. The targets specified under the policy are 1 gigawatt (GW) by 2020 and 2 GW by 2025. This is certainly ambitious considering Delhi's solar rooftop installed capacity is around 7 MW as of August 2015.[41] Discoms have also taken up DSM initiatives such as the promotion of LED usage, energy conservation campaigns in school, etc. The TPDDL in particular has taken the lead in implementing DSM measures such as the Appliance Replacement Program, and launched India's first large-scale integrated Auto Demand Response (ADR) programme with smart meters. If the ADR technology were to be adopted across the board, it is predicted to reduce consumption by approximately 7 per cent and reduce peak demand by 11.5 MW for TPDDL.[42]

The present phase is defined by certain watershed moments, which bring to fore the complexities of the Indian federal structure and the manner in which it is intrinsically linked to sectoral change. Likely, as a consequence of the Congress holding power at the centre from 2004 to 2013, Sheila Dixit's fifteen-year term was not marred by any external interference or conflict with the Central Government (see Table 3.1). In sharp contrast, the predicament of the AAP government bears witness to how the interplay of federal politics and an unfavourable interpretation of law granting administrative powers in Delhi to the LG has crippled state government machinery and consequently the power sector.

***

Privatization of electricity distribution in Delhi was implemented in part to insulate the sector from political pressures, but the tenor of the electricity sector debates in Delhi has been distinctly political, more revealingly so in the past few years. Delhi's distribution sector is unique in many ways: apart from being one of the few states with private discoms, the unique governance structure involving the state government, LG, and the central government adds another dimension to understanding how the power sector operates within the state and the additional pressure likely to ensue.

One of the themes that have emerged is the evolving nature of reform itself—transitioning from incumbent-led under Sheila Dixit's rule to a populist movement fuelled by a mobilized constituency under AAP. Privatization of the distribution sector in Delhi came in under the guise of a strong leader in Sheila Dixit, who subsequently used her incumbency advantage to implement the reforms over more than a decade. Privatization led to remarkable measurable improvements in both the quantity and quality of power supplied, which in early years were contributing factors to Dixit's stronghold over Delhi, evidenced by the Congress winning three consecutive state elections. Ironically, the nature of competitive populism allowed AAP to rewrite Dixit's narrative of the success of privatization to one of corruption and lack of accountability. AAP successfully channelized the public ire at the time to shift the dialogue from the obvious benefits of privatization to the cost of this success, which led to a pilfering of public money for private gain. The existing conflict between the LG and the AAP Government is another example of competitive populism at play, where consumers continue to benefit from major subsidies while tariffs remain stagnant and contribute to the mounting financial burden of discoms.

In the early post-privatization years, the sector suffered from various infirmities arising from GNCTD's interference in DERC's functioning and the latter's inability to stem political influences within its domain. However, the GNCTD's limited effort to ensure the success of the privatization model and attract private players led to an early stunting of the DERC's autonomy, leading to a loss of confidence among consumers and discoms. Perhaps in a bid to improve consumer faith in its functioning, the DERC, under the chairmanship of Singh, also adopted a populist stand, evidenced by the absence of tariff hikes despite increasing power purchase costs for nearly five years. This fomented a sectoral crisis with mounting RA for the discoms and major tariff shocks for consumers in the years to follow. At present, DERC continues to be caught in the crosshairs of the conflict between the state government and the LG, and has been functioning as a single-member commission without a chairman for nearly two years. The absence of a tariff order for FY 2016–17 and the resultant financial burden on discoms is a direct consequence of this conflict. The Delhi case study highlights the challenges of implementing large scale reforms and the long-term impact of negating the authority of key institutions such as the regulator over the years.

The price of reform in Delhi, in terms of legal and political battles, has been high, but the Delhi discoms also offer a story of innovation and the resuscitation of an ailing distribution sector. AT&C loss levels in Delhi are amongst the lowest in the country, with a significant improvement in the quantity and quality of power supply since privatization. While the political situation continues to be hazy, it remains to be seen if the Delhi discoms can sustain their performance despite the increasing pressure of competitive populism on the sector.

Notes and References

1. Navroz K. Dubash and D. Narasimha Rao, 'Delhi: Regulation in the Shadow of Privatisation', in *The Practice and Politics of Regulation: Regulatory Governance in Indian Electricity* (India: Macmillan Press, 2007), 145.

2. AT&C losses in the state are targeted to decrease to 12.5 per cent in FY 2018–19 from 14.2 per cent in FY 2014–15 according to the loss trajectory proposed by the Central Electricity Authority of India (CEA) to the Ministry of Power (MoP), which needs to be adopted by a state. Based on data for FY 2014–15, Tata Power Delhi Distribution Limited (TPDDL) is way ahead in loss reduction at 9.8 per cent, whereas BSES Rajdhani Power Limited (BRPL) and BSES Yamuna Power Limited (BYPL) have brought down AT&C loss levels to 14.7 per cent and 19.5 per cent respectively in their areas—*24×7 Power for All: A Joint Initiative of Government of India and*

Government of Delhi (New Delhi: Ministry of Power, GoI, 2016), 28: http://powermin.nic.in/sites/default/files/uploads/joint_initiative_of_govt_of_india_and_delhi.pdf (accessed on 14 March 2017).

3. Sudha Mahalingam, 'A Reform Fiasco in Orissa', *Frontline*, 11–24 May 2002, available http://www.frontline.in/static/html/fl1910/19100420.htm (accessed on 14 March 2017).

4. Sunila S. Kale, 'Power Steering: The Politics of Utility Privatization in India' (PhD dissertation, University of Texas, Austin, 2007), 140, available https://www.lib.utexas.edu/etd/d/2007/kaled56445/kaled56445.pdf (accessed on 14 March 2017).

5. Interview with Jagdish Sagar (last DVB chairman), 5 October 2016.

6. Dubash and Rao, 'Delhi', 145.

7. Daljit Singh, Shantanu Dixit, and Girish Sant, *A Critical Review of the Performance of Delhi's Privatized Distribution Companies and the Regulatory Process* (Pune: Prayas Energy Group, 2006), p. 4.

8. Furthermore, Delhi Power Company Limited (DPCL)- Holding Company, Delhi Transco Limited (DTL)—Transmission Company (Transco), and Indraprastha Power Generation Company Limited (IPGCL)—Genco were also formed.

9. The timing of the Policy Directions issuance is interesting. In May 2001, DERC rejected the GNCTD's multi-year tariff proposal. A few months later, in November 2001, the GNCTD found a way around any future conflict by issuing the Policy Directions.

10. Interview with retired senior IAS officer who was involved in the Delhi privatization process, 5 October 2016.

11. *Haldea* v. *NCT* (Writ Petition (Civil) No. 2705/2002 (Delhi High Court, 2 July 2007).

12. Singh, Dixit, and Sant, *A Critical Review*, 5.

13. Lalit K. Jha, 'Unreliable "BSES way behind Quality" NDPL', *The Hindu*, 22 May 2004, available http://www.thehindu.com/2004/05/22/stories/2004052209690400.htm (accessed 14 March 2017).

14. 'The Quiet Czarina', *Outlook*, 19 May 2003 available https://www.outlookindia.com/magazine/story/the-quiet-czarina/220186 (accessed on 14 December 2017).

15. Singh, Dixit, and Sant, *Critical Review*, 28.

16. 'Enhanced Power Charges Paid to be Adjusted: Discoms', *The Hindu*, 16 October 2005, available http://www.thehindu.com/2005/10/16/stories/2005101604760300.htm (accessed 14 March 2017).

17. The report referred to a specific case where DERC did not impose any penalty on the discoms when they claimed an excess rebate in violation of the Bulk Supply Agreement. Instead, it ordered that Transco would have

to pay penal interest if it did not calculate the rebate due to each Discom and make the payment within a day.

18. 'DERC Anti-consumer', *The Hindu*, 26 May 2006, available http://www.thehindu.com/todays-paper/tp-national/tp-newdelhi/derc-anticonsumer/article3138537.ece (accessed 14 March 2017).

19. There was a minor five-paisa tariff hike across consumer categories in 2007–8.

20. 'Comparative Executive Summary—BRPL, BYPL, TPDDL Petitions for True up for FY 2013–14, APR FY 2014–15 and ARR for FY 2015–16', Government of India, http://www.derc.gov.in/ordersPetitions/orders/Tariff/Tariff%20Order/Tariff%20Order%20for%20FY%202015-16/Executive%20Summary/COMPARATIVE%20STATEMENT%20OF%20BRPL,%20BYPL,%20TPDDL%20_Final.pdf. (accessed 14 March 2017).

21. Since tariff is estimated ex-ante, actual revenue realized may not cover the annual revenue requirement. This difference (or the RA) is to be adjusted while estimating the aggregate revenue requirement in the following year. However, in practice, the timeline for liquidation of RA is much longer.

22. Tariff Revision (Suo-Motu action on the letter received from Ministry of Power) (OP No.1 of 2011), (APTEL, 11 November 2011), available http://aptel.gov.in/judgements/OP%20NO.1%20OF%202011.pdf

23. 'Delhi Government Inks Power Purchase Deals', *The Hindu*, 20 April 2006, available http://www.thehindu.com/todays-paper/tp-national/tp-newdelhi/delhi-govt-inks-power-purchase-deals/article3150108.ece (accessed 14 March 2017).

24. Smriti Kak Ramachandran, 'BYPL Customers may have to Pay more for Electricity', *The Hindu*, 11 April 2007, available http://www.thehindu.com/todays-paper/tp-national/tp-newdelhi/bypl-consumers-may-have-to-pay-more-for-electricity/article1826862.ece. (accessed 14 March 2017).

25. Delhi discoms are procuring a total of 3,748.5 crore units (MU) annually from around forty-five power plants to cater the power requirement of Delhi consumers. Out of the total power, around 50 per cent of total long-term power is from plants like Dadri-II, Badarpur Thermal Power Station (BTPS), Aravali Power Company Pvt Ltd (APCPL), Bawana, Pragati, and GT. The average cost of power from these plants is higher in comparison to that of other plants and in the range of Rs 5.3 per unit to Rs 7 per unit.

26. Smriti Kak Ramachandran, 'Wait for Power Tariff Order Getting Longer', *The Hindu*, 5 May 2010, available http://www.thehindu.com/todays-paper/tp-national/tp-newdelhi/wait-for-power-tariff-order-getting-longer/article761546.ece (accessed 14 March 2017).

27. In May 2011, the Delhi High Court in *Nand Kishore Garg* v. *GNCTD and Others* held that the 2010 tariff order was invalid in law since key procedural requirements like placing the matter before the DERC and holding deliberations had not occurred. DERC itself, in a subsequent order dated 26 August 2011, said that the budget projection by the then-chairperson of a Rs 3,577 crore surplus was based on highly optimistic assumptions about the availability of the power to discoms.

28. 'BJP Raises the Pitch against Power Tariff Hike', *The Hindu*, 30 June 2012, available http://www.thehindu.com/todays-paper/tp-national/tp-newdelhi/bjp-raises-the-pitch-against-power-tariff-hike/article3587349.ece (accessed 14 March 2017).

29. Smriti Kak Ramachandran, 'BJP Leader Enacts High Drama, gets Little Support', *The Hindu*, 9 October 2012, available http://www.thehindu.com/todays-paper/tp-national/tp-newdelhi/bjp-leader-enacts-high-drama-gets-little-support/article3979965.ece (accessed 14 March 2017).

30. Gaurav Vivek Bhatnagar, 'Government, BSES deny allegations', *The Hindu*, 2 February 2013, available http://www.thehindu.com/news/cities/Delhi/government-bses-deny-allegations/article4371700.ece (accessed 14 March 2017).

31. 'No Change in Power Tariff for another Three Months', *The Hindu*, 31 December 2013, available http://www.thehindu.com/todays-paper/tp-national/tp-newdelhi/no-change-in-power-tariff-for-another-three-months/article5521393.ece (accessed 14 March 2017)

32. Mohammad Ali, 'Power Subsidy Ahead of Struggle for Power', *The Hindu*, 19 July 2014, available http://www.thehindu.com/news/cities/Delhi/power-subsidy-ahead-of-struggle-for-power/article6227606.ece (accessed 14 March 2017).

33. Gaurav Vivek Bhatnagar, 'Power Hike a Betrayal: Cong', *The Hindu*, 19 July 2014, available http://www.thehindu.com/todays-paper/tp-national/tp-newdelhi/power-hike-a-betrayal-cong/article6226947.ece (accessed 14 March 2017).

34. Shubhomoy Sikdar, 'DERC Rollback A Move to help BJP: AAP', *The Hindu*, 15 November 2014, available http://www.thehindu.com/todays-paper/tp-national/tp-newdelhi/dercs-rollback-a-move-to-help-bjp-aap/article6601329.ece (accessed 14 March 2017).

35. The 50 per cent subsidy has come under scrutiny since nearly 80 per cent of the households are eligible for it, a number which increases to 95 per cent in some months. The subsidy has also been characterized as regressive since it tends to benefit middle class households more than poor households. For example, the average household subsidy varies from a little over Rs 1,000/year for those who consume up to 100 units per month to over

Rs 9,000/year for those whose consumption is 300–400 units per month—Rahul Tongia, 'Delhi household electricity subsidies: Highly generous but inefficient?', *Brookings Institution*, 13 April 2017, available https://www.brookings.edu/research/delhis-household-electricity-subsidies-highly-generous-but-inefficient/ (accessed 18 April 2017).

36. 'DERC asked to Revoke Fuel Surcharge', *The Hindu*, 16 June 2015, available http://www.thehindu.com/todays-paper/tp-national/tp-newdelhi/derc-asked-to-revoke-fuel-surcharge/article7320079.ece (accessed 14 March 2017).

37. Sweta Goswami, 'No Increase in Power Tariff Rates', *The Hindu*, 23 July 2015, available http://www.thehindu.com/todays-paper/tp-national/tp-newdelhi/no-increase-in-power-tariff-rates/article7454165.ece (accessed 14 March 2017).

38. 'AAP takes Credit for Static Delhi Power Tariff', *The Hindu*, 25 September 2015, available http://www.thehindu.com/news/cities/Delhi/aap-takes-credit-for-static-delhi-power-tariff/article7689255.ece (accessed 14 March 2017).

39. TPDDL had the maximum surplus revenue amounting to Rs 323 crore, followed by BSES Rajdhani (BRPL) with Rs 92 crore and BSES Yamuna (BYPL) with Rs 37 crore—Sweta Goswami, 'Discoms Earn Surplus Revenue', *The Hindu*, 1 October 2015, available http://www.thehindu.com/news/cities/Delhi/discoms-earn-surplus-revenue/article7710277.ece (accessed 14 March 2017).

40. Josy Joseph, 'Discoms Inflated Dues by Rs 8,000 crore, says CAG', *The Times of India*, 18 August 2015, available http://timesofindia.indiatimes.com/city/delhi/Discoms-inflated-dues-by-Rs-8000-crore-says-CAG/articleshow/48520042.cms (accessed 14 March 2017).

41. To facilitate solar rooftop projects, DERC issued the DERC (Net Metering for Renewable Energy) Regulations in 2014 and the DERC (Terms and Conditions for Determination of Tariff for Procurement of Power for Grid-connected Solar Photovoltaic Power Projects) Regulations in 2013.

42. 'Demand Response: Honeywell and Tata Power Delhi Distribution', Metering and Smart Energy International, available https://www.metering.com/demand-response-honeywell-and-tata-power-delhi-distribution/ (accessed 14 March 2017).

4

SIDDHARTH SAREEN

Gujarat's Success in Efficient Electricity Distribution

A Call for Proactive Governance to Further Gains

The Gujarat story is an intriguing lens for analysing the subnational political–economic dynamics that characterize the development trajectories of Indian states. Home to a culture of commerce with a history of ocean trade[1] as well as a hub for domestic industry, Gujarat has long been a relatively wealthy region, and has remained among India's economically better off states ever since its formation in 1960, 13 years after national independence. Lately, it has become the poster child for the 'good governance' mantra championed by the Bharatiya Janata Party (BJP), which at the time of publication is in power both at the centre (since 2014) and in the state (since 1998). Yet this mainstream image has also been deftly critiqued, labelling the sort of state that Gujarat represents an ally of big capital,[2] and questioning its development model as one that has exacerbated inequity alongside achieving economic growth.[3] An analysis of reforms in the electricity distribution sector takes on added interest due to these competing narratives, especially since it is commonly acknowledged that power sector developments in India are deeply linked to state politics.[4] While the sectoral trajectory cannot be understood except in conjunction with political dynamics, emerging scholarship suggests that Gujarat represents a rare instance within India where a problem-driven approach has characterized sectoral evolution that is widely regarded as a best practice.[5] The state-level scale at which this chapter addresses the co-evolution of regional and sectoral political economies does not lend itself to a close examination of community- or household-level inequities, but the analysis does aim to capture the broad sweep of sociopolitical trends in relation to the suite of changes in the state's electricity distribution sector over the past quarter-century. Table 4.1 provides a brief overview of their co-evolution by highlighting some key changes.

TABLE 4.1   Timeline of Key Events: Gujarat

Political Events	Year	Power Sector Events
	1991	• First state to achieve 100 per cent village electrification (17,940/18,028 villages)
	1993	• Start of corporatization of electricity sector, GSECL incorporated
• BJP government comes into power in Gujarat, re-elected until date	1998	• Commercial operations of GSECL commence; central Electricity Regulatory Commissions Act
	1999	• GERC established
• Narendra Modi replaces Keshubhai Patel as CM, BJP re-elected in 2002	2001	• Agricultural share of consumption 43 per cent
	2003	• Central Electricity Act passed, ERC Act effective 10 June 2003, Gujarat Electricity Industry (Re-organisation & Regulation) Act passed
	April 2005	• GEB unbundled into six state electric companies under the holding company Gujarat Urja Vikas Nigam Limited (GUVNL): o Generation company: GSECL o Transmission company: GETCO o Four regional distribution companies:

(*Cont'd*)

Table 4.1   (*Cont'd*)

Political Events	Year	Power Sector Events
		o Uttar Gujarat Vij Company Limited (UGVCL)
		o Dakshin Gujarat Vij Company Limited (DGVCL)
		o Madhya Gujarat Vij Company Limited (MGVCL)
		o Paschim Gujarat Vij Company Limited (PGVCL)
	2005	• Jyotir Gram Yojana (feeder separation, later inspiration for Deendayal Upadhyaya Jyoti Gram Yojana (DDUJGY—national scheme)
• BJP re-elected under Chief Minister Modi	2007	• Wind Power Policy
	2009	• Solar Power Policy, prior to national policy, kicks off solar growth
	2010	• Principal GERC (Procurement of Energy from Renewable Sources) Regulations
• BJP re-elected under Modi	2012	
• Modi becomes Indian prime minister, Anandiben Patel (BJP) takes over as chief minister	2014	
	2015	• Gujarat Solar Power Policy (new), including net metering guidelines
	2015	• Gujarat joins Ujwal Discom Assurance Yojana (UDAY), tenth state to do so, with A+ ratings for all four of its public discoms
• Vijay Rupani takes over as chief minister	2016	• Gujarat Wind Power Policy (new)

Source: Author.

The narrative commences in 1990, a significant year in that it signalled a departure from political rule dominated by the Indian National Congress (henceforth Congress) since state formation, with several parties and even coalitions managing short-term stints throughout the following decade. During the same period, India sought to liberalize, privatize, and globalize its economy, opening up a power sector that had till then worked largely as a public utility, with exceptions such as two industrial cities in Gujarat that had been long served by private utilities.[6] From 1998, the BJP emerged as a clear political victor in the region. It has remained in power in Gujarat ever since, including an over thirteen-year period (2001–14) under the same chief minister, Narendra Modi, who now serves as India's prime minister. These political dynamics, particularly the continuing period of single-party dominance that has characterized nearly the past two decades, is crucial to an understanding of the regional political economy. This dominance by the BJP has been key to furthering Gujarat's reputation as a state with good governance and a strong culture of commerce. The evolution of the electricity sector over the past two decades reflects the magnitude of Gujarat's achievements from an economic perspective: reforms have changed it from an ordinary state electricity board to a sector whose performance has been consistently outstanding at a national level.

The electricity sector, including distribution, is critical in terms of inputs for the continuous-process industries that flourish in Gujarat, such as pharmaceuticals and textiles.[7] Thus, despite the geographic challenge of low population density in its vast western reaches, the state has had an enviable mix of relatively high-tariff industrial consumers as part of its load profile. From comprising 29 per cent of consumption in 1999–2000, industrial consumers have grown to account for 47 per cent of consumption and 62 per cent of revenue for the Gujarat Electricity Board, as per 2014–15 figures (see Figure 4.1). For the public utilities, industrial consumption stood at 34 per cent with an additional 16 per cent under low-tension medium demand, a category that primarily includes industrial consumers.[8] In physical terms, Gujarat has had to contend with unfavourable supply characteristics in terms of conventional energy sources, with little access to coal and hydropower, and a fair distance to high-quality pitheads in India's central belt.[9] However, it has managed to partly assuage this by commissioning five large-scale thermal plants through a so-called 'Ultra Mega Power Project' or the

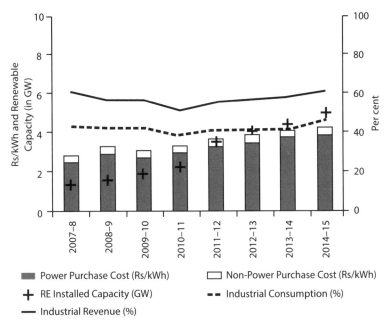

Figure 4.1   Physical and Financial Profile: Gujarat
Sources: CSO, *Energy Statistics* (New Delhi: Central Statistics Office, Ministry of Statistics and Programme Implementation, Government of India, 2010, 2012, 2014, and 2016); PFC, *Reports on Performance of State Power Utilities* (New Delhi: Power Finance Corporation Limited, 2011, 2013, 2015, and 2016).

Mundra UMPP, that provides 4 gigawatts (GW) in installed capacity based on coal imported primarily from Indonesia. The state moreover has high potential for renewable sources, and in addition to playing a long-term role in championing wind energy, became the first mover on solar power adoption in India a decade ago. Figure 4.1 reflects the steady rise in installed renewable energy.

The most vaunted aspect of electricity distribution sector development within Gujarat's overall economic reforms since the early 1990s, however, has been its success at bringing down Aggregate Technical and Commercial (AT&C) loss levels through the targeted implementation of efficiency measures that other Indian states have failed to execute as effectively. As Figure 4.2 shows, there has consistently been no revenue gap to speak of between the Average Revenue Realized (ARR) and the

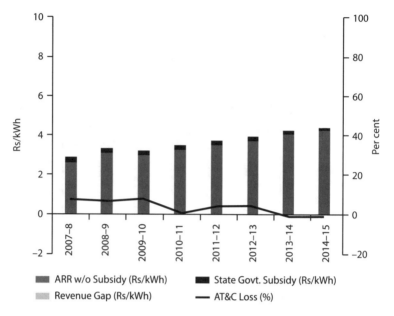

FIGURE 4.2   Supply-side Costs and Revenue Recovery: Gujarat
Source: PFC, *Reports on Performance of State Power Utilities* (New Delhi: Power Finance Corporation Limited, 2011, 2013, 2015, and 2016).

Average Cost of Supply (ACS). This has contributed substantially to the state's overall economic standing. Given that this vital sector typically constitutes a loss to the public exchequer in Indian states but is financially sound in Gujarat, its robust performance moreover performs a signalling function to industries keen on operating in regions with efficient administration, reliable infrastructure, and policy visibility.

The next section of this chapter delves into three periods in contemporary history to present an analysis grounded in the dynamic between the regional and sectoral political economies. The first of these periods is 1991–2001, during which power sector reforms were initiated at a time of political shifts that resulted in the BJP establishing a strong grip on the state that continues at present. The second period of 2001–8 unpacks the successfully implemented efficiency measures that are now regarded as key to the impressive performance of Gujarat's electricity distribution sector, starting with Modi's early years as chief minister. The third section, covering 2008–16, discusses the sector's performance across issues of current relevance such as competition, renewable energy, and public engagement, in the light of sustained financial and political stability. Here I focus on further ways in which the state can capitalize on the virtuous cycle in its distribution sector. A concluding section takes a step back to problematize the dynamic at play between the subnational and sectoral political economies, asking whether the trajectory can still be validly described as problem-driven today. While Gujarat has performed exceptionally well compared to other states, its current position should allow it to go even further towards providing inclusive and clean energy access, as envisaged in the national energy strategy. The conclusion argues that the political and techno-economic conjuncture that has enabled positive changes in the sector so far has more limited power to effect changes for further improvements and optimization towards these objectives. It calls for renewed visionary administrative and managerial leadership to drive the sectoral transformation that is within the state's grasp.

Historical Periods

1991–2001: The Slow Onset of Sectoral Reforms at a Time of Political Flux

The state of Gujarat, as well as the Gujarat Electricity Board (GEB) were established in 1960, inheriting a capacity of 315 MW catering to 1.4 million existing consumers. By 1991, Gujarat was quite exceptional among Indian states, being the first one to have already achieved near-full electrification (17,940 out of 18,028 villages), albeit based on having electrified every village rather than every household within each village. It also had acceptably low AT&C loss levels of 21.10 per cent during 1992–3, which were brought even lower to 18.20 per cent during 1996–7. In parallel, power sector reforms prompted the corporatization of the state's electricity sector, starting with the incorporation of the Gujarat State Electricity Corporation Limited (GSECL) in 1993. Having navigated the changing political landscape and bureaucratic administrative shifts of this period, GSECL began commercial operations in 1998, followed by another GEB-promoted subsidiary, the Gujarat Energy Transmission Corporation Limited (GETCL) in 1999. The same year saw the creation of the Gujarat Electricity Regulatory

Commission (GERC), which established the current regulatory framework.

When the GERC looked into the GEB's accounts in 1999–2000, it found a large mismatch between the GEB's claimed AT&C losses of around 20 per cent and its own determination of around 34 per cent. In October 2000, the GERC's first tariff order explained that a 'substantial quantity of agricultural consumption is shown by way of agricultural use and as such it is difficult to assess use of unauthorized power or loss of power by way of theft that might have been added or included in the use of agricultural sector'.[10] This was particularly significant given that the BJP, which came into power in 1998, found itself dealing with a 48 per cent agricultural share in power consumption in 2000 as per GEB figures, compared with 17 per cent three decades before that. The problem was compounded by the prevalence of flat-meter tariffs for rural power supply to agricultural pump-sets since 1983, making oversight of actual and attributed consumption for this burgeoning category of agricultural consumers nigh impossible. As a farmer association representative freely admitted, line theft by farmers awaiting agricultural connections was rampant, fashioning a device locally called a *teta* that uses capacitors to convert single-phase to triple-phase power.[11] Single phase power supply was essential for rural domestic consumers, yet impossible to monitor in a cost-effective manner with existing infrastructure and principal-agent problems in checking theft.[12] This was especially true in western Gujarat's scattered population of largely smallholder farmers. While a high share of subsidized agricultural power consumption placed a fiscal burden on state government coffers, line theft directly impacted sectoral finances. This constituted an incentive for the GEB to buttress agricultural consumption figures and increase its agricultural subsidy income to partially compensate for revenue ceded to high line theft before the GERC's intervention. Thus, more careful governance of the water–energy nexus was the need of the hour in 2001 in Gujarat and many other states.[13] At the same time, the ACS had gone up from Rs 1.10 during 1990–1 to Rs 2.77 during 1998–9, reflecting the poor financial status of the GEB during a period in which most capacity added was due to relatively more expensive private utilities, alongside plants commissioned by central utilities.[14] Assuming the role of chief minister in 2001, Modi certainly had his work cut out for him in terms of turning the sector around.

2001–8: Implementing Efficiency Measures and Sectoral Reconfiguration

In the light of the preceding decade's developments, this observation on Gujarat's power sector from 2003 makes for unsurprising reading: 'The problems are particularly acute in Gujarat state, which represents a microcosm of the key issues faced throughout India, where a complicated and overlapping regulatory structure and new entrant prohibitions have stifled new electricity sector investment'.[15] Yet it reads strangely in retrospect, given that what transpired next bears testament to the possibilities of efficiency that all too often remain latent within public sector enterprises.

First, the so-called unbundling of the sector in line with the national mandate was undertaken gradually, with the central Electricity Act 2003 being followed by the Gujarat Electricity Industry (Re-organisation and Regulation) Act, leading to the GEB being unbundled into six public electric companies in 2005, under the holding company Gujarat Urja Vikas Nigam Limited (GUVNL).[16] Concurrently, bureaucrats in the state energy and petrochemicals department found leeway to renegotiate some existing power purchase agreements (PPAs) with generators, capitalizing on prevalent low interest rates to restructure sectoral finances in concert with the Department of Finance.[17] Such coordination is a rarity in the Indian context, and was instrumental in providing the initial financial leverage under reforms. Moreover, the GERC brought about greater transparency in sectoral finances. According to a former senior GERC official, 'There was a lot of opposition as people didn't want the details to come out ... Our engineers were technically good but lacked financial accounting skills ... There was no commercial mindset in power in Gujarat'.[18] Thus, cooperation between government departments and capable management improved sectoral financial positioning and oversight.

Second, a massive investment of Rs 1,290 crore was made in the Jyotigram Yojana (JGY), a scheme to segregate rural feeders which installed a parallel network of lines to separate the technical infrastructure for rural domestic and agricultural supply. The government financed the bulk of this with Rs 1,110 crore; GUVNL furnished the rest. The JGY began with a pilot initiative in eight districts during 2003–4, with state-wide extension undertaken immediately thereafter and completed by 2008. This enabled 24-hour three-phase domestic supply and scheduled three-phase supply to agricultural users. A single elegant technical solution provided the basis for stemming line theft losses, improving the quality of rural power supply, and boosting operational efficiency and revenue realization. A GUNVL official summed it up retrospectively:

> The key aspects of JGY were regulating water drawal through segregation by bypassing the *teta* [phase converter based on capacitors] and using the SDT [Special Design Transformer] to supply rural domestic power in parallel ... With feeder separation, there is more transparency, so actual transmission losses are visible. This makes it easier to identify where the losses are, which vigilance teams and dedicated police stations are acting on.[19]

A former official from the energy department called JGY 'the biggest success anywhere you go. [Many] state teams came to learn, but I think only Madhya Pradesh learned. They have implemented JGY in about half their state now. The difference is that we invested ... and others are unable to do the same'.[20] He emphasized the role of a single farmer union, the Bharatiya Kisan Sangh, in this development, in concert with state politics. Another official currently at the same department independently confirmed the significance of the scheme to the state's sectoral success: 'JGY and unbundling happened simultaneously, which has benefitted the sector. That's the main development. JGY led to quality power supply'.[21] He emphasized the simultaneous role of political will and technical support, pointing out that the former Chief Minister is now trying to replicate the success of the scheme at the national level as India's Prime Minister.

Given the vote-bank politics typical of Indian states, with governments pandering to agricultural consumers, the political will to address line theft that accompanied the JGY, by way of police stations dedicated to identifying and penalizing abusers, is remarkable. The outcome of this multi-pronged approach is in keeping with studies that show that rural load segregation boosts sectoral performance with accompanying measures rather than in isolation.[22] This contextualized implementation of feeder reforms has been lauded as a best practice of socio-technical sectoral change.[23]

Thus, financial leverage within the sector, combined with stable political rule, created an opportunity for investment in upgrading and expanding physical infrastructure to bring about efficiency, shortly followed by positive political knock-on effects from the financial turn-around of a key sector. As a former official who had occupied senior roles within multiple discoms summed up, 'I used to sit with the farmers and hear their problems. The SDO [subdivisional officer], etc. take cuts everywhere possible and cheat the farmers. We optimized the rural electricity corporation norms in order to optimize performance knowing all this, in order to have better revenue in the long run through more satisfied consumers.'[24] Despite ACS continuing to increase during this period up to Rs 3.42 during 2010–11, revenue realization did indeed keep pace. In part, this can also be attributed to another innovative financial mechanism implemented in 2004: the Fuel and Power Purchase Price Adjustment (FPPPA). This enables marginal quarterly tariff adjustments and, thereby, a closer balancing between cost and revenue. This was brought in by the GERC with petition-based engagement by the utilities as part of a move towards multiyear tariffs under financial reforms.[25] This sort of nuanced approach, as opposed to the one taken in other states where even minor adjustments remain dependent on an elaborate tariff petition process via the regulatory body, underscores the smooth interface between technical, administrative, and financial management in Gujarat's distribution sector. Like the JGY, the FPPPA is now being replicated nationwide.

The above measures indicate awareness of the political dividend to be secured through a well-functioning electricity distribution sector, contrasting with frozen tariffs during similar periods in other states and a tendency to give out pre-election sops. There was certainly kowtowing to key vote-bank groups such as agricultural consumers in Gujarat as well, by offering a significant state government subsidy on agricultural tariffs that is widely regarded as essential.[26] Nonetheless, efficiency measures limited leakages that are typically associated with distribution in sparsely populated areas. Additionally, the large share of high-tariff consumers meant that there was sufficient financial cushion for the sector to grow. As Figure 5.1 shows, industrial consumption was 44 per cent of state wide consumption during 2007–8, and generated 62 per cent of the total revenue—proportions that have been maintained since. AT&C losses, with the GERC's oversight and feeder reform measures ensuring a closer match with reality, were at 23 per cent during 2007–8. A decade later, many other states would be happy with comparable achievements.

2008–16: Cashing in on Stable Politics and Finance

Since 2008, Gujarat's electricity distribution sector has capitalized on its sound financial standing and efficient performance. During 2014–15, AT&C losses had dropped to 16.06 per cent. From 1.26 GW during 2007–8, its installed renewable energy capacity shot up to 4.97 GW by 2014–15. Besides steady growth in wind energy, this has partly been due to its championing of solar energy even before the national solar policy came into force in 2011. During this period, efforts to introduce competition in the distribution sector, inspired by successful experiences in the electricity generation and transmission sectors, have opened up different power sourcing options to industrial consumers above 1 MW, posing new challenges for discoms that have long held the status of incumbent service providers. Gujarat already has Torrent Power Limited as a long-standing private licensee in its three urban centres of Ahmedabad, Gandhinagar, and Surat. The company has set the benchmark for efficient, financially successful operations throughout, implementing state-of-the-art technology to benefit from a profitable mix of relatively high-tariff industrial and urban domestic consumers and high population density. Yet unlike its neighbouring state Rajasthan, Gujarat's public discoms have not had to adopt a distribution franchisee model in any new areas. As a GERC official explained, 'They have avoided franchisees. There has been both technical and financial improvement, and both quality and amount of supply have gone up'.[27] Maintaining a strong public sector stake in distribution also suggests a greater likelihood of democratic participation in determining its trajectory, but in this regard there is some room to criticize Gujarat's handling of a key aspect, namely public engagement. This subsection details developments on open access and renewable energy during this most recent period, and reflects on public engagement.

In interviews, Chamber of Commerce representatives were both appreciative and critical of the manner in which open access has panned out. One reported that industrial consumers were happy with the quality of service the discoms had achieved, especially the state's major industries such as pharmaceuticals, textiles, and chemicals, for whom reliable power supply is key to avoiding disruptions in continuous processes and thus avoiding heavy losses.[28] Another reflected on the savings that industrial consumers switching to independent power producers (IPPs) or sourcing from the power exchange stand to make, 'Ground realities of social obligation dictate the need to safeguard the discoms. But they should consider an option of purchasing certain percentages from out-of-state and some from the discoms for private players'.[29] Thus, despite voicing some frustration at having to forego part of the benefits that would accrue to them under strictly competitive open access, industrial consumers did appreciate the social pact inherent in the cross-subsidy matrix, indicating some buy-in to the reform trajectory. The GUVNL employees, well aware that industrial consumers save approximately Rs 2 per unit despite paying various surcharges under the open access rules prevalent in 2016, did not entertain any ideas that might lessen demand from their high-tariff consumers. Approximate surcharges include Re 0.80 fixed charges, Rs 1.20 cross-subsidy charges, Re 0.60 as an additional surcharge, and Re 0.10 charges for estimated losses.

An energy department official justified the current balance by saying that discoms' 'supply management must not suffer due to frequent changes in demand by private consumers trying to always go after the best rate. So, transmission must prioritize the discoms. This is in accordance with the Electricity Act'.[30] On this basis, he justified the denial of short-term open access to applicants. A Torrent Power Limited expert on regulation was partly sympathetic, noting that short-term open access had led to gaming, disrupting discoms' ability to plan and balance distribution to a variety of consumers. 'So it is not only about the spirit of competition. It is a question of policy', he quipped.[31] Yet in the long run, policy should seek to address these problems in a manner cognizant of the much cheaper power exchange rates whose benefits, to a large extent, are foregone by industrial consumers at present. At least, that is what a future move to a truly competitive distribution sector requires.

One instance of the fallout of holding back competition came up in an interview with a GERC official. He noted that with the current savings of about Rs 2 per unit after surcharges, open access consumers 'still make good savings compared to industrial tariffs by buying from the power exchange, but unfortunately since wind is above Rs 4, it costs around the same as the industrial tariff [after adding open access surcharges]. Hence, nobody bothers to adopt it under open access.'[32] This cooling effect on renewable energy uptake is a retrograde policy outcome, protecting fixed cost recovery under inefficient PPAs and transferring the burden to consumers. Despite this policy jam, wind capacity addition has maintained a steady rate, even with relatively low purchase rates offered by the state. A senior GUVNL manager claimed this is because 'Signing a contract with GUVNL means lower costs for developers in terms of administration, financing and operational costs, since our system is working pretty much on auto mode'.[33]

Yet the roughly 4 GW of installed wind capacity is not without problems for energy planners, since it is characterized by high daily and seasonal flux. A senior official at the Gujarat Energy Development Agency (GEDA) quoted an intra-day high that was sub-1 GW and a low that was sub-300 MW, observing that 'regulations demand a PLF [plant load factor] of minimum 24 per cent but usually it stays below 20 per cent in practice'.[34] An official from the Chief Electrical Inspector Office, however, saw these as problems that can easily be overcome by optimizing the distribution and transmission system based on existing GETCO infrastructure, enabling local wind power consumption to minimize grid management effects. He envisioned smart grids and the setting up of micro-grids to maintain whole-grid stability by connecting multiple renewable energy projects and existing substations.[35]

With regard to solar energy, GEDA was instrumental in rapid uptake from 2009. A former official reminisced:

> We didn't have a single MW of solar energy around. We invited a series of stakeholders, then held a meeting with 35 of them. GERC confirmed Rs 15 per unit initial tariff and the costs associated with solar went down, so the rush began. We got 350 proposals from developers, which we evaluated on financial and managerial strength of the applicants rather than sectoral experience, which hardly anyone had with solar. We allotted in small capacity, a maximum of 25 MW and down to 2 MW. We didn't want to give big projects to a few big people which might misfire. Now the market has matured. Banks are willing to provide financial support for solar.[36]

These Rs 15 tariffs were locked in for the first 12 years, followed by Rs 5 per unit for the next thirteen years of the PPA, as an incentive strictly available only to those developers who commissioned plants within a short control period for up to 1 GW in installed capacity. Over 80 per cent met this timeline, beating expectations and tying the state into paying what, in retrospect, are exorbitant rates for increasingly affordable solar energy.

These negative economic consequences aside, Gujarat has been credited with kick-starting solar energy uptake prior to the national solar policy of 2011,[37] which commits India to 100 GW in installed solar capacity out of a total renewable energy capacity of 175 GW by 2022. Yet, even this growth powered by relatively small developers was spatially concentrated in land earmarked for the purpose by the state government, with fast-tracked clearances and licensing at Charanka solar park. This location in a remote area entailed heavy investment of $134 million in transmission infrastructure,[38] and has been critiqued for its distributive injustice.[39] Distributed solar capacity has grown much more modestly, with installation capped at 50 per cent of connected load for consumers and similar caps on transmission, severely limiting prospects for prosuming, that is, solar self-generation combined with distributed storage, and net metering. Even a successful demonstration rooftop solar project in Gandhinagar is on the MW scale and uses government institutional buildings in the state capital rather than targeting ordinary consumers.

Thus, the benefits of inclusion and increased access without infrastructure-intensive development have not accompanied solar uptake. A representative from the chief electrical inspector's (CEI) office elaborated:

> I have seen developers suffer. They have to approach CEI, GEDA, GETCO, and GUVNL separately; it is a big hassle for even a 1-kW project, which takes a minimum of three months to get approval for ... all [agencies] demand different sets of documents to provide their certifications. After that, to get the MNRE [central government Ministry for New and Renewable Energy] subsidy you have to submit all these certificates ... With single-window clearance, you could give all powers of different agencies to one authority and ask for the minimum documents online. GERC has the power to make this happen now![40]

Such exasperation at the complex and slow bureaucratic process was a recurring theme in more general observations about the sectoral trajectory beyond renewable energy matters.

For instance, a senior journalist with energy sector expertise criticized GERC's relocation from leased premises in central Ahmedabad in 2013 to swanky new offices in GIFT One City near Gandhinagar: 'There is no [public] bus, no direct transport—they have their own buses running, nobody knows where it stops, when it goes. This increases inaccessibility for the consumers'.[41] An energy auditor sagely observed, 'Consumers have got their main demands satisfied in terms of quality reliable power, so they are focussing on business. When people are busy with activity they generally don't disturb the system'.[42] While public participation by way of annual public hearings on tariffs has been undertaken since the GEB days and by all four discoms since 2006, engagement has been subdued and has typically comprised consumer representatives from industry and retired sector employees. Given the rise in quality and quantity of service, there is little pressure on the sector to undertake new initiatives at a radical departure from actions it is already performing. Yet this means that renewable energy uptake is being curtailed, and that discoms are being artificially protected from the consequences of efficiency gains from which open access consumers are deriving only partial benefits.

***

There is much to learn from Gujarat's performance, which has been stellar compared to most Indian states in terms of service quality and financial positioning despite far-from-ideal supply characteristics. Some factors such as the load profile have been in its favour, but others are outcomes of politically savvy decision-making and a sustained vision for the sector across various aspects that have been dealt with in combination. Yet there is a limit to how progressive these initiatives have been, and there seems to be less action than one might expect if the steering of the sector were to be truly informed by the objectives of 'clean and inclusive energy access' that constitute the mantra of the national electricity mission, and indeed of the United Nations' seventh Sustainable Development Goal. Sectoral development, despite being in good financial form, is understandably still motivated by conventional concerns of stability. However, these concerns lead to conservatism instead of a rapid transition to clean energy, which Gujarat is uniquely positioned to undertake among Indian states. For instance, it has been argued that Gujarat's success since the early 2000s was made possible not only by its achievements with distribution sector finances and rural load segregation, but also because of an astounding 166 percent increase in installed capacity from below 9 GW in 2004 to nearly 24 GW in 2013, based primarily on rapid growth in private generation from just over 2 GW to over 14 GW during the same period, leaving the public share of overall capacity at 25 per cent.[43] This was enabled by quick project commissioning in Gujarat's business-friendly environment. Yet at present, there is a definite lost opportunity for the integration of renewable sources in a massive way beyond the renewable purchase obligation (RPO, elsewhere known as renewable portfolio standards) targets through more ambitious, future-oriented grid coordination. Another sector that will benefit from a more integrated approach is solar energy infrastructure manufacturing, which there are signs of, as the major Gujarati industrial player Adani comes to the fore of installing facilities in India. A 2014 report shows that renewables can be a vital source of job creation in India's growing economy.[44] As a state with an entrepreneurial culture, Gujarat has historically been a master at capturing potential gains from nimbleness in the manufacturing sector, as evidenced in its successful foray into producing low-cost LED lamps en masse under the national Ujala scheme.

Zooming out, the general lesson from the Gujarat case for analyses of regional and sectoral political economic dynamics is that these can function in concert to produce virtuous cycles based on a host of factors. First, coordination between different governmental line agencies (in this case especially state departments of finance and energy) enabled restructuring of PPAs and enhanced transparency. Second, visionary leadership instituted systems of administrative accountability, such as police stations to tackle line thefts; these plugged leakages in sectoral functioning at lower levels to bring about efficiency. Third, innovative measures, ranging from physical infrastructural interventions such as feeder separation through JGY to sophisticated financial instruments like FPPPA, put in place a technological basis for efficiency. It is precisely because these strategies complemented each other that they led to improved performance, avoiding possible political pitfalls such as loss of popularity due to tariff hikes, accusations of poor governance if positive effects were not quickly visible, and changes in the commitment of the state's administrative machinery to ensuring sound implementation due to inconsistent policies.

On a more sobering note, these same political economic dynamics contain the potential to curtail progressive sectoral development by reaching a stable but suboptimal equilibrium. This manifests in a ban on short-term trading at the power exchange as a protectionist measure that favours discoms while limiting industrial consumers' prospective gains from competitive market measures; in caps on solar prosuming that limit distributed solar uptake; and in the failure to promote sufficient public engagement with the sector by painstakingly reaching out to and empowering consumers. The same problem-driven approach that the sector has been credited with for its recent accomplishments[45] does not seem to be at work in these cases where political gains are perhaps not perceived, leading to inaction that would otherwise enable significant substantive advances for the sector and the state.

These trends suggest that, while well ahead of the curve among Indian states, Gujarat's distribution sector and its most influential stakeholders are becoming complacent after having secured achievements that are remarkable among Indian states, rather than being driven by an insatiable urge to constantly improve and further optimize sectoral outcomes. Given the state and the sector's considerable success in overcoming the institutional memory of bureaucratic inefficiency from pre-reform days, is it wishful thinking to hope that the high potential in its electricity distribution sector to achieve truly transformative status will be grasped and championed by future visionary leaders in positions of either managerial or administrative influence, if not both?

Notes and References

1. Edward A. Alpers, 'Gujarat and the Trade of East Africa, c. 1500–1800', *The International Journal of African Historical Studies* 9(1), 1976: 22–44.
2. Nikita Sud, 'The Indian State in a Liberalizing Landscape', *Development and Change* 40(4), 2009: 645–65.
3. Christophe Jaffrelot, 'What "Gujarat Model"?—Growth without Development—and with Socio-Political Polarisation', *South Asia: Journal of South Asian Studies* 38(4), 2015: 820–38.
4. Sunila S. Kale, *Electrifying India: Regional Political Economies of Development* (Stanford: Stanford University Press, 2014).
5. Namrata Chindarkar, 'Beyond Power Politics: Evaluating the Policy Design Process of Rural Electrification in Gujarat, India', *Public Administration and Development* 37(1), 2017: 28–39.
6. The two exceptions, Ahmedabad Electric Company Limited and Surat Electric Company Limited, have operated as licensees since 1913 in Ahmedabad and Gandhinagar and since 1920 in Surat respectively. They

continue to operate in these urban regions as the company Torrent Power Limited.

7. Sudha Venu Menon, 'Drivers of Economic Growth in Gujarat', *Munich Personal RePEc Archive Paper No. 9233* (Munich: Munich University Library, 2008).

8. GUVNL, March 2016, figures displayed at SWITCH Global Expo, Vadodara, in October 2016.

9. Notably, this disadvantage was tempered by the freight equalization policy until the early 1990s.

10. GERC, *Tariff Order No. 19 of 1999* (Ahmedabad: Gujarat Electricity Regulatory Commission, 2000), 102. For a detailed discussion, see Christopher Joshi Hansen and John Bower, *Political Economy of Electricity Reform: A Case Study in Gujarat, India* (Oxford: Oxford Institute for Energy Studies, 2003).

11. Interview with Bharatiya Kisan Sangh representative, Gandhinagar, 27 September 2016.

12. This term from political science and economics refers to the moral hazard problem of an agent being motivated by interests contrary to those of the principal whom they act on behalf of, for example, utility field staff who might take a bribe rather than levying a fine for line theft on behalf of their employer.

13. See Jagadip Narayan Singh, 'Politics of Agriculture Interest Groups: A Case Study of the Bharatiya Kisan Sangh and Its Interaction with the Gujarat State Government Over Power (Electricity) Issues' (PhD dissertation, MS University of Baroda, 2005).

14. Priyadarshi R. Shukla, Debashish Biswas, Tirthankar Nag et al., 'Captive Power Plants: Case Study of Gujarat India', *Program for Sustainable Energy Development (PESD) Working Paper* 4 (2004).

15. Hansen and Bower, 'Political Economy of Electricity Reform', 2003.

16. These six companies included the existing generation (GSECL) and transmission (Gujarat Energy Transmission Corporation Limited [GETCO]) companies as well as four regional distribution companies, or discoms: Uttar (UGVCL), Dakshin (DGVCL), Madhya (MGVCL), and Paschim Gujarat Vij Company Limited (PGVCL).

17. For further details, see Siddharth Sareen, 'Energy Distribution Trajectories in Two Western Indian States: Comparative Politics and Sectoral Dynamics', *Energy Research & Social Science* 35, 2017: 17–27.

18. Interview with former GERC official, Gandhinagar, 11 October 2016.

19. Interview with GUVNL official, Vadodara, 8 October 2016.

20. Interview with former Department of Energy and Petrochemicals official, Gandhinagar, 28 September 2016.

21. Interview with Department of Energy and Petrochemicals official, Gandhinagar, 5 October 2016.

22. ASTAE (Asia Sustainable and Alternative Energy Program), 'Lighting Rural India: Load Segregation Experience in Selected States', *South Asia Energy Studies*, World Bank, Washington, DC (2014).

23. Tushaar Shah, Madhavi Mehta, Gopi Sankar, and Shankar Mondal, 'Organizational Reform in Gujarat's Electricity Utility: Lessons for Revitalizing a Bureaucratic Service Delivery Agency', *IWMI-Tata Water Policy Research Highlight* 6, 2012: 1–8, http://www.iwmi.cgiar.org/iwmi-tata/PDFs/2012_Highlight-06.pdf.

24. Interview with former discom official, Vadodara, 7 October 2016.

25. Muralidharan K. Iyer, 'Power Sector Reforms in India and Restructuring of Gujarat Electricity Board: A Case Study' (PhD dissertation, M.S. University of Baroda, 2007), 132.

26. Vidyut Joshi and Akash Acharya, 'Addressing Agricultural Power Subsidy: A Case Study of North Gujarat', *Centre for Social Studies Working Paper 2*, Veer Narmad South Gujarat University (2005).

27. Interview with GERC official, Gandhinagar, 21 September 2016.

28. Interview with Chamber of Commerce representative, Ahmedabad, 22 September 2016.

29. Interview with Chamber of Commerce representative, Vadodara, 9 October 2016.

30. Interview with Energy and Petrochemicals Department official, Gandhinagar, 5 October 2016.

31. Interview with Torrent Power Limited employee, Vadodara, 6 October 2016.

32. Interview with GERC official, Gandhinagar, 21 September 2016.

33. Interview with GUVNL official, Vadodara, 8 October 2016.

34. Interview with GEDA official, Gandhinagar, 23 September 2016.

35. Interview with Chief Electrical Inspector·Office official, Gandhinagar, 13 October 2016.

36. Interview with former GEDA official, Gandhinagar, 27 September 2016.

37. Interview with solar energy specialist, telephonic, 27 September 2016.

38. GETCO, *Initial Environmental Examination: Gujarat Solar Power Transmission Project* (Gujarat: Asian Development Bank, 2011).

39. Komali Yenneti, Rosie Day, and Oleg Golubchikov, 'Spatial Justice and the Land Politics of Renewables: Dispossessing Vulnerable Communities through Solar Energy Mega-projects', *Geoforum* 76, 2016: 90–9.

40. Interview with official from CEI office, Gandhinagar, 13 October 2016.

41. Interview with senior reporter, telephonic, 12 October 2016.

42. Interview with energy auditor, Ahmedabad, 29 September 2016.

43. Sudheer Pal Singh, 'Why Gujarat's Power Story Is Hard to Replicate', *Business Standard*, 18 June 2014, available www.business-standard.com/article/economy-policy/why-gujarat-s-power-story-is-hard-to-replicate-114061801337_1.html (accessed 21 August 2017).

44. CEEW-NRDC, *Re-energizing India's Solar Energy Market through Financing* (New Delhi/New York: Council of Energy, Environment and Water [CEEW] and Natural Resources Defense Council [NRDC], 2014).

45. Chindarkar, 'Beyond Power Politics', 28–39.

5

ROHIT CHANDRA

Extractive States and Layered Conflict

The Case of Jharkhand's Electricity Sector

Political Economy of Jharkhand

When Jharkhand was first formed in 2001, a sense of optimism pervaded the state. A unified, persistent social movement led by various, primarily tribal, groups in southern Bihar had finally achieved their own political and administrative entity separate from Bihar.[1] Given the developmental vacuum and divisive caste politics of Bihar, the political and bureaucratic elites of Jharkhand were hopeful that this separation would engender a decisive break from the past. The electrification gap between Jharkhand and Bihar was pronounced: the population density of north Bihar, the domination of Bihari politics by upper-caste groups, and the terrain complexity of south Bihar had resulted in the systematic deprivation of electricity to households in non-industrial Jharkhand. An autonomous Jharkhand could presumably make more claims on the plentiful natural resources within its borders to correct this historical imbalance. The confluence of geological circumstances made Jharkhand an ideal location for heavy industry: plentiful coal, abundant rivers and waterways, and large expanses of unsettled land.

Within a few years, however, it became exceedingly clear that Jharkhand would not experience the conflict-free transition once hoped for. Protracted disputes with the Bihar government prevented the electricity bureaucracy from settling into a comfortable rhythm of operations. Perhaps more importantly, the political climate within the state fractured much quicker than imagined; the unity displayed during the Jharkhand movement quickly dissolved into more localized identity-based (tribal and non-tribal) rivalries, creating an inhospitable ecosystem for long-term planning.[2] In the last fifteen years, Jharkhand has had ten chief ministers and two instances of President's rule. Whichever party or coalition came into power would often look to extract quick rents from the power system. The dominance of short-term political goals has taken its toll on the state's power system: Jharkhand still has one of the worst rural village electrification rates in the country (39 per cent),[3] its discom is ranked among the worst financial performers nationally,[4] and the state has been unable to resolve legacy issues with public sector enterprises (PSEs). The state unbundled its electricity board, Jharkhand State Electricity Board (JSEB) only recently, in late 2014.

Despite this dire situation, regulation in the power sector has provided a counterbalance to political manipulation. Within a year of the Electricity Act of 2003, Jharkhand mobilized its own regulatory commission, known formally as the Jharkhand State Electricity Regulatory Commission (JSERC). The JSERC started as an apolitical, progressive voice for electrification in a political environment where the political salience of electricity was questionable, especially amidst myriad other identity and developmental issues that have historically dominated the state's politics. Over time, the effectiveness and authority of JSERC has slowly eroded, but it still performs many critical functions that rein in excessive politicization of JSEB.[5]

Given the state's political origins, it is not surprising that Jharkhand politics is known for mobilization around tribal issues. Issues of tribal land rights, access to government schools, universities, and jobs, and tribal representation (or lack thereof) in government and business tend to dominate headlines. The rapid formation of Jharkhand from its Bihari remnants has unfortunately alienated the median tribal voter in the state in favour of a small, rotating tribal elite.[6] A consequence of this concentration of power has been the deprioritization of developmental issues, like electricity, in mainstream political campaigning.

Unsurprisingly, large capital projects have become ripe for patronage and rent-seeking, a symptom of Jharkhand's extractive mode of politics. This has affected both the retail level, where the JSEB has been buying increasingly expensive power, and the wholesale level, where revenue and physical losses necessitate large state budget subsidization of the JSEB (shown in Figures 5.1 and 5.2).

As a young state, Jharkhand is discovering its place in the federal politics of electricity, where it has control over distribution, some transmission, and little generation. The legacy of the state's interactions with the Damodar Valley Corporation (DVC), and various other Central Public Service Entities has left multiple layers of inherited conflict from which the state is still extricating itself. These problems dominate the administrative space, and understanding them will give insight into how the state's agency, particularly in the financial domain, has eroded over

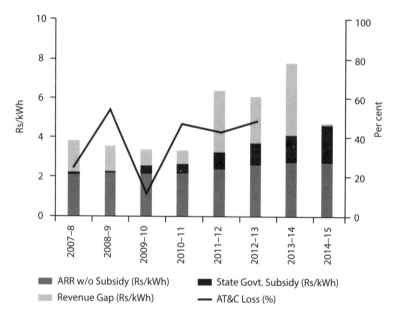

FIGURE 5.1   Physical and Financial Profile: Jharkhand
Source: CSO, *Energy Statistics* (New Delhi: Central Statistics Office, Ministry of Statistics and Programme Implementation, Government of India, 2010, 2012, 2014, and 2016); PFC, Reports on Performance of State Power Utilities (New Delhi: Power Finance Corporation Limited, 2011, 2013, 2015, and 2016).

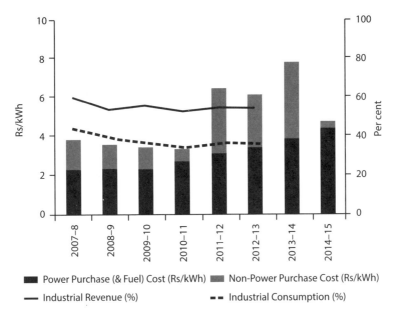

FIGURE 5.2   Supply-Side Costs and Revenue Recovery: Jharkhand
Source: PFC, *Reports on Performance of State Power Utilities* (New Delhi: Power Finance Corporation Limited, 2011, 2013, 2015, and 2016).

time. Between extractive politics affecting the retail domain, and layered jurisdictional conflicts affecting the wholesale procurement of power, Jharkhand's power sector has been plagued with inefficiencies since the state's inception.

Political Economy of the Power Sector

Political instability in Jharkhand has constantly threatened long-term state planning across sectors, paralysing bureaucracies, and their ability to operate. Bureaucratic risk-aversion to signing major orders meant that any large tender or purchase needs political authorization. Without a stable Energy Minister, procurement freezes.[7] The most productive periods for JSEB were when the chief minister (CM) kept the energy portfolio to prevent undue rent-seeking. The 2014 Jharkhand election was the first time that one party won an outright majority without power sharing, and the present government is the first in the state's history where the

CM will likely govern for an entire term. Consequently, it is no surprise that the extractive mode has dominated Jharkhand governments. Due to this bureaucratic risk aversion, the regulatory function became even more important in the early years of Jharkhand's formation.

Jharkhand's electricity timeline is best segmented by the tenures of three JSERC chairmen: S.K.F. Kujur (2003–8), Mukhtiar Singh (2008–12), and N.N. Tiwari (2014–present).[8] Political turnover was frequent (see Table 5.1) so JSERC chairmen ended up inhabiting various roles: consumer advocate, JSEB watchdog, grievance redresser, and political-bureaucratic coordinator, among others. Characterizing each of their tenures provides a broader sense of how the regulatory apparatus has evolved within the state, and illustrates how extractive politics have slowly chipped away at state institutions including the JSERC.

The JSERC was initially a bulwark against the extractive mode, protecting the power sector from its most corrosive practices. The first four to five years were a honeymoon period, when JSERC exercised its authority without major political blowback. S.K.F. Kujur's initial insistence on transparency ruffled many feathers—especially amongst licensees and power sector bureaucrats unused to scrutiny—resulting in swift legal challenges to most of his orders.[9] But Kujur's style of governance also allowed JSERC to grow in the absence of sanctioned opposition by the political class. Consumer advocates and the media began to see JSERC as a potential ally, rather than yet another government department needing to be cajoled and lobbied.[10]

As JSEB and other licensees learned about the new regulatory system, however, they found ways to gradually undermine it. Furthermore, the political cover that had been afforded to Kujur was not available to his successors. This is evident particularly from the Mukhtiar Singh period when licensees and JSEB began disengaging from the regulatory process. The JSERC was undermined in many ways: deprival of office space, legal challenges to JSERC rulings,[11] and delayed and falsified responses to data requests. Such wilful undermining of a statutory regulator is impossible without some degree of tacit support from state leaders. Traditional punitive measures for non-compliance, financial penalties by the JSERC grew ineffective as the financial situation of JSEB deteriorated: JSERC's levied penalties were negligible in comparison to the crushing interest payments and outstanding generation dues that JSEB had accumulated. By this point, the JSERC's tactics had become

TABLE 5.1   Timeline of Key Events: Jharkhand

State Politics		Power Sector Events
• August: Jharkhand State created through Bihar State Reorganisation Act • BJP wins election, Babulal Marandi becomes the Chief Minister	2000	
	2001	
	2002	
• Arjun Munda becomes the Chief Minister	2003	• Electricity Act passed • SKF Kujur appointed JSERC Chairman
	2004	
• November: JSEB Offices ransacked by BJP party workers in response to power s/hablertages	2005	
• Madhu Koda becomes the Chief Minister	2006	• CERC brings DVC under regulated tariff
	2007	
	2008	
• Jan–Dec: President's Rule invoked	2009	• Mukhtiar Singh appointed JSERC Chairman
• June–Sept: President's Rule invoked • BJP wins election, Arjun Munda becomes the Chief Minister	2010	
	2011	
	2012	• CESC and Tata appointed distribution franchisee for Ranchi and Jamshedpur
• Power sharing agreement between BJP and JMM breaks down • Jan–Jul: President's Rule invoked • JMM wins election, Hemant Soren becomes the Chief Minister	2013	• December: JSEB unbundles under pressure

(Cont'd)

TABLE 5.1 (*Cont'd*)

State Politics		Power Sector Events
• BJP wins December election, Raghubar Das becomes the Chief Minister	2014	• N.N. Tiwari appointed JSERC chairman
	2015	• CESC and Tata contract cancelled
• Jharkhand becomes first state to buy into UDAY	2016	• April: NTPC JV takes over Patratu TPS

Source: The State Politics timeline excludes the following Chief Ministers because of visual constraints. Shibu Soren (JMM) 2 March 2005–12 March 2005, Shibu Soren (JMM) 27 August 2008–18 January 2009 (bookended by President's Rule), Shibu Soren (JMM) 30 December 2009–31 May 2010, President's Rule 18 January 2013–12 July 2013.

relatively ineffective. In addition to regulatory decline, Jharkhand has faced major jurisdictional and territorial disputes with multiple state entities, which have severely impacted the state's financial agency.

The Honeymoon Period (2003–8)

S.K.F. Kujur was a career Indian Administrative Service (IAS) officer. A Jharkhand local, he played a major role in state bifurcation as Principal Accountant General of Bihar. Trusted by the political establishment in Jharkhand, he was appointed Member (Finance) and shortly thereafter, Chairman of JSERC. He knew that he had a short window of opportunity to discipline a still nascent electricity bureaucracy and establish the regulator's authority. Through the mid-2000s the state was preoccupied with the legacies of bifurcation, and therefore did not realize how drastically the Electricity Act had upended existing power relations within the sector. Arbitrary tariffs, inefficient operation, and slow progress towards performance targets were all issues for which the regulator was now authorized to exercise discipline on JSEB. Kujur did just that.

With his knowledge of law and finance, and his trust among the political class (particularly the Energy Minister at the time Lalchand Mahto),[12] Kujur established JSERC as a legitimate entity. Using JSERC as a platform, he disciplined JSEB by cutting their tariffs massively. He publicized tariff proceedings and pushed for unprecedented audits of JSEB records. Flustered by his onslaught, JSEB wrote a letter to the Ministry of Power asking to be 'exempted from the terms of the Electricity Act, 2003', an expression of their then-administrative and legal naiveté. More importantly, Kujur tried to proactively involve himself in all aspects of JSEB activities. He hired outside consultants to assess tariff orders, established a State Advisory Committee (SAC) of smart consumer advocates, and ensured JSERC's financial independence.[13] An assertive regulator dealing with an inexperienced state apparatus, he shaped many practices outside of JSERC's formal jurisdiction.

Kujur's most promising but ultimately failed project was the revamp of Patratu Thermal Power Station (PTPS). One of Bihar's oldest power plants, PTPS was commissioned in the early 1970s with Soviet assistance with a nameplate capacity of 840 megawatt (MW). In a state procuring over 70 per cent of its power from external sources, PTPS was a valuable asset in the early 2000s providing cheap instate generation. However, over the 2000s, as plant load factors fell due to unit downtime and maintenance costs rose, the economic logic behind keeping the plant operational slowly disappeared.[14] Currently, only two out of the ten units are in operation, with a combined load factor of about 15 per cent. Multiple regulators, JSEB chairmen, and the CEA tried to push for plant closure or transfer,[15,16] but were unsuccessful because of political support for excessively optimistic modernization and revenue targets. PTPS renovation and modernization (R&M) expenditures have been a regular item on the Energy Ministry budget, sometimes reaching Rs 200 crore per year.[17] Despite this, PTPS plant efficiencies have not changed significantly in the last ten years; in fact, most insiders believe that the R&M funds have gone primarily into employment costs for workers, making PTPS renovation essentially a patronage strategy. Unsurprisingly, various multi-year R&M budgets were passed by different parties in power, each eager to milk the dying asset. The PTPS was finally handed to National Thermal Power Corporation (NTPC) in April 2015, further eroding the state's control over its generation assets. The new entity has a 76:24 shareholding structure between NTPC and the state government. While not explicitly stated as such, this transfer was likely part of a larger settlement with NTPC over dues as well.

Why are politicians able to assert control over these institutions with such impunity? One problem is that the political visibility of electricity is still relatively low. One common observation is that promises by politicians to increase electrification are never taken seriously, particularly in rural Jharkhand. As one regulatory official put it, '[On electricity], the government has zero credibility to deliver on its promises'. In a state where only 46 per cent of households had electricity in 2011 (see Table 5.1), many other issues loom much larger: identity and self-respect, land and forest rights, food and water availability, access to basic healthcare services, road penetration, and so on.[18] In an elaborate sixteen-page manifesto, one of the state's most prominent tribal parties (the Jharkhand Mukti Morcha) mentioned electricity and solar power in only two minor bullet points.[19]

Urban middle class lobbying for reliable electricity supply has been far more effective than rural mobilization in Jharkhand. The most well-known case occurred in the mid-2000s, when a couple of judges annoyed by regular power cuts at courthouses took *suo motu* action against JSEB, summoning the Chairman, Member (Technical), and Energy Secretary to account for the erratic power supply in Ranchi.[20] Although not reported publicly, it seems JSEB was selling some power meant for Ranchi to other, higher-paying consumers in the short-term market in order to shore up their finances. The ensuing verdict allocated 150 additional MW of generation to the city which improved reliability considerably.

While political interference has partially undermined the effectiveness of JSEB, what is more problematic is the myriad state and central disputes that remain unresolved. Jharkhand has always had a mosaic of electricity suppliers. Before India's grid truly became somewhat national (from the early 1990s with the creation of Power Grid), most regions had isolated sub-grids with limited transmission between cities, industrial corridors, and generating plants. Part of the state was under the DVC service area, villages in the coal belt were supplied power through Central Coalfields Limited, the larger area around Bokaro received power from the SAIL power plant, and areas around Jamshedpur received power from the Tatas. While the BSEB was still the distribution company, in practice there were financial exchanges between these electricity suppliers and the BSEB to compensate them for their cost of supply.

After the Electricity Act, most licensees were state-owned entities, so JSEB could continue earlier financial practices adapted for the licensee regime. However, Kujur took a bold step early on in his tenure as JSERC chairman that had far reaching consequences. Jamshedpur Utilities and Service Company (JUSCO), the Jamshedpur utility run by the Tata Group, applied for a parallel license in Seraikela Kharsawan district; many of Tata's ancillary suppliers in Adityapur were unsatisfied with the quality of service provided by JSEB, and were hoping that JUSCO would be more reliable. Before the government understood the implications of parallel licensing, Kujur approved JUSCO's application, effectively creating competition in this district from late 2006. The result was catastrophic for JSEB; 65 per cent of consumers in the district, most of them HT industrial, switched to JUSCO immediately despite higher prices.[21]

JSEB had received its first taste of competition, and did not like it. Open hostilities took root as legal challenges were mounted against JUSCO's parallel license, and further attempts by JSERC to issue parallel licenses were stymied. It was clear that the political establishment and JSEB were not willing to cede operational and financial control of the electricity system. One thin silver lining is that this parallel license became an early exemplar of Electricity Act success, cited by regulators throughout India as an example of localized competition drastically improving the quality of service for consumers.[22] From the events of this period, however, the backlash of the state against the regulatory apparatus began, only intensifying under the next JSERC Chairman.

Disengagement and Political Instability (2008–13)

Mukhtiar Singh, a Bihar/Jharkhand cadre IAS officer, succeeded Kujur in July 2008 during the most unstable period in Jharkhand's short political history. Within six months of his appointment, the state entered a year of President's rule and later again for three months in 2010. Singh had strong political roots in Bihar, where he served as Collector of Patna, acquainting himself with the major political actors in the state. The political class, meanwhile, began to appreciate JSERC's power and the importance of having a sympathetic, pliant regulator. While Singh was headstrong, political instability, and other delays ensured that no other Members were appointed to JSERC for years; he served half of his tenure alone, struggling to convince licensees to file tariff petitions on time. The JSEB, DVC, and other licensees delayed tariff filings, reluctant to concede that tariff determination was outside their control. Not to be outmanoeuvred, Singh passed a *suo motu* tariff order for DVC and JSEB without petition or any public hearings, a wakeup call for the other licensees trying to bypass JSERC. After this incident, licensees gradually became more cooperative.

Like Kujur, Singh was extremely outspoken against the JSEB, excoriating them for excessive losses and inefficiencies during public hearings and SAC meetings. He continued JSERC's strong tradition of consumer advocacy by limiting JSEB efforts to recuperate losses through tariffs, given that their AT&C losses exceeded 40 per cent. As much as he could, Singh tried to force typically office-bound JSEB engineers into the field. With the appointment of the Member (Technical) T. Munikrishnaiah in June 2010, Singh also encouraged energy audits, more systematic transformer maintenance, and other technical fixes.[23] Kujur and Singh established JSERC's control over the sector; no licensee or generator could ignore the institution anymore. As one former JSERC official put it, 'the JSERC were treated like *maha-babus* (super-bureaucrats), once we were appointed it was hard to put very much pressure on us. We could pass tariff orders as frequently as we liked'.[24]

Another promising initiative stifled by political interference during this period was the hiring of distribution franchisees. Like most government agencies in India, JSEB is naturally possessive: ceding operational responsibilities to a private contractor is anathema, financial reasoning notwithstanding. However, by mid-2012, the Arjun Munda-led government managed to overcome political and institutional opposition and bid out distribution franchisee contracts. In late 2012, during the Singh period, Calcutta Electric Supply Corporation (CESC) in Ranchi and Tata Power in Jamshedpur were appointed as distribution franchisees.[25] Jamshedpur was home for the Tatas, making their job easier. The CESC, meanwhile, had to invest considerable resources in their franchise over its first year: surveying the entire city and its load patterns, taking inventory of existing distribution assets, scouting locations for new infrastructure, and installing payment machines, consumer grievance centres, and other services.

Unfortunately, Munda was ousted from coalition leadership within two months of the franchisee appointments. This preceded a rapid succession of governments: six months of President's rule, then one and a half years of rule under CM Hemant Soren, and finally a new Bharatiya

Janata Party (BJP) government in late 2014. All existing arrangements between appointed franchisees and political parties were renegotiated after each election. When the franchisees refused to meet the BJP government's terms, JSEB proceeded to cancel their contracts in May 2015, almost two and a half years after their disbursement. As one former regulator put it, 'It seems that the state was not really committed to these reforms in the first place. The unions were not the main reason these were rolled back; the graft potential is so high in distribution that taking on distribution reforms takes serious will.'[26] Here the state was alienating the private sector. However, its bigger jurisdictional battles were being fought with central or out-of-state PSE giants, primarily the DVC.

DVC exists in a legal grey area because of the unique conditions of its incorporation: it was established in 1948 by the DVC Act, itself approved by the Governor-General because Parliament did not yet exist. Consequently, no real deliberation over state rights occurred, and the Corporation was given widespread power over its service area,[27] including 7 districts within present-day Jharkhand. At the time this decision made sense: DVC was working in a developmental vacuum and needed to swiftly develop power infrastructure that India urgently required. However, nearly seventy years later, DVC retains far-reaching powers that severely restrict states' ability to make decisions about their own electricity and water.

Therefore, there are perpetual tensions between the Jharkhand government and DVC. Over the 2014–15 financial year, almost 45 per cent of JSEB's power purchase budget (Rs 2,127.90 crores) went to purchasing 36 per cent of its total power (4,316.22 million units) from DVC, indicating the latter's market power. Unsurprisingly, every few years a high-profile financial dispute emerged between JSEB and DVC, which was usually temporarily resolved through executive negotiations.[28] There are few representatives from Jharkhand at the highest levels of central government, making it very difficult for the state to advocate for itself in Delhi. Furthermore, little power is consumed in Jharkhand compared to other states, making it impossible for JSEB and the Jharkhand government to assert themselves as large consumers.

The common site of these disputes is the legal or the quasi-judicial regulatory system. Unhappy with JSERC's tariff orders, DVC filed a case in 2009 with the central regulator challenging JSERC's authority over

DVC. This case stalled until Central Electricity Regulatory Commission (CERC), under pressure from the Appellate Tribunal for Electricity (APTEL), finally passed a tariff order for DVC. In fact, under APTEL's ruling, DVC was forced to retroactively return money to consumers it had overcharged via its inflated tariffs. The DVC's appeal is still pending at the Supreme Court, while the company continues to financially underperform.[29] Unsurprisingly, since the Electricity Act, DVC has developed a reputation as a litigious entity, causing one former regulatory official to describe it as 'basically a bully in its service area'.[30] While Jharkhand is partially to blame for its consistently late payments, it continues to be hampered by restricted financial agency.

The only way to continue extracting from existing state institutions for 15 years is to undermine the presumed supremacy of finance and financial logic. Extant financial rules, therefore, are increasingly being intentionally ignored. Looking through CAG reports on PSEs in Jharkhand, the auditor expresses palpable exasperation with JSEB for not having ever placed its audited accounts in front of the State Legislature.[31] From gaming PTPS R&M expenditures to wilfully ignoring certain large consumers' power dues, to manipulating tenders towards favoured contractors, JSEB has established strong norms that prioritize short-term gains and place the power bureaucracy in a very difficult position. In the words of one senior JSEB official,

> We are an orphan child here at JSEB. *Humein bhojan bhi theek se nahin milta* (We don't even get fed properly). I am losing Rs 20 crores a month simply because no government office ever pays its power bills. We can't even ask them to pay. And if government offices don't pay, then what example does that set for everyone else? It severely undermines our authority.
>
> I have an operational budget of about Rs 100 crores annually. I have to split this among the 28 verticals of the JSEB. Think about how many consumers I have to meter. There are about 25 cities in Jharkhand with an average of 2 lakh consumers each. That's 50 lakh consumers. A new meter costs around Rs 1,500. I would need a budget of around Rs 900 crores just to meter everyone. I just don't have the money to spend on meters even if I wanted.[32]

Now add to this the out-of-state pressures. The JSEB pays almost half of its power procurement budget to DVC. As of September 2015, it was in arrears of over Rs 5,000 crores to DVC.[33] Between debt service, power procurement costs, and the little money it pours into generation, JSEB is constantly scrambling for working capital (Figure 5.1 shows the magnitude of this problem). It desperately tries to recover money from the consumers it can successfully bill to cover its monthly expenses. It loses money on most of the power it procures because JSERC does not allow it to recover a higher tariff (albeit for good reasons). On top of this it has private companies infringing on its service area and potentially taking over its distribution centres. The profit motive is a distant illusion in this setting; loss minimization is the order of the day.

Regulatory Decline and the Dominance of Large Corporations (2014–Present)

Justice N.N. Tiwari's appointment as chairman of JSERC in 2014 was a surprising choice. While JSERC is a quasi-judicial body in theory, technical knowledge and political experience have often been more important for work the chairman does in addition to his statutory responsibilities. Judges tend to be socially and politically isolated; as one lawyer familiar with Tiwari's style commented, 'Tiwari is quite a legalistic, by-the-books Chairman. He is not capable of the backroom conversations, the off-the-record negotiations, the assertiveness that Kujur and Mukhtiar Singh were known for.'[34] Given his legalistic preference for conflict avoidance, Tiwari seemed to be the very intentional choice of a government seeking to maintain the status quo.

Jharkhand's electricity sector boasts a large industrial load, and industrial customers are known to experience unequal treatment. This was apparent during the SAC meeting on 20 July 2016, when the few outspoken consumer advocates present were representatives of small industry associations, rather than large corporations.[35] While industry electricity consumers as a group have historically held a privileged position in Jharkhand (see Figure 5.2), clear differentiation within the group has emerged. Large industrial consumers like Tata, SAIL, HEC, and so on, have financial leverage over and backdoor political access to JSEB, while smaller industrial consumers do not. Consequently, the most vocal objections to current policy in the SAC meeting came from representatives of flour mills (Dhanbad), small metal works (Deoghar), and ancillary parts providers to Tata (Adityapur).

Consumer groups clearly have dealt with the extractive mode of Jharkhand politics in different ways. Middle-class and urban consumers often have powerful state institutions (like the courts) acting on their behalf to discipline JSEB, and thus have rarely needed to organize politically. Industrial consumers, on the other hand, have tried to use the SACs and regulatory processes when possible, but smaller companies have often struggled during individual negotiations. Rural consumer activism is notably absent. Local political representatives have shown up at regulatory hearings during the Tiwari period, but it is not clear whether their views ever percolate upwards to Ranchi. The changing load profile of Jharkhand towards domestic consumption has benefited primarily urban consumers, yet industrial consumers still account for more than 50 per cent of JSEB's revenue. Even with this cross-subsidization, JSEB's finances remain dismal.

The erosion of the state government's financial agency has bred pessimism in its electricity bureaucracy regarding the efficacy of any of the Central government's new policy initiatives. In this cost-constrained environment, how can JSEB even consider buying additional expensive renewable power? Although bids for renewable capacity projects were entertained recently, the state government is already dragging its feet on signing PPAs.[36] While the Ujwal Discom Assurance Yojana (UDAY) may temporarily transfer the accumulated debt of JSEB to the state government, this is unlikely to resolve the financial haemorrhaging described earlier. The state government is happy to accept UDAY debt transfers as they delay a JSEB default, but ultimately UDAY has merely delayed the inevitable for one year without provoking serious operational changes.[37] According to JSEB insiders, Restructured Advanced Power Development and Reforms Programme (R-APDRP) and Rural Electrification Corporation (REC) funds are used primarily to make bankrupt JSEB solvent, transferring of funds from the centre to the state wholesale without monitoring, accountability, or directed spending, a trend corroborated by the litany of CAG-reported irregularities.[38] Traditionally the central government has imposed strong conditionality on fund transfers to states, but conditions expressed on paper have frequently been ignored or undermined.

***

So much of Jharkhand's electricity related cognitive space is occupied in managing either political interests or its relationship with out-of-state organizations (NTPC, PowerGrid, MoP, DVC, and so on), that it is failing its ultimate constituents: its citizens. Consultants sitting in JSEB offices are busy coming up with complicated timelines and highly impractical plans for UDAY and Power for All to satisfy the central government while basic maintenance and repairs are neglected on the ground. For already understaffed organizations like JSEB, it is not clear whether this top-down approach is helping to improve service delivery.

While the state did have a credible, uncaptured regulator in JSERC, the state electricity bureaucracy and successive ruling coalitions have eroded its powers and influence over time. In turn, the state is often so embroiled in short-term crises that there is little to no bandwidth for planning or long-term investment, compounded by the extreme scarcity of working capital for system improvements. Rapid political turnover has undermined private sector projects and confidence in the state's power sector. Generation seems to be one exception, but this is primarily due to the ability of generators to sell a portion of their power to other states that have more predictable governments and finances.

For Jharkhand to emerge from this entangled situation, it needs to single-mindedly extricate itself from its operational and financial conflicts with various entities, particularly the DVC. Even partial resolution of these conflicts will lead to expanded financial agency of the state's various institutions, which in turn will elongate their time horizons. If this can happen with stable, centre-aligned government, then maybe service delivery and quality of service can become priorities.

Ultimately, Jharkhand's situation serves as a warning of how helpless states can be in the Indian federal electricity system. This is not just a state-level failure, but one of India's federalism. As Weingast has influentially argued, thriving markets in federal structures require cooperative federalism, where state governments give up some of their power and commit to preserving the rules of markets within their territory in return for access to a common market regulated by the centre.[39] In electricity, this includes actions like shuttering failing state-owned power projects, limiting borrowing from state banks to pay utility dues, and procuring cheaper power from national markets when possible, rather than expensive power from legacy contracts or short-term markets. Jharkhand has not yet reached this point. Given that the political salience of electricity seems unlikely to change in the short-term, it is worth considering more interventionist moves by the Central government to force the state electricity bureaucracy into action. Forces within the state have proved incapable of doing this so far.

Notes and References

1. In 2011, 26.2 per cent of the Jharkhand population was officially ST, as compared to 1.3 per cent in Bihar. More importantly, seven out of 24 districts in Jharkhand have 50 per cent tribal population, making them electorally much more significant. http://tribal.nic.in/WriteReadData/userfiles/file/Demographic.pdf (accessed on 11 August 2016).

2. Stuart Corbridge, 'The Ideology of Tribal Economy and Society: Politics in Jharkhand, c. 1950-80', in Stuart Corbridge, Sarah Jewitt, and Sanjay Kumar (eds), *Jharkhand: Environment, Development, Ethnicity* (Oxford: Oxford University Press, 2004).

3. According to the 'eHabitation Details' table available http://garv.gov.in/garv2/dashboard (accessed on 6 January 2017).

4. 'State Distribution Utilities: Fourth Annual Integrated Ratings', Power Finance Corporation, 6 January 2017, available http://projects.teamgrowth.net:8083/DocumentRepository/ckfinder/files/GoI_Initiatives/4th_rating_booklet_Final_20-6-16.pdf (accessed on 12 September 2016).

5. After unbundling in late 2014, JSEB was split into a holding company, a genco, a transco, and a discom. Practically, these companies still occupy the same physical and bureaucratic spaces. It is not a stretch of the imagination to consider them as de facto unified, although de jure separate entities. For brevity, I will refer to them collectively as JSEB in this chapter.

6. Alpa Shah, '"Keeping the State Away": Democracy, Politics, and the State in India's Jharkhand', *Journal of the Royal Anthropological Institute* 13(1), 2007: 129–45.

7. This became particularly true after the conviction of Madhu Koda, a former Chief Minister of Jharkhand, in 2009 for disproportionate assets and money laundering. A collaborative investigation between the Enforcement Directorate, the State Vigilance Commission and the Income Tax Department found evidence of various financial improprieties against Koda.

8. This chapter focuses primarily on the electricity politics of Jharkhand after the state was formed in 2000.

9. The details of these challenges are available on the web archived first annual report of the first JSERC available at https://web.archive.org/web/20060503065152/http://jserc.org/annualreport.html (accessed on 27 January 2017).

10. 'More Power Players for Brighter Days', *The Telegraph*, 2 January 2006, https://www.telegraphindia.com/1060102/asp/ranchi/story_5669260.asp (accessed on 27 January 2017).

11. The last few years of daily orders on the JSERC website show a pattern of continuations (due to counsel unavailability), institutional non-response, forum shopping (particularly between JSERC and Appellate Tribunal for Electricity [APTEL]) and more.

12. Given the amount of contestation that existed between ministries in early Jharkhand governments (see http://indiatoday.intoday.in/story/turf-war-between-ministers-bureaucrats-bothers-jharkhand-cm-babulal-marandi/1/232097.html accessed on 27 January 2017), this was definitely an anomaly.

13. S.K.F. Kujur, Interviewed by Rohit Chandra, Ranchi, 19 July 2016.

14. JSEB, 'MYT Petition of Generation Function for the First Control Period FY 2012–2013 to 2015–2016', Ranchi, 2012, available http://archive.jharkhand.gov.in/Notice/Notice/73/N2012000035.pdf (accessed on 17 January 2017).

15. JSERC, 'Section 6—Directions to the JSEB', *Tariff Order 2003-2004 For JSEB*. Ranchi, 2003, available http://web.archive.org/web/20080720142730/http://www.jserc.org/pdf/tarriff_period/tarriff_03-04/tarifforder-Section6.pdf (accessed on 31 October 2016).

16. Ranjan Dasgupta, 'Centre Calls for Patratu Handover', *The Telegraph*, 7 January 2008, https://www.telegraphindia.com/1080107/jsp/jharkhand/story_8751521.jsp (accessed on 24 March 2017).

17. Department of Energy, 'Detailed Power Sector Analysis of Jharkhand', Ranchi, 2012, http://archive.jharkhand.gov.in/New_Depts/energ/pdf/Detailed%20Power%20Sector%20Analysis%20of%20Jharkhand.pdf (accessed on 27 January 2017).

18. Census of India, 'Households by Main Source of Lighting', 2011, http://www.censusindia.gov.in/2011census/Hlo-series/Hl-data/DDW-HH2507-0000.xls (accessed on 14 January 2017).

19. 'JMM Manifesto', 2014, http://www.jharkhandmuktimorcha.org/jmm-manifesto.pdf (accessed on 21 February 2017).

20. Chandrajit Mukherjee, 'Courts Lash at JSEB on Ranchi Power Cut', *The Telegraph*—Ranchi edition, 14 May 2005, http://www.telegraphindia.com/1050514/asp/ranchi/story_4737912.asp (accessed on 15 January 2017).

21. B.N.P. Singh, interviewed by Rohit Chandra, Ranchi, 2 August 2016.
22. Pramod Deo, interviewed by Rohit Chandra, New Delhi, 4 July 2016.
23. Former JSERC Personnel, interviewed by Rohit Chandra, Ranchi, 9 August 2016.
24. Former JSERC Member, interviewed by Rohit Chandra, Ranchi, 17 July 2016.
25. 'Jharkhand State Electricity Board Signs Pact with CESC, Tata Power', *The Times of India*, 6 December 2012, http://timesofindia.indiatimes.com/city/ranchi/Jharkhand-State-Electricity-Board-signs-pact-with-CESC-Tata-Power/articleshow/17500542.cms (accessed on 20 March 2017).
26. Former Regulatory Official, interviewed by Rohit Chandra, Ranchi, 17 July 2016.
27. This included the rights to supply electricity and control water in the Damodar Valley, to set its own tariffs, and other administrative powers in its service area without explicit permission from state governments.
28. In one of the more egregious examples narrated to me, DVC unilaterally cut off power to Steel Authority of India's (SAIL's) Bokaro Steel plant because of financial arrears, causing hundreds, maybe even thousands of crores in losses to SAIL. Steel making is particularly sensitive to power cuts because of the necessity of maintaining high temperatures to ensure that the steel stays consistent and in liquid form.
29. For example, read this ruling by APTEL in a recent *DVC v. JSERC* case (http://aptel.gov.in/judgements/A.No.%20255%20of%202014.pdf) (accessed on 15 October 2016). It took almost one and a half years for the APTEL to rule on the disputed tariff order which was issued by JSERC in September 2014.
30. Former Regulatory Official, interviewed by Rohit Chandra, Ranchi, 1 August 2016.
31. Government of Jharkhand, 'Report of the Comptroller and Auditor General of India on Public Sector Undertakings for the Year Ended 31 March 2015', http://cag.gov.in/sites/default/files/audit_report_files/Jharkhand_Public_Sector_Undertakings_Report_2_2016.pdf (accessed on 17 October 2016), p. 22.
32. Senior JSEB Official, Personal Communication, 22 July 2016.
33. 'DVC Likely to Recover 5,000 cr Dues from Jharkhand', *BusinessLine*, 9 September 2015, http://www.thehindubusinessline.com/companies/dvc-likely-to-recover-5000-cr-dues-from-jharkhand/article7633870.ece (accessed on 15 February 2016).
34. Senior Lawyer in Ranchi High Court, interviewed by Rohit Chandra, Ranchi, 22 July 2016.

35. Rohit Chandra, 22 July 2016. Notes taken at the public meeting of the State Advisory Committee, Ranchi, Jharkhand.

36. 'Solar Power: Jharkhand Discoms Seek Additional Upfront Subsidy', *Financial Express*, 19 October 2016, http://www.financialexpress.com/economy/solar-power-jharkhand-discoms-seek-additional-upfront-subsidy/423490/ (accessed on 20 February 2016).

37. 'Jharkhand Electricity Board Continues to Lose Despite UDAY', *Business Standard*, 28 January 2017, http://www.business-standard.com/article/news-ians/jharkhand-electricity-board-continues-to-lose-despite-uday-117012800691_1.html (accessed on 18 December 2016).

38. 'Report of the Comptroller and Auditor General of India on Public Sector Undertakings for the Year Ended 31 March 2015' (13 March 2017): 34–47.

39. Barry R. Weingast, 'The Economic Role of Political Institutions: Market-Preserving Federalism and Economic Development', *Journal of Law, Economics, & Organization* 11(1), 1995: 1–31.

6

MEERA SUDHAKAR

Efficiency and Welfare

The Tightrope Walk in Karnataka's Power Sector

While India's economic reforms have liberalized investment rules, capital markets, and trade policy, they have not been able to reform sectors that affect a large number of people directly. Reform planning has often been limited to bureaucratic consensus alone, without either an explicit political articulation of benefits and losses or a debate about its winners and losers.[1] Karnataka's experience with power sector reforms is an illustrative case—an ongoing process of negotiation between the bureaucracy and the politics of development in the state. The state's electricity sector was a major contributor to its dismal fiscal situation by the 1990s, locked into a cycle of loss-making utilities and chronic underinvestment in infrastructure. When the state embarked on the path of power sector reforms in 1999, there was broad-based bureaucratic acceptance of what was considered the 'standard model' of reform—corporatization and eventual privatization of the electric utility—as the answer to the woes in the sector. While the reform process unbundled the Karnataka Electricity Board (KEB) and created five geographically delimited, state-owned companies, with the eventual objective of privatization and distancing of the government from the sector, several existing structural and political constraints forced it to suspend this course and instead, adopt a gradual, incremental approach that was more sensitive to the developmental politics of the state.

In this chapter, I argue that although Karnataka set out on a path of drastic reforms through privatization, the reforms were initiated by mobilizing bureaucratic support alone. The shape it eventually took was determined by the development process that was already playing out in the state—its economic geography, influenced by historical processes and the politics of development that emerged from it. The electricity sector has always been deeply entrenched in Karnataka's development planning, and it serves as a tool to mediate between the perceived development deficits across various regions of the state, as well as between rural and urban areas. Far from distancing the government from the sector, reforms have created a set of highly interdependent government-owned companies that play a crucial role in how the state is managing its rural–urban transition. A relatively new equilibrium is emerging for power sector governance whereby new interventions, especially mandates from the centre are accommodated through intra-bureaucracy negotiations in the state. This impacts how tariffs are set, how government subsidies are distributed, and how renewable energy (RE) mandates are allocated between the electricity supply companies. The constraints and opportunities created by this still-unfolding incremental approach to reforms are crucial to understanding the fate of future interventions in the power sector.

With the objective of tracing this reform process, the first section outlines the macro political economy in Karnataka that formed a backdrop to reforms in the sector and influenced its implementation. The second section traces the key trends and actor constellations in the power sector that influenced the reform process across three key periods, and the final section concludes with implications for future interventions in the sector.

Political Context for Reforms

The historical diversity amongst Karnataka's varied regions has heavily influenced the shape that reforms have taken. In 1956, Karnataka was formed by unifying very diverse Kannada-speaking regions—districts from the erstwhile Bombay Province and the princely state of Hyderabad were merged with the princely state of Mysore. While

Mysore state, consisting of southern parts of present-day Karnataka, had a well-developed pre-independence industrial base enabled by hydroelectric power capacity,[2] the northern districts were largely rural and depended on rain-fed agriculture. Mysore was seen as a model state with an efficient and autonomous bureaucracy that had facilitated state-led industrialization and canal-based irrigation. It was expected that the benefits of state-led development would flow to northern Karnataka after unification.[3]

The politics in the state since unification that demanded responsiveness to agrarian issues have shaped the power sector significantly, leaving the sector in a position where privatization of distribution would have been unsustainable by the time of a major intervention in the form of power sector reform in the late 1990s. A timeline of key events in state's politics and power sector is outlined in Table 6.1.

TABLE 6.1   Timeline of Key Events: Karnataka

State Politics	Period	Power Sector
• Devraj Urs, a loyal regional leader in INC, comes to power; implements land reform in KA	1971–9	• Thrust for rural electrification and completion of major irrigation schemes • Bhagya Jyothi and Kutir Jyothi programmes started to extend free electricity to poor and backward-caste households
• Devraj Urs exits INC and joins Janata Party, INC's Gundu Rao becomes CM	1980–2	• Rise of Karnataka Rajya Raitha Sangha (KRRS), a farmers' movement and that mobilized interest groups on price-related issues and protested against alleged neglect of rural interests. Reduction of electricity tariff for agriculture was one of several demands
• First non-Congress government by Janata Party, under CM Ramakrishna Hegde, a protégé of Devraj Urs.	1983–8	• The new government decides to cap supplies to power-intensive high-tension (HT) users and to shift the emphasis of KEB to energization of agricultural pump sets. • First thermal plant owned by the state generation company (KPCL) is built at Raichur. Karnataka's entire capacity was hydroelectric until then

(Cont'd)

TABLE **6.1** *(Cont'd)*

State Politics	Period	Power Sector
• INC returns to power under CM Veerendra Patil, followed by Bangarappa and Veerappa Moily in a power struggle within INC	1989–94	• Karnataka signs power purchase agreement with Cogentrix, an American company, under an array of early IPP projects in the country, fast-tracked by the Centre. The cost negotiations went on for seven years and the company cancelled the project in 1999
• Deve Gowda leads a unified JD(S) to victory and becomes CM	1994–7	• Government publishes policy statement referring to future privatization of electricity distribution in order to improve operational efficiency of distribution and to enhance customer service quality
		• Committee set up under the chief secretary of the state to execute restructuring and privatization
• Legislative elections in which INC under S.M. Krishna comes to power	1999–2001	• Karnataka Electricity Reform becomes an Act
		• Karnataka Electricity Regulatory Commission (KERC) established under the provisions of Karnataka Electricity Reforms Act (KERA)
		• KEB unbundled and corporatized into two separate companies: a T&D company, Karnataka Power Transmission Corporation limited (KPTCL) and generating company, Vishwesharayya Vidyut Nigam Ltd. (VVNL). VVNL had only 230 MW after this unbundling, and later merged with Karnataka Power Corporation Limited Karnataka Power Corporation Limited (KPCL).
	2002–3	• KPTCL unbundled into five electricity supply companies (ESCOMs) based on geographically delimited zones. KPTCL became a transmission only company but

(Cont'd)

TABLE 6.1 (*Cont'd*)

State Politics	Period	Power Sector
		retained bulk power purchase and acted as a wholesale trader
• Legislative elections in which INC under S.M. Krishna suffered a major defeat. Although BJP is the largest party, a coalition government is formed with Dharam Singh from INC as CM and Siddaramaiah from JD(S) as Deputy CM	2004–7	• Electricity Act 2003 passed by Parliament • KPTCL could not trade electricity as per Electricity Act 2003, so PPA is assigned to ESCOMs in proportion to the share of each ESCOM in consumption • Power Company of Karnataka Limited (PCKL) formed as an Special Purpose Vehicle (SPV) to facilitate capacity procurement and competitive bidding on behalf of ESCOMs
• Siddaramaiah expelled from JD(S); JD(S) withdraws support from the coalition government and supports BJP with an arrangement for sharing CM post between BJP and JD(S)		
• Legislative elections in which BJP forms government under Yeddyurappa	2008	• Free power to 15 lakh pump sets below 10 HP • KERC introduces open access to all HT consumers with contract demand more than 1 MW

(*Cont'd*)

TABLE **6.1**   *(Cont'd)*

State Politics	Period	Power Sector
		• First IPP-based thermal plant with 90 per cent of its share tied-up in long-term PPA with ESCOMs
	2009– 12	• KERC asks government to pay the agricultural subsidies upfront to ESCOMs
		• RPO targets of 10 per cent for three major ESCOMs and 7 per cent each for two other ESCOMs by KERC
		• KA provides thrust to solar capacity in its solar policy 2011–16
• Legislative elections in which INC, under Siddaramaiah comes to power	2013– 16	• FiT for solar rooftops by KERC. • GoK revises earlier solar policy with an objective of rapid capacity addition—to add 2,000 MW (1,600 utility scale and 400 MW rooftop) in a phased manner until 2020
		• 300 MW of PPA for land-owning farmers; guidelines for implementation stipulate allocation for SC/ST farmers separately, apart from a general category
		• 1,200 MW solar plants in the state to be allocated through bids across 60 taluks with a max cap of 20 MW in each taluk, only one bid per taluk and project location change only within taluk
		• KERC revises tariffs; 30–40 per cent increase in cross-subsidy surcharge for industry and commercial
		• Karnataka joins UDAY

Source: Author.

The 1970s saw the rise of regional leaders who were loyalists to then Prime Minister Indira Gandhi and her redistributive politics. In keeping with this trend, Karnataka's most acclaimed chief minister, Devraj

Urs, came to power in 1972. Although land reforms were implemented very early on in his tenure, they had very little effect on fundamentally changing the agrarian structure.[4] Karnataka followed a much more centrist approach in its redistributive policies, and was driven by pragmatic reasons rather than ideology.[5] By the late 1970s, public sector-led industrialization had led to rapid urbanization of Bangalore,[6] and there was growing discontent amongst the farmers, due to the perceived neglect of agriculture. In 1980, this discontent found its most strident expression in the protests of Karnataka Rajya Ryota Sangha (KRRS), a lobby group for farmers who demanded that the Indian National Congress (INC) government declare agriculture as an industry, intervene in pricing, and extend all facilities enjoyed by industrial labour to agriculturists.

In the state assembly, agriculture-heavy northern districts had an upper hand, and traditionally offered steadfast support to the INC and its policies. However, the government's insensitive handling of the farmers' rebellion led to a decline of faith in the INC in the north. In the 1983 assembly elections, the KRRS explicitly called for defeat of the INC, and supported the Janata Party under Ramakrishna Hegde, who was from the northern region and had a large support base in the rural constituency. The region's allegiance later alternated between the Janata Dal (JD)[7] and INC (Figure 6.1) as both parties projected regional leaders from northern Karnataka, usually from the dominant Lingayat community.[8] By the mid-1990s, infighting in the JD had led to a split and weakening of the party. This brought the INC into power in 1999, despite it being under the leadership of S.M. Krishna, who was seen as having no connection to the rural voter base. In the 1999 elections, the agricultural constituency in northern Karnataka had banked heavily on the INC's promise of correcting regional imbalances in the state.

In response to growing resentment in the northern districts, Krishna appointed a high-power committee for redressing regional imbalances in October 2000, with D.M. Nanjundappa, a noted economist from the state, as chairman. The backwardness of northern Karnataka was acknowledged by the findings of this committee in 2002.[9] These development narratives of regional imbalances had the effect of severely constraining the options for the bureaucracy during power sector reforms. Krishna also claimed credit for the booming information technology and biotechnology industries in Bangalore. By the 2004 elections, Krishna was seen as a modernizer who excessively relied on a

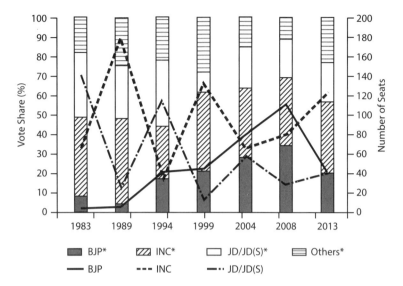

FIGURE **6.1**   Number of Seats Won by Three Major Parties in Assembly
Elections (1983–2013)
Source: Statistical Report on General Election to the Legislative Assembly of
Karnataka, Election Commission of India 1983, 1989,1994, 1999, 2004, 2008, and 2013.

Bangalore-centric development model. The right-wing Bharatiya Janata
Party (BJP) emerged as the largest party in the legislature in 2004, and
although the INC retained power by forging a coalition government
with the Janata Dal (Secular), this was an unstable arrangement; the
JD(S) withdrew its support after two years, and instead partnered with
the BJP to form the government.

The years 2004–13 saw intense political competition between three
major parties: the INC, BJP, and JD(S) as shown in Figure 6.1. Similar
to the strategy followed by the neighbouring state of Andhra Pradesh's
chief minister Y.S. Rajasekhara Reddy in 2004, all political parties in
Karnataka promised free power to farmers during the 2008 elections.[10,11]
No party could alienate either the rural voter base or the demand for
power for growth centres in the state. The approach to reform, therefore, has been uniform across party regimes—a shift in focus from drastic privatization to internal reform, maintaining the overall fiscal health
of the state while ensuring that the key growth centres receive quality
power supply even amidst rising costs.

Karnataka sees itself as a progressive state with regard to power sector reform implementation. It stays under the radar of the central power ministry by instituting regular tariff revisions and seeing lower regulatory assets and aggregate technical and commercial (AT&C) losses compared to other states (Figure 6.2). However, performance across state-owned electricity supply companies (ESCOMs) varies greatly, mainly due to vastly different proportions of paying consumers. Due to this, the regulator must work in coordination with the five ESCOMs to allocate the tariff burden, the state's budgetary support for agricultural consumption, and the state's RE commitments under a power sector regime that is seeing increasing power purchase costs (Figure 6.3). Far from reducing the government's role in the operations of utilities, this has enhanced its role in coordinating this fine balancing act through intra-bureaucracy negotiations. The next section traces the major trends in the state's power sector in three periods that saw key shifts in the political economy of the state.

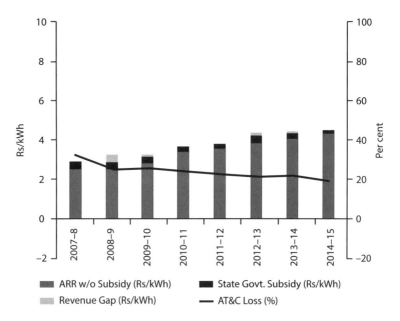

FIGURE **6.2** Supply-side Costs and Revenue Recovery: Karnataka
Source: PFC, *Reports on Performance of State Power Utilities* (New Delhi: Power Finance Corporation Limited, 2011, 2013, 2015, and 2016).

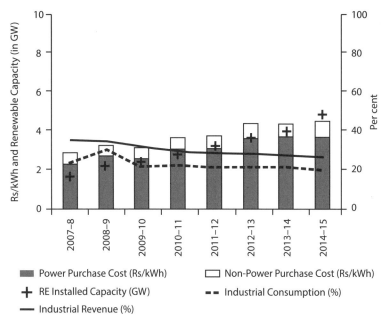

FIGURE 6.3 Physical and Financial Profile: Karnataka

Sources: CSO, *Energy Statistics* (New Delhi: Central Statistics Office, Ministry of Statistics and Programme Implementation, Government of India, 2010, 2012, 2014, and 2016); PFC, *Reports on Performance of State Power Utilities* (New Delhi: Power Finance Corporation Limited, 2011, 2013, 2015, and 2016).

Power Sector Political Economy

1970–99: Consolidation of the Farm Lobby

At the time of India's independence, Mysore State enjoyed more than 60 megawatt (MW) of generation capacity, including the first hydroelectric generation station in Asia. Even before Karnataka's formation in 1956, this pre-existing infrastructure in the southern districts had facilitated state-led industrialization of the region, including a thriving electrical industry.[12] The northern districts, on the other hand, were arid and drought-prone, and had to wait until the 1970s for irrigation from the Krishna river project. This disparity generated the first friction between the unified state and its rural constituency, and, as detailed in the previous section, a growing farmer's movement in politics. The rise to power of the Janata government had major consequences for the power sector. As soon as it came to power in 1983, the Janata Party government decided to provide preference for pump-set energization over industries. This decision led to most large-scale industries leaving the grid in favour of captive generation, drastically altering the consumer mix of the state distribution company (KEB) over the period 1985–95. During this period, the share of agriculture which was around 8 per cent of the total sales in FY85 climbed to 46 per cent. Correspondingly, the industries' share of sales fell from 67 per cent in FY85 to 34 per cent in FY95.[13]

Flat-rate tariffs for agricultural consumers based on pump set rating was enabled by the ready availability of inexpensive hydroelectric power in the state until the mid-1980s. This relatively successful equilibrium would be disrupted by a rapid increase in demand for power from the growing service industry and from commercial and domestic consumers in Karnataka's cities, mainly Bangalore. Other comparatively expensive supply sources, such as thermal generation, had to be rapidly added in a state that had relied exclusively on hydroelectricity until 1985. Between 1995 and 1999, the cost of power purchase for the state distribution company (KEB) more than doubled. Even as Bangalore became the single significant hub of growth for the state, worsening power crises, especially in summer months, were blots on its success story. The city faced power cuts that lasted three hours at a stretch.[14]

The non-remunerative consumer mix that the state utilities were left with, combined with the Bangalore-centred development strategy in the 1980s and 1990s, was to have the effect of constraining the privatization option during the power sector reform process as detailed in the next section.

2000–4: Constancy Amidst Attempts to Reform

The liberalization of the Indian economy altered how state governments searched for capital for infrastructure investment; instead of lobbying the centre for funds, states now needed to take measures to attract private capital. Soon after foreign direct investment (FDI) was enabled in the power sector in 1991, the central government attempted to work with states to facilitate private investments in the sector. Karnataka's actions during this period were driven by an urgent need for private capital in order to add generation capacity. In October 1999, INC returned to power under Chief Minister S.M. Krishna, in whom the reform process found a champion. By November 1999, the Karnataka Electricity Regulatory Commission (KERC) was constituted and approval was accorded for the formation of two new state-owned companies, separating generation from transmission and distribution.[15] This reform process was driven by the bureaucracy, with active involvement by the government under Krishna. In 2000, the state constituted a steering committee under the chief secretary to restructure and privatize distribution companies through an open and competitive bidding process.

Attempts to engage private capital, both in generation and distribution, met with initial setbacks. The government's efforts to attract independent power producers (IPPs) ended in failed negotiations with Cogentrix, which was one of the eight IPP-based projects fast-tracked by the centre. Although there was considerable pressure from Delhi to attract FDI in the sector, Karnataka could not endorse the Cogentrix project due to prolonged litigation that accused the government of malfeasance in contracting high-cost power.[16] With this failed attempt at private investment in thermal generation, Karnataka continued to rely on state-owned thermal capacity by expanding its lone thermal plant in the northern district of Raichur. On the distribution side, a consultant's report submitted to the government in 2001 endorsed eventual privatization of distribution companies, and by June 2002 distribution was unbundled into four regional government-owned companies.[17] However, the logic of unbundling based on geography left some ESCOMs in highly disadvantageous positions. The regions that belonged to northern Karnataka—Gulbarga Electricity Supply Company (GESCOM) and Hubli Electricity Supply Company (HESCOM)—served districts that were relatively less developed, faced lower average demand, and had close to 50 per cent of their sales from agricultural consumption. By contrast, the state's dependence on a services-led industrialization strategy in the 1980s, with a single-minded focus on Bangalore city, resulted in Bangalore Electricity Supply Company (BESCOM) having a disproportionately large load centre and a much larger share of higher-paying customers.

KERC had by now instituted a culture of regular and systematic tariff revisions and a technical scrutiny processes; the first tariff order and public consultation on tariffs happened within a year of its creation. The commission, in what was still an evolving experiment in independent regulation in India, aspired to be a neutral institution that distanced tariff setting from political interference. Its guiding principles were to allow full cost recovery and to improve operational efficiency by disciplining the utilities to reduce losses, thus reducing the amount of cross-subsidy required from subsidizing consumers. This meant that the regulator started off on a confrontational regulatory style in its early days.[18] As with regulators in other states with high agricultural consumption, lack of accuracy in pump set consumption created early friction between KERC and utilities. In the tariff order in 2002, the regulator disallowed tariff increases to KPTCL, demanding the utility to improve its revenue through reduction in losses. The KERC has mobilized public participation and transparency regarding technical matters of tariff-related negotiations and uses consumer objections to calibrate the technical aspects of the tariff-setting process. Farmer groups have often pointed out to potential malpractices in agricultural estimation by utilities in the tariff hearings.[19]

By 2003, it was becoming clear that Karnataka's peculiar development trajectory posed a significant barrier to its utility privatization plans. The deliberations and expressions of interest from the private sector indicated that privatization would have takers only in Bangalore. KERC also criticized the government's proposal that allowed private companies to pass on cost increases to consumers, thus bypassing the regulator.[20] Once it was clear that the government would have to continue carrying the burden of tariff subsidies and demand risk in other regions of the state apart from Bangalore, privatization was put on the backburner.[21] Chief Minister Krishna attempted internal governance reforms through civil society engagement and by improving the responsiveness of government agencies; initiatives which saw some success under his government through the Bangalore Agenda Task Force. The period from 1999 to 2003 saw marked improvements in public service delivery across several government services, albeit restricted to Bangalore. These practices attempted to shift the focus of the reforms from privatization of ownership to adopting private sector best practices in government agencies.[22]

The final blow to the privatization strategy was arguably dealt in 2004, when the incumbent chief ministers of Karnataka and its neighbouring state of Andhra Pradesh suffered major electoral defeats. Both S.M. Krishna and his Andhra counterpart Chandrababu Naidu were seen as pro-reform modernizers who prioritized fiscal prudence over populist measures. In a year affected by droughts across the region, Naidu's opposition to free power for farmers over grounds of practicality and his enthusiasm for reforms were widely perceived to have led to his defeat in the 2004 elections.[23] This narrative left a lasting impact on Karnataka's collective political memory.[24] Imposing drastic increases in power tariff revisions for agriculture was seen by the political class as risky, and it was widely perceived that privatization attempts would fuel a rural backlash.[25]

2005–16: Incrementalism under Rising Costs

One policy principle that emerged from deliberations during the reform process was to abandon the notion of separate tariffs for each utility, commensurate with the cost of supply to the region, in favour of a uniform tariff for the entire state as a development imperative.[26] Rather than operating as autonomous companies, the government initiated several formal and informal practices to coordinate between ESCOMs. On the power-purchase side, a new institution, the Power Company of Karnataka Ltd (PCKL), was created in 2007 using a Special Purpose Vehicle (SPV) to enable power purchase at scale for all ESCOMs together. Experts in the sector justify this by arguing that negotiation for contracts is better on a large scale instead of each ESCOM separately contracting fragmented capacities, especially since BESCOM services more than 50 per cent of the peak demand in the state.[27]

Within a month of the first BJP government formation in 2008, free power to all pump sets below 10 HP was announced, as promised in the party's manifesto. This resulted in free electricity to an estimated 15 lakh pump sets, for which Rs 2,050 crores were budgeted.[28] In order to prevent cash-flow problems for ESCOMs, KERC directed the government to pay the revenue due to the ESCOMs owing to the free power policy, at the start of the year based on estimated agricultural consumption provided by them. As the agricultural consumption was already unmetered and calculated as a residual, a substantial portion of utility revenues in the form of government subvention furthered the lack of transparency in apportioning the unmetered residual between agricultural consumption and distribution losses. All ESCOMs in Karnataka reported a steep reduction in losses in 2008–9, only for losses to increase later on, suggesting that the loss-reduction was not fully due to system-level improvements (see Figure 6.3).

As the utilities are under pressure from both KERC as well as national-level monitoring to report lower AT&C losses, the free power policy has directly resulted in the subsidy burden of the Government of Karnataka (GoK) increasing threefold in the period from 2008 to 2016. The subsidy bill touched Rs 8,000 crores in the 2016 financial year, rising from Rs 2,000 crores in 2008. This reduces the fiscal space available for the state government and is also a cause for interdepartmental battles in GoK between the finance department and energy department. Although these subsidies are widely acknowledged as unsustainable, the idea of free power to farmers as a legitimate welfare policy for reducing rural–urban inequality—similar to subsidies on other agricultural inputs such as seeds and fertilizers—is now entrenched in the energy bureaucracy, with a member of the commission opining that the subsidy of 8,000 crores looks high only when seen in the context of the power sector.[29] The focus of the finance department is to ration and set an upper limit for subsidies rather than eliminate them entirely, for which technology interventions were adopted; Karnataka was one of the early adopters of the feeder separation policy in 2008–9, with the objective to control electricity supplied to agriculture consumers, and at the same time to improve supply to non-agricultural consumers in rural areas. However, even after two phases of implementation of the programme and after several directives issued by KERC to produce better estimates of IP-set consumption on separated feeders, KERC has seen very little success in ensuring transparency of this data.

KERC's stance towards utilities has transitioned from the earlier abrasive style to one that acknowledges the multiple challenges facing utilities. In doing so, 'it acts like an accommodating parent who guides utilities to self-discipline'.[30] This approach is evident in several instances—KERC issued a directive to GoK to withhold 10 per cent of the subsidy towards projected agricultural consumption in the annual tariff revision process in 2016 until utilities produce accurate data from separated feeders. However, it had to relent in the face of noncompliance, allowing utilities more time to report accurate estimates for agricultural consumption. In order to limit the subsidy burden on the government, KERC disallows the reported agricultural consumption if it is above what was approved by them at the start of the year. All of these supervisory measures have meant that quality of supply to the cities and district headquarters has improved.

Ironically, the reform process that created ESCOMs with an intent to insulate utilities from the government has necessitated much closer coordination between KERC, GoK, and utilities in the wake of recent pressures in the sector, chiefly rising power purchase costs as the sector becomes more market-oriented, the mandate to increase the share of RE, and the need to limit the subsidy burden. In order to do this, the government uses the better cash flow positions of ESCOMs with more paying consumers (BESCOM and MESCOM)[31] to compensate ESCOMs in northern Karnataka. A consensus has evolved in KERC to ensure that the weaker ESCOMs get a higher share of the government subsidy allocated for agricultural consumption. This is done through a formula for commission-determined tariff (CDT) for agricultural consumers; a higher CDT is usually set for GESCOM and HESCOM, the cited reason being that lower ground water levels in the northern region disincentivize groundwater extraction.[32] In practice, however, since consumers do not face this tariff, it does not affect groundwater extraction. Instead, the ESCOMs in the northern region, with more than 50 per cent of their sales to going to non-paying consumers, receive a higher share of the state government's budgetary support for agricultural consumption.

This consensus on how the costs are to be distributed across regions is reflected in KERC's RE regulations as well; KERC issued a renewable purchase obligation to all ESCOMs in the 2012 financial year, and they meet this obligation at the state-level. However, the RE obligations for GESCOM and HESCOM are set lower than those for other ESCOMs. From 2007 to 2015, Karnataka rapidly increased its renewable energy capacity (Figure 6.3). This increase of renewable energy capacity in the supply mix has required better coordination between distribution companies, often involving the regulator, seeing as the load centre is concentrated in the southern regions. Interest in solar energy is increasing; solar energy is being integrated with the state's regional development plans, and solar policies are being designed to include farmers by providing landowning farmers a chance to set up grid-connected solar energy for very high preferential rates. These guidelines also stipulate separate allocations for SC/ST farmers. In 2015, the state nodal agency

Karnataka Renewable Energy Development Ltd (KREDL) allocated 1,200 MW solar plants with a cap of 20 MW per taluk, to create a regionally distributed capacity in solar energy. This might have the effect of aggravating the current situation, as more than 50 per cent of the load during the daytime falls under BESCOM. While the ESCOMs where the RE generation capacity is located typically sign power purchase agreements and pay higher preferential tariffs for RE, most of the consumption happens in BESCOM. This is currently settled between ESCOMs at the lower rates of inter-settlement pegged at average pooled power purchase cost. The load profile is such that there are distinct morning and evening peaks, and a shortage in summer months. ESCOMs have resorted to costly short-term power purchases to manage these daily peaks. To tide over the summer months, GoK imposes Section 11[33] to ensure that all IPPs in the state supply power to the state grid during the summer months, in a direct breach of the open access contract.[34]

Almost 50 per cent of the sales of HESCOM and GESCOM belong to the non-paying consumer category that is fully-subsidised by the government. All ESCOMs have witnessed a decline in the share of sales to industrial consumers (Figure 6.3), and there has been an increase in the share of domestic consumers for utilities supplying southern parts of the state. Since 2011, tariffs for commercial and industrial consumers have been revised upwards. Cross-subsidy surcharges that make the open access option unviable for industry and commercial consumers have seen an unexpected return in 2015, in contrast to the earlier reducing trend. Recent tariff orders also suggest that costs will be increasingly passed on to domestic consumers in urban areas. Overall, the reform process has generated more transparency for tariff and cross subsidy-related negotiations, where KERC avoids any drastic action and opts for incremental changes while the government has become more entrenched in the wholesale political economy in the distribution sector.

***

Power sector reforms were driven by the bureaucracy in Karnataka alongside discourses of efficiency and fiscal prudence in the larger context of liberalization. This went head-on against the politics of development that were already playing out in the state: the narrative of regional imbalances between the southern and northern parts of the state, as well as the perceived neglect of rural concerns in development planning. These two competing concerns and narratives surrounding them are still unresolved in the sector, and have led to the reforms taking a gradual and incremental process of adaptation to new rules and institutions rather than the drastic privatization and distancing of government from the sector, as was originally envisaged. If anything, the reforms have brought Karnataka's regional divisions into sharper relief, through unbundling into regionally delimited ESCOMs. To mitigate this, the government and the regulator had to institute new rules for how government subsidies would be apportioned and how tariff burden would be allocated between consumer categories. While the policy of cross-subsidization is well known, there is an emerging consensus in the bureaucracy that a combination of government subsidies, industrial and commercial consumers, and more recently urban domestic consumers, will continue to subsidise agricultural and rural consumption as a welfare policy, even if there is a need for better 'targeting'.

ESCOMs in Karnataka have managed to stay 'under the radar' relative to those in other states in terms of financial performance; tariffs have been regularly revised, and regulatory assets have been absorbed in a phased manner, taking off pressures from their own books. However, this relative self-sufficiency has come at the cost of increasing budgetary support for the sector, which eats into the fiscal space for other developmental expenditures. Although these concerns are acknowledged, the state has managed to absorb the subsidy through its better fiscal position and also through using technological interventions to limit the subsidy.

Reforms have improved the quality of supply in the state, especially in cities and district headquarters. However, the state also faces one of the highest costs of power for commercial and domestic consumers, especially in the urban centre of Bangalore. Large industries rely on captive power, and hence the challenges to higher tariffs come from citizen groups in Bangalore, commercial consumers, and small industries. The response has been a one-step-here-two-steps-there approach of managing the interests of these consumers through retail tariff negotiations, for which KERC is the venue. There is a view that better physical infrastructure and land allocation in industrial parks will sustain the growth momentum and attract industries that are less sensitive to the cost of power.[35] The fairly well-entrenched balancing act between the state government, KERC, and utilities to mitigate the impacts of ESCOMs serving vastly different regions in terms of their socio-economic potential means that any institutional reform like separation of distribution and supply are unlikely to be acceptable; the current strategy is to use the better cash-flow positions of urban ESCOMs to keep those serving rural consumer bases viable. Power sector interventions will need to accommodate these dynamics of ESCOM interdependence, as the electricity sector plays a crucial role in how Karnataka manages its rural-urban transition strategy through an incremental and internal reform process.

Notes and References

1. Jeffrey D. Sachs, Ashutosh Varshney, and Nirupam Bajpai (eds), *India in the Era of Economic Reforms* (New Delhi: Oxford University Press, 2000).
2. Sunila S. Kale, 'Structures of Power: Electrification in Colonial India', *Comparative Studies of South Asia, Africa and the Middle East* 34(3), 25 January 2015: 454–75.
3. Janaki Nair, 'The "Composite" State and Its "Nation": Karnataka's Reunification Revisited', *Economic and Political Weekly* 46(47), 2011: 52–62.
4. Narendar Pani, *Reforms to Pre-Empt Change: Land Legislation in Karnataka* (Delhi: Concept Publishing Company, 1983).
5. James Manor, 'Pragmatic Progressives in Regional Politics: The Case of Devaraj Urs', *Economic and Political Weekly* 15(5/7), 1980: 201–13.
6. Bangalore was officially renamed as Bengaluru in 2014. For the sake of uniformity across the periods, this work will use the old name, Bangalore.
7. Formed by merging Janata Party with several minor state parties.
8. T.V. Sivanandan, 'Forgotten Lessons', *Frontline*, May 2008, available http://www.frontline.in/static/html/fl2510/stories/20080523251003000.htm (accessed 20 August 2017).
9. S. Rajendran, 'Regional Imbalance and Shoddy Implementation of Plan', *The Hindu*, 3 January 2015, available http://www.thehindu.com/todays-paper/tp-national/tp-karnataka/regional-imbalance-and-shoddy-implementation-of-plan/article6750438.ece (accessed 20 August 2017).
10. Vicky Nanjappa, 'BJP Promises Free Power, K'taka Facelift', *Rediff*, 24 April 2008, available http://www.rediff.com/news/2008/apr/24kgovt2.htm (accessed 20 August 2017).
11. 'Siddaramaiah Harps on Free Power to Farmers', *The Hindu*, 14 April 2008, available http://www.thehindu.com/todays-paper/tp-national/tp-karnataka/Siddaramaiah-harps-on-free-power-to-farmers/article15203020.ece (accessed 20 August 2017).

12. Sunila S. Kale, 'Structures of Power: Electrification in Colonial India', *Comparative Studies of South Asia, Africa and the Middle East* 34(3), 25 January 2015: 454–75.
13. Antonette D'Sa and K.V. Narasimha Murthy, 'Karnataka's Power Sector & Suggested Ways Forward', *International Energy Initiative, Discussion Paper*, 2002, http://iei-asia.org/IEIBLR-Kar-WayForward.pdf (accessed on 10 November 2016).
14. D'Sa and Narasimha Murthy, 'Karnataka's Power Sector'.
15. KEB was unbundled into Vishwesharayya Vidyut Nigam Ltd. (VVNL), a generation company and Karnataka Power Transmission Corporation Limited (KPTCL) that owned transmission and distribution.
16. Stephen David, 'Procrastinated Power Play Short-Circuits Cogentrix Project yet Again', *India Today*, 27 December 1999, available http://indiatoday.intoday.in/story/procrastinated-power-play-short-circuits-cogentrix-project-yet-again/1/254463.html (accessed 20 August 2017).
17. In 2005, this became five as Mangalore Electricity Supply Company (MESCOM) was further bifurcated into MESCOM and Chamundeshwari Electricity Supply Company (CHESCOM).
18. Interview with former chairman of KERC, Bangalore, 10 September 2016.
19. Navroz K. Dubash and D. Narasimha Rao, *The Practice and Politics of Regulation: Regulatory Governance in Indian Electricity* (New Delhi: Macmillan India, 2007).
20. Dubash and Narasimha Rao, *The Practice and Politics of Regulation*.
21. Interview with senior partner, consultants to GoK, Bangalore, 16 September 2016.
22. James Manor, 'Successful Governance Reforms in Two Indian States: Karnataka and Andhra Pradesh', *Commonwealth & Comparative Politics* 45(4), November 2007: 425–51, doi:10.1080/14662040701659860.
23. Praveen Chakravarty, 'Twin Demons of 2004—Chandrababu Naidu's Loss and Wrong Lessons', *IDFC Institute*, 18 July 2015, available http://www.idfcinstitute.org/knowledge/publications/op-eds/twin-demons-of-2004-chandrababu-naidus-loss-and-wrong-lessons/ (accessed 20 August 2017).
24. Interview with Special Officer, Reforms, Department of Energy, Bangalore, 3 September 2016.
25. Interview with Special Officer, Reforms, Department of Energy, Bangalore, 3 September 2016.
26. Interview with Special Officer, Reforms, Department of Energy, Bangalore, 3 September 2016.
27. Interview with senior partner, Consultants to GoK, Bangalore, 16 September 2016.

28. 'Farmers to Get Free Power', *Business Standard India*, 18 July 2008, available http://www.business-standard.com/article/economy-policy/farmers-to-get-free-power-108071801005_1.html (accessed 20 August 2017).

29. Interview with Member, KERC, Bangalore, 13 October 2016.

30. Interview with Member, KERC, Bangalore, 13 October 2016.

31. Accounting for 58 per cent of electricity sales in the state.

32. This is according to a provision in the national tariff policy.

33. Section 11 is an emergency provision in the Electricity Act 2003, whereby the generating stations are required to act in accordance with direction of government. GoK cites shortages in the State to use Section 11 to prevent inter-state open access sales of electricity.

34. B.S. Satish Kumar, 'Section 11 of Electricity Act to Be Invoked in State', *The Hindu*, 30 January 2012, available http://www.thehindu.com/todays-paper/tp-national/tp-karnataka/section-11-of-electricity-act-to-be-invoked-in-state/article13387237.ece (accessed 20 August 2017).

35. Interview with former chairman of KERC, Bangalore, 10 September 2016.

7

ASHWINI K. SWAIN

Poverty in the Midst of Abundance

Repressive Populism, Bureaucratization, and Supply-side Bias in Madhya Pradesh's Power Sector

Electricity reforms in Madhya Pradesh (MP) remain underreported, despite some atypical outcomes. The once well-performing MP Electricity Board (MPEB) fell into insolvency in the 1990s as its cheap pithead generation failed to keep pace with growing demand, which it unsuccessfully tried to address through high-cost short-term power purchases. Declining revenue realization due to defaulting consumers protesting unreliable supply as well as free power for agriculture further worsened the problem. In the mid-1990s, MP initiated reform planning, independent of any external push. State reorganization in 2000 and subsequent resource allocation further deteriorated power sector health, making reforms inevitable. Asian Development Bank (ADB) assistance and interventions made way for the global model of electricity reforms. Despite no significant resistance to it, the reform process had been long-drawn-out, and resulted in complete institutional restructuring, bureaucratization, and de-electrification, but not many operational efficiency gains. Subsequently, the state has prioritized supply-side augmentation, with an industrial aspiration. While expectations are far from realization, surplus capacity is adding to the financial burdens of the distribution companies (discoms). In 2016, the state joined the Ujwal Discom Assurance Yojana (UDAY), seeking to turn around the finances of discoms.

This chapter examines the political economy of transitions in MP's power sector, with the objective of identifying drivers of policy choices and their outcomes. Drawing on the findings, this paper explains how intensive institutional restructuring has resulted in bureaucratization and consolidated state control over the sector, and discusses the resulting outcomes. It also analyses the implications of past experiences for ongoing and future reforms.

MP holds an important position in India's subnational political economy, owing to its geographic, demographic, economic, and political prominence. Over the two state reorganizations in 1956 and 2000, it has remained the largest Indian state by size. In its current form, it is the second largest state by size, with the fifth-highest population. The state has an agrarian economy, with 72 per cent of the population living in rural areas and being primarily dependent on agriculture for their livelihood.[1] For a long period, MP has been seen as a symbol of uneven development in economy and society.[2] The state has historically been at the lower end of regional disparities in the country, and a part of the infamous 'BIMARU' states.[3] Despite an acceleration of economic growth in the 1990s following a slower than average growth rate in the 1980s,[4] MP could not attract much domestic or foreign investment during the 1990s. Although it was a frontrunner in terms of economic growth, the state did not get much success from economic liberalization, at least in the first decade. The state economy further deteriorated when it lost a good part of its natural resources to Chhattisgarh in the 2000 state reorganization. Until the mid-2000s, the state had a poor industrial development record.[5] It continued to reel under fiscal deficits until the early 2000s. MP's poor economic performance, especially during the 1990s, is partly blamed on the state's ineffective articulation of its interest at the centre.[6] Beginning in 2004–5, there have been significant improvements in the economy, with a recorded revenue surplus. Over this most recent decade, there has been constant growth, often at a higher level than the national average. Industrial promotion has been prioritized, with an emphasis on promoting ease of doing business and attracting private capital investment.[7] Yet, the industrial contribution to net state value added (NSVA) lags behind agriculture.[8]

Politically, the state has been vibrant. It was one of the first states to express resistance to the Congress hegemony in the 1960s; Samyukta Vidhayak Dal, an anti-Congress coalition, came to power in 1967 and ran the state government for two years. The state has experienced healthy electoral competition and stable elected government, except during brief stints of President's Rule. During the first decade of economic reforms, from 1993 to 2003, Congress was in power under the leadership of Digvijay Singh. Since 2003, the Bharatiya Janata Party (BJP) has been in power, mostly under the leadership of Shivraj Singh Chouhan. Along with economic development issues, the inclusion of marginalized groups in the state's power structure seems to have dominated state politics in MP.[9,10] Without any significant social movement, however, economic, and political inclusion of weaker social groups continues to dominate political discourse in the state.

MP's power sector shares the fate of wider economic reforms in the state. Though it has been an early mover in response to reforms, it did not achieve much success in the power sector until 2000. State reorganization in 2000 left MP's power sector in despair with an unfavourable share of resources and liabilities. Subsequently, there have been major developments in the sector. On the physical front, installed generation capacity has increased five-fold since 2000. As of June 2017, MP has achieved an installed capacity of 19,766 megawatts (MW), accounting for 6 per cent of national capacity.[11] Most of the new capacity has been put up by private sector, which owns about 46 per cent of the total generation capacity in the state.[12] The electricity grid has been extended to almost all villages. Paradoxically, despite an increase in the availability of power and grid extensions, the state has recorded a reduction in household access to electricity, from 70 per cent in 2001 to 67 per cent in 2011.[13] The de-electrification is mainly reported in the rural areas, reflecting state failure to assimilate weaker regions and communities. As of June 2017, about 4.5 million (that is, 40 per cent) households in the state are yet to be electrified.[14] Subsequently, per capita electricity consumption in the state was just 739 kilowatt-hours (kWh) in 2014–15, far below the national average of 1,010 kWh[15] and better than only Bihar and Uttar Pradesh.

The consumer mix in the sector reflects the structure of the state economy. Corresponding to agriculture's prominence in the state economy, with 1.42 million irrigation pumps, the sector accounts for the largest share of electricity demand (39 per cent), followed by domestic (23 per cent) and industry (21 per cent). Over the last decade, the agricultural share of total electricity sale has increased, whereas the industrial share has decreased, reflecting the trend in both sectors' contribution to gross state domestic product (GSDP).[16] Yet, the burden of revenue contribution is placed upon the industrial consumers (Figure 7.1). MP seems to have one of the higher cross-subsidy rates. Although there was some initial reduction in cross-subsidy, it remains higher than the prescribed 20 per cent.[17] Interestingly, domestic consumers in the state also cross-subsidize the agricultural consumers. In 2014–15, domestic

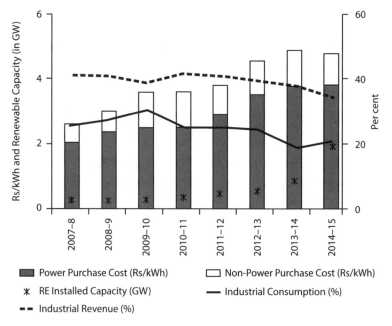

FIGURE 7.1   Physical and Financial Profile: Madhya Pradesh
Source: CSO, *Energy Statistics* (New Delhi: Central Statistics Office, Ministry of Statistics and Programme Implementation, Government of India, 2010, 2012, 2014, and 2016); PFC, *Reports on Performance of State Power Utilities* (New Delhi: Power Finance Corporation Limited, 2011, 2013, 2015, and 2016).

consumers contributed 28 per cent of the revenue while consuming 23 per cent of total power sold. The average revenue realized (ARR) from domestic consumers was Rs 5.04 per kWh, while the average cost of supply (ACS) was Rs 4.79 per kWh. The major part of the revenue gap comes from agricultural consumption, which contributed just 16 per cent of revenue while accounting for 39 per cent of consumption.[18]

The revenue problem is further worsened by a high level of aggregate technical and commercial (AT&C) losses (Figure 7.2) at a varied level across the three discoms. As a result, the discoms have recorded increasing financial losses over the years, amounting Rs 5,000 crore for the three discoms in 2014–15. The gap between ACS and ARR was Rs 0.98 per kWh after subsidy was received, which was significantly higher than the national average of Rs 0.70 per kWh.[19] The three discoms had an accumulated debt of Rs 33,400 crore as of March 2015. Interestingly, about 81 per cent of this debt has come from the state government, as the discoms lack the creditworthiness to access other

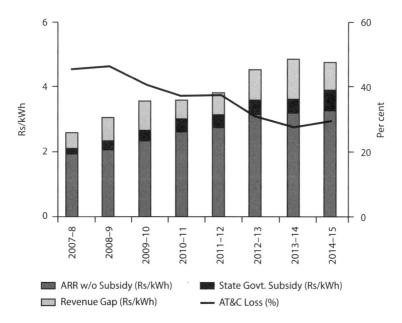

FIGURE 7.2 Supply-side Costs and Revenue Recovery: Madhya Pradesh
Source: PFC, *Reports on Performance of State Power Utilities* (New Delhi: Power Finance Corporation Limited, 2011, 2013, 2015, and 2016).

finances, including public agencies. GoMP's loans to the three discoms account for 47 per cent of the total loans from state governments to the electricity sector at the national level.[20] The three discoms have consistently been rated 'Poor' in an annual integrated rating of the discoms. In the fifth version of these ratings, Madhya Pradesh Pashchim Kshetra Vidyut Vitaran Co. Ltd. (west discom) got B+, Madhya Pradesh Poorv Kshetra Vidyut Vitaran Co. Ltd. (east discom) got B, and Madhya Pradesh Madhya Kshetra Vidyut Vitran Co. Ltd. (central discom) got C+, implying moderate to low operational and financial performance capability.[21]

From Abundance to Scarcity and Bankruptcy in MPEB (1991–9)

MPEB was established in 1956 immediately after the first state reorganization. From the beginning, the Board performed well in terms of electrical expansion and financial viability. Blessed with the good fortune of sizeable coal reserves, MPEB was able to set up pithead plants at strategic locations. A low cost of generation enabled the Board to supply power at a low tariff rate and yet bear some level of loss. Central schemes provided financial assistance for electrical and grid expansion. These schemes also carried a 'work charge' of 2–3 per cent, which covered part of the operational expenses of the Board. During the first three decades, MPEB was profitable and was in a position to use the profit for various experiments. As a retired Chairman of MPEB would recall, the Board 'was pioneer in doing things, before the others. It would do things and others would learn and follow. There were good leaders and passionate people in the Board then.'[22]

The very first operational challenge faced by the Board was power shortage in the early 1980s. At that point, the challenge was grid connectivity: areas with surplus generation were not well connected with high-demand areas. At the same time, monsoon failures affected hydro generation in the state. Power shortages persisted for years. By the early 1990s, though the Board was financially comfortable, the power shortage scenario had worsened, and the quality of service started deteriorating.[23] The Board was not in a position to meet the rising power demand from consumers. Power purchases from central generating stations started increasing, yet they could not meet the demand. The low tariffs in the state did not support power procurement from central plants. On the other hand, because of supply interruptions, consumers started defaulting on their bills. By 1992, the Board was running losses and sought subvention from the state government. Commercial losses of the Board increased from Rs 4,930 million in 1992–3 to Rs 26,550 million by 1998–9; correspondingly, revenue subsidy from state government increased Rs 3,800 million to Rs 16,970 million (from 19 per cent of revenue from sales to 40 per cent) over the period.[24]

When the GoI opened up electricity generation for private participation MP was one of the first takers and issued IPP contracts in 1992. However, these contracts did not mature, owing to bureaucratic mishandling and lack of clarity about the process.[25] The power situation in the state worsened, year by year. This development also coincided with reduced funds from Rural Electrification Corporation (REC) and Power Finance Corporation (PFC), as the Board's commercial losses were increasing and thereby reducing its creditworthiness. This led to a chronic challenge. As the Board started incurring financial losses and could not raise funds, it did not have the resources to invest in generation and transmission and distribution. The Board became dependent on the state government for subventions in order to meet operational expenses.

As the debate on distribution reforms was initiated, MP joined the bandwagon. However, it chose to plan its reforms at the state level, rather than following the World Bank model. In 1996, GoMP appointed an Expert Committee, headed by N. Tata Rao, to prepare a reform plan for the power sector in MP. The Committee submitted its report in 1997, recommending fundamental changes in institutions, policies, and procedures in the sector. Keeping with the global trend, major recommendations of the Committee included a functional division of the Board, private sector investment in all three functional areas, establishment of an electricity regulatory commission, reform and transparency in subsidy, a single distribution network and quality for rural and urban consumers, and uniform tariffs across the discoms.[26] Following the Committee's recommendations, GoMP approached the Asian Development Bank (ADB) for assistance on the reforms. GoMP, GoI, and the ADB agreed to start with a set of studies as groundwork before the reforms were introduced.

Despite the emergent financial crunch occurring in the Board, in 1994, MP had its advent of populism in the sector. Within three months of coming to power the Congress government, led by Digvijay Singh, introduced free supply of power to agricultural consumers with pumps rated below five horsepower. In addition, it offered free single-light point connections to below poverty line (BPL) households.[27] The free power policy was very much in line with the ruling party's repressive and co-optive strategy to limit political mobilization among the peasant and subaltern classes in MP, a trend that was already being experienced in neighbouring northern states.[28] The giveaway came when there was no such organized demand and people were willing to pay user charges. However, echoing the political undercurrents, the then-chief minister claimed, 'Pricing is not just a matter of people's willingness to pay. It's also a matter of politicians' willingness to charge.'[29]

MP also saw a push for renewable energy (RE) deployment in the early 1990s, possibly to get out of the power availability crisis. In 1994, the state government promoted a joint sector company called MP Wind Firms Limited in order to facilitate and expedite wind energy deployment, the preferred renewable energy technology at the time. However, it has not been very successful. The company started its first project in 1995, which took four years to complete.[30]

Following the enactment of the Electricity Regulatory Commission Act, MP was one of the first states to establish a State Electricity Regulatory Commission in August 1998.[31] However, the momentum of power sector reforms was somewhat slowed over the next two years, owing to preparations for state reorganization. During this phase, the major drivers for change were the increasing power crisis in the state and the compounding loss of MPEB. There was seemingly no political push or resistance to the reform planning. Even after the Tata Rao Committee report was submitted and made public, Congress could return to power in the 1998 state assembly election. There is no evidence of resistance to the Tata Rao Committee Report.

A Long-Drawn-Out Restructuring and Stealthy Bureaucratization (2000–12)

In 2000, the state was reorganized to carve out Chhattisgarh. Consequently, MPEB was split into two parts to create two new Boards, Madhya Pradesh State Electricity Board (MPSEB) and Chhattisgarh State Electricity Board (CSEB). While the division of assets was based on project locations, the division of non-project liabilities was based on population share, thereby favouring Chhattisgarh.[32] The condition of MPSEB was much worse than its predecessor.

At that point, the GoI was consolidating a national-level power sector reform strategy and preparing for the new legislation. Soon, GoMP signed a memorandum of understanding (MoU) with the MoP to expedite power sector reforms. Keeping with the Tata Rao Committee recommendations, the MoU suggested unbundling of the Board and corporatization of new utilities, but did not advise MP regarding privatization of the discoms. The Centre agreed to allocate an additional 100 MW of power from Central generating stations, promised more power to commercially viable discoms, offered financial support to upgrade the sub-transmission and distribution network and rural electrification, and eased the financing requirements of the PFC.[33] Subsequently, the Madhya Pradesh Vidyut Sudhar Adhiniyam was enacted in 2001. This Act was largely based upon the recommendations of the Tata Rao Committee and studies commissioned by ADB. Although MP chose to have a reform strategy and process independent of the World Bank guidelines and with some state-level thinking, the prevailing global model found its way into the process through ADB interventions in the sector. The Act, in line with the prevailing trend and oblivious to Odisha's experience until then, emphasized restructuring, independent regulation, universal meterization, tariff rationalization, and the budgetary allocation of subsidies. Immediately, ADB approved a US$ 350 million loan for a power sector development programme in MP. The loan was to be disbursed in a phased manner, based on achievement of restructuring and reform milestones.

MPERC came out with its first tariff order in 2001. As opposed to MPSEB's request for a 53 per cent tariff hike to cover the revenue gap, MPERC allowed an average hike of 31 per cent to cover 75 per cent of the ACS. Free power supply to farmers was revoked, except for scheduled caste (SC) and scheduled tribe (ST) farmers, and a flat tariff was restored.[34] The order also allowed time-of-day tariff for industrial high-tension (HT) consumers. The Commission also questioned the Board's projection of agricultural consumption, asked the Board to conduct sample studies for estimating agricultural consumption, and highlighted the need for proper metering.[35] However, the Commission never followed up on these issues. As a first step towards these reforms,

MPSEB went through a functional division, creating five companies under the Board in 2002. These companies include MP Power Generation Corporation Limited (MPPGCL), MP Power Transmission Corporation Limited (MPPTCL), and three discoms. However, these companies were not yet independent, and operated as agents of the Board. In its second tariff order issued on 30 November 2002, MPERC again raised the retail tariff for domestic and agricultural consumers. Interestingly, the tariff order—possibly strategically—came just two days after the 2003 state assembly elections and before the results were announced.

Nevertheless, Congress lost power and BJP formed the state government. Clearly, the state government supported the tariff hikes, as evidenced by its support for the 1999 hike by MPEB and a major revision in 2001 by MPERC. However, the support was less because of political will for reforms, and more because of a compulsion to meet the ADB loan conditionality, which required regular tariff revisions for the disbursement of loan instalments. Interestingly, these major tariff hikes did not lead to any mass resistance and public unrest like they did in other states. Jan Sangharsh Morcha, an NGO, called for a state-wide protest.[36] Some farmer leaders gave statements to the media opposing the tariff hike. However, the opposition never fermented into a mass agitation like those seen in Andhra Pradesh. This could be explained by absence of organized consumer groups, social engineering by the state government and limited engagement of the media in crystallizing the anti-reform sentiments. Historically, the leading parties have successfully managed to subdue mass mobilization through social engineering involving political co-option and proactive allocation. However, this social engineering backfired in the 2003 state assembly election, when a wider discontent was experienced around failure of the political structures. The BJP propagated prevailing power shortage as a failure of the Congress government in crystallized voters' discontent.

Even though electricity played a role in Congress's election failure in 2003, their loss was not due to the tariff hikes. Roads and electricity were important in BJP's election campaign and emerged as effective influences on voters' behaviour. The discontent was more about power shortages.[37] After several years of drought, MP had a good monsoon in 2003; water was finally available for irrigation, but there was no power to pump it to the fields. Other consumers, especially commercial and industrial, were hit hard by frequent load shedding affecting their operations.[38] Although there was some resentment against the hike in electricity charges, 'Charges had less impact than the problem of supply, but they sharpened discontent over shortages because voters now got less power and also had to pay'.[39] Defaulting consumers were disconnected as part of a drive that launched under a reform programme in 2001 and was implemented with some degree of seriousness. Although then CM Digvijay Singh wished to waive the pending bills of farmers and the urban poor in the weeks before polling, the Election Commission prevented the move.[40]

The new government carried the reforms forward. In the subsequent years, MPERC issued important regulations for electricity utilities and significant tariff revisions (see Table 7.1). Following the guidelines of the Electricity Act, in 2005 GoMP issued an order to make the five utilities independent companies. MPSEB remained the holding company for three discoms and acquired the additional responsibilities of bulk purchase and cash flow management. In 2006, MP Power Trading Corporation Limited (Tradeco) was set up with the responsibility of bulk purchase and cash flow management, thus reducing the role of MPSEB significantly. After six years, in 2012, Tradeco was rechristened as MP Power Management Corporation Limited (MPPMCL), which now served as the holding company for three discoms and absorbed the MPSEB. This marked the end of institutional reorganization in the MP power sector.

Despite institutional and procedural reforms, the sector did not adequately develop its physical infrastructure. Installed capacity increased to 7,000 MW by 2011, but it was not enough to meet the growing demand. As a result, the quality of power supply kept deteriorating. The 2011 census recorded a dip in electricity access in the state. Commercial entities were asked to shut down early in the evening to reduce the peak load. Industrial consumers were levied a peak surcharge for power consumption from 18:00–22:00 hours. Yet, the discoms recorded a high expenditure on short-term power purchases. These short-term purchases cost Rs 10–12 per kWh in 2007. MPERC pushed the discoms to negotiate long-term power purchase agreements in order to reduce power purchase costs.[41]

TABLE 7.1   Timeline of Key Events: Madhya Pradesh

State Politics	Year	Power Sector Events
• INC in power since 1993; Digvijay Singh is the Chief Minister	1996	• Appointment of an expert committee, headed by N. Tata Rao, to prepare a reform plan for power sector in MP
	1997	• Tata Rao Committee submitted the report
• INC returns to power; Digvijay Singh continues as Chief Minister	1998	• Establishment of MP Electricity Regulatory Commission
• State reorganization; Separation of Chhattisgarh	2000	• MPEB was split into MPSEB and CSEB • GoMP signs MoU with MoP, GoI to expedite power reforms
	2001	• *Madhya Pradesh Vidyut Sudhar Adhiniyam* (Madhya Pradesh Electricity Reform Act) • ADB approved $350 million loan for power sector development programme • MPERC issued first retail tariff order (with 31 per cent tariff hike) • Free power to farmers revoked
	2002	• Functional division within MPSEB: five companies created under MPSEB (one genco, one transco, and three discoms)
• BJP won state assembly election; Uma Bharati becomes Chief Minister	2003	
• Babulal Gaur replaces Uma Bharati as Chief Minister	2004	• MPERC issued first wind tariff order (with feed-in tariff) • MPERC (establishment of Forum and Electricity Ombudsman for Redressal of Grievances of the Consumers) Regulation

(Cont'd)

TABLE 7.1   (*Cont'd*)

State Politics	Year	Power Sector Events
		• MPERC (Conduct of Business) Regulation
• Shivraj Singh Chouhan replaces Babulal Gaur as Chief Minister	2005	• As per E Act guidelines, five power companies were made independent through an order • MPERC (Terms and Conditions for Intra-State Open Access in MP) Regulation
	2006	• Establishment of MP Power Trading Company Limited (Tradeco)
• BJP won state assembly election; Shivraj Singh Chouhan continues as Chief Minister	2008	• MPERC (Cogeneration and Generation of Electricity from Renewable Sources of Energy) Regulation
	2011	• MP Small Hydel Policy
	2012	• MP Wind Power Project Policy • Tradeco rechristened as MP Power Management Company Limited and absorbed MPSEB • MP Investment in Power Generation Projects Policy • MP Solar Power Policy
• BJP won state assembly election; Shivraj Singh Chouhan continues as Chief Minister	2013	• MP Solar Park Policy • MP Biomass Based Power Policy
	2015	• MPERC (Demand Side Management) Regulations (Draft)
	2016	• MPERC issued latest wind tariff order, with a major cut in tariff (from Rs 5.92 to Rs 4.78/kWh) • MP initiated UJALA (LED lights) Scheme • MP joined 24×7 Power for All • MP joined UDAY

Source: Author.

Industrial Aspirations and Generation Bias (2013–17)

At the time, the institutional restructuring was completed, the electricity sector was still grappling with its past problems, notably power shortage and deteriorating discom finances. The state government decided to focus on electricity generation. Between 2011 and 2013, the GoMP established multiple policies to promote private sector participation in electricity generation. The MP Investment in Power Generation Projects Policy came out in 2012 to promote independent producer projects (IPPs) in conventional power generation. On the renewable energy front, there were five separate policies focused on small hydro, wind power, solar power, solar park, and biomass, respectively. Although power shortages were the immediate driver of generation prioritization, the state's failure to promote industries was also a key factor.

Although policy documents do not claim so, the state gradually considered electricity generation to be a primary industry. Considering the endemic power shortages in neighbouring states like UP and the growing demand in Delhi, the MP state government put high hopes on interstate power trade. As the REC market was promoted, renewable energy generation also became an area of aspiration. In fact, the Industrial Promotion Policy of 2014 lists renewable energy as one of the ten priorities of MP.[42] Thanks to this focus on generation, MP has more than doubled its installed capacity within a period of four years.

However, the abundance of electricity has come at a very high cost. In 2015–16, MPPGCL reported a loss of 3,332 MkWh, owing to discoms' back down. For 2016–17, MPERC has projected a surplus of 23,122 MkWh, which is about 28 per cent of total available generation from the total contracted capacity of the three discoms. The cost of backing down was Rs 2,200 crore, which was about 28 per cent of the total fixed costs paid[43] and about 9 per cent of total revenue requirement of three discoms in 2015–16. The cost of surplus power in 2016–17 is expected to rise to Rs 2,800 crore, accounting for 10 per cent of the approved revenue requirement.[44] In addition, surplus power seems to be constraining renewable energy and open access in the state. More recently, discoms have avoided new PPAs with renewable energy producers and allegedly disrupting connectivity during peak production hours.[45] On the other hand, open access and captive generation is discouraged through high additional surcharges.[46]

This period also saw what many critics refer to as the bureaucratization of the sector. With completion of institutional restructuring in 2012, all the new institutions are headed by Indian Administrative Service (IAS) officers. Even the MPERC has been led by a retired IAS officer. There is a clear divide between the bureaucrats and technical manpower in the sector. Both blame the other for failures: Top management blames them on a lack of will to change and outdated mindsets among technical and field staff. Technical staff blames them on bureaucrats' lack of technical knowledge and wishful thinking. It is also claimed that bureaucrats are often dependent on and driven by consultants who tend to promote a one-size-fits-all western model of reform and planning which has already failed across the Indian states.[47] However, with new bureaucratic heads and interlinked hierarchy, the state government has managed to exert greater control over the new institutions.

The condition of MPERC is more appalling. As in other states, while the initial set of regulators were proactive, later appointments have been made in such a way as to ensure compliance with the government. The Commission's capacity is further limited by a lack of in-house staff. Most of the staff are drawn from the regulated utilities on deputation.

During this period, the state has taken several protective measures for various sectors. Although the discoms suffer from commercial losses and a lack of creditworthiness to raise capital investment, the state has consistently provided assistance in the form of subsidies, low-interest loans, and equity investments to mitigate the revenue gap. However, keeping with the provisions of the National Tariff Policy, a major part of the subsidy provided to the discoms is recovered from consumers in the form of an electricity duty.[48] On the other hand, as seen in the Rewa solar project case, the GoMP has extended state guarantee for the interstate sale of power from private developers. Although the latter are aligned with the government's industrial aspirations in the sector, the former seem to have reduced the discoms' incentives to improve their operational and commercial efficiencies.

Against this backdrop, and after some contemplation, GoMP joined UDAY in August 2016. GoMP has agreed to convert 75 per cent of its outstanding debt into equity over a period of five years. As a result, the interest burden of discoms will go down. However, this will not lead to the desired financial turnaround, as interest has been a small fraction (less than 4 per cent) of total costs. Expectations of discoms' performance efficiency are considered ambitious for the time frame. Moreover, technocrats in the sector seem to mistrust the Centre's intent regarding the scheme. Although the UDAY scheme is seen as a strategy to liquidate the discoms' liabilities to central banks and financial institutions, such debts constitute less than 20 per cent of the accumulated total. Debt takeover will have some positive impacts, yet financial turnaround of the discoms in MP will depend more on their loss reduction performance.

★★★

MP's experience with power sector reform is long-drawn-out and has some atypical outcomes (See Table 7.1 for key events). Though the state opened doors for IPPs in 1992, success came after two decades. Similarly, institutional reforms initiated in 2001 continued till 2012, evolving in multiple stages. The results are complex; the boons are outweighed by the banes. On the institutional front, a monolithic Board has been unbundled resulting in a complex network of highly bureaucratic institutions, prone to political capture and manoeuvring. The focus on improving availability and overcoming scarcity has undermined access and affordability for consumers. On the operational side, the old challenges—high losses, poor billing, and collection efficiency—persist. Direct subsidy from the state government still accounts for an important part of the discoms' revenue (18 per cent in 2014–15).

An early ardent of reform idea, MP's initial reform planning had an internal push and was home grown. While there were many internal drivers for reform, including acute power shortage, increasing financial loss, and stress on the state exchequer, external push was limited by discontinued external funding channels. However, the global model of electricity reforms found its way to the state through ADB assistance for reforms. Despite rigorous tariff reforms, resulting in 200 per cent hike for domestic consumers over three years, MP has successfully managed to contain public resistance through creative politics. However, reforms did not result in significant operational gains, instead tariff hikes and disconnection of defaulters have reduced household access to electricity over the reform period.

The MP experience also suggests how the state uses allocation and protection as tools to exercise political control. In addition, by appointing bureaucrats as head of utilities and agencies, the state has consolidated its control over the sector. This has been facilitated by the state's allocations to the sector, in the form of subsidies, soft loans, and equity investments. However, it seems to have resulted in a clash between the bureaucrats and technocrats, resulting in delays and lack of coordination. While technocrats constitute the permanent staff of utilities, the bureaucrats in top management are there for fixed tenure, which limits the institutional memory as well as creates trust gaps within the organization. The bureaucrat–technocrat divide and the race to fail each other may constrain future reforms in the sector.

The success of power reforms in MP seems to come from augmentation of generation capacity, pulling it out of the acute power availability crisis. But, this success has come at a high cost. Although power availability has resulted in improved supply to existing consumers, it has not improved the access scenario. By burdening the ailing discoms with high power purchase costs, surplus power is limiting investments in the sector and other reform measures. The future of MP's power sector will depend on how it manages the surplus power and success of its industrial goals from the sector.

Notes and References

1. 'Census of India 2011', Government of India, available http://censusindia.gov.in (accessed 11 July 2017).

2. M. Shah, 'Ecology, Exclusion and Reform in Madhya Pradesh', *Economic & Political Weekly* 40(48), 2005: 5009–13.

3. In the 1980s, Ashish Bose coined the acronym 'BIMARU', which stands for Bihar, Madhya Pradesh, Rajasthan, and Uttar Pradesh. The term has a resemblance to the Hindi word *bimar*, meaning sick, and implied economic sickness of the four states. Poor economic performance of the BIMARU states had been blamed for dragging down India's gross domestic product, especially during the 1980s and 1990s. K.P.N. Kumar, 'Ashish Bose: The Man Who Coined the Term "Bimaru"', *Mint*, 2 August 2007.

4. M.S. Ahluwalia, 'State Level Performance under Economic Reforms in India', in *Economic Policy, Reforms and the Indian Economy*, in A.O. Krueger (ed.) (New Delhi: Oxford University Press, 2002): 91–122.

5. N.R. Jalal, 'Industrial Growth in Madhya Pradesh: Structure and Economic Backwardness' (PhD dissertation, Cochin University of Science and Technology, 2004).

6. Shah, 'Ecology, Exclusion, and Reform'.

7. According to Assessment of Implementation of Business Reforms, MP has significantly improved in the 'Doing Business' indicators and retained its high rank at fifth position; DIPP, *Assessment of State Implementation of Business Reforms, 2016* (New Delhi: Department of Industrial Policy and Promotion, Ministry of Commerce and Industry, Government of India, 2016). In the recent Global Investors Summit, held in October 2016, the state has received an expression of interest in investment to the tune of Rs 5.6 trillion; S. Trivedi, 'Rs 6-lk-cr Investment Promised to State', *Business Standard*, 24 October 2016.

8. In 2014–15, industrial contribution to NSVA was 22 per cent, whereas the agriculture and service sectors contributed 37 per cent and 40 per cent, respectively. It was not only lower than the high-income states (for example, 42 per cent in Gujarat and 33 per cent in Maharashtra), but also below Rajasthan (28 per cent) and Uttar Pradesh (25 per cent), two other BIMARU states; RBI, *Handbook of Statistics on Indian Economy* (New Delhi: Reserve Bank of India, 2016).

9. See S. Gupta, 'Socio-Economic Base of Political Dynamics in Madhya Pradesh', *Economic and Political Weekly* 40(48), 2005: 5093–100. Here he explains the limits of state initiatives for inclusion of subalterns in MP and the political and social barriers.

10. The demography of MP includes a high share of socially marginalized populations. The state population includes 21 per cent Scheduled Tribes, 16 per cent Scheduled Castes, and about 51 per cent from Other Backward Classes (GoI, *Census of India 2011*, New Delhi: Government of India, 2011). A total of 32 per cent of the population, largely from these socially marginalized communities and living in rural areas, are living below the poverty line. See Planning Commission, *Press Notes on Poverty Estimates, 2011–12* (New Delhi: Planning Commission, Government of India, 2013).

11. CEA, *All India Installed Capacity (in MW) of Power Stations* (New Delhi: Central Electricity Authority, June 2017).

12. CEA, *All India Installed Capacity*.

13. GoI, 'Census of India 2011'.

14. 'GARV Portal', Government of India, available https://garv.gov.in (accessed 25 July 2017).

15. GoI, *24×7 Power for All: Madhya Pradesh* (New Delhi: Ministry of Power, Government of India, 2016).

16. Industry contribution to GSDP in MP declined from 27 per cent in 2004–5 to 26 per cent in 2013–14 and 25 per cent in 2014–15 (GoMP, Madhya Pradesh Economic Survey 2015–16. Bhopal: Directorate of Economics and Statistics, Government of Madhya Pradesh, 2016). Although agricultural growth rate at the national level is dropping consistently, MP recorded an

agricultural growth of 20 per cent in 2011–12 and 2012–13, and 24 per cent in 2013–14, highest among the states (ToI, 'MP Creates Record, Clocks 24.99 percent Agricultural Growth Rate', *Times of India*, 2014).

17. National Tariff Policy of 2006 required to bring down cross-subsidy surcharge progressively to a maximum of 20 per cent of average cost by 2010–11.

18. Power Finance Commission (PFC), *Report on Performance of State Power Utilities for the Years 2012–13 to 2014–15* (New Delhi: Power Finance Corporation Limited, 2016).

19. PFC, *Report on Performance of State Power Utilities*.

20. PFC, *Report on Performance of State Power Utilities*.

21. MoP, *Fifth Annual Integrated Ratings of State Power Distribution Utilities* (New Delhi: Ministry of Power, 2017).

22. Interview with an ex-Chairman of MPEB, Indore, 18 October 2016. All interviews were conducted by the author on a not-for-attribution basis.

23. In 1991 and 1992, the state was facing a power deficit of 6 per cent and a peak deficit of 21 per cent, which increased to 12 per cent and 29 per cent, respectively, by 1996–7. Planning Commission, *Annual Report on the Working of State Electricity Boards & Electricity Departments* (New Delhi: Planning Commission, Government of India, 2002).

24. Planning Commission, *Annual Report*; N. Abhyankar, 'Power Sector Restructuring in Madhya Pradesh', *Economic & Political Weekly* 40(48), 2005: 5038–55.

25. In the early 1990s, MP signed memoranda of understanding with 22 IPPs adding up to a proposed capacity addition of 8,235 MW, about two and a half times the existing capacity at the time. However, none of these projects could reach commercial operations owing to procedural lapses and lack of power system planning; Abhyankar, 'Power Sector Restructuring in Madhya Pradesh'.

26. Asian Development Bank, *India: Madhya Pradesh Power Sector Development Program Evaluation Study* (Manila: Asian Development Bank, 2011).

27. Abhyankar, 'Power Sector Restructuring in Madhya Pradesh'.

28. MP had seen strong peasant mobilizations during the early post-independence years. With 88 per cent of its population falling into the categories of SC, ST, or OBC, the state had a strong potential for a political awakening among subaltern groups in the post-Mandal era. The state government tried to contain this through a social engineering based on repressive and co-optive strategies in which 'supply' preceded the 'demand'; A.K. Verma, 'Decline of Backward Case Politics in Northern India: From Caste-Politics to Class-Politics', in Sudha Pai (ed.), *Handbook of Politics in Indian States: Region, Parties, and Economic Reforms*, (New Delhi: Oxford University Press, 2013).

29. R. Vinayak and R. Saran, 'Power Ploy', *India Today*, 2005, available http://indiatoday.intoday.in/story/punjab-cm-amarinder-singh-re-introduces-sad-bjp-giveaway-announces-free-power-for-all-farmers/1/193053.html (accessed 10 March 2017).

30. Interview with a senior official of CECL, Bhopal, 9 November 2016.

31. Interestingly, MPEB revised its tariff in March 1999, without approval from the MP Electricity Regulatory Commission (MPERC). The new tariff was challenged in MPERC and the Commission stayed its implementation. The matter was then moved to the High Court by MPEB and the court stayed MPERC's order. Later, GoMP made a provision in the reform act to legalize the tariff change; Abhyankar, 'Power Sector Restructuring in Madhya Pradesh'.

32. Abhyankar, 'Power Sector Restructuring in Madhya Pradesh'.

33. The MoU is available http://powermin.nic.in/en/content/madhya-pradesh (accessed 10 March 2017).

34. As a result, many farmers could not pay their bills and faced disconnections. Within a year, about 0.75 million of 1.2 million agricultural consumers were disconnected. However, the government later brought in a reconnection scheme (Samadhan Yojana) to settle the bills at a discounted rate and to restore connections. Abhyankar, 'Power Sector Restructuring in Madhya Pradesh'.

35. By that time, it was known that agricultural load is being overestimated in many cases and there was some thinking to recalculate it.

36. The call for protest is available www.narmada.org/nba-press-releases/december-2002/tariff.html (accessed 10 March 2017).

37. J. Manor, 'The Congress Defeat in Madhya Pradesh', *Seminar* 534, 2004: 18–23.

38. The power crisis at this point was aggravated by Chhattisgarh government's refusal to supply power to MP, as agreed to under the state reorganization arrangement, owing to the longstanding feud between Chhattisgarh Chief Minister Ajit Jogi and Digvijay Singh. While GoMP's attempt to divert scarce funds to purchase from other states was not sufficient, the crash programme to develop a hydro project could not materialize before the elections; Manor, 'The Congress Defeat in Madhya Pradesh'.

39. Manor, 'The Congress Defeat in Madhya Pradesh'.

40. Manor, 'The Congress Defeat in Madhya Pradesh'.

41. Interview with ex-chairperson of MPERC, Noida, 5 November 2016.

42. The recent development around the Rewa ultra mega solar power project boosts MP's industrial aspirations in the renewable energy sector. Although the project has been in the news for its lowest tariff, its major success lies in the arrangement to sell power outside the state. The 750

MW project has signed an MoU with Delhi Metro Rail Corporation to sell 363 MkWh/year power (60 per cent of the latter's daytime demand) for 25 years; U. Bhaskar, 'India's Solar Power Sector Turns a Corner, Thanks to Rewa Record Tariff Bid', *Mint*, 14 February 2017.

43. Prayas (Energy Group), *The Price of Plenty: Insights from 'Surplus' Power in Indian States* (Pune: Prayas Energy Group, 2017).

44. Interview with a senior official of PSERC, Bhopal, 20 October 2016.

45. Interview with a wind power producer, Bhopal, 9 November 2016.

46. Historically, owing to weak distribution network and frequent break-downs, industrial consumers in MP have preferred on-site captive generation over open access for better reliability.

47. Interview with a senior administrative staffer of a discom, Indore, 18 October 2016; interview with two senior technical staffers of a discom, Indore, 18 October 2016; interview with a senior administrative staffer of a discom, Bhopal, 8 November 2016; interview with a senior technical staffer of a discom, Bhopal, 8 November 2016.

48. MP has one of the higher electricity duties. Domestic consumers with consumption less than 100 kWh/month, commercial consumers with consumption less than 50 kWh/month, and industrial low-tension (LT) consumers are charged the lowest duty of 9 per cent; domestic consumers with higher consumption are charged 12 per cent; commercial consumers with higher consumption and industrial HT consumers are charged 15 per cent. Agricultural consumers and railways are charged no electricity duty; Central Electricity Authority, *Electricity Tariff & Duty and Average Rate of Electricity Supply in India* (New Delhi: Central Electricity Authority, 2016). To roughly estimate, in 2014–15, electricity duties collected would have contributed to 62–5 per cent of subsidies disbursed to the discoms.

8

KALPANA DIXIT

Paradoxes of Distribution Reforms in Maharashtra

The trajectory of electricity development in Maharashtra closely relates to state politics. The developmental state considered electricity an engine of growth, to be employed for the achievement of economic and political objectives. This mindset has resulted in the development of select rural areas[1] and strengthened the manoeuvring capability of the state. After the introduction of reforms in 1991, a host of new issues complicated the trajectory of electrification and provision. The chapter explores these issues and attempted responses, focusing particularly on distribution reforms.

Electricity development in Maharashtra is best characterized by state attempts to accommodate both industrial and agricultural interests. Politics in Maharashtra—one of the most industrialized and urbanized states in India—has historically been shaped by agricultural interests which dominated the state Congress Party. The development of cooperative sugar factories provided a strong institutional foundation for Congress rule and helped initiate early rural electrification in the western part of the state. The state government provided subsidies for agricultural consumers which mainly strengthened a small class of rich farmers.

Over time, however, the power of cooperative firms declined, and the pro-Congress Maratha–Kunbi voting bloc fragmented due to factionalism within the Congress. In its place, the Shiv Sena (SS) and the Bharatiya Janata Party (BJP) came to power, receiving strong support from the disgruntled Maratha leaders who successfully lobbied for continued power subsidies. Table 8.1 provides a timeline of important political events in the state, along with important milestones in the electricity sector.

TABLE 8.1   Timeline of Key Events: Maharashtra

State Politics	Year	Power Sector Events
• Establishment of Maharashtra State; Congress Party won the election	1960	• Establishment of Maharashtra State Electricity Board (MSEB)
	1977	• MSEB adopted flat rate tariff for agricultural consumers
	1992	• Maharashtra government signed MoU with Enron Development Corporation
• Shiv Sena–BJP alliance came to power	1995	
	1996	• Shiv Sena–BJP government first cancelled the agreement with Dabhol Power Corporation, but renegotiated it later
	1998	• Shiv Sena chief Bal Thackeray declared free power to farmers
• Congress–Nationalist Congress Party alliance came to power	1999	• Maharashtra Electricity Regulatory Commission was established
	2001	• MSEB restated the agricultural consumption as a result of CSO's intervention in public hearing process • MSEB rescinded the contract with Enron citing failure of company to abide by contract conditions

(Cont'd)

TABLE 8.1   (*Cont'd*)

State Politics	Year	Power Sector Events
	2003	• Internal Reform Agreement between the government, MSEB, and trade unions • Private utilities came under regulatory purview after CSO's intervention
• Congress–Nationalist Congress Party alliance came to power	2004	• Ruling and opposition coalitions announced free power to farmers in view of upcoming elections
	2005	• Dismantling of MSEB into four companies • Demand–supply gap increased leading to heavy load shedding in the state
	2006	• Adoption of 'load shedding protocol' by the MSEB • Adoption of 'Pune Model' to achieve zero load shedding in few cities by MSEDCL
	2008	• Supreme Court judgement in favour of parallel licensing in Mumbai
• Congress–Nationalist Congress Party alliance came to power	2009	
	2010	• Agitation in the state to protest frequent tariff increase in spite of heavy load shedding
• Government appointed Committee suggested 10–20 per cent reduction of tariff across categories	2013	• Power-loom owners went on strike protesting tariff hike
• BJP–Shiv Sena alliance came to power	2014	
	2016	• Maharashtra joined UDAY scheme

Source: Author.

Reforms began with the ambitious Enron project, which started an era of high-cost power in Maharashtra. The financial strain caused by the Enron project, which will be discussed at length later, still afflicts the sector. The regulatory reforms of the late 1990s led to greater civil society activism and an increase in transparency.

More recent trends in the electricity sector demonstrate challenges before the sector (see Figures 8.1 and 8.2). Especially noteworthy is rising power costs, now among the highest in India (see Figure 8.1). The share of industrial consumption declined from 45 per cent in 2007–8 to 31 per cent in 2014–15 as Figure 8.1 shows, due to sluggish industrial growth and a policy of open access. Consequently, industrial revenue decreased by 15 per cent during the same period. The installed capacity of renewable energy (RE) reached 6.40 GW: an impressive achievement, but one that has come at a higher cost (Figure 8.1).

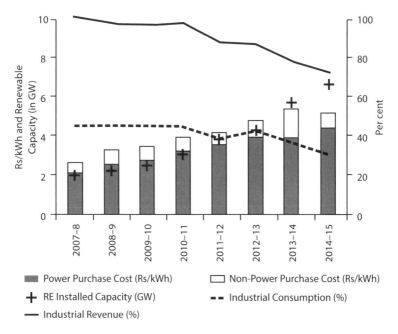

FIGURE 8.1   Financial and Physical Profile: Maharashtra
Source: Power Finance Corporation, *Report on Performance of State Power Utilities* (2011, 2013, 2015, and 2016); Central Statistical Office, *Energy Statistics* (2010, 2012, 2014, and 2016).

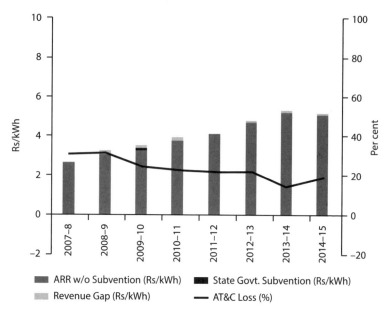

FIGURE 8.2   Supply-side Costs and Revenue Recovery: Maharashtra
Source: Power Finance Corporation, *Report on Performance of State Power Utilities* (2011, 2013, 2015, and 2016).

Increasingly expensive power led to an increase in annual revenue requirement from Rs 2.67/kilowatt hour (kWh) in 2007–8 to Rs 5.11/kWh in 2014–15 (see Figure 8.2). Subsidies to agricultural and power-loom consumers have increased from Rs 493 crore in 2001–2 to Rs 10,500 crore in 2014–15, indicating growing pressure on state finances. The revenue gap of Maharashtra State Electricity Distribution Company Ltd. (MSEDCL) has remained relatively low since 2007, thanks to frequent tariff hikes by Maharashtra Electricity Regulatory Commission (MERC). Furthermore, there was a consistent decline in aggregate technical and commercial (AT&C) losses from 31 per cent in 2007–8 to about 20 per cent in 2014–15, an impressive achievement as shown in Figure 8.2. However, as will be discussed later, these figures have created controversy. Many civil society organizations (CSOs) challenge the public utility's claim of having reduced losses.

Overall, recent developments suggest stagnation and even decline of the sector in some respects. With growing structural constraints, the state seems to be grappling with the legacy of past reforms, instead of proactively undertaking new ones. The following section discusses the trajectory of the electricity sector in Maharashtra across different time periods.

Early Days: Balancing Industrial and Agricultural Interests

The Maharashtra State Electricity Board (MSEB) took over nearly 90 private electricity companies upon its establishment in 1960. While the most lucrative customer bases of Maharashtra remained out of MSEB's jurisdiction—particularly the city of Mumbai, served instead by the Bombay Suburban Electricity Supply company (BSES) and the Tata Power Company (TPC)—the state provided strong support for the development of electricity infrastructure. The state Congress leadership, motivated by the twin objectives of industrialization in urban centres and agro-industries in rural areas, invested large resources for electricity development. The introduction of electric pump sets in the late 1960s proved immensely beneficial for the production of cash crops like sugarcane and provided further impetus for rural electrification. By the 1980s, the public grid reached almost 90 per cent of villages in Maharashtra.[2] Electricity consumption by farmers increased substantially over the years that followed, from 1.5 crore kWh in 1961 to 6,604 kWh in 1991.[3] However, irrigation-related electricity consumption remained highly concentrated in western Maharashtra, which consumed 75 per cent of the total agricultural consumption in 1973–4.[4] Industry tariffs were initially low. However, with growing industrial consumption and increased revenue needs, the government raised tariffs for HT industrial and commercial consumers, thus instituting the policy of cross-subsidy from industry to agriculture.

In 1977, MSEB adopted flat rate agricultural tariffs to address the problem of low billing efficiency in rural areas.[5] Relatively well-off farmers were the largest winners, as the cost of growing water-intensive crops like sugarcane was reduced substantially.[6] Amid attempts to extend the grid, problems with metering and billing received less priority. Furthermore, rapid grid expansion without adequate strengthening of the transmission and distribution network adversely affected the quality of supply.

In the late 1970s, the organizational strength of the Congress Party declined and factionalism within the party grew.[7] Furthermore, the importance of urban centres and service sectors in the economy grew. The SS–BJP coalition, which hosted its traditional base in cities, slowly started spreading into rural areas, especially the backward regions of Vidarbha and Marathwada.[8]

1992–8: The Rise of Competitive Populism

Larger global trends towards private participation in electricity generation influenced Maharashtra in the mid-1990s. The state avoided privatization of utility in the early 1990s to protect agricultural interests,[9] instead adopting generation reforms such as the controversial Enron project and ushering in an era of high-cost power. A 2,015-megawatt (MW) Enron project amounted to a 20 per cent expansion of total installed capacity in Maharashtra at that time.[10] Various central and intergovernmental agencies, including the Central Electricity Authority and the World Bank (WB) opposed the project, questioning its financial viability and suitability.[11] In its evaluation report, the WB condemned the project as 'not viable' and refused to provide financial assistance.[12] In spite of the heavy criticism from various quarters, political and bureaucratic elite went ahead with the project. Underestimation of the project's adverse impacts[13] and the possibility of large kickbacks were some of the motivating factors driving the elite to seal the sector's fate.[14]

In response to the deal, an anti-Enron movement emerged in Maharashtra composed of groups across the ideological spectrum. The SS–BJP leaders successfully took advantage of this backlash, making Enron one of their major campaign issues in the 1995 state assembly election and coming to power for the first time in Maharashtra. The new government initially cancelled the agreement with Enron; however, after dramatic negotiations between Enron and SS party leader Bal Thackeray, the deal was renegotiated and even expanded in terms of duration and scope.

The commencement of the Enron project in 1999 led to a five-fold increase in government electricity subsidy, from Rs 355 crore in 1998–9 to Rs 2,084 crore in 1999–2000. The hitherto profit-making MSEB reported losses of Rs 1,689 crore in 2000.[15] Crucially, the high-cost Enron project constrained MSEB's ability to add new capacity for nearly a decade (1995–2005), leading to a huge demand–supply gap after 2005.[16]

The Congress Party's influence steadily declined over the 1990s. The mismanagement of many sugar factories led to their financial demise, resulting in growing unrest among sugarcane farmers. The pro-urban policies of the Congress government and reservation to other backward classes in local government bodies further alienated the Maratha elite.[17] One important reason of the SS–BJP victory in 1995 was unprecedented rebellion in the Congress Party.[18] As a result, the Maratha–Kunbi caste voting bloc split in a decisive manner for the first time in Maharashtra.[19]

Patronage for agriculture and industry interests continued under the SS–BJP government. In 1998, SS leader Bal Thackeray declared free electricity for farmers in order to placate rural unrest,[20] while the government also provided financial assistance for indebted cooperative spinning mills.[21] These development policies attested to the enduring influence of rural interests in shaping state's public policy.

1999–2007: Regulatory Reforms and the Effective Role of Civil Society

The regulatory reforms in the late 1990s institutionalized consumer participation avenues which in turn facilitated effective civil society interventions in electricity governance. The SS–BJP government lost power in 1999 due to performance failure at various levels[22] and inadequate measures adopted to placate rural interests.

The state government, wary of ceding power to independent regulatory authorities, established MERC under the Regulatory Commission Act (RCA) in 1999 only after the High Court issued an order responding to petition by consumer groups in Maharashtra.[23] After the establishment of MERC, CSOs in Maharashtra used various provisions in the act to enhance transparency as well as spaces of participation in the sector. In the very first tariff revision process, the Prayas Energy Group (PEG), a Pune-based public advocacy organization, revealed that MSEB's estimation of agricultural consumption was highly inflated, allowing the board to hide 20 per cent of its losses.[24] Confronted with close scrutiny of data by CSOs, MSEB had to revise its estimation of transmission and distribution (T&D) losses from 18 per cent to 39 per cent. Public hearings on tariffs at six locations in Maharashtra and technical validation sessions provided opportunities for holding public utility accountable.[25]

Responding to the pressure from MERC and CSOs, MSEB adopted an internal reform programme which resulted in a tripartite agreement between the government, MSEB, and trade unions to improve the performance of MSEB.[26] Accordingly, the trade unions formed committees at various levels to combat electricity theft, and demanded application of the Government Employee Protection Act to effectively deal with threats and physical assaults by influential consumers during anti-theft drives.[27] However, this agenda of internal reform lost steam over time mainly due to a lack of political support. It is telling that from 1998 to 2006, the government changed a chairperson or managing director (MD) of public utility nine times.[28] The CSOs alleged that honest and efficient officers were transferred frequently.[29] Although various measures were employed to curb theft, such as a separate police station and dedicated staff, procedural shortcomings hampered the process of punishing wrong-doers.[30] During one of its public hearings, MSEDCL stated that there should be 'practical improvement trajectories rather than unachievable targets' and that 'one has to be sensitive to ground realities'.[31] Slow pace of agricultural metering installations and high loss levels mark this phase.

The demand–supply gap in Maharashtra increased post-2005, as MSEB failed to add new capacity after the Enron debacle. By the year 2005–6, the peak deficit reached 23 per cent of the total demand. The MERC accepted CSOs' suggestion to adopt a procedure deciding load restrictions for rural and urban areas known as 'load-shedding protocol'.[32] The MSEDCL also undertook separation of agricultural feeders from the rest of the demand in 2006, reducing the impact of load-shedding on rural households.[33]

With load-shedding reaching its peak, the Confederation of Indian Industries proposed that industry-owned captive power plants and standby generating sets in Pune generate electricity during peak hours to alleviate load-shedding. MERC accepted this proposal, levying an additional 'reliability charge' to recover the increased cost of power with an exemption for small consumers. This 'Pune Model' was adopted to avert load-shedding in few other cities, however, various issues pertaining to power costs and monitoring led MSEDCL to discontinue it after two years.[34]

During the 2004 state assembly election campaign, both opposition and ruling party coalitions promised free power for farmers.[35] This period witnessed the further decline of the cooperative sugar factories and eroding credibility of Maratha leadership;[36] however, the Congress–Nationalist Congress Party (NCP) coalition retained power, mainly due to the inability of SS–BJP to function effectively as opposition parties. Following the central government's 2003 passage of the Electricity Act mandating the unbundling of state public utilities, the GoM unbundled MSEB into four companies with the objective of improving its performance. The trade unions initially opposed this move, fearing imminent privatization; however, lacking broader public support, they eventually conceded. In response to newfound pressure to achieve fiscal solvency, the unbundled companies widened their consumer base by regularizing illegal connections, collecting dues from consumers, and developing profit-enhancing strategies. Within management, however, was no real change in terms of increased autonomy or independence.[37]

The revival of the Enron plant cost the public exchequer around 6,000–8,000 crore.[38] Unfortunately, the project could not salvage the state from an ensuing long spell of shortages. In 2007, MSEDCL adopted the distribution-franchisee model in Bhivandi, a power-loom hub and high T&D loss area. The distribution franchisee, Torrent Power, successfully reduced losses with infrastructure improvements and strict action against defaulters. The company enlisted the cooperation of local political leaders and police staff in its anti-theft drives.

Regulation of Private Utilities

Maharashtra is one of the few states in India with long-standing, well-functioning private utilities, which posed a challenge for newly established regulatory commission. The private utilities were brought under regulatory purview after an intervention by the Mumbai-based consumer organization Mumbai Grahak Panchayat and PEG. During its first tariff hearing process, MERC reduced TPC tariffs by 9.2 per cent and Reliance Infrastructure Ltd. (RInfra) tariffs by 8.5 per cent, saving Rs 300 crore per annum for Mumbai consumers in the process. In MERC's 187-page tariff order to the TPC, the PEG was mentioned ninety-nine times,[39] while the 139-page order to RInfra referred to

PEG's submission 77 times.[40] MERC went on to further restrict the ad hoc nature of private utility operations.

Overall, the early and mid-2000s brought turmoil to Maharashtra's electricity sector, but also laid the foundation for strong civil society action. Public hearings were almost deliberative in nature. However, esoteric regulatory proceedings and limitations to forging collective action prevented large-scale mobilization to tackle critical sectoral issues. Although they held the public utility accountable for governance failures, CSOs failed to adequately address collusion between the state and societal actors. Rising power costs and Enron debacle restricted the state's ability to manage demand, however, a substantial industrial load and high economic growth enabled the state to continue heavily subsidizing agricultural power and neglect large losses and arrears.

2008–13: New Interests in the Electricity Sector

Three major developments characterize the years following the early and mid-2000s: (a) renewed distributive conflicts between industry and agriculture; (b) strong market competition between private utilities in Mumbai; and (c) the increasing role of private power producers. As will be discussed below, the role of Appellate Tribunal for Electricity (APTEL) and the Supreme Court (SC) often proved to be decisive, as electricity-related litigation increased.

Competition in Mumbai Distribution

Debates about open access and competition have played out starkly in Mumbai, as the city has been served by private utilities from the advent of its electricity sector. In a landmark decision in 2008, the Supreme Court granted the right to the TPC to supply power in the RInfra licensed area, sparking competition between the two providers. Consequently, many large industrial firms shifted to TPC due to its lower tariffs.[41] After RInfra complained about cherry-picking by the TPC, the MERC applied various surcharges for migrating consumers, and also put restrictions on TPC's use of RInfra's distribution network.[42] As a result, the ability of Mumbai consumers to choose their distribution utility was largely curtailed, while an increase in TPC's tariff further discouraged would-be switchers.[43] Both the companies challenged various orders by MERC in APTEL, which kept tariff-related matters sub judice for many months.[44]

The situation of Mumbai's power sector has become highly complex, with a number of regulatory orders and court decisions providing contradictory interpretations of legal provisions. Both TPC and RInfra have failed to contract power through competitive bidding; in fact, according to one senior activist, MSEDCL has often pursed bids more successfully than the private utilities.[45] The CSOs continue to face funding and time constraints on pursuing higher-level litigation to improve sector governance.[46] Consequently, consumers are increasingly inadequately represented as decision-making takes a more legalistic turn.

Increasing Role of Private Power Producers

MSEB avoided adding capacity for many years after the setback of Enron project, ignoring directives from the commission. The worsening shortage situation led MSEDCL to contract 6,115 MW of capacity through competitive bidding with private power producers.[47] However, Adani Power and Jindal South West (JSW) Group demanded tariff increases after promising the lowest price in the competitive bidding process. Though MERC rejected tariff revisions, it still granted compensatory surcharge to these companies.[48] Upon litigation by CSOs, the issue went to APTEL which disallowed compensatory tariffs.[49] In the meantime, many projects in Maharashtra filed cases before the MERC seeking revision of tariffs set under bidding competition.[50] Tariff increases appear increasingly likely as a result, although a 2017 SC judgement now limits compensatory tariffs to private power producers.[51]

The issue of T&D losses became controversial during this phase as CSOs countered MSEDCL's claims of rapid loss reduction and instead alleged manipulation of data by MSEDCL.[52] Thus, the question of actual loss levels in Maharashtra is far from settled.

Electricity shortages severely impacted the quality of service during this phase and led to high-cost supply lock-ins. In spite of dismal service provision, MERC undertook timely tariff revisions and entertained frequent true-up proposals. These measures kept utility finances on track, but frustrated CSOs whose interventions failed to mitigate the rising cost of power. Disputes over compensatory tariffs further highlighted the challenges of governance amid the growing clout of private power producers.

2014–16: New Challenges: Open Access and Rooftop Net Metering

The BJP–SS coalition came to power in Maharashtra in 2014 amid a sea change in both national and state-level electoral politics. In this election, both the parties made far-reaching inroads into western Maharashtra, the traditional stronghold of the Congress–NCP coalition. Many Maratha leaders joined the BJP in this process, consolidating the party's rule and indicating the continued influence of agricultural interests on state government.[53]

In the last few years, challenges faced by the MSEDCL have acquired new dimensions and can be separated into four storylines: (a) excess capacity addition and declining demand; (b) a growing number of big consumers procuring electricity through open access; (c) the rising cost of public utility power; and (d) increasing pressure from the central government to increase the share of renewable energy in the overall energy mix, including rooftop solar with net metering. The MSEDCL proposed to buy 7.4 per cent of its total power from the renewable sources at the rate of Rs 5.77/kWh in its most recent tariff proposal.[54]

Thanks to a large capacity addition by the MSEDCL over the course of 2007–12, the state no longer faces perpetual power shortages. However, due to sluggish industrial growth and the high cost of power, demand has fallen short of MSEDCL projections. In response to the ensuing power surplus, some MSPGCL plants had been backed down over the past few years. Thus, as elsewhere in India, there exists in Maharashtra a paradox of both surplus power and non-electrified households.

Recently, GoM joined the central government Ujjwal Discom Assurance Yojana (UDAY), under which it committed to take over 75 per cent of the Discom's non-capital expenditure debt—approximately Rs 6,600 crore—during 2016–17. Maharashtra is expected to receive a net benefit of Rs 9,725 crore in return.

***

After 25 years of reforms, the electricity sector in Maharashtra continues to struggle with a range of issues: high-cost power, high subsidy burden, the flight of subsidizing consumers, mounting arrears, and surplus power. The objective of ensuring universal, affordable, and quality electricity supply still has to be fulfilled, while some of the attempted reforms have themselves bred new problems.

Historically, electricity policy in Maharashtra has been closely tied to state party politics because of the crucial role of the cooperative movement in the Congress Party's base of support. Over the years, this close connection weakened as the cooperative movement declined and the political significance of industrial interests grew. However, the vote-mobilizing abilities of rich farmers ensured the continuation of agricultural power subsidies and accommodation of growing arrears by the state.

The generation reforms initiated an era of high-cost power in Maharashtra burdening state finances and restricting state's ability to add capacity. The resultant heavy shortages led MSEDCL to contract large private power. This pattern of periodic high-cost supply lock-in regularly puts pressure on Discom finances. Now there is a pressure of expensive renewable energy. Together, these developments restrict the ability of the state to manage increasing demands of consumers.

Declining industrial demand post-2007 due to economic slow-down and open access policies has affected Discom finances and curtailed its ability to cross-subsidize as Figure 8.1 shows. The large capacity addition and ensuing demand shortfall has led to a situation of power surplus which compelled MSPGCL to shutdown some of its plants. Surplus power and loss of cross-subsidy create structural constraints which affect the state's ability to address political pressure.

There has been marked reduction in AT&C losses since 2007 (see Figure 8.1). However, debates over the proper methodology for estimating agricultural electricity supply highlight the difficulty in reaching to any conclusion on this issue. According to recently launched UDAY, AT&C losses in Maharashtra are 28.54 per cent.[55] The story of losses in Maharashtra shows that the state is still pursuing its old strategy of placating dominant interests by allocating them explicit and implicit subsidies.

The reform process has not achieved many of its stated objectives, but it has unintentionally opened the door to civil society and enhanced sector transparency. The CSOs have positively influenced vital decisions by representing the hitherto neglected concerns of consumers; however, the prevailing regulatory framework has made it difficult for the CSOs to address the perpetual bias of policy makers towards dominant interests. Amid the increasing role of private power producers and novel experiments like market competition in Mumbai's distribution sector, electricity governance has recently taken an overtly legalistic turn. The role of regulatory agencies, moreover, has become increasingly critical as role of private actors continues to grow.

Power sector reforms in India, while adhering to a standard global model, have neglected to account for specific political economy contexts. Consequently, there has been selective implementation of broadly promulgated reform measures. While reforms have aimed to change the relationship between government and utilities, they have not attempted to influence either the relationship between utilities and consumers or between government and consumers.[56] As a result, a large portion of sector politics continues to elide reform efforts, thus limiting the possibility of fundamental change.

Notes and References

1. Sunila S. Kale, *Electrifying India: Regional Political Economies of Development* (Stanford, California: Stanford University Press, 2007), 62–99.
2. Ashwini Chitnis and Ann Josey, *Review of Maharashtra Power Sector Policy and Regulation: Lessons, Challenges and Opportunities* (Pune: Gokhale Institute of Politics and Economics, 2015), 5.
3. GoM, *Economic Survey of Maharashtra, 2009–10* (Mumbai: Directorate of Economics and Statistics, Planning Department, 2010), 8.
4. Kale, *Electrifying India*, 91.
5. Flat-rate tariff means charging consumers on the basis of the size of the pump set instead of metered consumption.
6. Girish Sant and Shantanu Dixit, 'Beneficiaries of the IPS Subsidy and the Impact of Tarff-hike', *Economic and Political Weekly* 31(51), 1996: 3315–17, 3319–21.
7. Suhas Palshikar and Rajeshwari Deshpande, *Maharashtra: Electoral Competition and Structures of Domination* (University of Pune: Occasional Paper Series II: 1, 1999), 25.
8. Palshikar and Deshpande, *Maharashtra: Electoral Competition*.
9. Kale, *Electrifying India*, 93.
10. Enron was divided into two phases of 695 MW and 1,320 MW.
11. Maharashtra had adequate base load capacity in 1991 and needed power to fulfill peak load demand.
12. Quoted in Abhay Mehta, *The Power Play: A Study of the Enron Project* (Hyderabad: Orient Blackswan, 2000): 38–9.

13. Interview with senior activist on 24 August 2016.

14. Mehta, *The Power Play*.

15. Madhav Godbole, 'MSEB's Tariff Revision Proposal: Unconscionable Burden on Consumers', *Economic and Political Weekly* 36(38), 2000: 3583.

16. On the Enron controversy, please see Subodh Wagle, *The Enron Story: Controversial Issues and the Struggle* (Pune: Prayas Monograph Series, 1997); Madhav Godbole, 'Resolving Dabhol Tangle', *Economic and Political Weekly* 39(23), 2004: 2329–34.

17. Suhas Palshikar, 'Manipulative Politics Continues', *Economic and Political Weekly* 34(13), March 27, 1999: 743.

18. The number of rebel candidates reached 200, out of which 35 were elected. Additionally, the division of votes caused the defeat of Congress candidates in 43 districts. See Rajendra Vora, 'Shift of Power from Rural to Urban Sector', *Economic and Political Weekly* 31(2–3), 1996: 171–3.

19. Palshikar and Deshpande, *Maharashtra: Electoral Competition*.

20. 'Maharashtra: Wooing the Farmers the Wrong Way', *Economic and Political Weekly* 33(44), 1998: 2761.

21. Madhav Godbole, 'Cooperative Sugar Factories in Maharashtra: Case for a Fresh Look', *Economic and Political Weekly* 35(6), February 5, 2000: 420.

22. Palshikar, 'Manipulative Politics'.

23. Interview with senior activist, Mumbai, 22 September 2016.

24. Prayas Energy Group, *Supplementary Submission before MERC, Case 1/99* (Pune, 5 February 1999), 8.

25. After CSOs pointed out glaring gaps in the data provided by MSEB, MERC began the process of validation of data in which it invited selected CSOs.

26. MERC, *Three Years of MERC: A Report* (Mumbai, 2002), 8.

27. Interview with MSEDCL official, Pune, 1 September 2016.

28. Interview with senior activist, Pune, 29 September 2016.

29. Interview with senior activist, Pune, 29 September 2016.

30. Interview with senior activist, Pune, 29 August 2016.

31. MERC, *Tariff Order for MSEDCL for FY 2006–07* (Mumbai, 2006), 35.

32. Prayas Energy Group suggested a range of options to develop a well-articulated procedure for sharing of load restrictions in urban and rural areas.

33. Feeder separation allowed MSEDCL to discontinue the supply to agriculture without affecting the rest of the consumers.

34. Interview with ex-official of MSEDCL, Pune, 16 September 2016.

35. M.K. Datar, 'Maharashtra's Finances: Too Good to Be True?', *Economic and Political Weekly* 40(18), April 30, 2005: 1812.

36. B.S. Baviskar, 'Cooperatives in Maharashtra: Challenges Ahead', *Economic and Political Weekly* 42(42) 2007: 4219.

37. Interview with ex-official, MSEDCL, Pune, 16 September 2016.
38. Chitnis and Josey, *Review of Maharashtra Power Sector*, 6.
39. MERC, *Tariff Order for TPC—FY 2003–04 and FY 2004–05, Case no. 30 of 2003* (Mumbai, 11 June 2003).
40. MERC, *Tariff Order for BSES—FY 2003–04 and FY 2004–05, Case no. 18 of 2003* (Mumbai, 1 July 2004).
41. Chitnis and Josey, *Review of Maharashtra Power Sector*, 30.
42. Forum of Regulators, *Indian Experience in Retail Consumer Choice* (New Delhi, 2014), 2.
43. Chitnis and Josey, *Review of Maharashtra Power Sector*, 13.
44. Interview with senior activist, Pune, 29 September 2016.
45. Interview with senior activist, Pune, 29 September 2016.
46. Interview with senior activist, Pune, 29 September 2016.
47. For the review of the process of competitive bidding, pl. see Chitnis and Josey, *Review of Maharashtra Power Sector*, 11–15.
48. Chitnis and Josey, *Review of Maharashtra Power Sector*.
49. 'APTEL Disallows Compensatory Tariff for Adani Group's Plants', *Economic Times*, 12 May 2016.
50. Chitnis and Josey, *Review of Maharashtra Power Sector*, 13.
51. Samanwaya Rautray and Rachita Prasad, 'Tata, Adani Can't Charge Compensatory Tariff: Supreme Court', *Economic Times*, 12 April 2017.
52. Pratap Hogade, *Suggestions on MSEDCL MYT Petition, Case No. 48 of 2016* (Ichalkaranji, 2016), 2.
53. Suhas Palshikar, 'Maharashtra Assembly Elections: Farewell to Maratha Politics?', *Economic and Political Weekly* 49(42), 18 October 2014.
54. MERC, 'MYT Order of MSEDCL for the period from FY 2016–17 to FY 2019–20' (Mumbai 2016): 40.
55. See https://www.uday.gov.in/home.php#modal-three (accessed on 27 December 2017).
56. Sumir Lal, *Can Good Economics Ever Be Good Politics: Case Study of the India Power Sector*, World Bank occasional paper no. 83 (Washington DC, 2006), 24.

9

MRIGAKSHI DAS
MAHAPRAJNA NAYAK

Endless Restructuring of the Power Sector in Odisha

A Sisyphean Tale?

Odisha was the first state in India to restructure its state-owned electricity sector and privatize the distribution business. Around 1992–3, the World Bank initiated the electricity reform process wherein the Orissa State Electricity Board (OSEB) was unbundled into separate entities like generation, transmission, and distribution in order to secure financial viability for the debt-ridden power sector. It was also the first time in India that a regulatory body within the sector was set up to ensure independence and accountability of the sector, freeing it from possible political interference. Hence, the Orissa Electricity Regulatory Commission (OERC) was formed in 1995. To rationalize the distribution sector, privatization was recommended, which came into effect in 1999, when the Bombay Suburban Electricity Supply (BSES) took over the utilities in Northern Electricity Supply Company of Orissa (NESCO), Western Electricity Supply Company of Orissa (WESCO), and Southern Electricity Supply Company of Orissa (SOUTHCO), and Applied Energy Services Transpower (AES) won the bid for Central Electricity Supply Company of Orissa (CESCO). AES left CESCO in

2001, leaving behind huge debt. The debacle of AES and thereby the conditions leading to the failure of private player participation in distribution was discussed in the Kanungo Committee report, which came about in 2001. Ten years after that, the restructuring of the power sector took recourse to franchising as a model to rehabilitate the distribution company, Central Electricity Supply Utility (CESU). The struggling franchisees Feedback Energy Distribution Company (FEDCO), Enzen Global Solutions, Bhubaneswar (ENZEN), and Riverside Utilities Power Limited (RUPL) form the latest leg of the discourse of distribution challenges in the post-reform power sector in Odisha.

Historicizing Sectoral Development

The power sector story in Odisha revolves around a sense of urgency accorded to industrial development interspersed with a narrative of neglect for agriculture. Between 1990–8 there was visible decline in the percentage consumption of electricity in the agricultural sector, which reflected the lack of attention for agriculture in reform debates.[1] From the industrial policy of 1980 until the Orissa Electricity Reforms Act in 1995, government formed by both Indian National Congress (INC) and Janata Dal (later named Biju Janata Dal) focused policy attention on mobilizing Odisha's rich natural reserves for industrialization and encouraging capital intensive metal-based industries, rather than the small industries that might have yielded large-scale employment.[2] The state's focus on extractive industries coincided with India's economic reforms in the 1990s, which opened up market to private players and global players. The privatization and corporatization of the power sector in Odisha is embedded in these developments.

Consistently characterized as one of India's most 'backward states', Odisha, in the last two decades since the power reforms, has continued to fall short on indicators of development like health, education, and per capita consumption of food. The distribution of economic development and political power in the state is uneven across caste, social groups, and geography. According to the 2011 census, the Scheduled Tribe (ST) population in Odisha is 22.8 per cent and the Scheduled Caste (SC) population is 17.1 per cent, both of which are higher than national averages. These communities remain socioeconomically marginal compared to other states.[3] Most striking among Odisha's development indicators is the historical neglect of agriculture. Successive state governments have been unable to link industrial development to the development needs of the state's rural population, whose livelihood remains heavily dependent on agriculture fact, over the decades, power consumption has seen a sharp decline from 3.1 per cent in 2001–2 to 1.56 per cent in 2013–14 for lack of dedicated electric feeder.[4]

Against this economic backdrop, the prevalence of a privatized power regime in a potentially profit-contentious space was bound to fail. The impetus of power sector reforms seems to have been an attempt to restore the finances of a debt-trapped government. The state lacked a significant structurally conducive pretext to embark on privatization other than an impending debt of 334 crores.[5] In the first half of the 1990s immediately prior to the reforms, the annual subsidy invested in the power sector amounted to about 250 crores and average Transmission and Distribution (T&D) losses hovered around 46 per cent. Institutional inefficiency, low capital expenditure (CAPEX), and improper tariff setting led to poor and inadequate power supply. The state's main utility, OSEB, suffered due to low revenue generation and high cost of supply. Generating plants were inefficiently run at 36 per cent (1993–4), and the T&D losses were around 60 per cent. The lack of a technologically sound documentation system and the continued practice of manual accounting of revenue records was reflected in the utility's billing efficiency, which was about 17 per cent.[6]

The World Bank compelled the Odisha government to restructure the sector by linking a loan for a large-scale hydro project in the state with rehabilitation of OSEB.[7] Hence, beginning in the early 1990s, Odisha became the first state in India to secure a World Bank financial reform package that stipulated the mandatory unbundling of the vertically integrated OSEB followed by privatization of the distribution enterprise. For the Odisha government, the 350 million dollar grant was meant to attend to the state government's inability to assure financial sustainability of the State Electricity Board (SEB) and ensure the ongoing operation and management of utilities.[8]

The process of reform, restructuring, and privatization was accepted by political elites because it was perceived as the surest route for massive industrialization.[9] In this, there was an alignment of interests between the dominant development vision held by political leaders within the state to the model of utility reform and management that was taking hold globally and among reform leaders in New Delhi. However, reforms as they have unfolded in Odisha have not been a success. Twenty years since the reforms began in 1995, the state's power sector has mired in spiralling debt, lacks sufficient investment, and is unable to provide universal and adequate electricity access and supply. This chapter focuses on mapping and understanding modes of institutional restructuring in the power sector, from the initial reforms of the 1990s to the more recent adoption of the recent franchise model of electricity distribution. For this latter development, where Odisha has progressed further than many other states in experimenting with distribution franchising, we consider how franchising would be integrated with the state's broader development policies and goals. We have tried to map out the possible structural reinventions or makeovers in Odisha pertaining to the business of distribution of electricity in particular and ideological views that have underwritten these reinventions. A recurring question that motivates the chapter is why does the Odisha government seek recourse to privatization even after instances of massive failure, first with AES, then with Reliance, and now with private franchisees?

A key challenge facing the sector as a whole and distribution franchising in particular comes from the state's rapid expansion of rural electrification in the past decade. To ensure financial sustainability of CESU (the distribution company briefly taken over and then abandoned by AES in 2001) and manage efficiency in billing and collection, Odisha's franchisee model was invested in catering to rural consumers more than the urban base. The viability of franchising as a model is delicately balanced on the success and failure of these companies' being able to establish the idea of electricity as a 'commodity' among rural consumers through efficient services and ensuring collections across a rural landscape that is geographically uneven and continues to have large numbers of low- and very low-income consumers.

A Brief Contextualization of Events

From 1990–5, the power shortage during peak period was around 37 per cent and T&D losses were around 60 per cent.[10] Indian policymakers at that time were embracing ideas of liberalization, privatization, and globalization, and opening up core economic sectors to private players. This created space for capital-rich entities to scout for investment-friendly, resource-rich developing economies.[11] The political leadership in Odisha from J.B. Patnaik in the 1980s and late 1990s to Biju Patnaik in the early 1990s, and now Navin Patnaik since 2000, has single-mindedly pursued capital-intensive development.[12]

The first steps towards power sector reform were taken in the early 1990s, under the chief ministership of Biju Patnaik of the Janata Dal, who held the position from 1990 to 1995. A war hero and beloved local politician, Patnaik was also a strong supporter of reforms as the best mechanism for drawing capital for industrial development. Initial consultations for unbundling OSEB into generation, transmission, and distribution included retired employees of OSEB. There was an urgent need for the distribution entities to change the existing culture and approach to management.[13] This was in reference to the complacency of the workforce that had seeped into the public sector, which necessitated corporatization of the distribution utility in hopes of efficiency in billing and collection and better management of the workforce.

A key enabling factor of Odisha's reforms programme was that, unlike other states, whether Punjab, Maharashtra, Haryana, or Andhra Pradesh where the agricultural share in electricity consumption was about 40 per cent, in Odisha it was barely 6 per cent and remains an insignificant share. The social profile of agriculture labour in Odisha comprises mostly Dalit and tribal populations who have been unsuccessful in breaking the hegemony of the upper caste, upper class in electoral politics. Historically, local-level resistance to the economic reforms has been time-bound with solely anti-industrial and anti-displacement objectives that dissipated after the project was halted. Unlike in other parts of India, in Odisha there was no concerted agricultural lobby to impede the privatization process. The lack of public involvement is evident in the regulatory arena, where even the tariff hearing documents of the late 1990s, at a time of steep tariff hikes, do not mention instances of public resistance or protest.[14]

Biju Patnaik's reform agenda for the power sector was furthered by the Congress government in 1995 under the chief ministership of J.B. Patnaik. As this seamless transition suggests, electricity governance, electricity tariffs, and access to electricity are not politically salient in the state, nor have politicians contested elections with promises for free power or more access as they do in other states. In 2000, the Janata Dal, renamed the Biju Janata Dal, returned to power under the chief ministership of Naveen Patnaik (son of Biju Patnaik), who has held the post since then. The party initially ruled in a coalition with the Bharatiya Janata Party (BJP), but has garnered enough seats to rule on its own since 2009. Naveen Patnaik's political support rests heavily on his image as a corruption-free politician and is further bolstered by a host of welfare programmes targeting Odisha's most socio-economically marginalized. Despite these populist measures, though, electoral politics remains dominated by the state's upper caste, urban elite, as many scholars of the state have pointed out.[15] See Table 9.1 for a timeline of the key events in the power sector of Odisha.

Reformation: Organizing Decentralization in the Early 1990s

Following the recommendations from the consultants hired by the World Bank, the assets of Odisha Hydro Power Corporation Ltd. (OHPC) and Grid Corporation of Odisha Ltd. (GRIDCO) were overvalued by almost 200 per cent as part of the structural readjustment of finances. This created a need for a huge amount of capital allocation to meet depreciation expenditure.[16]

Also, high debt: equity ratio implied a huge amount of interest expenditure, which increased the liability of GRIDCO, leading to a further increase in Average Cost of Supply and then the tariff. But this was not commensurate with the desired reduction in distribution losses, making the sector's operation and finances more precarious.

To make up for the outstanding debt of OSEB and ease GRIDCO's finances, the Talcher Thermal Power plant was sold to National Thermal Power Corporation (NTPC) for 356 crores[17] on 3 June 1995, AES was given a side deal of 49 per cent stake in Orissa Power Generation Corporation Ltd. (OPGC) through government divestment, and retail tariffs were hiked by about 17 per cent (Figure 9.1).

With the objective of distancing the government from the tariff-setting process, Odisha became the first Indian state to set up an independent regulatory commission in 1996. Most important, it was an attempt at creating a formidable technocratic institution, detaching regulatory activities from political processes.

However, the intent of regulating political interference in the sector by investing power in the OERC was weakened when bureaucrats became

TABLE **9.1** Timeline of Key Events: Odisha

State Politics		Power Sector Events
Congress government	1985–90	• Pushed for industrial development
• J.B. Patnaik as prominent Chief Minister		
• Biju Patnaik of Janata Dal comes to power	1990–5	• Consultation begins for restructuring the power sector • World Bank comes to the scene
	1995	• Orissa Electricity Reforms Act • TTP sold to NTPC
	1996	• OERC formed
	1998	• Process for privatizing the distribution sector began
	1999	• Privatization of discoms
• BJD–BJP Alliance comes to power • Naveen Patnaik as Chief Minister	2001	• Centre's Rajiv Gandhi Grameen Vidyutikaran Yojana for rural electrification launched • AES quits CESU
	2005	• CESU has CEO and board members for lack of buyers • Central Government scheme RGGVY was implemented in Orissa in the month of April
	2007–8	• BGJY—rural electrification drive launched by BJD government.
	2010	• CAPEX programme launched
	2012	• Franchisee model adopted for CESU area
	2015	• The license of Reliance was revoked due to non-performance
	2017	• In the month of August, OERC won the case against Reliance and the three discoms (WESCO, NESCO, SOUTHCO) are now managed by GRIDCO with OERC as the custodian

Source: Author.

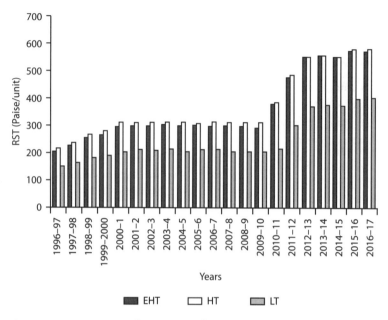

FIGURE 9.1   Percentage Change in Tariff over Time
Source: OERC, 'Odisha Power Sector and Tariff for 2016–17'.

central to the functioning of the Commission, centralizing power in the hands of the political executives, quite contrary to the objective of a regulatory authority. So far, all the prolific positions in OERC have been held by retired Indian Administrative Services (IAS) officers. The director of tariff at OERC explained that it is a travesty of ethical governance that retired administrators occupied a space meant for experts and professionals, which seemingly blurred the distinction between a manager in a corporate entity and administrator under a government.[18] Under such circumstances, there was no tariff revision for almost a decade, from 2001 to 2010, a period in which BJD had stable electoral power riding on populist policies. According to a senior professional from ENZEN, a newer franchisee operating in the state, OERC went on a 'tariff revision holiday' that caused irreversible damage to the sector.[19]

Quite clearly, the sector is stuck in the colonial legacy of supervision and control in methods of governance. As of September 2017, there is no Chairman of OERC, and members of the regulatory board are yet to be appointed. Within these structural factors, the political interference in the tariff-setting process coupled with a lack of political will to ensure fair operation of privatized services proved detrimental for the commercial standing of the distribution companies.

Privatizing Distribution: Post-1999

Discom privatization in Odisha had three key motivations: operational efficiency, quality service to the consumers, and commercial sustainability. The decisions about the proportion of stakes to be sold and the valuation of assets relied on the expectation that a private investor would be able to invest sufficient capital in the system to reduce transmission and distribution losses. Following the competitive bidding process in 1998, the Indian utility company BSES acquired a 51 per cent stake in three discoms (NESCO, WESCO, and SOUTHCO), and the American utility AES acquired CESCO. The government utility, GRIDCO, retained a 49 per cent stake in each of these (OERC 2011). Along with the distribution assets, a 600-crore liability was transferred to the discoms (OERC 2011). The private players paid a premium price to GRIDCO following the up-valuation of the assets.

AES started its operation with a net worth of 139.17 crore and debt capital worth Rs 216.57 crore, apart from 174 crore borrowed from GRIDCO under the condition of return on operational improvements. But these expected improvements never materialized (OERC 2011). In July 2001, in clear violation of the shareholder's agreement, AES sought GRIDCO's permission to sell the 51 per cent stake in CESCO to a third party or even GRIDCO before the contractual period of five years had ended. Over these disagreements, AES abandoned CESCO in 2001 with arrears amounting to 577 crores and having made no investment in upgrading the system. In 2005, OERC, through an executive intervention, came up with the CESU scheme, dismantling CESCO. Since then CESU has been managed by a board of directors and a CEO appointed by OERC. However, none so far has received a return on equity owing to recurring losses in the distribution business.[20]

The first decade of privatization may not have been promising for discom performance, but the abundance of power helped the sector negotiate questions of viability within the sector for subsequent years. Analysis of the financial statements of the discoms reveals that the utilities have remained financially weak owing to huge accumulated losses and heavy dependence on debt capital.[21] This has affected the liquidity position of both generating companies, as their balance sheets showed huge current assets in the form of receivables, as well as public sector banks in the form of non-performing assets.

Until 2007–8, GRIDCO drew from the advantage of abundant hydro-power in the state to meet more than 60 per cent of its demand. Cheaper hydro-power ensured stability in the average cost of supply and thereby ensured tariff control (Figure 9.1). This is evident from the power purchase cost as shown in Figure 9.2. Owing to low average cost of supply, the gap between revenue and cost could be maintained at a moderate level (Figure 9.3).

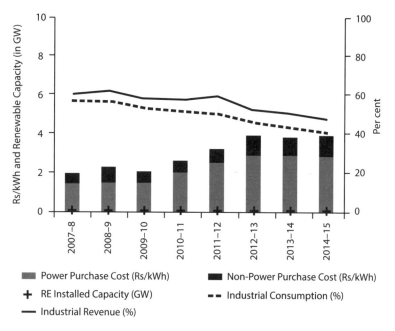

FIGURE 9.2   Physical and Financial Profile: Odisha
Sources: CSO, *Energy Statistics* (New Delhi: Central Statistics Office, Ministry of Statistics and Programme Implementation, Government of India, 2010, 2012, 2014, and 2016); PFC, *Reports on Performance of State Power Utilities* (New Delhi: Power Finance Corporation Limited, 2011, 2013, 2015, and 2016).

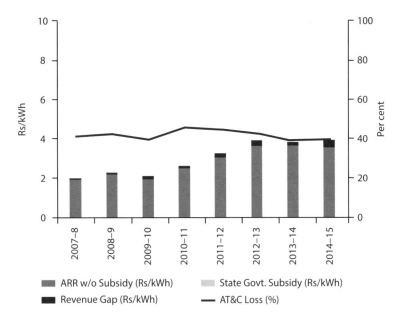

FIGURE **9.3**   Supply-side Costs and Revenue Recovery: Odisha
Source: PFC, *Reports on Performance of State Power Utilities* (New Delhi: Power
Finance Corporation Limited, 2011, 2013, 2015, and 2016).

The ready availability of hydro-power also enabled GRIDCO to earn
profits from interstate power trading, further enabling it to sell power
to discoms at low RST.[22] In the meanwhile, to ensure efficient performance of power utilities, OERC in 2003 started following the multi-year
tariff principles. A normative calculation of distribution losses, which is
around 15 per cent lower than the actual losses, was taken into consider-
ation while setting tariff. The gap from the actual losses was to be borne
by the discoms. This was a step taken by Commission to encourage the
discoms to make their operations more efficient.

For two years, 2005–6 and 2006–7, the two distribution utilities
NESCO and WESCO managed to earn profits because of the large
numbers of industrial consumers in their load profiles. However,
their balance sheets have continued to show huge accumulated losses.
Several developments post-2009 pulled GRIDCO and the discoms back
to fiscal difficulties. Around 2010–11, the power scenario was in a state

of transition owing to massive rural electrification and diminishing hydro-power.

During the 11th five-year plan, approximately 12,204 unelectrified villages were electrified, 22,660 villages were intensively electrified, and 2,404,798 below poverty line (BPL) households were electrified under Rajiv Gandhi Grameen Vidyut Yojana (RGGVY) and Biju Gram Jyoti Yojana (BGJY), central funds granted to states to fund rural grid extensions.[23] The state's hydro-power was reduced because of silting of water reservoirs and erratic rainfall, leaving no surplus for GRIDCO's interstate trading. In addition, the absence of tariff hikes over for nine long years increased the gap in average revenue realized (ARR) and average revenue realized of GRIDCO to around Rs 2,995.14 crores by 2010, which is an increase of almost 85 per cent since 2005–6.[24] The situation went downhill with the rise in demand of the existing consumer base as well as new consumers joining the grid after rapid expansion of networks (especially in rural areas). In the absence of financial support from the state government, GRIDCO borrowed funds from nationalized banks and other financial institutions to meet the gap in annual revenue requirement.

In order for the state grid to function properly given substantial rural expansion, the system required capital to strengthen distribution and transmission infrastructure. However, because the discoms in Odisha were, on record, private enterprises, they were not eligible for financial assistance or grants under the Restructured Accelerated Power Development and Reforms Programme (R-APDRP). Hence, in 2010, the Government of Odisha charted a CAPEX plan of Rs 2,400 crore to fund system improvements in the distribution sector, out of which the state government's investment was Rs 1,200 crore, and discoms were asked to arrange the remainder independently. According to the terms of the CAPEX agreement, failure on the part of the discoms to reduce Aggregate Technical and Commercial (AT&C) losses by least 3 per cent per annum would result in part of the grant being converted into a loan. In a break from the pre-reform practice of subsidies, the government strong-armed the discoms into improving their performance. However, the financial fallout of this was the further addition to the liabilities of the discoms in the form of interest expenditures. Simultaneously, by this point the sector's heavy dependence on high-cost thermal power priced at more than Rs 3.5 per unit,[25] during a period of rising coal prices and the surfacing of a coal allocation scam, was badly timed. This period also marked the rising relevance of Captive Power units in the market that would continue until 2013–14.

Following the Electricity Act 2003, which specified that generation from Captive Power Plants (CPPs) should be encouraged and the power be fully utilized to meet the growing demand in the country, there was an acceleration of the dependence of GRIDCO on CPPs by almost 59 per cent from 2008–9 (Table 9.2).[26]

In 2009, OERC came up with its order on pricing of CPPs, which had the provision that a commitment for supply of power for a period of more than three months up to one year would entail that a CPP be considered a supplier of firm power of electricity from their CPPs and the state utilities shall be obliged to pay them a rate more than 110 per cent of the cost of generation of such power.[27] The Commission fixed the rates at Rs 3.00/kWh for surplus power from CPPs, which was further revised to Rs 3.10/kWh in 2010–11.[28] OERC also increased the

TABLE 9.2 Percentage of Power Supply from Different Sources and Megawatts of Power Available for Trading to Other States

Year	Availability of Power from Different Sources (MW)			Sold to Other States (MW)
	State	Central	Captive	
2001–2	1,271	98	54	0
2002–3	869	440	62	0
2003–4	1,269	481	76	0
2004–5	1,459	498	69	517
2005–6	1,275	525	62	250
2006–7	1,543	435	92	207
2007–8	1,563	736	82	311
2008–9	1,375	763	130	32
2009–10	1,157	773	485	50
2010–11	1,295	814	729	128
2011–12	1,136	1,170	225	49
2012–13	1,226	1,221	239	136

Source: Government of Odisha, Economic Survey, 2014.

tariff by approving 5 crores in favour of each discom in 2015–16, failing which there would have been a further increase in regulatory assets, in turn further burdening future consumers.

Although ATC losses declined, the average across discoms was still approximately 40 per cent in 2012 (see Figure 9.3), which is still towards the higher end. Also, because of the rapid expansion of rural networks, cases of theft and wastages increased, according to reports from the Energy Police Station.[29] For the last two years, 2015–16 and 2016–17, again OERC did not increase tariffs. Even before the state government provided power at subsidized rates to agricultural and BPL consumers, tariffs for domestic consumer categories had always been fixed much below the average cost of supply until 2010–11. Hence, it was felt that, given the rapid expansion of rural networks, a marginal increase wouldn't create any burden on the consumers. The government funded only the initial cost of the asset requirement under RGGVY and BGJY, whereas the responsibility of repairing and maintaining the network rests with the discoms.

Private to Public: Failure of a Decentralized Entity (1999–2015)

In March 2015, OERC revoked the three discom licenses of BSES (which in 2003 became part of Reliance Power) citing violations under section 19(1) of the Electricity Act 2003. Between 1999 and 2013, the net worth of Reliance-owned Odisha discoms eroded by 6.5 times and the debt capital increased by 10 times.[30] In the three distribution zones in which Reliance operated, despite the presence of high number of high-tension (HT) and extra high-tension (EHT) consumers, they were mired with financial and operational inefficiencies, barring the period from 2005 to 2007. The negative net worth and the resultant increasing debt capital was the consequence of inadequate capital investments from their own sources,[31] which was a clear contravention from the terms and conditions of privatization during the reforms.[32] Reliance sought relaxation of escrow terms several times as they were not able to earn and towards the end of 2013, owed Rs 2,649.95 crores in dues to GRIDCO. The discoms' losses increased substantially after both the state and central governments introduced new measures from 2007 onward to finance network expansion. Discom finances further deteriorated owing to the simultaneous rise of captive power units by EHT consumers.

This affected GRIDCO's financial viability as well, which borrowed heavily from state government and other financial institutions to pay generators. The burden was on the private discoms to increase their collection efficiency, decrease distribution losses through investments, and make system improvements through implementing administrative checks and balances. The discoms' precarious conditions exempted them from reaping the benefits of loans from financial institutions, and hence they resorted to the stubborn demand to relax escrow terms.[33] Ultimately, OERC charged Reliance with wilful default of escrow arrangements and highly unsatisfactory performance in areas such as energy audit, repair and maintenance of lines, and billing inefficiency. For their part, the discoms have invariably blamed inadequate governmental support. However, because funding by the state government had never been a precondition for privatization, and because they were supposed to make capital investments from their own sources to improve the system, the discoms' arguments about the lack of governmental support and inadequacy of tariff revisions were deemed hollow by the Commission. In 2015, Reliance filed a counter petition with the Supreme Court citing erroneous tariff setting as a major hurdle for discom performance. The matter is sub judice as of August 2017.

In 2015, OERC handed over the management of all three discoms to GRIDCO. The Managing Director of GRIDCO is the administrator of all utilities, in some sense re-inaugurating the model of vertically integrated, state-owned utilities that Odisha was the first state to reject. As of now, the four distribution companies owe Rs 5,000 crore to GRIDCO for bulk power supply, leaving it in deep financial crisis.

The Rise of Franchisees: The most Recent Experiment in Institutional Decentralization

In Odisha, the massive expansion of rural electrification beginning in 2007 served as a key motivation for state utilities to explore distribution franchising. Given the fact that rural electrification was supported by funds from RGGVY and BGJY, low tension sales increased by 46 per cent in WESCO, 39 per cent in CESU, 29 per cent in SOUTHCO, and 11.9 per cent in NESCO from 2012 to 2016 (OERC 2016).[34] All of these gains to grid expansion and household electrification took place without an adequate mechanism in place to ensure the requisite billing and collection. Even though the efficacy of the franchisee model is still under debate,[35] it has been implemented in several states, including Maharashtra, Bihar, and Uttar Pradesh. The Input Based Franchisees with Incremental Revenue Sharing (IBF-IRS) Model was used in Odisha with the hope that it would bring an infusion of capital and upgrading of the system in territories that have had a history of financial laxity. Franchisees were expected to perform three key roles: make CAPEX and operating expenditure (OPEX) investments, improve operational efficiency, and institute a grievance redressal system.

As the consumer strength of CESU increased from 4 lakhs in 2005 to 16 lakhs by 2012, energy sales increased and it was imperative to upgrade network infrastructure. The history of unsustainable financial health forced the discom to consider OERC's recommendation that franchisees be inducted into the system on the basis of the IBF-IRS model. At the time of these deliberations in 2011–12, the discom's cumulative loss was approximately 1,500 crores and the ATC losses hovered around 50 per cent. CESU declared that it lacked adequate cash to invest in activities like metering, aerial bundled cabling, and automated meter reading systems. Citing the recommendations from the Shunglu Commission Report of 2010, CESU decided that the extra revenue generated from franchising would be shared between CESU and prospective franchisees in a mutually agreed ratio.

In 2012, three franchise operators—FEDCO, RUPL, and ENZEN—were taken onboard to cater primarily to the rural consumer base within the CESU area. They were charged with overseeing the quality of service, ensuring revenue returns, and attending to consumer needs.[36] FEDCO and ENZEN had prior experience in Odisha. While FEDCO worked as consultants to the government of Odisha on implementation of the franchisee model for billing and collection, ENZEN previously had taken subdivisions from Reliance to look after metering, billing collection, and overall customer services from 2008 to 2012.

An earlier input-based distribution franchise model was first adopted in Bhiwandi, Maharashtra, in 2007. Odisha found its own unique way of franchising, keeping in view its distinct sectoral needs. While Bhiwandi is an industrial area (ensuring consistent revenue in a contracted period spanning ten years), in Odisha, the IBF-IRS model was brought into loss-making pockets of the central utility for a period of five years to encourage the franchisee to improve performance over time.

The equation between CESU and its franchisee hinges on three factors—limited autonomy of the franchisee over decisions on crucial expenditures, no provision for ownership of distribution assets irrespective of their investment, and performance-based incentive conditional on meeting yearly targets.

The extra revenue earned over the base year provided would be shared on a 60:40 basis; 60 per cent of the revenue remains with the franchisee and 40 per cent with CESU. During the initial bidding, financial parameters weighed heavily over the technical or operational parameters. The franchisees agreed to bring in CAPEX, OPEX, and metering, and to set a target to reduce AT&C losses to 15 per cent within 60 months.

Three years after their operation, the average ATC losses have come down hardly by 6 per cent as of 2016–17. Over several interviews with CESU, there was a general consensus that franchisees have significantly improved billing efficiency from around 50 per cent in 2011–12 to about 70 per cent in 2016–17. Similarly, collection efficiency has improved from around 90 per cent in 2011–12 to around 99 per cent as of FY 2016. However, they could not bring down losses uniformly in all divisions.

Franchisees were supposed to invest a total of at least 750 crores in five years. By now they should have invested at least 400 crores. According to a senior manager in CESU, as of early 2017, the franchisees have invested only 50 crores total, which is only 10.5 per cent of the expected amount. However, FEDCO claimed to have invested approximately 93–4 crores towards CAPEX as of 2016.[37]

There is considerable variation in the functioning of the three franchisees. Whereas RUPL is running losses, FEDCO has fared well, with huge success in the Nayagarh division. The ENZEN is barely managing revenue returns. The difference in revenue generation has been attributed to temperament of the consumers and conduciveness to function without political interference. In Nayagarh, consumers were said to be prompt in paying their dues, whereas consumers in Puri and Khorda had resisted the presence of FEDCO. By involving previously existing local bodies for collection activities, FEDCO could secure its services at the local level, while ENZEN's negotiations with local organizations has been less successful.

From the perspective of the franchisees, successful operations require strong governmental support. Even greater is the challenge to break the collusion of political mafia with the local people. As long as technology operates with human intervention, the state and institutions of governance must work together to bring about a sense of responsibility in consumer practices. Franchisees must work together with CESU to synchronize field data across divisions and overcome CESU's shortcomings in documentation.

Impending Developments in the Sector: The Way Ahead

The future of the power sector will necessarily engage with the growing importance of renewable energy. In the previous decade, when Odisha had a surplus of hydropower and solar power costs were much higher than conventional sources, there was little motivation within the state to compel a comprehensive plan for harnessing power from nonconventional sources. To meet its Renewable Purchase Obligation (RPO) compliance, 57 MW of power is harnessed from micro hydro projects and 20 MW from biomass. A total of 140 MW of renewable energy is harnessed by Odisha as of now. A policy document for accelerated development of solar energy in the state was released in 2013. Between 2010 and 2016, a couple of schemes under Odisha Renewable Energy Development Agency (OREDA) have been purchased but most of the policy initiatives for solar energy are yet to be implemented.[38] The RPO percentage is around 4.5 per cent, which according to senior utility and government officials is a substantial increase from the 1 per cent compliance in 2011–12. Of the 4.5 per cent, only 1.5 per cent is from solar and 3 per cent is from non-solar, which includes wind, hydro, biomass, solid waste, and so on.[39] Currently, the government has mandated all government buildings of the twin cities—Cuttack and Bhubaneswar—to install rooftop solar panels and bidirectional meters to push surplus power into the system.

It seems this has been a point of contention for the discoms. The distribution companies would lose out on consumers who are on the 'economically higher side' if the latter chose to adopt renewables and the discoms would be left with consumers with lower consumption slab.[40] Hence, the rise of renewable energy would increase competition and the lack of a guidelines would challenge the commercial interests of the discoms.

***

At the crux of reforms lay attempts by the government to dissociate itself from managerial and financial obligations of a utility. The attempts unfolded through transfer of power to private entities then to the energy-police mechanism and eventually to ushering in franchisees. The alleged lack of political will could be attributed to the absence of political competition. Spanning four terms, the BJD government under Naveen Patnaik has parried the questions of sustenance of discoms, while offering to enable access across the marginalized communities. Loss attributable to theft is far from being addressed.

The Energy police station set-up to monitor theft has been dismantled for logistical reasons. Over the decades, the political leadership has failed to put the idea of energy access within the larger political economic regime it espouses, by equating it to blind entitlement. Even as we talk of Access, under current circumstances the discoms are functionally public utilities, having failed to convince private entities to invest in the discoms.

It is deemed that a reduction in 1 per cent loss would help discoms gain 80 crores. In Odisha, steps were being taken by OERC to manage the increasing demand through implementation of Intra State ABT in 2012, with the objective of minimizing the fluctuations in frequency that arise from disorderly withdrawal of power. However, the discoms are wanting in infrastructure for better real-time analysis and forecasting.

For all the talk of successful rural electrification, the chronically backward regions and communities are yet to have quality access to electricity, and rural areas bear the brunt of demand-side management.

Notes and References

1. OERC, *Annual Revenue Requirement and Tariff Orders for FY 1998*, http://www.orierc.org/Orders/1998/C-19-1998.htm (accessed on 6 April 2018).

2. S.S. Kale, *Electrifying India* (California: Stanford University Press, 2014), 110–13. Kale talks about the dichotomy between actual socioeconomic reality and the developmental agenda pursued. Odisha is notably socio-economically backward with predominant dependence on agriculture. But the route to development has been industrialization.

3. Kale, *Electrifying India*.

4. *Odisha Agriculture Statistics, 2013–14*, Government of Odisha, 16. http://agriodisha.nic.in/content/pdf/Agriculture%20Statistics_2013-14.pdf

5. OERC, *Odisha Power Sector—At a Glance* (Bhubaneswar, 2011) also available at http://www.orierc.org/Status_of_Power_Sector_of_Orissa_Till_Sept_2011_-_Final.pdf (accessed on 14 April 2018).

6. OERC, *Odisha Power Sector—At a Glance*.

7. Government of India, *Annual Report on the Working of State Power Utilities and Electricity Departments* (Planning Commission, 2011, 13). (Notes: The argument about manual documentation was based on the blog post by Anish De, Partner and Head, Strategy and Operation Management, KPMG, India [on first hand experiences of having worked through the Reform process of the Orissa Model] on LinkedIn).

8. S. Mishra, 'Power Sector Reforms in India: A Critical Appraisal of Orissa's Reforms Experience' (PhD dissertation, Utkal University, Bhubaneswar).

9. Kale, *Electrifying India*.

10. OERC, *Odisha Power Sector—At a Glance*.

11. B. Mishra, 'Agriculture, Industry and Mining in Orissa in the Post-Liberalisation Era: An Inter-District and Inter-State Panel Analysis', *Economic and Political Weekly* xlv(2), 2010: 53; M. Mohanty, 'Persisting Dominance: Crisis of Democracy in a Resource-rich Region', *Economic and Political Weekly* xlix(14), 2014: 39.

12. Interview, Birendra Nayak, 10 September 2016. Nayak mentions how in the 1980s, J.B. Pattnaik of the Congress talked about 1,000 industries worth 1,000 crores in 1,000 days. The present Chief Minister talked about 1,000 start-ups in five years. He pointed out that there is 'absolute continuity' in the political economy. 'The changes are only rhetorical due to technology coming in.'

13. Interview, K.C. Pujari, Retd. Chief Engineer, OSEB, 13 August 2016.

14. Interview, Birendra Nayak, 10 September 2016, and interview, ex-regulator of OERC, 12 September 2016.

15. Mohanty, 'Persisting Dominance'.

16. S. Mahalingam, 'The Unravelling of the Reform Experiment in Orissa: A Case of Facile Assumptions, Glaring Fallacies, and Unrealistic Targets', Presented in the Event on the Power Sector Reforms, organised by Prayas and Focus on the Global South, Mumbai, India, December 2000.

17. Government of India, *Annual Report on the Working of State Power Utilities and Electricity Departments* (Planning Commission, 2011).
18. Interview, Priyabrata Pattnaik, Chairman OERC, 9 September 2016.
19. Interview, Faruk Garari, Enzen Global Solutions, 22 November 2016.
20. OERC, *Odisha Power Sector–At a Glance*. An analysis of the financial statements of all the power utilities operating in Odisha revealed the same.
21. OERC, *Odisha Power Sector—At a Glance*.
22. OERC, *Odisha Power Sector—At a Glance*, 143.
23. DDUGJY, 'Status of Rural Electrification in Odisha', Table III A, http:// garv.gov.in/assets/uploads/reports/statesnaps/Odisha.pdf (accessed on 6 April 2018).
24. OERC, *Odisha Power Sector—At a Glance*, 453.
25. Government to Stand Guarantee on Gridco Loan, *The New Indian Express*, 4 December 2011, http://govtpress.odisha.gov.in/pdf/2010/488.pdf
26. Government of Odisha, *Economic Survey of Odisha* (2014), 257.
27. Odisha Electricity Regulatory Commission, *Determination of Procurement Price of CGPs* (2009).
28. OERC, *Annual Revenue Requirement and Tariff Orders* (2010), 103.
29. Interview, Chandrasekhar Sahoo, Inspector in charge, Energy Police Station, 2 August 2016.
30. OERC, *Annual Revenue Requirement and Tariff Orders for FY 2015–16* (Bhubaneswar, 2011), 465 (the accumulated losses of the discoms eroded their net worth and because power companies are heavily capital intensive, the heavy dependence of the discoms on debt capital increased their debt capital by almost 10 times).
31. OERC, *Odisha Power Sector—At a Glance*, 390.
32. OERC, *Annual Revenue Requirement and Tariff Orders for FY 2015–16*, 461.
33. OERC, *Annual Revenue Requirement and Tariff Orders for FY 2015–16*.
34. Annual Retail Tariff Order for the year 2016–17 published by Orissa Electricity Regulatory Commission. Available http://www.orierc.org/ order.html (accessed on April 14 2018).
35. For our understanding, we have drawn significantly from participants to connect the dots in the franchisee story.
36. Central Electricity Supply Utility, *Engagement of Input Based Franchisees with Incremental Revenue Sharing (IBF-IRS) Model in Fifteen Divisions of CESU* (Bhubaneswar, 2012) also available http://www.cescoorissa.com/franchisee/Base_Paper.pdf (accessed on 15–18 November 2016).
37. Interview, Manoj Singh, Senior General Manager, AT&C Cell, CESU, 17 August 2016.
38. Interview, P.K. Pradhan, Retired Finance Manager, GRIDCO, 24 August 2016.

39. GRIDCO, *Status of Renewable Energy, Odisha*, 3 February 2016. Document presented before the CM by GRIDCO.

40. Interview, Manoj Singh, General Manager, AT&C Cell, CESU, 17 August 2016.

10

ASHWINI K. SWAIN

Protecting Power

The Politics of Partial Reforms in Punjab

Punjab's power sector, known for its agricultural embeddedness and chronic subsidy challenges, was one of the least attractive and pragmatic choices for reform advocates. Considering a feeble external push and forceful internal resistance, the state has undertaken partial electricity reforms to comply with legislative mandates from the central government. Despite limited reforms, Punjab has made substantive progress on electricity access, quality of supply, and some operational efficiencies. It was one of the first states to achieve universal household access, and has a per capita consumption nearly double the national average. While pioneering agricultural electricity subsidies, the state also has targeted subsidies to half of its households, especially those from socially and economically weaker sections. Expedited generation capacity expansion has enabled Punjab to overcome power shortage and improve quality and reliability of supply for consumers. However, these successes came with their own costs, and have created new lock-ins in the sector. Unsolicited yet unbridled populism has been straining the state exchequer, though part of these costs is gradually being passed on to consumers as electricity duty. Additionally, stagnant industrial loads, costs of unutilized generation capacity, and delayed subsidy disbursement have been pulling down an otherwise well-performing distribution utility (discom). In 2016, Punjab joined the central government's Ujwal Discom Assurance Yojana (UDAY), seeking to turn around its discom's finances.

This chapter analyses how the power sector has evolved in Punjab, especially through institutional restructuring and policy reforms, with the objective to examine the policy choices, outcomes, winners, and losers at the state level. It analyses the political–economic drivers for these policy choices and how they deviate from or comply with signals from the central government. Building on these findings, it also discusses the implications of past experiences and prevailing power dynamics for ongoing and future reforms.

Despite its small size, Punjab holds an important position in India's economy and politics. Building on the success of the Green Revolution and subsequent agricultural growth, by 1993–4 Punjab recorded the highest per capita income among major states, and held this position for a decade. However, Punjab failed to gain from economic liberalization,[1,2] and subsequent declines in agricultural growth and the economy caused the state to slip to the tenth position by 2014–15.[3] Land shortage, land-locked geography, lack of industrial labour, and overpriced and unreliable industrial electricity supply not only restricted the entry of new industries into Punjab, but also constrained the expansion of existing industries. Consequently, the industrial sector's contribution to Net State Value Added (NSVA) has been declining consistently in Punjab. By 2014–15, industrial activity accounted for 22 per cent of NSVA, whereas the agriculture and service sectors contributed 29 per cent and 49 per cent respectively.[4]

The state has experienced equal amounts of political dynamism over the last five decades. It was one of the first states to have a non-Congress government as early as 1967. Aside from several periods of President's Rule in the 1980s, politics from 1992 onwards have reflected a healthy electoral competition between the Indian National Congress (INC) and the Shiromani Akali Dal (SAD).[5] Following low voter turnout in the 1992 elections, all of the state's parties prioritized cadre building through distributive politics and populism, thus undermining economic policymaking and institutional consolidation. Moreover, the state has been through social turmoil, terrorism, and civil disorder in 1990s and drug abuse from late 2000s onwards, that have dominated the political and policy space. While the state has followed central policy guidelines,[6] the lack of state-level thinking and adaptation and the dysfunctionality of public institutions compromised its ability to make policy changes suitable to local dynamics.[7] The legacy of agricultural success has limited political decisions to diversify to the secondary sector. From the early 2010s, political will and efforts to promote private industries in the state have been constrained by corruption and rent-seeking that became entrenched during the decade without an elected state government.[8]

Despite sluggish industrial growth, Punjab has seen striking growth in its electricity generation capacity. With 14,178 megawatts (MW) of installed capacity, it accounts for 4.3 per cent of national capacity. The electricity grid has been extended to all villages, connecting all households and 12.7 lakh irrigation pumps. Universal access is ensured through the state sponsorship of monthly 200 kilo watt hour (kWh) free power to more than half of the population, including those belonging to Below Poverty Line (BPL), scheduled caste (SC), and other backward class (OBC) households, and daily eight hours of free power supply is given to all agricultural connections. 'Urban pattern supply' to rural consumers has been ensured by separating agricultural feeders from rural feeders. Consequently, Punjab has recorded the highest per capita electricity consumption among states: in 2014–15, consumption was 1,858 kWh, compared to the national average of 1,010 kWh.[9]

The state has a balanced consumer mix; in 2014–15, industrial consumers accounted for 34 per cent of consumption, followed by domestic consumers (28 per cent), agricultural consumers (26 per cent), and others (12 per cent).[10] Expectedly, industries contribute the largest share of revenue (Figure 10.1). The state government pays for the cross-subsidized cost of free power.[11] Punjab has a peculiar annual load curve, with peak summer demand being almost four times that of off-peak winter demand.[12] Unlike many discoms catering to large rural and agricultural demands, Punjab State Power Corporation Limited (PSPCL) has achieved moderate operational efficiency. Aggregate technical and commercial (AT&C) loss has been below the national average (Figure 10.2), and PSPCL has recorded high collection efficiency, at 98 per cent in 2014–15.[13] As a result, the gap between average cost of supply (ACS) and average revenue realized (ARR) has gradually been alleviated. Following small profits over two years, PSPCL again plunged into commercial loss in 2014–15 (Figure 10.2), mainly attributed to gaps in subsidy disbursement. Otherwise, between 2007–8 and

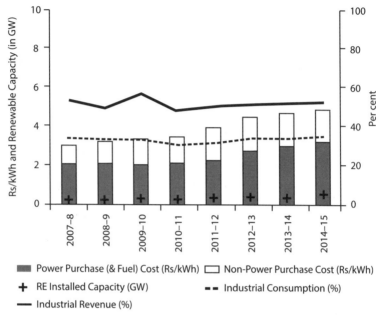

FIGURE 10.1   Physical and Financial Profile: Punjab
Source: CSO. *Energy Statistics*. New Delhi: Central Statistics Office, Ministry of
Statistics and Programme Implementation, Government of India, 2010, 2012,
2014, and 2016; PFC. *Reports on Performance of State Power Utilities*. New Delhi:
Power Finance Corporation Limited, 2011, 2013, 2015, and 2016.

2014–15, ACS has increased by 60 per cent (Figure 10.1), largely driven
by rises in power purchases, employees, and interest costs. The PSPCL
has a higher non-power purchase cost (as a share of ACS) compared to
most discoms. In 2014–15, interest costs accounted for more than 10
per cent of total expenditure.[14] The utility received a 'B+' grade in the
Fifth Annual Integrated Rating of Distribution Utilities, which implies
'moderate operational and financial performance capability'.[15,16]

Punjab remained averse to economic reforms until the late 1990s.
While many other states had initiated reforms by this time, Punjab was
grappling with terrorism, political instability, and vote-bank politics.
However, faced with a rising fiscal deficit, in 1999 the Government of
Punjab (GoP) and Government of India (GoI) agreed on fiscal reforms,
followed by the creation of various committees and commissions to look
into the problems of revenue mobilization, expenditure management,

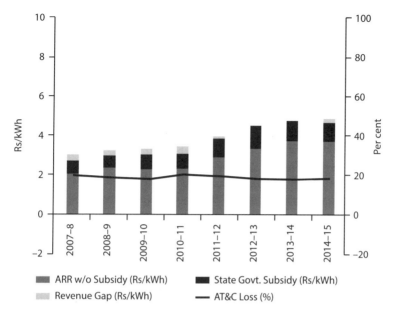

FIGURE **10.2** Supply-side Costs and Revenue Recovery: Punjab
Source: PFC, *Reports on Performance of State Power Utilities*. New Delhi: Power
Finance Corporation Limited, 2011, 2013, 2015, and 2016.

and state public sector enterprises (SPSEs). As the largest SPSE, Punjab
State Electricity Board (PSEB) received extensive attention. The following sections discuss the evolution of the electricity sector in Punjab over
three periods (See Table 10.1 for a chronology of power sector events
in the state).

TABLE **10.1** Timeline of Key Events: Punjab

State Politics	Year	Power Sector Events
• State Assembly Election: SAD Government; Parkash Singh Badal as Chief Minister (CM)	1997	• Free power for agriculture • 50 kWh/month free power for SC households
• *GoP signs MoU with GoI to promote fiscal reforms in the state*	1999	• PSERC established
	2001	• GoP signs MoU with GoI to expedite power reforms

(Cont'd)

TABLE 10.1   *(Cont'd)*

State Politics	Year	Power Sector Events
• State Assembly Election: INC Government; Amarinder Singh as CM • *Directorate of Disinvestment Established under the Department of Finance*	2002	• PSERC issues first retail tariff order • Free power for agriculture is removed; flat-rate-tariff restored
	2003	• Report of the Expert Group on Power Sector Reforms in Punjab
	2005	• Punjab Electricity (Duty) Act, 2005 • PSERC (Conduct of Business) Regulations • PSERC (Forum and Ombudsman) Regulations • 'Energy Bonus' scheme for small farmers is proposed and scrapped before coming into force • Free power for agriculture restored
	2006	• Free power to SC households is increased to 200 kWh/month
• State Assembly Election: SAD Government; Parkash Singh Badal as CM	2007	• PSEB fails to file annual revenue requirement petition; PSERC issues a *suo moto* tariff order • Free power of 200 kWh/month to non-SC BPL households
• Sukhbir Singh Badal joins state government as Deputy CM, in charge of Power Department	2009	• PSERC (Harnessing of Captive Power Generation) Regulations
	2010	• Unbundling of PSEB into PSTCL and PSPCL • Power Generation Policy • PSPCL files first annual revenue requirement petition for 2011–12

(Cont'd)

TABLE 10.1 *(Cont'd)*

State Politics	Year	Power Sector Events
	2011	• PSERC (RPO and its Compliance) Regulation • PSERC (Terms and Conditions of Intra-State Open Access) Regulation
• State Assembly Election: SAD Government; Parkash Singh Badal as CM; Sukhbir Singh Badal as Deputy CM, in charge of Power Department	2012	• PSERC (DSM) Regulation • New and Renewable Sources of Energy Policy
• Emergence of AAP as a third political alternative in Punjab in 16th general election	2014	• Policy on net metering for Grid Interactive Roof-Top Solar Photo Voltaic Power Plants • PSERC (Electricity Supply Code and Related Matters) Regulations
	2015	• Farmers Solar Power Scheme • PSERC (Grid Interactive Rooftop Solar Photo Voltaic Systems based on Net Metering) Regulations
	2016	• Punjab joins 24×7 Power for All initiative • Punjab joins UDAY • Reduction in industrial tariff, elimination of PLEC, but open access surcharge is increased • Free power of 200 kWh to OBC households
• State Assembly Election: INC Government; Amarinder Singh as CM	2017	• CMD of PSPCL resigns and Principal Secretary (Power), GoP assumes charge • Chairman of PSERC resigns

Source: Author.

Populism, Free Power, and Financial Decline of PSEB (1992–8)

The PSEB was set up in 1959 and was later revamped in 1967, following the state's reorganization.[17] Punjab, at its birth, was ahead of many states in electrical development, with 553 MW of installed capacity (while national capacity was 9,027 MW in 1966),[18] nearly 40 per cent of villages electrified (while national average was below 25 per cent),[19] and a per capita consumption one-and-half times higher than national average.[20] At this point, Punjab received most of its power from cheap hydropower sources and enjoyed a significant amount of surplus,[21] which in turn enabled it to pursue intensive rural electrification in following years.

In 1976, Punjab became the second state (after Haryana) to achieve 100 per cent village electrification, and most households were electrified by the late 1990s.[22] Adoption of Green Revolution farming techniques increased agricultural electricity demands to draw groundwater. Irrigation pumps were energized expeditiously, especially from the 1960s onward; the number of electrified tube wells reached 800,000 by the late 1990s, surpassing the estimated ultimate potential in the state.[23] This was further bolstered by Punjab's pioneering step in 1968 to remove meters from agricultural connections and simply charge a flat-rate tariff on the basis of pump capacity. While critics considered the measure to be regressive and punitive as it would benefit rich farmers more,[24] advocates, including international development agencies, defended the move on the grounds that metering geographically dispersed agricultural connections was not economically viable.[25] As agricultural demand ballooned year after year, the flat-rate tariff failed to reflect the rising costs of supply.

The state's heavily agrarian economy required electricity access in farms in order to draw groundwater, a key input for the success of the Green Revolution. The initial success of agriculture-led economic growth justified aggressive pump energization in the state. A flat-rate tariff system was also economically justifiable in the prevailing context, as it reduced operational burdens and costs of the PSEB, and was also backed by an emerging global narrative. The alleged economic measure was later politically misappropriated to create a vote-bank of farmers. However, rapid village electrification and pump energization were

enabled by supply-side characteristics of the sector, especially the availability of cheap surplus power. Moreover, the state's economic prosperity allowed it to invest more in the sector.[26]

By the 1990s, the sector began displaying signs of a looming crisis.
Though Punjab had increased its installed capacity by nearly 10 times
over this period, it started facing chronic seasonal shortages during
summer; peak power deficits during the 1990s hovered around 10 per
cent. The Board catered to the peak demand from agricultural consumers by load-shedding to industrial consumers, in keeping with Punjab's
prioritization of agriculture over industry. While transmission and
distribution losses (in the range of 17–18 per cent) were among the lowest, total cost recovery was between 65–80 per cent. By 1992–3, PSEB
recorded a commercial loss of Rs 600 crores, which increased to Rs 900
crores by 1997–8. By 1996–7, the gross subsidy burden on PSEB was
Rs 1,200 crores, largely comprising of subsidies to agriculture (Rs 1,000
crores) and households (Rs 200 crores). While a small part of this total
(Rs 300 crores) was mitigated through cross-subsidy, the state government did not provide any direct subvention, leaving PSEB with a net
subsidy burden of Rs 900 crores.[27]

Despite the financial crisis in the sector, the 1997 state assembly elections featured promises of free power supply to agricultural connections. After poor voter turnout in the 1992 elections, political parties
sought to build support from the strong and mobilized peasantry class by
offering electoral freebies, including subsidized electricity supply. After
coming to power in 1997, the SAD government immediately ensured
free power supply to all agricultural connections and provided 50 kWh/
month free power to SC households (which comprise more than 30 per
cent of Punjab's population, the highest percentage in the country).[28]
Subsequently, PSEB's subsidy burden rose to Rs 1600 crores (gross) and
Rs 1,300 crores (net), pushing it into further financial degeneration.

A Decade of Reform Planning, Resistances, and Status Quo (1999–2009)

By 1999, Punjab's finance was in a depleted state. Overdrafts with the
Reserve Bank of India reached a peak and the state was in dire need of
the central government's assistance.[29] In that backdrop, GoP signed a
comprehensive MoU with GoI, seeking to promote fiscal reforms in the

state. The agreement between the two governments was facilitated by a political alliance between SAD and the Bharatiya Janata Party (BJP) at the centre and the state. The power sector, accounting for a major share of SPSEs in size and investment, received priority in reform planning. As an initial step to reforms, the state government established the Punjab State Electricity Regulatory Commission (PSERC) in March 1999. In 2001, GoP signed an MoU with the central Ministry of Power to expedite power reforms, with the objective that PSEB would break even by the end of March 2003. In the absence of external pressure (from organizations like World Bank), these symbolic developments in Punjab were seen as an outcome of pressure and persuasion from SAD's ally in the central government as well as an emulation of Haryana, a first mover on both fronts. However, neither PSERC performed its core functions, nor the targets of the 2001 MoU were pursued. The 2002 state assembly elections saw a change of power; despite its populist moves, SAD lost the election, and INC formed the government. The new government not only carried forward the reform agenda, but also took some substantive measures immediately after coming to power; PSERC issued its first retail tariff order in 2002. The Commission, on the state government's advice, discontinued free power supply to agriculture and restored flat-rate tariffs, while raising tariffs for other consumers. However, the free power for SC households was continued. An expert committee, headed by Gajendra Haldea, was appointed in the same year to prepare a power sector reform plan for Punjab.

The Expert Committee's report, replicating proposals of the Electricity Bill 2001, suggested that unbundling of PSEB, corporatization, and privatization of utilities was necessary, but not enough. The committee stressed the need to promote open access for real competition (thus attracting private investment in the sector), phase out cross-subsidies in a timely manner, target subsidies for social objectives, and rationalize tariffs.[30] The report received widespread media coverage and was perceived as GoP's plan of action for the power sector, thereby making electricity reforms a public concern.

Though it caused some degree of public discontent, the 2002 tariff order interestingly did not result in mass agitation. A possible explanation for this could be the low share of electricity costs, at flat-rate tariff, in total input costs for farming. Moreover, by this time, Punjab's farmers were shifting away from demands for input services, instead demanding a higher minimum support price that would be reflective of increasing input costs.[31] On the other hand, marginal tariff hikes for household consumers seemed to have little impacts on high-income households, while the poorest continued to receive some amount of free supply. However, the reform plans faced strong resistance from employees' unions, predominantly from the PSEB Engineers' Association (PSEBEA). The PSEBEA claimed that the desired operational efficiencies could be achieved without structural reforms and privatization, while employees were worried about the likely degradation of service conditions and benefits following privatization. Simultaneously, there was a fear that unbundling would split the union and reduce their political clout.[32] In its opposition to reforms, PSEBEA managed to mobilize other employee unions and some farmer groups. As the idea of privatization was losing support in the face of this resistance, GoP deferred unbundling of the Board, which was by then made mandatory for Indian states under the Electricity Act 2003. In a desperate move to avoid a political backlash in the upcoming elections, the INC government restored free power for agriculture in 2005 and increased the free power allocation for SC households to 200 kWh/month in 2006. However, INC lost the 2007 elections and SAD returned to power in the state. Seeking to pursue institutional restructuring, the SAD government tried to negotiate with the PSEBEA, but without much success.

Despite a high-level agreement (from both SAD and Congress governments) and the central government's push, institutional restructuring was resisted mainly by PSEB employees. Nevertheless, the state managed to achieve multiple transformations in distribution infrastructure and consumer experience, utilizing central assistance under various schemes. During this period, there was a modest increase in state-owned generation capacity. Demand growth had mostly levelled out, as most of the household demand was already met at the beginning of the period and industrial demand was almost stagnant. Yet, the seasonal deficit continued, along with unreliability in the industrial supply. Under the Rajiv Gandhi Grameen Vidyutikaran Yojana, by providing electricity access to the remaining unelectrified household, Punjab became the first state to achieve universal household access. The state also extended 200 kWh/month of free power to BPL households, and the separation of rural feeders from agricultural feeders resulted in improved supply to rural households. Relocation of meters outside household premises helped to check pilferage by household consumers. The consumer complaint-handling process was modernized, with call centre facilities.

During this decade, although the state failed to accomplish centre-prescribed structural reforms, PSEB made a progressive move towards desired outcomes like universal access, round-the-clock supply, and loss reduction. Punjab's inability to implement institutional reforms, despite repeated reminders from the centre, pushed it to pursue the central government's transmission and distribution network strengthening schemes[33] to display some degree of compliance. On the other hand, successful implementation of these schemes was the only way PSEB engineers could have proved PSEBEA's position that efficiency gains could be achieved without unbundling. Moreover, given that Punjab had already achieved the electrification goals which continue to be political focus in most other states, it could afford to prioritize the consumer experience of electricity service.

Institutional Restructuring and Consolidation of Political Control (2010–17)

After seeking 13 extensions from the central government, the SAD government finally unbundled the erstwhile PSEB in April 2010. The central Ministry of Power, in its letters to the state government, had been sending clear signals that Punjab would forfeit central assistance to the sector unless it complied with legislative mandates. Having benefited from various central schemes to consolidate its distribution network, GoP could not risk losing central funding. Two corporations were carved out of the Board: PSPCL retained the major part of the business involving generation and distribution, while Punjab State Transmission Corporation Limited (PSTCL) received the transmission business. All of PSEB's generation and distribution assets, liabilities, and staff were retained by the PSPCL. The PSTCL received the ownership of the transmission infrastructure and was operated by a dedicated management.[34]

Though the unbundling was a compromise of desired restructuring, it catered to many interests. Unbundling protected the PSEBEA's interests by keeping all of the PSEB staff under one corporation and retaining service conditions. On the other hand, it has also allowed the state government to have firm control over the sector. Both corporations are now managed by a separate Board of Directors, directly appointed by the government without a proper process and tenure.

Following the restructuring, there has been a boom in private sector participation in electricity generation. From a lack of any private sector participation at the time of unbundling, the private sector now accounts for 45 per cent of Punjab's capacity. However, this is an outcome of shifts in state politics and changes in economic policy rather than restructuring of the sector. With the induction of Sukhbir Singh Badal[35] into state politics in 2009, the developmental approach of the state shifted away from only agriculture. Badal has been instrumental in developing a vision and strategy for industrial promotion and agricultural diversification in the state, which were long overdue. The new leadership recognized that availability and reliability of power supply are necessary to attract industrial investment to the state. In the Industrial Policy of 2009, with the stated objective to make Punjab a power surplus state and ensure reliable power supply to industries, the GoP proposed to add six new power plants of 7,520 MW generation capacity under private sector ownership.[36] Keeping the objective intact, through a Power Generation Policy issued in 2010, the GoP revised the ambitious target to three plants adding up 3,840 MW generation capacity.[37] While most state governments have restricted their policies to setting broad goals for capacity addition and offering incentives for IPPs, GoP went overboard to specify the quantum, ownership, technology and location of the generation capacity to be added. Eventually, the state has achieved the revised target, while bagging 1,819 MW capacity from six other IPPs outside the state.

Capacity addition as a way out of the power availability crisis received support from both the older and younger generations of leaders in the SAD government. While the former supported it for catering the peak agricultural demand, the latter saw capacity addition as a prerequisite for industrial promotion. On the other hand, critics point to the possibilities of corruption in independent power producer (IPP) promotion and private capacity utilization.[38]

On the positive side, additional capacity has ensured service quality improvements. Since 2014, all consumers have been ensured round-the-clock supply, while agricultural connections have been ensured reliable eight hour/day supply. However, there are many adverse consequences.

Besides additional costs for the strapped discom, surplus capacity has emerged as a barrier for demand-side management, open access, and renewable energy deployment, jeopardizing facilitating regulations from PSERC. In 2015–16, fixed charges paid by PSPCL for unutilized capacity accounted for 12 per cent of its revenue requirement for the year.[39] Renewable energy deployment has been stalled as there is no need for more power.[40] Demand-side management is not included in the state's policy goals, owing to high marginal costs; rather, the focus is on increasing demand. Open access has been discouraged through prohibitive surcharges to retain high-paying consumers with utility.[41] Moreover, high-cost, long-term power purchase agreements with coal-fired private plants have locked the state into expensive power procurement, while it is forced to surrender its share in lower-cost central generating stations.[42]

Despite emergent financial burdens, populism was sustained and flourished throughout the reforms. In the 2017 state assembly elections, there was a consensus among the three leading contenders (Aam Aadmi Party, Congress, and SAD) on free power supply. Prior to the elections, the ruling SAD government extended 200 kWh/month free power to OBC households.[43] Despite pioneering free power for farmers and SC households in 1997, SAD lost the elections in 2002. Similarly, restoration of free power after a brief pause and the enlargement of subsidies for SC households did not help Congress in winning the 2007 elections. Yet, unsolicited populism continues, even without any organized demand for it. During the 2017 assembly elections, all of the parties promised to not only continue the subsidies, but to extend the quantum. While, farmers are demanding high quality power, that quality remains only in rhetoric.

The paradox of unsolicited populism can partly be explained by the limits of state capacity and the options that state governments have to assist farmers. Farmers' demands are organized around better minimum support price (MSP), improved procurement conditions, better access to institutional credits, and input subsidies. Most of these items—including MSP, a large part of food procurement, fertilizer subsidies, and conditions for institutional credit—are under the jurisdiction of the central government, where the state government has a very limited role. States, including Punjab, have offered loan waivers for farmers and attempted to improve market linkages, but without much success. The electricity subsidy, in this context, appears to be most tangible giveaway. Moreover, the burden of this subsidy on the state government is not as large as it has been perceived. In 2014–15, GoP recovered about 70 per cent of the subsidies disbursed to PSPCL, in the form of electricity duty and cess.[44]

Despite efficiency gains, PSPCL had accumulated a debt of Rs 20,800 crores as of September 2015,[45] accounting for more than 15 per cent of the state's total outstanding liabilities.[46] Seeking a way out, in May 2016, Punjab joined UDAY, with the aim to achieve a financial turnaround for PSPCL. Sceptics continue to express doubts about the outcome of this scheme as well as the intent of the state government. In 2012, Punjab declined to join the Financial Restructuring Plan as it was offering central incentives based on actual performance. However, the advance incentive offered under UDAY may have been a driver for joining the scheme.[47]

Defying the objective of institutional autonomy and limited government interference, restructuring has rather consolidated state control over the sector. With the power to appoint senior officials, the government has been able to appoint their aides[48] and exercise command over sectoral institutions. The directors of the two utilities have often been appointed 'till further order' (no fixed term), without following proper procedure.[49] While a selection procedure for the regulators is defined by the Electricity Act, it is alleged that the state government manages to steer through the process and appoint their supporters, often identified prior to the selection process.[50,51] This has resulted in politically motivated economic decision-making in the sector. For example, over last 15 years, PSERC either did not raise the tariff or reduced it in the tariff order preceding state assembly elections. Transparency gain, a much-desired outcome of the independent regulatory process, is neither visible nor valued in the state, owing to absence of an active civil society. The opportunity to participate in regulatory proceedings is valued, but is also considered futile, as public interventions are almost never reflected in regulatory decisions.

★★★

Punjab has complied with the central government's checklist of mandatory reforms in the electricity sector, but these changes are only skin-deep;

the power dynamic in the sector continues as usual. Defying its key objectives, institutional restructuring has allowed for more political influence in the sector, through the appointment of close aides as institutional heads. While reforms led to few changes in sector governance, there have been substantial gains in access, quality of service, and some aspects of discom performance. The utility employees' resistance to central government-backed unbundling seems to have driven them to meet efficiency targets.

Beginning in 2009, with the influx of young leadership, the state economy has made a gradual shift towards industry, while holding on to its agrarian roots. To power its industrial aspirations, Punjab has made momentous investments in the supply side with private sector participation. While increased power availability has resulted in improved quality of supply for all, it has brought in new challenges, stifling the options for renewable energy, demand-side management, and open access. Attracting industrial investment with a reliable supply and low tariffs has added to the state's existing burden of subvention to the sector. However, it has manoeuvred to pass on a substantial part of that burden to consumers, in the forms of high electricity duty and cess. While competitive populism is gradually losing its electoral and welfare value, state politics is still locked into agricultural subsidies.

Though appearing to be populist, the state government and ruling political parties have used power sector reforms to cater to elite interests. Through multiple channels, including appointments to newly established institutions, manipulation of the tariff process, awarding of IPP contracts, and the allocation of subsidies, the state has managed to protect the power dynamics between the government, utility, regulator, and consumers. The existing *partial reform equilibrium* seems to be favourable a small group of short-term winners.[52]

Punjab's experience reveals the limits of the Centre's influence on state action. Political alignment between the state and central government, on multiple occasions, has enabled broad policy consensus on reform measures. Yet, actual implementation has been driven by local considerations, catering to vested interests, and state-level dynamics, often in conflict with the centre's position and broad consensus.[53] Despite the state government's consent, the resistance of local interest groups has not only delayed unbundling but also diluted its basic thrust. What have worked are those central policy prescriptions with upfront budgetary allocations—or threats to discontinue these.

Notes and References

1. Upinder Sawhney, 'Subnational Reforms and Public Policy Issues in Punjab', *International Journal of Punjab Studies* 19(1), 2012: 49–66; Nirvikar Singh, 'Punjab's Economy: What Went Wrong?', *The Tribune*, 12 August 2016, available http://www.tribuneindia.com/news/comment/punjabs-economy-what-went-wrong/279303.html (accessed on 12 September 2017).

2. Bucking the prospects of economic convergence, over the economic reform period, high-income states in India have shown higher growth rates than low-income states and the national average, resulting in a phenomenon of divergence and rising inequality across states (Montek Singh Ahluwalia, 'State Level Performance under Economic Reforms in India', in Anne O. Krueger (ed.), *Economic Policy, Reforms and the Indian Economy* (Chicago: University of Chicago Press, 2002): 91–128; Utsav Kumar and Arvind Subramanian, 'Growth in India's States in the First Decade of the 21st Century: Four Facts', *Economic & Political Weekly* 47(3), 2012: 48–57; Planning Commission, *Data-Book Compiled for Use of Planning Commission* (New Delhi: Planning Commission, Government of India, 2014).

   Notwithstanding the trend, Punjab lagged behind the national average growth rate throughout the 1990s and 2000s. During 1992 to 2012, Punjab's economy grew at the rate of 5.6 per cent per annum, while average annual national growth rate was 6.9 per cent. Lakhwinder Singh, 'Resurrecting Punjab's Economy', *Hindustan Times*, 6 January 2015, available www.hindustantimes.com/chandigarh/resurrecting-punjab-s-economy/story-G8GKxxbauvLije5LF6mJlO.html (accessed on 12 September 2017).

3. RBI, *Handbook of Statistics on Indian Economy* (Reserve Bank of India, 2016).

4. Neighbouring Haryana recorded a 29 per cent NSVA from industrial activities, while Gujarat and Maharashtra (two important high-income states) recorded a 42 per cent and 33 per cent industrial share in NSVA, respectively. RBI, *Handbook of Statistics*.

5. Over about 51 years of existence, the state has been governed by SAD for more than 20 years, around 19 years of Congress rule, and has been under President's Rule for more than eight years.

6. Sawhney, 'Subnational Reforms and Public Policy'.

7. Singh, 'Resurrecting Punjab'.

8. Singh, 'Punjab's Economy'.

9. MoP, *Tripartite Memorandum of Understanding Amongst Ministry of Power, Government of India and Government of Punjab and Punjab State Power Corporation Limited (UDAY)* (Ministry of Power, 2016).

10. PFC, *Report on Performance of State Power Utilities* (New Delhi: Power Finance Corporation Limited, 2016).

11. During 2005–16, the regulator approved Rs 44,700 crore as a subsidy requirement of the discom and the government paid Rs 40,500 crore (ToI, 'Punjab's Free Power Bill is Rs 40,538 crore in 13 Years', *Times of India*, 13 March 2016, available http://timesofindia.indiatimes.com/city/chandigarh/Punjabs-free-power-bill-is-Rs40538-crore-in-13-years/articleshow/51384863.cms [accessed on 12 September 2017]), which is about double the amount of discom's outstanding debt and more than 1.5 times its revenue requirement for 2016–17. PSERC, *Tariff Order for PSPCL FY 2016–17* (Chandigarh: Punjab State Electricity Regulatory Commission, 2016).

12. PEG, *The Price of Plenty: Insights from 'Surplus' Power in Indian States* (Pune: Prayas Energy Group, 2017).

13. PSPCL, *Management Information Report (Quarter Ending March 2016)* (Patiala: Punjab State Power Corporation Limited, 2016).

14. PFC, *Report on Performance of State Power Utilities*, 2016.

15. MoP, *Fifth Annual Integrated Ratings of State Power Distribution Utilities* (New Delhi: Ministry of Power, 2017).

16. The utility has mostly received a 'B+' grade, except in the third rating, when it received the highest grade 'A+', after two subsequent years of net profit. PSPCL officials are highly critical of the rating methodology, which gives more weight to financial performance. As a senior PSPCL official pointed out, 'They judge our efficiency from our balance-sheet. This is not the right approach. Our balance-sheet reflects inefficiency of the [state] government. Had the government paid the committed subsidy amount, PSPCL would have made a profit.' (Interview with a senior PSPCL official, 11 August 2016, Patiala).

17. In 1966, erstwhile East Punjab state of India was trifurcated on linguistic grounds to create two states, namely, Punjab and Haryana, and the union territory of Chandigarh.

18. Navjot Kaur, *Managing Power Systems: Efficient Supply Planning and Optimal Pricing of Electricity* (New Delhi: Deep & Deep Publications, 2006).

19. R.P. Bhagat, *Rural Electrification & Development* (New Delhi: Deep & Deep Publications, 1993).

20. Sunila S. Kale, *Electrifying India: Regional Political Economies of Development* (Stanford: Stanford University Press, 2014).

21. In 1967, PSEB had a mere capacity of 62 MW, while remaining capacity came from Punjab's share in Bhakra Dam. In 1967–8, the state consumption (including exports) was 701 MkWh, while it generated 1,136 MkWh. Kaur, *Managing Power Systems*, 2006.

22. Though household electrification in 1998 is unknown, by 2001, 92 per cent of households in Punjab were using electricity as source of lights, the highest among major states. GoI, *General Census of India* (New Delhi: Government of India, 2011).

23. Anindita Sarkar and Arijit Das, 'Groundwater Irrigation-Electricity-Crop Diversification Nexus in Punjab: Trends, Turning Points, and Policy Initiatives', *Economic & Political Weekly* 49(52), 2014: 64–73.

24. Kale, *Electrifying India*, 2014.

25. Ashwini K. Swain and Olivier Charnoz, 'In Pursuit of Energy Efficiency in India's Agriculture: Fighting "Free Power" or Working with It?', *AFD Working Paper 126* (Paris: Agence Française de Développement, 2012).

26. During the 1970s and 1980s, the power sector accounted for about 86 per cent of state investment in SPSEs. Sawhney, 'Subnational Reforms and Public Policy' 2012. Until the 8th Five Year Plan, the power sector used a larger share of the planned expenditures in the state, often higher than the outlay. Planning Commission, *Annual Report on the Working of State Electricity Boards & Electricity Departments* (New Delhi: Planning Commission, Government of India, 2002); Kale, *Electrifying India* 2014.

27. Planning Commission, *Annual Report on the Working of State Electricity Boards* 2002.

28. At this point, there was an emerging national consensus on charging for electricity services. The Common Minimum National Action Plan for Power, evolved out of two conferences of CMs in 1996, suggested to charge at least 50 paisa/kWh to the agricultural consumers, and over three years, move towards charging 50 per cent of the cost of supply. Owing to the political stakes and sensitivity, there was a shift in position by 1998, asking the state governments to pay for subsidies (Ashwini K. Swain, 'Political Economy of Distribution Reforms in Indian Electricity', *Working Paper*, Initiative on Climate, Energy and Environment [New Delhi: Centre for Policy Research, 2016]). However, GoP did not pay for the subsidies, until it was reintroduced in 2005.

29. Upinder Sawhney, 'Fiscal Reforms at the Sub-National Level: The Case of Punjab', *NIPFP Working Paper 05* (New Delhi: National Institute of Public Finance and Policy, 2013).

30. NCAER, *Report of the Expert Group on Power Sector Reforms (Headed by Gajendra Haldea), Executive Summary* (New Delhi: National Council of Applied Economic Research, 2003).

31. Interviews with three farmer leaders on 11 August 2016, 15 September 2016, and 3 January 2017, in Patiala, Chandigarh, and Ludhiana, respectively.

32. Interview with three office bearers of PSEBEA, 10 August 2016, Patiala.

33. See Swain, 'Political Economy of Distribution Reforms', (2016) for a detailed analysis of various Central Government schemes on transmission and distribution network upgradation.
34. Until 2016, PSTCL received field staff from PSPCL on deputation.
35. Sukhbir Singh Badal, son of Parkash Singh Badal, was already appointed as SAD President in January 2008, had been elected three times to the Lok Sabha (11th, 12th, and 14th), and had been nominated once to Rajya Sabha (2001–4). When he joined state government in 2009, he was a sitting member of the 14th Lok Sabha and was later elected into the state Assembly in August 2009.
36. GoP, *Industrial Policy-2009*, Chandigarh: Department of Industry and Commerce, Government of Punjab, 2009.
37. GoP, *Power Generation Policy*, Chandigarh: Department of Power, Government of Punjab, 2010.
38. Interview with a journalist, 11 August 2016, Patiala; interview with an academic, 25 August 2016, Chandigarh.
39. PEG, *The Price of Plenty*, 2017.
40. An innovative Farmer Solar Power Scheme launched in 2015 was never implemented, as PSPCL faced with surplus power challenge and decline to purchase any additional power. The Scheme details available http://peda.gov.in/main/farmer_solar_scheme2015.html, (accessed on 6 September 2017).
41. Punjab had 485 open access consumers in 2016–17, fifth largest among the states, with power exchanges (CERC, *Report on Short-term Power Market in India: 2016–17* [New Delhi: Central Electricity Regulatory Commission, 2017]). With the objective to get back the industrial load, in 2016, PSERC eliminated the archaic peak load exemption charge on industrial consumers for consumptions beyond their contracted load during the evening peak hours. It also offered a lower than ACS tariff for new industries and additional consumption of existing industries. The revenue loss in lieu on low industrial tariff will be borne by the state government. PSERC, *Tariff Order*, 2016.
42. In 2016, GoP offered to surrender 336 MW of its share in four NTPC plants. PEG, *The Price of Plenty*.
43. HT, 'Power Sop: OBCs to get 200 Units Free in Punjab', *Hindustan Times*, 11 August 2016, available www.hindustantimes.com/punjab/power-sop-obcs-to-get-200-units-free-in-punjab/story-IVS3BwkbUCMnZJ832HaiJN.html (accessed on 12 September 2017).
44. Punjab has one of the high electricity duties, at 13 per cent (CEA, *Electricity Tariff & Duty and Average Rate of Electricity Supply in India* [New Delhi: Central Electricity Authority, 2016]) and additional infrastructure

development cess, at 5 per cent, charged equally to all consumers on their
billed amount. Both the amounts have historically been adjusted against
the subsidy booked by PSPCL. Moreover, electricity bills in the state
include extraneous charges like cow cess, a water charge, and an octroi
tax, to generate revenue for ineffective government bodies (M. Rajshekhar,
'Why Punjab's Power Bills Include a Cow Cess and Water Charges',
Scroll.in, 13 January 2016, available http://scroll.in/article/802014/why-
punjabs-power-bills-include-a-cow-cess-and-water-charges [accessed on 13
February 2017]). The National Tariff Policy allows the state governments
to use electricity duty to provide subsidy to needy consumers, but as a
substitute to the cross-subsidy. While cross-subsidization continues, these
additional charges have increased the landed price of electricity service.
45. MoP, *Tripartite Memorandum*.
46. RBI, *Handbook on Statistics of Indian States* (Reserve Bank of India, 2017).
47. Interestingly, Punjab, with the most advanced rural electricity distribution network, received a Rs 800 crore central grant to upgrade rural grid,
months ahead of signing UDAY MoU. IE, 'Punjab Gets Rs 800 Crore to
Upgrade Rural Power Sector', *Indian Express*, 11 August 2015, Chandigarh.
48. After Congress came into power in 2017, the head of PSPCL and PSERC
Chairman resigned from their position at an early stage of their tenure.
The fact that both the officers were appointed by the previous SAD government and resigned immediately after change in government backs
the allegations of political alignment between these positions and state
government.
49. Vishal Rambani, 'Punjab Power Sector's "Powerless" Bosses', *Hindustan
Times*, 4 August 2016, available http://www.hindustantimes.com/pun-
jab/punjab-power-sector-s-powerless-bosses/story-hjgWKRVFxQP5eG-
BEtMC6vL.html (accessed on 12 September 2017).
50. Interview with a senior journalist, 11 August 2016, Patiala; interview with
an academic, 25 August 2016, Chandigarh.
51. Media reports on previous PSERC Chairman's resignation in May 2017
reported the likely successor's name, much before the position was adver-
tised (HT, 'Kusumjit Sidhu likely to Replace DS Bains as Punjab Power
Regulatory Commission Chief', *Hindustan Times*, 12 May 2017, available
http://www.hindustantimes.com/punjab/kusumjit-sidhu-likely-to-
replace-ds-bains-as-punjab-power-regulatory-commission-chief/story-
DjGcIBDHv5QpNpAnexZa8L.html [accessed on 12 September 2017]).
The same person's appointment as PSERC chief in August 2017 points to
government interference in regulatory appointment.
52. Drawing on economic reforms in post-communist transitions, Hellman
argues that while short-term losers are seen as major obstacles to

economic reforms, short-term winners are the most common obstacles to the progress of reforms. The latter is a small constituency of early winners who seek to stall the process in a *partial reform equilibrium* that generates concentrated rents for few, while imposing higher costs for the rest of the society. Joel S. Hellman, 'Winners Take All: The Politics of Partial Reform in Post-Communist Transitions', *World Politics* 50(2), 1998: 203–34.

53. For example, the introduction of free power in 1997 and its restoration in 2005 came in the face of the central government's push for charging a reasonable cost to all consumers, including farmers.

11

SIDDHARTH SAREEN

Electricity Distribution in Rajasthan

Unbundling the Recurrent Failures of a Politicized Sector

From single-party rule dominated by the Indian National Congress (Congress) following state formation in 1949, since 1990 Rajasthan has witnessed healthy electoral competition, with power regularly alternating between the two main national political parties (see Table 11.1). National power sector reforms commenced in the year 1990; Rajasthan declared its intent to follow suit in 1993, and issued a Broad Reform Policy Statement in 1995. This statement was revised twice before the Rajasthan Power Sector Reforms Act was passed in 1999. The Congress came back in power in Rajasthan in 1998, the same year that the Electricity Regulatory Commission Act was adopted. With the subsequent establishment of the Rajasthan Electricity Regulatory Commission (RERC) in 2000, the Rajasthan State Electricity Board (RSEB) was one of the first in India to be unbundled. Yet, the broader electoral trend of alternating but stable Congress and Bharatiya Janata Party (BJP) state regimes has meant that the incumbent party sees little incentive for long-term planning. Both parties have failed to set a policy course that sticks for the desert state's power sector.

238 | *Siddharth Sareen*

TABLE 11.1   Timeline of Key Events: Rajasthan

Political Events	Year	Power Sector Events
• State's first BJP government	1990	• Power sector reforms commence
• Congress back in power	1998	• Central Electricity Regulatory Commission Act
	1999	• Rajasthan Power Sector Reforms Act passed

	2000	• Rajasthan Electricity Regulatory Commission (RERC) established; RSEB unbundled into five state electric companies:
		• Generation company: Rajasthan Rajya Vidyut Utpadan Nigam Ltd. (RVUN)
		• Transmission company: Rajasthan Rajya Vidyut Prasaran Nigam Ltd. (RVPN)
		• Three regional distribution companies each serving 10–12 of 33 districts:
		  o Jaipur Vidyut Vitran Nigam Ltd. (JVVNL)
		  o Ajmer Vidyut Vitran Nigam Ltd. (AVVNL)
		  o Jodhpur Vidyut Vitran Nigam Ltd. (JdVVNL)

• BJP back in power with Raje	2003	• Central Electricity Act passed, ERC Act effective 10 June 2003; RERC poised to play more significant role
	2007	• RERC (Renewable Energy Obligation) Regulations
• Congress back in power with Gehlot	2008	
	2010	• RERC (Renewable Energy Certificate and Renewable Purchase Obligation Compliance Framework) Regulation

TABLE 11.1   (*Cont'd*)

Political Events	Year	Power Sector Events
	2011	• Rajasthan Solar Energy Policy
• BJP back in power with Raje	2013	• Approval of PPAs signed for 1,975 MW with power companies
• Raje government raises tariff rates by 16 per cent in 2015–16 after elections	Aug 2016	• RERC approves cancellation of seven out of nine PPAs, worth 1,475 MW
• Raje government joins UDAY; Rajasthan first state to adopt it	Dec 2015	• State discoms struggle to stay afloat
	2016	• Rajasthan State Electricity Distribution Management Responsibility Act passed for discom accountability
	Mar 2016	• Rajasthan issues Rs 28,455 crore in bonds to 26 banks under UDAY to clear part of sectoral debt

Source: Author.

As in most other Indian states, the past quarter century has seen dizzying growth for Rajasthan's power sector. From 201 kilowatt hour (kWh) in 1990, per capita power consumption rose by two-thirds to 335 kWh in 2000.[1] At this point, when the RSEB was unbundled into one generation, one transmission, and three distribution utilities, the total installed capacity was 1,872 megawatt (MW). Compare this with 17,924 MW by mid-2016, an almost ten-fold increase.[2] Such a major expansion, however, has not come without its own peculiar problems. The most worrying of these problems is a persistent combination of high costs and low revenue in recent years. This has led to repeated financial trouble and debt restructuring, including a massive bailout that exceeded Rs 80,000 crore in 2015–16.

Several factors are stacked against Rajasthan's power sector. It is a low-income state with a large proportion of traditionally low-tariff consumers, especially agricultural consumers. In a region with a low water table, the need to power agricultural pumps constitutes a large share of demand. Population density is low by Indian standards, which implies a dispersed load and makes service provision expensive due to increased infrastructural outlay, maintenance, and monitoring requirements. Moreover, Rajasthan is physically ill-disposed for harnessing cheap power from conventional sources such as hydropower and coal-based thermal power. Finally, to reiterate the point made above, robust electoral competition has meant that political decisions favour a short-term calculus of potential costs and benefits of change, rather than affording the luxury of long-term planning. This short-term thinking has characterized the development of the state's electricity distribution sector over the past quarter century.

The three distribution companies (discoms) Jaipur Vidyut Vitran Nigam Limited (JVVNL), Ajmer Vidyut Vitran Nigam Limited (AVVNL), and Jodhpur Vidyut Vitran Nigam Ltd (JdVVNL), have considerably different load profiles due to varying population density distribution across regions. The JVVNL covers 2.56 crore people with a density of 354 persons per sq. km., AVVNL serves 2.29 crore people (density 263), and JdVVNL caters to 2.03 crore people (density 112), compared to a national average of 382 persons per sq. km.[3] Despite these differences, the same tariff is levied state wide, approved by the RERC. This places a greater burden on JdVVNL, whose highly dispersed load is more expensive to serve than that of JVVNL with its relatively higher consumer density.

Moreover, tariffs vary across consumer categories, and increase by consumption slab within each category. For instance, in 2014–15, non-domestic consumers paid the highest energy charges ranging from Rs 6.75 to Rs 7.85, followed by industrial rates between Rs 5.35 and Rs 6.50, while domestic rates ranged from Rs 3.50 to Rs 6.40 and agricultural tariffs were between Rs 4.50 and Rs 5.70.[4] The last category is, however, largely subsidized by the state government. In 2013–14, metered farmers supplied in block hours paid a share of Re 0.90 per unit, while those supplied outside block hours were charged Rs 2.10 per unit; many agricultural consumers pay monthly flat rates of Rs 15 per horsepower to operate pumps during block supply hours.

Percentage sales of power across consumer categories are also different between the three discoms. The JVVNL and ANNVL have reasonable shares of high-tariff industrial consumers in terms of sales of power (31 per cent and 29 per cent respectively in 2014–15), whereas JdVVNL's industrial consumer share that year was 13 per cent. By contrast, JdVVNL has the highest low-tariff agricultural consumer share: 55 per cent in 2014–15, compared to 30 per cent for JVVNL and 37 per cent for AVVNL.[5] Thus, JdVVNL faces the toughest challenge in terms of matching average revenue realized (ARR) with average cost of supply (ACS).

Besides factors related to load profiles, the discoms face several supply-side challenges. A critical factor that interfaces directly with consumers is the aggregate technical and commercial (AT&C) loss level. This includes both technical losses during transmission and distribution as well as losses due to line theft, inadequate billing, and revenue recovery. The structural power sector reforms instituted in the state from 2000 onwards have been partially informed by intent to facilitate efficiency measures; in the years immediately following the unbundling of the RSEB, Rajasthan struggled with AT&C losses of over 40 per cent. Since then, sectoral reforms have managed to lower this level to some extent. However, Figure 11.2 shows that AT&C losses continue to be high, having dropped from 33 per cent in 2007–8 to 29 per cent in 2014–15, despite a dip to 20 per cent in 2012–13. The ACS rose from Rs 3.26 to a worrying Rs 6.02 per unit during the same period, with a high of Rs 7.13 in 2010–11. The ARR in 2007–8 was Rs 2.22 per unit, and after government subsidy of Re 0.39, the revenue gap was Re 0.65. At its peak in 2010–11, the revenue gap was an incredible Rs 4.53 per unit, meaning the discoms were actually losing considerably more money on average per unit sold than the ACS just three years prior in 2007–8! By 2014–15, the ARR was up at Rs 3.91, but the revenue gap remained problematically high at Rs 1.84. Figures 11.1 and 11.2 present graphical depictions of movements in these key indices from 2007–8.

Understanding these developments requires an explanation grounded in both the regional as well as the sectoral political economy within which various policies and other interventions have shaped the trajectory of Rajasthan's power sector. In an attempt to furnish such an explanation, the next section moves through three historical periods, offering some background on the early sectoral reform period during the 1990s, sectoral developments in the immediate aftermath of unbundling in 2000, and the sectoral trajectory over the most recent decade from 2007–8, which, as mentioned, is highlighted in Figures 11.1 and 11.2. It shows how the state went from looking solid during the early reform period to being on much shakier ground when restructuring brought about more transparency regarding operations and finances.

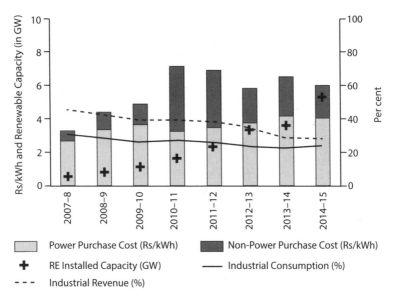

FIGURE 11.1   Physical and Financial Profile: Rajasthan
Sources: CSO, *Energy Statistics* (New Delhi: Central Statistics Office, Ministry of Statistics and Programme Implementation, Government of India, 2010, 2012, 2014, and 2016); PFC, *Reports on Performance of State Power Utilities* (New Delhi: Power Finance Corporation Limited, 2011, 2013, 2015, and 2016).

This prompted attempts to increase efficiency, but these never seem to have been implemented across the board in an effective manner, with numerous leakages continuing unchecked. Struggles to fulfil rising demand led to suboptimal decision-making on the supply side, escalating costs without a concurrent revenue increase.

Two indicators point to a simple explanation for these developments. First, tariffs stagnated for years on end even as the sector bled losses, an outcome that can only be explained as the political determination of what should have been a primarily technical matter. Second, AT&C losses did not decrease steadily despite various efficiency measures being instituted, indicating inadequate effort to tackle the core problem of line theft. In a context where electricity provision holds electoral significance, and given alternating political rule, these phenomena suggest that both parties leaned on the sector, courting constituencies to its financial detriment. Meanwhile, repeated financial leniency freed

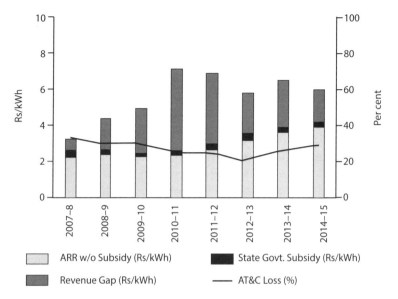

FIGURE 11.2   Supply-side Costs and Revenue Recovery: Rajasthan
Source: PFC, *Reports on Performance of State Power Utilities* (New Delhi: Power
Finance Corporation Limited, 2011, 2013, 2015, and 2016).

the sector from pressure to reform, with no firm incentives in place to
achieve what were essentially moving targets. The sector's recent performance illustrates the perils of unchecked sectoral growth without
sufficient oversight and planning despite political competition.

Historical Periods

1990–2000: The Early Years of Sectoral Reform: Balancing Finances, Agriculture, and Politics

A key trend in the early power sector reform period in Rajasthan was
the declining share of industrial consumption in the total sale of power,
from 40 per cent in 1995 to 28 per cent in 2002. This was paralleled by
an increase in agricultural consumption, from 30 per cent to 40 per cent
of total consumption during the same period. By 2000, the increase in
agricultural consumption was visible in the required state government
subsidy having swollen to Rupees 37 crores for that year. It was in this

context that the state went about implementing the Rajasthan Power Sector Reforms Act from 1 June 2000. This was supported by Rupees 18 crores World Bank Rajasthan Power Sector Restructuring Project and reflected a wider trend of power sector reforms.

These reforms targeted a strategy of attracting investment, improving efficiency, and enabling growth, very much echoing the liberalization philosophy that had become so fashionable in India and globally during the 1990s. Yet, right from the outset there were some signs of turbulence within the sector's changing dynamics. These were linked with the state's three-quarters rural population, which is predominantly agricultural; farmers constitute a vote bank that wields enormous political significance for both the Congress and the BJP. The emergent bone of contention was agricultural connections. These became a conjuncture of financial pressure on the state through subsidy burden and infrastructure expansion; resource management issues linked with the sustainability of pumping groundwater in arid and semi-arid environments; and electoral success based on power sector concessions to the farmer vote bank.

During the mid-1990s, with pending agricultural connections burgeoning into the lakhs, the BJP promoted a so-called 'nursery scheme'. This encouraged relatively affluent farmers to jump the queue, by (a) paying the full Rs 50,000 installation costs instead of the usual subsidized Rs 5,000 amount; and (b) acquiescing to premium tariffs. This proved popular in terms of uptake; about 85,000 connections were allocated under the scheme, which contributed to grid expansion to the tune of 10,000 new transformers. The perverse equity effects of such schemes can be debated, as is the case with critiques of targeting under more recent solar pump subsidy schemes.[6] Power Line magazine named the chairman of the RSEB at the time, P.N. Bhandari, a 'hero of 1997' for having more than doubled the public utility's monthly revenue from Rs 130 crore to Rs 300 crore. Yet with state elections coming up in 1998, mindfulness of the tendency to offer agricultural connections as political largesse to win votes seems to have led to the chairman's ouster.[7]

With the Congress assuming power in 1998, the 'nursery scheme' was discontinued, to be replaced by a promise of a lakh free connections a year. While this obviously catered to smallholder farmers in a way the former scheme neglected, an experienced energy consultant explained its drawbacks thus: 'It depleted the already low water table very quickly. Plus it unduly increased the number of subsidized connections. The major income source was industry. But the major consumers became subsidized agricultural users'.[8] This example of swerving from the commodification of power based on market principles, in this case by the BJP, to the electricity-as-public-good model subsequently pushed by the Congress, characterizes sectoral development during the early reform period, in that it lacked a consistent political vision for policy to cohere around.

2000–7: Developments Immediately after Sectoral Unbundling: Change and Resistance

In 2000, Rajasthan began implementing power sector reforms, unbundling the RSEB in one fell swoop into five public utilities. Its transmission and distribution losses continued to be in the 43–45 per cent range during 2002–6, falling to 37 per cent in 2006–7. Until 2007, the state's attempts to raise efficiency were regarded as fairly successful in this sector. But a study carried out shortly subsequent to this period on JVVNL—the discom with the load profile most conducive to good financial performance—reveals that employee productivity remained well below that of national and private sector utilities, contributing an employee cost of Re 0.51 per unit during 2009–10. Private company Torrent Power compares at Re 0.12 in the same year, while even Gujarat's worst-performing public discom on this front had an employee cost of Re 0.23 per unit during 2013–14.[9] The study notes that 'the majority of JVVNL's O&M [operations and maintenance] costs are directed towards employees and administration'.[10] Research from this period shows insufficient measures and a lack of individual incentives at the ground level to prevent theft from power lines.[11] Such accounts point towards mismanagement rather than steady optimization of sectoral structures and processes. By contrast, the neighbouring state of Gujarat, having taken a more gradual approach to unbundling, firmly implemented an agricultural feeder separation scheme during the same period to put a definitive stop to line theft in rural areas, strengthening its financial position, and expanding sectoral infrastructure.[12]

A former discom employee who worked during this period stated that entrenched politics had led to him stepping down shortly after commencing a senior position: 'While the electricity sector has been described as autonomous, it has never been so … Even decisions like whether or not to even *make* a substation are up to political party people'.[13] Interviewees additionally attributed persistent inefficiency to a lack of skill upgrades, manpower shortages, and transfers. A former RERC employee noted that this situation did not improve with the introduction of the RERC in 2003. Since discoms' directorial boards continued to largely consist of government representatives, he explained, even the annual revenue requirement and tariff petitions put forward by the discoms to the RERC were already politically modulated.[14] These insights suggest that unbundling did not restructure the sector as much in reality as it did on paper, leading to it hurtling towards massive indebtedness. A senior journalist expressed shock at having observed that the chief engineers from this period have continued to receive two-year extensions without promotion while the superintending engineers responsible for financial disaster remain in charge, quipping that 'restructuring is not possible with the same workforce'.[15]

Nonetheless, a new initiative did emerge during this period thanks to a national policy push: Renewable Purchase Obligations (RPOs), known elsewhere as renewable portfolio standards. In 2006–7, RERC specified an RPO of 2 per cent for wind-sourced power and 0.50 per cent for biomass-sourced power. By 2010–11, these had gone up to 8 and 3.25 per cent respectively, and a further component was introduced for solar-sourced power for discoms. Compliance was lax and not stringently enforced during these initial years, with a high of 3.02 per cent for wind in 2010–11 and 0.45 per cent for biomass in 2008–9. However, a Supreme Court ruling from the case of *Hindustan Zinc Ltd. v. RERC* (Civil Appeal No. 4417 of 2015) mandated RPOs nationally, with compliance by both discoms and captive power plants rising dramatically thereafter. This set the stage for Rajasthan to regularly make the news in recent years for installing new solar energy capacity at record-breaking low rates.

Thus, this initial period after unbundling saw efforts to increase efficiency and decrease losses with modest gains, but also signs that, despite reforms, political interference in the sector had not been addressed in the manner envisaged, and that changes in sticky processes at multiple levels were in order to turn around its loss-making trajectory.

2007–16: Sectoral Trajectory in Recent Years: Old Wine in New Bottles?

The past decade has made it abundantly clear that Rajasthan has failed to address fundamental issues in its approach to sectoral unbundling.

Despite recognition of internal managerial problems, the discoms have been unable to effect change. According to employees from various discoms, it is only recently that they are starting to use individual incentives and undertake feeder-level renovation. In 2016, the chairman (who is common across discoms, while each has its own managing director) issued a host of standing orders to this effect, putting in place linemen-in-charge on 11 kilo Volt (kV) rural feeders (medium voltage distribution lines) and measures to act on feeders with AT&C losses exceeding 15 per cent while training field staff and instituting anti-theft measures such as a vigilance squad, following Gujarat's successful example. Yet, as a former RSEB employee wryly summarized: 'there is still so much political patronage. Even a senior engineer will have greater loyalty to his local MLA [member of legislative assembly] than to his MD [managing director], who can do nothing. Even if he wants to have the engineer transferred, he will have to go via the chairman who will end up going to the MLA.'[16]

It thus remains to be seen whether the bevy of efforts to improve organizational culture within the discoms will yield results, ranging from the uptake of consultant inputs towards efficiency by staff to feeder-level incentives and disincentives. The latter are aimed at increasing billing and collection, for instance by tracking AT&C losses at the feeder level and, in case a ceiling is transgressed, levying penalties on the linemen-in-charge and eventually restricting supply unless consumers cooperate in meeting targets at the feeder level, presumably by stopping line theft.

In contrast to these budding efforts, some things have undoubtedly changed. After years of low tariffs, several hikes between 2011 and 2016 at an average of 10 per cent per annum brought Rajasthan's ARR up to a relatively high level. These tariff hikes were prompted by runaway losses based on the aforementioned high ACS, which peaked at Rs 7.13 in 2010–11 during Congress rule. Competitive populism in the form of tariff freezes was set aside by both parties due to the monumental need to increase revenue realization as sectoral debt spiralled. Despite frequent tariff hikes, losses piled up at frightening speed, compounding debt accumulated during years of high-rate short-term power purchases to make up national grid shortages. In 2012, Rs 38,000 crore of short-term liabilities were recast under a Financial Restructuring Plan. Yet in 2012–13, banks declined a Rs 8,300 crore loan to the state discoms.[17]

With little fundamental change in operations, debt tripled between 2010 and 2015, and in September 2015 Rajasthan signed up for a central government scheme known as Ujwal Discom Assurance Yojana (UDAY). This involved a Rajasthan government takeover of three-quarters of the discom debt of Rs 80,500 crore, with the remainder to be issued as state-backed bonds. In return, the discoms were expected to cut AT&C losses along a strict timeline—one which they have already not managed to stick to. With AT&C losses nudging 30 per cent in recent years, the discoms will be hard-pressed to meet the target of 15 per cent by 2020 mandated under UDAY.

Addressing creeping inefficiencies and the exorbitant ACS levels are not the state's only challenges. Along with higher tariffs come consumer expectations of higher service levels. A Department of Energy representative emphasized the importance of 24×7, affordable, good quality power, with easy-to-get connections, convenient bill payment, and grievance redressal options. 'The consumer', he said, 'is not concerned with finance. He wants a service.'[18] However, a business association representative voiced exasperation at the lack of good administrators within utilities, based on his engagement with bureaucratic procedures handled by the technical engineers he said were in charge.[19] The capacity and will of utilities to manage dynamic change processes remains doubtful, especially given this take on UDAY by a senior discom employee: 'Losses will not come on the government in any case, because the central government is not counting this debt on the state's balance sheet. We can only think of servicing debt after the moratorium. Anyway, there is no pressure, maybe after UDAY 1, UDAY 2 will come'. This indifferent attitude and brazenness, born of a sense that failure is inconsequential in terms of any culpability or personal indictment, was also noted by interviewees with regard to procurement processes. A project management consultant attributed a lack of transparent technical assessment procedures for state tenders in the sector to the absence of expertise and independence among members of scoring committees, elaborating that discoms 'just pull in known members who don't understand the technical aspects' and allow politics to take over in lieu of objective criteria.[20]

But one aspect of the reforms has been to enable a demand-side push for change if supply-side factors fail to suffice. Having existed as a quasi-judicial independent authority for some years, the RERC has signalled an intent for public engagement to come of age and co-determine the sectoral trajectory by instituting consultation processes and forums such as public hearings. Yet, these forums have taken the form of annual tariff hearings limited primarily to the state capital of Jaipur, as well as petitions to the RERC. Most consumer groups' engagement is curtailed by their relative inability to pose arguments couched in technical jargon, while industrial consumers customarily hire experienced advocates to petition the RERC. While agricultural consumers ostensibly lack an organized farmer group in the state capital, their dispersed lobbying through political representatives seems to have been very successful in maintaining subsidized agricultural power supply, while still contending with an agricultural connection pendency numbering over three lakhs.

The one seeming exception to civil society's lack of systematic engagement with the sector has been Rajasthan's Consumer Unity and Trust Society (CUTS). Yet, having been the first such organization to be included on the RERC's State Advisory Committee, at the time of fieldwork they had been unceremoniously dumped, with a staff member exclaiming that 'the current committee has no non-state members for the first time'.[21] Thus, there is some element of public involvement through established procedures and platforms, but rather than increasing in strength in a systemic manner, it seems to be sporadic and contingent on factors such as people's access to expertise, the level of social organization on electricity-related issues, and consistent top-down willingness to entertain public inputs.

Another aspect of change during this period has been Rajasthan's renewable energy profile, which has continued to grow, with approximately 4 GW of installed wind capacity (but with considerable daily and seasonal flux) and a fast-growing solar energy component which commenced in 2011, surpassed 800 MW in 2015, and doubled over the subsequent year. Using reverse e-auctions, the state raised bids for instituting 420 MW in solar capacity at Rs 4.34 energy charge per unit through six 70 MW plants in the landmark year 2015, signalling the technology's competitiveness against traditional sources such as coal.[22] Two years on, these figures are already becoming outdated, with bids for hundreds of MW coming in at levels as low as Rs 2.44 per unit.[23]

With an 18 per cent tax set to be levied on solar power under India's new Goods and Services Tax (GST) regime, it will be interesting to observe whether there is a cooling effect on this accelerating market.

The main form solar growth has taken is that of spatially concentrated large-scale solar parks, placing an infrastructural development expense burden on the state and time lag for building evacuation capacity, as opposed to a distributed generation model which would have been strategic for Rajasthan's large low-density stretches. Experienced sectoral stakeholders noted that 1–10 MW project developers have been shut out of the solar market,[24] while solar power systems in the 10s and 100s of kilowatt (kW) have been left to private solar companies to develop and promote rather than being supported by any state schemes. The Rajasthan Renewable Energy Corporation Limited has been focusing on 37 W and 100 W solar modules that target households in remote villages. It serves to channel subsidies rather than boasting the manpower and strategic initiative requisite for grounded engagement and for setting the terms of the solar growth trajectory.[25] While net metering guidelines arrived in 2015, the implementation of feed-in tariffs remains a rarity, with no proactive enablement by discoms and a number of barriers (hard-to-access subsidies, foot-dragging by discoms on installing bidirectional meters) that severely restrict uptake.

A final change relates to the introduction of competition in the sector during the past decade, firstly in the form of permitting 1 MW-plus consumers to source power from outside the state or set up captive power plants (a phenomenon known as open access), and second by way of distribution franchisees, which have just been introduced in Bharatpur and Kota regions, with Kolkata-based Calcutta Electric Supply Corporation (CESC) winning both tenders. Open access poses a potential threat to the discoms' already-ailing economy, especially given Rajasthan's recently acquired status of having sufficient installed capacity and flagging demand over the past two years compared to demand projections. However, this has been dealt with by imposing high fixed charges for wheeling, carriage, cross-subsidy, and as an additional surcharge, allowing industrial consumers who opt for open access a marginal benefit due to the low power exchange rates (compared to the much higher tariffs within Rajasthan) without diverting too much revenue from this high-tariff consumer category away from the state coffers. In effect, this hardly amounts to 'competition' in the true spirit of the term.[26] An advocate with industrial clients was quick to point out that 'the more discoms push industry, the more industries run away. The discoms are losing them ... RERC is also hand-in-glove with the discoms'.[27] For now, after a fair bit of contention, the RERC seems to have had its say.[28] However, significant increases in captive power plants, which so far do not comprise a large share of installed capacity in Rajasthan, could well change this.

The franchisee model has been introduced as a hybrid version, with the licensee CESC having had to agree to conditions such as a minimum level of investment in infrastructural development during its two 20-year leases. The two franchisee divisions that succeeded in attracting bidders are both in urban areas with high AT&C losses and a good mix of high-tariff consumers, whereas Ajmer, a region with only 15 per cent AT&C loss (and therefore less room to show improvement), has thus far failed to attract bidders. Assigning such prime areas to a private franchisee risks setting up a dual-track sector where the licensee harvests the benefits of easy pickings from loss reduction, through measures to stem rampant line theft. Yet for the discoms it constitutes a lowered management burden and assured steady revenue flow for two decades for chronically problematic areas, which management sees as a bargain worth making at present.[29] Both open access and franchising bring out complexities of the fix that the sector has got itself into in Rajasthan, and show that there is no easy way out, regardless of any central directives to usher in competition or employ more effective efficiency measures. Rather than generating synergies and cross-learning that bring down ACS and boost up ARR for discoms, competition in these cases is being treated as yet another navigable obstacle by a sector struggling to come to terms with itself.

Political Undercurrents and Technical Oversight

This brief foray through the past quarter-century of Rajasthan's electricity distribution sector trajectory has shown how its regional and sectoral political economies have been linked, and have together constituted the context within which interventions both internal and external to the sector have shaped its development. There has been a significant increase in both service quality and access to power since 1990, but it has come at a mind-boggling cost to the state exchequer. While agricultural subsidies remain, power tariffs since 2011 have generally begun to reflect something resembling the actual cost of supply, rather than being kept artificially low to avoid the feared negative political fallout.

Despite repeated massive bailouts, the combined lack of public outcry and strong sustained public engagement with the sector is remarkable. This underscores the unique nature of the power sector and its vital importance in peoples' everyday lives: as long as there is progress and the quality and reliability of power continues to increase, people are willing to maintain a distant interest with the nitty-gritty of the sector's travails. Yet, the trade-off is often a political bargain that takes the form of unabated line theft which, to a large extent, keeps the sector from reaching acceptable performance levels. Such developments run the risk of setting up a dual-track economy, selectively involving the private sector on cushy terms if needed, while maintaining political constituencies serviced by the incumbent public utilities at a loss to the exchequer.[30] In Rajasthan, both parties seem to be taking turns playing this game of competitive populism.

Part of the explanation for Rajasthan's abject failures lies in the relatively difficult task the sector faces in this state. The agricultural mix in Rajasthan's load profile has increased since 1990 without being compensated by a similar rise in industrial consumption, which has stagnated at a level below one-third of the gross state domestic product. A difficult period of power shortages in the late 2000s rendered sectoral finances worse than ever, which has led to discoms functioning in a seemingly endless catch-up mode, with new challenges by way of open access and RPOs cropping up. The coming-of-age of solar technologies can be a potential positive development given the conducive physical conditions of Rajasthan's desert environment, but the current steering of the nature of solar growth and its integration in the sector display a lack of political imagination and technical rigour. The extent to which regional and sectoral political economies manage to come together and envision a change dynamic to cohere around in relation to this development will play a key role in determining the future of Rajasthan's electricity sector.

The impact of non-sectoral policies pertaining to agriculture, water management, and financial access on the electricity distribution sector is profound, with tariffs, distributed generation, and infrastructure development in the sector contingent upon them. These non-sectoral policies also impact the quality of access to power in remote regions of the state that remain relatively neglected, despite Rajasthan's newfound 'energy-surplus' status in terms of installed capacity. Similarly, sectoral interventions such as unbundling, managerial reforms, participatory measures, and most recently franchising play potent roles in enabling different stakeholders to determine the sectoral trajectory and its differentiated outcomes. At present, as in recent years, consumers appear to be bearing the brunt of the discoms' internal resistance to structural change and process optimization. In the absence of strictly applied disincentives for fiscal and technical mismanagement, it seems unlikely that efficiency and other improvements will come about. Indeed, the past quarter-century bears witness to the course that things take if a sector is stealthily driven by politics while claiming to be technically oriented.

Notes and References

1. Planning Commission (Power and Energy Division), *Annual Report (2001–02) on The Working of State Electricity Boards & Electricity Departments* (Government of India), available http://planningcommission.nic.in/reports/genrep/seb/ar_seb02.pdf (accessed 24 March 2017).

2. Government of India (2016), 'Power Sector—June 2016', Central Electricity Authority, New Delhi, available http://www.cea.nic.in/reports/monthly/executivesummary/2016/exe_summary-06.pdf (accessed 28 May 2018).

3. Rajasthan Electricity Regulatory Commission, *Annual Report, Financial Year 2014–15*, available http://rerc.rajasthan.gov.in/AnnualReports/Rpt15.pdf (accessed 23 August 2017).

4. Rajasthan Electricity Regulatory Commission, *Annual Report*.

5. Power Finance Corporation Ltd. (2016), 'Report on the Performance of State Power Utilities for the Years 2013–14 to 2015–16', p. 134, available http://www.pfcindia.com/Default/ViewFile/?id=1505210724491_Report%20on%20Performance%20of%20State%20Power%20Utilities%20for%20the%20years%202013-14%20to%202015-16.pdf&path=Page (accessed 28 May 2018).

6. Avinash Kishore, Tushaar Shah, and Nidhi Prabha Tewari, 'Solar Irrigation Pumps', *Economic & Political Weekly* 49(10), 2014: 55–62.

7. 'The Heroes of 1997', *Power Line*, February 1998, 10.

8. Interview with energy consultant, 9 August 2016. Unless noted otherwise, all interviews referenced here were conducted by the author on a not-for-attribution basis, and took place in Jaipur, Rajasthan.

9. Gujarat Electricity Regulatory Commission, 'Tariff Order for Uttar Gujarat Vij Company Limited', 31 March 2015.

10. CRISIL Infrastructure Advisory, *Study of Various Power Distributions in India (July 2011)*, available http://planningcommission.nic.in/reports/genrep/hlpf/ann6.pdf (accessed 24 March 2017).

11. Sudhir Kumar Katiyar, 'Political Economy of Electricity Theft in Rural Areas: A Case Study from Rajasthan', *Economic and Political Weekly* 40(7), 2005: 644–8.

12. Siddharth Sareen, 'Energy Distribution Trajectories in Two Western Indian States: Comparative Politics and Sectoral Dynamics', *Energy Research & Social Science* 35, 2017: 17–27.

13. Interview with former discom employee, 17 August 2016.

14. Interview with former RERC employee, 5 August 2016.

15. Interview with senior journalist, 18 August 2016.

16. Interview with former RSEB employee, 9 August 2016.

17. Rohit Parihar, 'Rajasthan CM Ashok Gehlot Bankrupts His Power Companies, Banks Deny Loan', *India Today*, 6 August 2012, available http://indiatoday.intoday.in/story/rajasthan-cm-ashok-gehlot-bankrupts-his-power-companies/1/212052.html (accessed 23 August 2017).

18. Interview with Department of Energy employee, 5 August 2016.

19. Interview with PHD Chamber of Commerce and Industry representative, 11 August 2016.

20. Interview with project management consultant, 7 August 2016.

21. Interview with CUTS employees, 10 August 2016.

22. Kunal Anand, 'For the First Time in Modern India's History, Solar Energy is Cheaper Than Coal', *India Times*, 27 January 2016, available http://www.indiatimes.com/news/india/for-the-first-time-in-modern-india-s-history-solar-energy-is-cheaper-than-coal-249907.html (accessed 23 August 2017).

23. Tom Kenning, 'Yet Another India Solar Tariff Record of 2.44 Rupees in Rajasthan', *PV Tech*, 12 May 2017, available https://www.pv-tech.org/news/yet-another-india-solar-tariff-record-of-2.44-rupees-in-rajasthan (accessed 23 August 2017).

24. Interviews with Rajasthan Solar Association representative, 16 August 2016, and with former Rajasthan Renewable Energy Corporation Limited employee, 23 August 2016.

25. Interview with researcher, 22 August 2016, and with private solar developer, 24 August 2016.

26. Sidharth Sinha, 'Introducing Competition in the Power Sector: Open Access and Cross Subsidies', *Economic and Political Weekly* 40(7), 2005: 631–7.

27. Interview with advocate, 9 August 2016.

28. See http://rerc.rajasthan.gov.in/TariffOrders/Order237.pdf (accessed 24 March 2017).

29. Interview with Department of Energy official, 17 August 2016, and discom official, 8 August 2016.

30. Kelli Joseph, 'The Politics of Power: Electricity Reform in India', *Energy Policy* 38(1), 2010: 503–11.

12

HEMA RAMAKRISHNAN[*]

Tamil Nadu Power Sector

The Saga of the Subsidy Trap

Tamil Nadu is amongst the top ranking states of India in terms of its economic strength, its urbanization, and its human development. The electricity sector in Tamil Nadu has the third highest generating capacity, has achieved near total electrification of all its households, and can boast of the highest capacity for renewable electricity generation among the Indian states. At the same time, in terms of financial performance, Tamil Nadu's power sector has been among the worst performing three utilities in the country in recent years.[1] Annual Integrated Rating of State Distribution Utilities—which is an integrated rating exercise based on a range of parameters covering operational, financial, regulatory, and reform aspects—has given the distribution company in Tamil Nadu a score of B (below average) or C+ (low) for its operational and financial performance capability during 2015–17.[2]

During the 1950s and 1960s, in spite of having significant expansion of rural electrification and also subsidizing the consumption of rural

* The author would like to thank K. Vishnu Mohan Rao and Ashwin Ram at the Citizen Consumer and Civic Action Group, Chennai, for their inputs.

consumers, the utility was able to generate a modest surplus without any subvention from the state government. However, since 1970–1 it has been incurring losses on account of the subsidized rates for electricity to certain consumer groups, as required by the state government. The state government's subvention provided to the utility was adequate to compensate for this till 2000–1 after which it has been inadequate. The continuously deteriorating financial position of the utility has adversely impacted the cost and quality of access, with the utility having to resort to power cuts at different points of time.

Why did this happen in a sector whose financial performance was good till the 1970s, within a state that had good economic and human capabilities? This chapter provides an account of the evolution of the power sector in Tamil Nadu as institutionalized through the provisions in India's Constitution, its Directive Principles for State Policy and relevant legislations, and as shaped by state level political economy aspects relating to its governance. The analysis focuses on how the interplay between group interests, political aspirations, technological factors, and the nature of control afforded to the state government over this sector have influenced, and in turn have been influenced, by the performance outcomes in this sector. The narrative is divided into specific time periods that have been chosen to capture significant shifts in the nature of political influence and in institutional arrangements (Table 12.1). The impact of the sector's performance (measured in terms of service quality, financial viability, and load composition) on the state economy as also on the opportunity costs for the society is analysed. This analysis is based on data, literature, media reports, interviews, and interactions with experts, practitioners, and civil society organizations as also the author's research on the sector.

Early History

The public electrification programme in Tamil Nadu started as early as the 1920s when it was the Madras Presidency under British rule. The Public Works Department initially developed the hydroelectric potential. In 1927, the Electricity Department was created and generation and transmission of electricity came under its monopolistic control. Distribution was mostly under the Department though a few areas were served by municipal licensees. Generation and transmission

TABLE 12.1   Timeline of Key Events: Tamil Nadu

State Politics	Period	Power Sector
• Madras Presidency under British	Early History 1920–57	• 1927: Electricity Department established
• 1947: India's Independence		• 1930: Rural Electrification started
• 1946–67: INC rule		• 1957: Formation of TNEB
		• 1963: Start of the peasant movement in Coimbatore demanding concession
• 1967–71: DMK rule under Annadurai and then Karunanidhi	Rule of Dravidian Parties 1967–2003	• 1973: Formation of Thamizhaga Vivisayigal Sangam
• 1971–7: DMK under Karunanidhi		• 1984: Free power for small farmers and fixed charges for other farmers
• 1977–89: AIADMK under MGR		• 1988: Metering of agricultural consumption discontinued
• 1989–91: DMK under Karunanidhi		• 1998: TNERC constituted
• 1991–6: AIADMK under Jayalalitha		• 2003: Electricity Act came into force
• 1996–2001: DMK under Karunanidhi		
• 2001–6: AIADMK under Jayalalitha		
• 2006–11: DMK under Karunanidhi	Post EA 2003	• 2010: TNEB unbundled into TANGEDCO (Gen and Distn) and TANTRANSCO (transmission)
• 2011–16: AIADMK under Jayalalitha		• 2015: Tamil Nadu signs up for UDAY scheme
• 2016: AIADMK under Jayalalitha		

Source: Author.

capacity expanded significantly and by 1944 the Madras Presidency had one of the largest electricity systems, in terms of capacity and sales, in British India. A two-pronged strategy to increase power generation as well as to expand its reach to more areas and more consumer groups was adopted. Rural electrification programmes began in the 1930s and by 1940 groundwater irrigation accounted for over five per cent of total consumption in the state.[3]

Post-independence, the Indian National Congress (INC) governed the Madras State and was in power till 1967. The Tamil Nadu Electricity Board (TNEB) was formed in 1957 in pursuance of the Electricity (Supply) Act, 1948 (EA 1948) legislated by the Union government. The TNEB was a government-owned statutory monopoly which was responsible for the integrated operations of generation, transmission, and distribution of electricity within the state. The overarching objective was to expand electricity access with an emphasis on serving rural areas and ensuring equitable access for all. Industrial and agricultural consumption expanded. The TNEB had a uniform pricing policy for all areas though it was cheaper to service urban areas. Electricity used for irrigation pumps was charged at rates lower than costs to promote agricultural productivity and rural incomes. The TNEB also earned positive net income without receiving any subsidy from the state government. Efficiency and equity aspects were thus well managed.

Expanding Subsidies, Dwindling Resources, and Shortages (1967–2003)

Start of Dravidian Rule

'Dravidian' refers to a member of the Tamil-speaking native population in south India. In 1925 Tamil Nadu witnessed the start of the Dravidian Movement—also known as the Self Respect Movement—that was founded by E.V. Ramaswamy, earlier a member of the INC. This was a movement to fight against the oppression faced by the non-Brahmans in a hierarchical caste-based society dominated by the Brahmans. It sought to achieve equal status for all castes and classes as well as gender equality. This movement transformed into an anti-Brahmanist one and later became anti-North Indians, anti-Hindi, and anti-religion.

The movement joined with the Justice Party and the Dravida Kazhagam (Dravidian Federation referred to as DK in short) was formed out of this in 1944. The DK wanted a separate Dravida Nadu (Dravidian Land) and was not in favour of contesting elections. This led to a split in the party and the Dravida Munnetra Kazhagam (Dravidian Progress Federation referred to as DMK in short) was formed in 1949. In 1967, the DMK, led by Annadurai, came to power in the state and since then this party or its break-away parties have been in power in Tamil Nadu.

According to Subramanian, the Dravidian movement was characterized by organizational pluralism which comprised of cadre autonomy, supporter autonomy, and strategic flexibility on the part of the leadership.[4] This combination of flexibility and autonomy enabled two strategic shifts in the Dravidian movement's organization. The first was a turn towards populism that was associated with the formation of DMK. The second was the emergence of diverse populisms associated with the formation of ADMK. These strategic shifts made the Dravidianist constructions of political economy more inclusive.

The DMK's discourse distinguished the popular Tamil community—the 'people', from the other ethnic and social categories (North Indian and Brahman)—the 'elite'. The DMK was primarily associated with 'assertive' populism which urges supporters towards militant action to open hitherto restricted spaces and creates entitlements to education, jobs, loans, subsidized producer goods, and so on. Due to the scarcity of such goods, groups with social power and key supporters of the movement are best able to compete for these entitlements.

When M.G. Ramachandran (MGR) broke away from DMK he embraced 'paternalistic' populism which promised that a benevolent leader or party will provide the poor and powerless subsidized wage goods and protection from the repressive elite. Lower strata and women are its main supporters and they are encouraged to assume an attitude of reverence and gratitude towards the party and its leader. The centrality of a charismatic leader implies a weak party organization with limited cadre autonomy. During MGR's tenure, the administration became individualized and highly centralized. Sanjivi Guhan finds that during the eighties the fiscal system in Tamil Nadu worked in the interest of the richer members of the society and actually taxed the poor. The public dole for the poor was, to a significant extent, paid for by themselves through tax payments. The welfare schemes of ADMK had very little impact in terms of redistribution of income and wealth.[5] In spite of this, he was very popular with the masses and had an uncanny hold on them because of his screen image of the hero who championed the cause of the downtrodden.[6] Many believe that Jayalalitha, MGR's successor, was the only contemporary leader who had built a near indelible personality cult through welfarism.[7] During her last decade in power she established a patron-client relationship with her 'people'. Pulapre Balakrishnan argues that it is part of a political strategy to lull the populace into quietude, strip them of any consciousness of citizenship, with which comes an awareness of politics and governance. At the same time, the slightest criticism of the government's policies is dealt with a heavy hand.[8]

Both the DMK and the AIADMK parties started distributing private goods like fans, gas stoves, mixers, television sets, laptops, bicycles, and so on. Pulapre calls this distributivism, as distinct from social protection, and indicates that it is carried out with strategic political intent. On one hand the expansion of democratic inputs is to be celebrated. But on the other hand, it has led to the rise of potentially unsustainable subsidies, not always optimally targeted. Both sides of this dynamic are the result of the kind of two-party populist electoral contest that has come to characterize Tamil Nadu since the formation of the DMK in 1967 and its offshoot AIADMK in 1977.

Green Revolution and Peasant Movement (1967–77)

Tamil Nadu has historically been an agrarian economy and the Cauvery delta region is considered the 'granary of South India'. Today Tamil Nadu is the second largest producer of rice in the country. Farming had largely been dependent on monsoon rains and surface water. During the 1960s, Tamil Nadu became one of the first few states where the green revolution was introduced. These new methods of farming required higher capital investments, intensive use of fertilizers, and assured water supply. With the state being largely dependent on surface water, when the rains failed, productivity was affected. Thus the cost of farming went up and so did the risks. The impact of this technology also worsened the income distribution since it was tougher for the economically weaker farmers to withstand the risk of crop failure. Access to electricity for irrigation became crucial and those in areas with lower water tables were at a disadvantage.

These factors gave rise to a strong peasant movement around issues relating to electricity, crop based agricultural income tax, deferral of loan repayment, and removal of agricultural income tax. The farmers were basically allowed to use the subsidized electricity only for irrigation and some limited lighting facilities. In 1963, a delegation of farmers from a taluk (subdivision) in Coimbatore district approached the Electricity Minister and the Chairman of TNEB and demanded that subsidized electricity be allowed for additional domestic lighting uses. Their initial efforts met with success and strengthened by this experience the movement expanded its organizational base to the entire district.

In 1967, the DMK government imposed severe penalties on illegal use of subsidized electricity for domestic water pumping and small scale agro processing. Again the peasant movement made a representation and got the penalties revoked. They also were permitted to use the subsidized electricity for domestic and small scale industrial activities. In 1970, when Karunanidhi (Annadurai's successor) hiked the electricity tariff by 2 paise/kWh and also introduced a crop-based agricultural tax, a district-wide agitation was organized and this time it involved hunger strike, massive rallies, and non-cooperation. When the police tried to repress them, it turned violent. Eventually, the tariff was lowered and the crop-based agricultural tax was revoked. By 1973, the organization expanded to the entire state and the Thamizhaga Vivasayigal Sangam (TVS), meaning Tamilian Agriculturists Association was formed.[9]

The TVS was a non-political organization having both rich and poor farmers as well as landless labourers as members. It had a four-tier structure with the units at the village, block, district, and state-level. In addition to the President and Secretary it also had a formal agitation committee. The TVS escalated matters by refusing to pay electricity dues, forcibly reconnecting if disconnections were imposed for non-payment, and became more militant when negotiations failed. During the Emergency in 1975–6, the agitations of the TVS were repressed and using this opportunity the DMK government raised the agricultural tariff.[10]

During this period the state government also offered a lot of concessions to power-intensive industries. The TNEB's generating capacity in hydro plants had expanded and so these concessions were offered with a view to promote industrial development by exploiting the cheaper hydro-power availability. Large subsidies were also offered to low income domestic consumers. However, starting from 1972–3 the power sector started experiencing a lot of shortages. An estimate made of the days of work lost due to this over the five years from 1972–3 to 1976–7 indicates that about 832 days were lost for the industries and 410 days were lost for large commercial consumers.[11]

Rise of MGR and Expansion of Subsidies (1977–89)

In 1977, the Anna Dravida Munnetra Kazhagam (ADMK), which was a splinter group from DMK led by MGR, a very charismatic and popular movie star, came to power. Since then, the DMK and the ADMK (which later became the All India Anna Dravida Munnetra Kazhagam referred to as AIADMK) have been the only two parties that have been elected to govern. Of these, AIADMK has won a majority seven times and has ruled for the longest time.

In 1978, the TVS hardened its stand and resolved not to pay electricity tariffs, cooperative credits and land taxes. When the government was not sympathetic statewide agitations ensued involving a lot of violence. As a result of which, the MGR government grouped the farmers into two categories—small farmers and other farmers and fixed a lower rate for the small farmers compared to others. Political machinations saw the dismissal of the MGR government in 1980.

Realizing that the support of TVS would be crucial for him to get re-elected, MGR negotiated a deal with them agreeing to meet their charter of demands in return for their support. However, after winning the elections in 1980, he rejected their demands. Instead, MGR announced free power for the small farmers and a fixed charge for the other farmers. Additionally, for the small farmers the 'taccavi' loans with penal interests—that is, loans extended by the government to tackle crop damage crises caused by natural calamities—were waived and they were allowed more time to pay back the term loans. He also initiated a programme to construct houses for the landless labour, mostly from the Dalit community. As a result the support of the small farmers and landless labourers for TVS started to weaken.[12]

MGR was voted back to power for the third time in 1984. During this term, subsidies were provided to additional categories of consumers.

Free lighting was provided for huts in villages and to tribal colonies. In order to partially cover these costs, the tariffs for the large industrial and commercial consumers were hiked. The power shortages were also increasing and these consumers had to resort to high-cost diesel-based captive generation. It also accelerated the flight of big industries from TNEB.

It was in 1988, during AIADMK's third term, that metering of agricultural consumption was discontinued. The argument was that while TNEB had to incur a lot of expenses in recording consumption it was not earning any revenue from agricultural uses. At this time agriculture accounted for about 25 per cent of the total consumption.

Farmers started exploiting the groundwater in an indiscriminate manner by using multiple pumps and choosing water intensive cropping patterns. Traditional crop rotation methods were replaced by cultivating paddy for all three seasons. Acreage under water-intensive sugarcane and banana increased while area under traditional millets and groundnut decreased.[13] This could not be sustained by the local water tables and groundwater levels started depleting. In coastal areas, this caused sea water intrusion and adversely affected productivity. The falling groundwater levels worsened the plight of the small and marginal farmers who could not afford to have deep bore wells. This spawned informal water markets and the poorer farmers had to pay heavily to buy water from their richer counterparts. Cheaper and energy inefficient irrigation pumps were used which raised the energy output ratio for the economy.

Due to the lack of metering of agricultural consumers, TNEB's knowledge about the shares of agricultural consumption, technical transmission & distribution (T&D) losses, and theft, in its unaccounted energy became increasingly inaccurate. This encouraged a lot of illegal drawing of power. Prior to the supply of free power, the T&D losses were around 18 per cent. Hence, TNEB continued to assume 18 per cent as T&D losses and the rest of the unaccounted energy was treated as agricultural consumption. The TNEB then claimed the entire shortfall in its revenue as subvention from the government on account of the free power supplied. Thus, the supply of free power for agricultural and for low income domestic consumers provided a convenient cover for the state to hide theft and inefficiencies. The nature of state control in this sector thus helped financial and political rent-seeking by the party in power to flourish. According to a former Chairman of a State Electricity Board rent-seeking in the power sector was the worst.[14]

The financial performance of TNEB started significantly deteriorating during MGR's rule. In addition to the free power for farmers, domestic tariff rates (except for high consumption slabs) remained mostly stagnant during this decade. The average tariff rates for industrial and commercial consumers on the other hand nearly doubled as they were partly cross-subsiding the agricultural and domestic consumers. In spite of growth in capacity, power shortages were witnessed.

During the 1980s, the central government started to promote wind-based power generation and Tamil Nadu was among the states with very good wind potential. The TNEB started setting up wind farms in Muppandal in the mid-1980s on a demonstration basis and later the capacity here expanded to 19 megawatt (MW) by 1993–4. The state government decided to encourage private sector to set up captive wind generation facilities by providing a lot of incentives. The facility could be set up at the site with wind potential and the power could be wheeled through TNEB's grid to their industrial unit. Any excess power generated could be sold to TNEB. This brought on board some additional wind-based capacity from the private sector. As a result some of the high paying industrial demand moved out of TNEB.

'Amma' Takes Charge (1989–2003)

After MGR's demise, DMK came back to power in 1989 but did not complete its term as the state was brought under President's rule. In 1991, J. Jayalalitha, a popular actor who had starred with MGR in many movies and had been greatly influenced by him, led the AIADMK to govern the state. However, in the next election held in 1996 the AIADMK had a crushing defeat and DMK came back to power led by Karunanidhi.

In the elections held in 2001, Jayalalitha was actually barred from contesting as she was found guilty of appropriating state-owned property and was convicted to five years imprisonment. In spite of this the AIADMK won the elections and she was anointed the Chief Minister as a non-elected member of the state Assembly. However, within a few months of her assuming office she was disqualified by the Supreme Court on grounds that she could not hold that office while criminal cases were pending against her. Six months later she was acquitted, resumed her position as the head of the government and went on to complete her term until 2006.

During the 1990s the financial performance in the power sector worsened further with the subsidy burden mounting and with the state government finding it increasingly difficult to raise the needed revenue. On one hand, the state government had to pay subsidies to the Board and on the other hand the Board had to pay interest to the government for loans borrowed from it. Consequently, the subsidy due from the government was adjusted against the interest payable by TNEB. Subsequently the government's loan amount with TNEB was also written down in order to adjust for subsides payable. By 1999, the state government's loan to TNEB was completely wiped out. The government then created an equity share of about Rs 200 crores in the utility.

Wind energy capacity in the private sector expanded but TNEB did not have adequate transmission capacity to evacuate the power. The fact that capacity expansion was concentrated on generation while transmission was neglected was pointed out by a few of the interviewees. To a certain extent, the central government and private sector participated in the generation segment. In case of transmission, it was solely the state government's responsibility and Tamil Nadu had insufficient funds. Tamil Nadu could not attract enough Independent Power Producers (IPP) in generation. According to an Ex-TNEB employee, Independent Power Producers were reluctant to come to Tamil Nadu as they felt they may not realize profits here, since the utility was known to delay payments to wind energy generators by more than a year.[15]

The Story Post-Electricity Act 2003

In 2006, the DMK, led by Karunanidhi, came back to power based on an anti-incumbency mood in the state. His family's role in India's 2G telecom auctions scam was used by the AIADMK's election campaigns and in 2011 Jayalalitha came back to power. The post-poll predictions for the 2016 elections indicated that the DMK would come to power but Jayalalitha had a surprise victory.

Figure 12.1 gives a broad idea of the physical and financial performance of TNEB between 2007 and 2015. The inadequacy in transmission capacity has been removed and in 2014, 100 per cent of the wind energy generated in the state could be evacuated. Between 2008 and 2012 severe

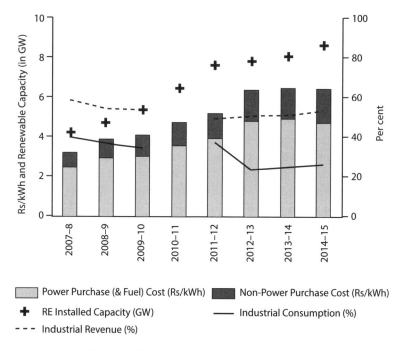

FIGURE 12.1   Physical and Financial Profile: Tamil Nadu
Source: CSO, *Energy Statistics* (New Delhi: Central Statistics Office, Ministry of Statistics and Programme Implementation, Government of India, 2010, 2012, 2014, and 2016); PFC, *Reports on Performance of State Power Utilities* (New Delhi: Power Finance Corporation Limited, 2011, 2013, 2015, and 2016).

power shortages were witnessed and the utility was able to meet only two-thirds of the maximum demand. The industrial sector bore the brunt of this shortage and while Chennai suffered two hour power cuts for a period of time other areas faced 12–14 hours of power cut. A higher proportion of the energy sold to the consumers came from power purchased at a higher cost compared to the cost of TNEB's own generation. The net losses, without subsidy, for 2014–15 was eighteen times the losses suffered during 2002–3. Also, as shown in the accounts of TNEB, the subvention provided by the state government was adequate to cover all expenses only until 2000–1 after which the net surplus was negative even after taking into account the subvention amount. For the period 2002–3 to 2014–15, the subvention from the government covered only 29 per cent of the utility's losses, on an average. The cumulative amount of uncovered losses at the end of 2014–15 was close to Rs 90,000 crores. TNEB's debt burden was about 50 per cent of the state's debt in 2013–14. Figure 12.2 gives an idea of the uncovered gap. The government's strategy of free power to agriculture and higher charges to industry has actually resulted in a decline of both their shares in the energy consumed because the opportunity costs in both these sectors have gone up.

Tamil Nadu was a forerunner in promoting renewable based electricity. As of October 2017, it has RE capacity of 10.7 gigawatt (GW) and almost all of it is in the private sector. In 2013, the state government launched a scheme to promote roof-top solar for domestic consumers by offering a subsidy component towards the capital cost in addition to the Ministry of New and Renewable Energy's (MNRE's) subsidy. The roof-top solar was to be grid connected with net-metering facility and Tamil Nadu Generation and Distribution Corporation (TANGEDCO) would pay for the net energy that might be supplied to the grid. There

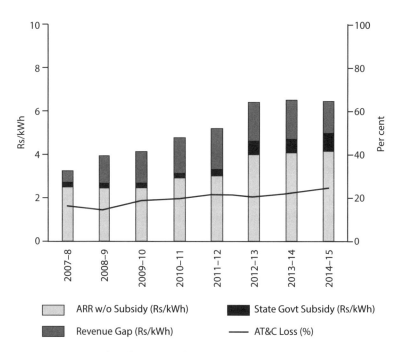

Figure 12.2 Supply-side Costs and Revenue Recovery: Tamil Nadu
Source: PFC, *Reports on Performance of State Power Utilities* (New Delhi: Power Finance Corporation Limited, 2011, 2013, 2015, and 2016).

was a good response to this and within the first few weeks 1,050 applications were received.[16] However, availing the capital subsidy entailed huge transaction costs and the ambitious project which targeted 10,000 installations had only 460 connections by March 2015.[17]

Recently, the state government has made plans to reduce the payment for the net energy it receives which is eroding the attractiveness of this option. Most of the rooftop solar in the state is now on a stand-alone basis as the transaction costs of availing net metering facility were a huge deterrent. One of the biggest policy challenges facing the solar energy sector in Tamil Nadu is the scaling up of the net metering. 'Tamil Nadu is one the first states to implement net-metering policy but now it lacks the driving force and net-metering has been totally stalled. The reason is that TANGEDCO does not want to lose its consumers and the profit.'[18]

Reforms That Weren't

The legislation of the Electricity Act in 2003 required all State Electricity Boards to be unbundled into generation, transmission, and distribution entities. The TNEB was among the last states to do so in 2010. The generation and distribution functions were hived off into TANGEDCO, the transmission function into Tamil Nadu Transmission Company (TANTRANSCO) and TNEB Limited became the holding company for both.

Regulation

The Tamil Nadu Electricity Regulatory Commission (TNERC) was constituted in 1999 but was without a Chairman till 2002. The members and staff of the Commission have mostly been chosen from ex-TNEB employees. In the opinion of an ex-TNEB employee, the TNERC was a puppet of the state government.[19] The only advantage of the Commission is that it has brought in some transparency.[20] Starting from the late 1980s, adequate information about the power sector was not easily available in the public domain.

The TNERC issued its first tariff order in 2003. In this order, TNEB was directed to get all consumption metered, including those of agricultural pumps and huts, within three years and to issue new connections only on a metered basis. As of 2017 this has not yet been implemented.

Between 2003 and 2010, TNEB did not seek any tariff revisions and did not submit the mandatory Annual Revenue Requirements.

When the state was witnessing significant power shortages between 2008 and 2012, crippling restrictions and control measures were imposed on industrial consumers and that too for an indefinite period (APTEL Judgement dated 11 January 2011). According to the Electricity Act 2003, such measures could be adopted only in an emergency or when the state load dispatch centre directs. However, the TNERC allowed TANGEDCO to impose a 40 per cent cut on the energy consumption of High-Tension industrial and commercial consumers. Additional restrictions on demand during peak hours were imposed along with penal charges if these restrictions were violated.

The TNEB had implemented open access in the state even before EA 2003 because private industries were encouraged to set up wind-based generation for their captive use and feed any excess power into the grid. The wind energy generators could also sell the excess to third parties. Given TANGEDCO's high tariff rates for large industries and with falling wind energy generation costs, it was cheaper for them to purchase through open access even after the cross-subsidy surcharges and wheeling charges. Most of the open access has been intrastate.[21]

There is no ex ante scrutiny of TNEB's investment decisions by TNERC. The decisions are made by the state government and agreements are signed by the Chief Minister. Earlier, when TNEB was a Board these decisions were scrutinized and deliberated upon in the Assembly and this information was also available in the public domain. Now, TNEB is a company and being a fully government-owned entity it does not rely much on the market for its investment finances and hence for its financial discipline. Power purchase agreements are decided by the government. The public have no information on this and no effective forum to raise their concerns let alone influence decision making. The only avenue is to participate in tariff hearings and once the major investment decisions are made marginal tinkering with the tariff rates is all that is possible.

The accumulated amount of TNEB's uncovered losses in 2014–15 were Rs 90,000 crores. The TNEB has petitioned the Commission to treat this as deferred income and book them under Regulatory Assets. The EA 2003 allows for Regulatory Assets to be created only under exceptional circumstances or constraints—for example, arising due to natural calamities. The Commission made the argument that trying to recover it now would pose a huge burden on the consumers. At the same time the state government is not in a position to pay. Hence, TNERC has approved converting about Rs 25,000 crores of the accumulated losses into regulatory assets in 2017 and has indicated that an additional amount of Rs 39,717 crores could be proposed in TNEB's annual revenue requirement petition for 2017–18. Thus the problem is postponed to the future.

Administration

All the former employees in the electricity sector who were interviewed were of the opinion that governance and administration in this sector has become highly inefficient. The utility staff lack basic knowledge of rules, regulations, and procedures, and there is apathy among the bureaucrats. There is no clarity on amendments to rules and the players in the segment incur huge transaction costs. In the opinion of an ex-Chairman of an SEB, policies are made without any idea of the problems on the ground and they lack clear objectives.[22]

Corruption

One issue that everyone interviewed had mentioned was the level of corruption involved in the electricity sector in Tamil Nadu. 'Worst form of rent seeking happens in this sector', 'TANGEDCO is in crisis purely because of decades long corruption', 'the government is corrupt and hence there is no policy taken to promote competition in the sector', 'the major reason for TANGEDCO's losses is the corruption at procurement stage and also the ineffective government policies of subsidies and free power', 'TNEB is the most corrupt state utility', 'the only agenda for politicians in this sector is using TANGEDCO for their personal rent-seeking' and so on. The CMS-India Corruption Study 2017[23] has ranked Tamil Nadu the third most corrupt state in the country.

Summing Up

The evolution of the power sector in Tamil Nadu started in the early part of the twentieth century embedded in an environment of decentralized political powers and shaped by the mutual objectives of the supplier and the consumers. Post-independence, it witnessed significant expansion with the efficiency and equity objectives well balanced. During the sixties, given the increased risks and unequal economic impact of green revolution on the farming community, a well-organized peasant movement managed to avail of a lot of concessions. Subsequently, the sector became a means to gain political popularity and financial rents at the same time, by subsidizing consumers in an indiscriminate manner, while the utility went deeper and deeper in the red. There is a path dependency in this process that seems to be difficult to escape. Having gone down this path, both vested interests and competitive politics constrains political will to reverse the trend.

UDAY Scheme

Tamil Nadu has been forced to sign up for this scheme because its credit rating is very low and its avenues for loans are drying up. However, it has to be seen if it will meet the efficiency improvement requirements by metering agricultural consumption.[24] Tamil Nadu is not even implementing annual revisions for tariffs and one is not sure if they will go ahead with the quarterly revisions.[25]

Prospects for the Future

No big change regarding improvements in the financial performance of the sector can be expected within the next five years. Maybe in 10 years the sector's performance will hit rock bottom after which it cannot but improve. The power sector cannot be neglected forever.[26]

At the national level renewable energy, mostly wind and solar, will be 15–20 per cent of the grid supply. Tamil Nadu is already there and the growth is likely to plateau. The benefits of free power are largely flowing to the landed farmers and smaller enterprises are subsidizing the large industries. This situation has to change and given today's technology and with the introduction of Aadhar, the subsidies to farmers could be provided as Direct Benefit Transfers.[27]

Notes and References

1. Power Finance Commission, *Report on Performance of State Power Utilities*, Power Finance Corporation Limited, Government of India, 2013.

2. Ministry of Power, *State Distribution Utilities Annual Integrated Rating* (Government of India, 2015, 2016, and 2017).
3. Sunila S. Kale, 'Structures of Power: Electrification in Colonial India', *Comparative Studies of South Asia, Africa and the Middle East* 34(3), 2014.
4. John, Harriss, 'Populism, Tamil Style, Is It Really a Success?', Development Studies Institute, *LSE Working Paper Series*, No. 01–15 (2001).
5. Harriss, 'Populism, Tamil Style, Is It Really a Success?'.
6. India Today, 'Tamil Nadu: A Decade of Decay', 31 July 1987
7. BBC News, 'Jayalalitha: The Downfall of India's "Mother" Politician', 3 October 2014.
8. The Hindu, 'Public Policy, Private Gain', 17 December 2015.
9. See, 'The Historical Background of Thamizhaga Vivasayigal Sangam', available http://shodhganga.inflibnet.ac.in/bitstream/10603/16237/9/09_chapter%203.pdf (accessed on 15 November 2017).
10. 'The Historical Background of Thamizhaga Vivasayigal Sangam'.
11. R. Hema, 'An Optimum Rate Structure for Electricity in Tamil Nadu' (unpublished PhD thesis, University of Madras, 1988).
12. 'The Historical Background of Thamizhaga Vivasayigal Sangam'.
13. M.E. Sivagnanaselvi, 'An Estimate for Electricity Consumption in Tamil Nadu' (unpublished Masters Dissertation Thesis, Madras School of Economics, 2003).
14. Interview with a retired Chairman of a State Electricity Board, 10 August 2016.
15. Interview with an ex-TNEB employee on 23 August 2016.
16. U.N. Sushma, 'Tamil Nadu's Solar Rooftop Scheme Gathers Pace', *The Times of India*, 27 March 2014.
17. R. Srikanth, 'Shadow over Solar Power Scheme', *The Hindu*, 19 March 2015.
18. Interview with a solar based Independent Power Producer on 13 June 2017.
19. Interview with an ex-TNEB employee on 23 August 2016.
20. Interview with the MD & CEO of an EPC company in Chennai, 30 October 2017.
21. Interview with the MD & CEO of an EPC company in Chennai, 30 October 2017.
22. Interview with a retired Chairman of a State Electricity Board, 10 August 2016.
23. CMS-India Corruption Study 2017, *Perception and Experience with Public Services & Snapshot View for 2005–17* (New Delhi: CMS Research House, 2017).
24. Interview with a retired TNERC Director, 2 November 2017.
25. Interview with a journalist, 20 August 2016.

26. Interview with a retired TNERC Director, 2 November 2017.
27. Interview with the MD & CEO of an EPC company in Chennai, 30 October 2017.

13

JONATHAN BALLS

Stalled Reform in the Face of Electoral Fears

Uttar Pradesh's Electricity Distribution Sector

The power sector in Uttar Pradesh (UP) has faced the persistent problem of its public electricity distribution companies (discoms) reporting poor operational performance, and suffering high annual financial losses since the 1980s. At a time of state-level financial crisis, in 1999 the then-Bharatiya Janata Party (BJP) government initiated a reform programme for the power sector, aided by the World Bank. The reform approach adopted was the New Delhi and the World Bank-supported vertical separation and privatization model.[1] The Uttar Pradesh State Electricity Board (UPSEB) was split up, and action was taken to invest in transmission infrastructure, facilitate private investment in generation, and institute independent tariff-setting. Plans were also initiated to privatize the state's distribution companies. Reform stalled after the BJP lost power in the 2002 state elections, as a subsequent period of Presidents Rule was then itself followed by two weak coalition governments. Five public discoms were created during this period, but plans for privatization repeatedly failed.

These reforms did not successfully engineer a turnaround of the state discoms' operational or financial performance. From 2007 onwards, UP has had majority single party governments, first Bahujan Samaj Party (BSP), and then Samajwadi Party (SP) government. Both avoided large-scale reform of the power sector instead making largely unsuccessful moves to privatize distribution. Both governments were arguably spared having to push through major reforms by the cushion of central government bailout schemes launched in 2012 and 2016. Through the late 2000s and 2010s, financial losses at the state's discoms have remained high, and aggregate technical and commercial (AT&C) losses have not been significantly reduced.

This chapter argues that explaining the persistence of problems in the power sector requires an understanding of UP's overall political economy. Since the 1990s, UP has had a competitive multiparty political environment.[2] Four main parties contend for power: the Congress, BJP, SP, and BSP. Between the late 1980s and 2007, the state experienced a frequent succession of chief ministers (CMs) and shifting coalition governments. The BSP and then the SP won majorities in 2007 and 2012, but neither consolidated longer-term power. Amid intense political competition, governments have adopted populist policies on tariffs and subsidies to win public support,[3] and have been reluctant to embrace power sector reforms that might be painful for the state's electorate. The power sector has been a political bellwether, with promises of electrification, subsidized power, and increased hours of supply often used to win support.[4] While tariffs have been raised periodically, they are never increased in the run-up to elections, and agricultural and domestic tariffs have been kept well below cost of supply. The state's discoms have not been allowed to operate independently.[5] Theft is often informally politically protected, with legislative assembly politicians more likely to win re-election when electricity theft has increased in their constituencies.[6]

This chapter also argues that the large base of domestic and agricultural consumption that UP's discoms serve, coupled with a low base of industrial consumers and expensive power purchasing costs, makes financial solvency very difficult to engineer. Domestic and agricultural consumers pay tariffs well below the actual cost of supply, and a relatively small industrial base is relied on for cross-subsidization. Raising the tariffs of these consumer groups is politically and socially problematic. Poverty in UP is high, with a per capita annual income of only Rs 42,249, much lower than the national average.[7]

The situation in UP highlights the challenge of reform in a politically competitive state, but also points to how structural realities can leave few good options on the table. The populist approach of several governments has clearly harmed the power sector. At the same time, the space for governments to act proactively has been limited. UP has experienced slow economic growth for decades and holds high levels of debt, meaning governments have operated within a limited fiscal space. There is no strong industrial base or source of cheap power to give UP breathing room.[8] Examples of successful discoms, such as the privately run Noida Power Company and neighbouring Uttarakhand's public discom highlight the importance of industrial demand and cheap power: the Noida Power Company, with industry constituting 59 per cent of its energy sales,[9] is a profitable business, while Uttarakhand's public discom, with high industrial revenue and cheap hydro-power, has experienced very low overall losses in recent years.

Three periods are considered in this chapter. The first section analyses the run-up to reforms that began in 1999, and then the reform period itself. The second section examines the stalling of reforms between 2002 and 2007. The final section looks at the years since 2007, during which only minor reforms have been attempted while two significant financial bail-outs took place. Table 13.1 outlines a timeline of key events in UP. Figure 13.1 shows the financial and physical profile of UP's power sector since 2007–8, while Figure 13.2 shows supply-side costs and revenue recovery since 2007–8. Per capita energy consumption in UP is 450 kilowatt hour (kWh), compared to a national average of 884 kWh.[10] In November 2016, UP had a total available installed capacity of 19,388 megawatt (MW),[11] while household electrification in 2011 was 37 per cent.[12]

Fiscal Crisis Opens a Window for Reform: 1990–2002

Prior to 1999, the power sector in UP was vertically integrated, meaning the publically owned UPSEB had responsibility for generation, transmission, and distribution. At the start of the 1990s, supply was still primarily restricted to urban, industrial, and agricultural connections.

TABLE 13.1   Timeline of Key Events: Uttar Pradesh

State Politics		Power Sector Events
	1993	• Noida Power Company established
• Kalyan Singh (BJP) becomes Chief Minister (CM)	1997	
	1998	• Uttar Pradesh Electricity Regulatory Commission (UPERC) established
• Ram Prakash Gupta (BJP) becomes CM	1999	• Power sector reform started • Bids invited for soon to be created Kanpur Electricity Supply Company (KESCO)
• Rajnath Singh (BJP) becomes CM	2000	• KESCO established, privatization sees no bidders
• Elections see no majority; 56 days of President's Rule before Mayawati (BSP) becomes CM	2002	• World Bank withholds funds due to lack of progress on reforms
• Mulayam Singh Yadav becomes CM	2003	• Mayawati creates four discoms, to operate under the UPPCL, provides Rs 1,340 to the UPPCL, and takes on pension liabilities; World Bank lifts suspension of support • 2003 UP Power Policy focuses on investment, private involvement, rural electrification • After forming government, the SP government increases house of supply to rural areas; World Bank cancels support for reforms
	2004	• UPPCL invites bidders for state's five discoms, but privatization does not happen
	2005	• Open Access Regulations set out by the UPERC
	2006	• New flat-rate power tariff for loom weavers announced by SP

(Cont'd)

TABLE 13.1 (*Cont'd*)

State Politics		Power Sector Events
• BSP wins election; Mayawati becomes CM	2007	
	2009	• 2009 UP Energy Policy focuses on new private generation, private involvement, electrification • Torrent awarded franchises to distribute on Agra and Kanpur
	2010	• Renewable Energy Obligation (RPO) requirements set out • Torrent takes over distribution in Agra, but is unable to do so in Kanpur because of protests
• SP wins election; Akhilesh Yadav becomes CM	2012	• SP promises free electricity to weavers if elected; but does not deliver on this promise • Financial Repackaging Programme for UP agreed • Plan to privatize distribution in four cities announced, but sees little progress
	2013	• UP Solar Power Policy launched
	2015	• SP government cancels Torrent's Kanpur franchise • Rooftop Solar PV policy launched
	2016	• UP signs up to UDAY • Mini-grid policy launched • All parties make promises to increased house of supply, and to provide cheaper power in run up to state elections
• BJP wins election	2017	

Source: Author.

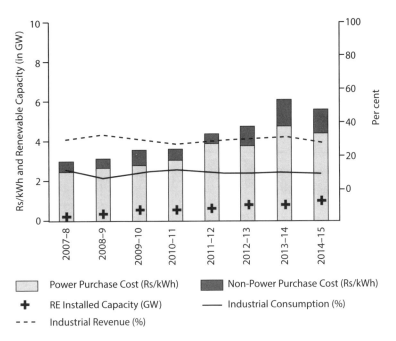

FIGURE 13.1   Financial and Physical Profile: Uttar Pradesh
Source: PFC, *Reports on Performance of State Power Utilities* (New Delhi: Power Finance Corporation Limited, 2011, 2013, 2015, and 2016).

The power sector suffered from shortages of supply, and load shedding was commonplace. Domestic and agricultural tariffs were kept below the cost of supply, with industry cross-subsidizing these consumer groups.

The 1990s were a decade of change and growing problems in the power sector. Following the rise of low-caste representing parties in the state, electrification of domestic rural households had become a key political priority, leading to the number of domestic consumers expanding rapidly, while industrial demand largely flat-lined. The Bahujan Samaj Party (BSP), in particular, accelerated village electrification, especially in the constituencies of BSP legislators.[13] Between 1991–2 and 1998–9, UP saw its domestic consumer load increase from 28 to 43 per cent of overall load, while industrial load declined from 34 to 26 per cent.[14] Over multiple years, successive UP governments increased tariffs for domestic consumers at below inflation rates, allowing

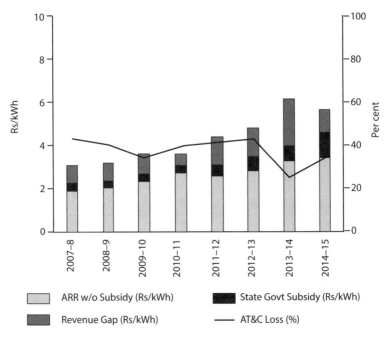

FIGURE 13.2   Supply-side Costs and Revenue Recovery: Uttar Pradesh
Source: CSO, *Energy Statistics* (New Delhi: Central Statistics Office, Ministry of Statistics and Programme Implementation, Government of India, 2010, 2012, 2014, and 2016).

cross-subsidization by industry to increase. Revenue from domestic customers only grew from 16 to 17 per cent of total revenue between 1991–2 and 1998–9, during which period the ratio of the average domestic tariff to the average tariff for all consumers decreased from 75 per cent to 56 per cent.[15] Industrial consumption grew marginally in real terms, while the share of revenue from industry declined from 53 to 49 per cent. In response to the burdens placed upon them, industry increasingly turned to captive power plants.[16,17]

The financial position of the UPSEB deteriorated throughout the 1990s. The UPSEB and the state government did not have the necessary capital to invest in transmission infrastructure and generation capacity. Low revenue realization, poor billing levels, high AT&C losses, and politically determined tariff-setting were key problems.[18]

As this situation unfolded, successive governments considered power sector reform. The World Bank was engaged repeatedly from the late 1980s, and a plan for a US $350-million World Bank-supported reform programme was formulated, and seriously considered several times.[19] However, with successive weak coalition governments in place through the 1990s, the political environment was not conducive to reform.[20,21] One experiment with privatization did take place: the Noida Power Company was established in 1993 as a private distribution company supplying electricity to the Noida areas.

Uttar Pradesh was facing a serious state level fiscal crisis by the end of the decade. Its economy was growing slowly, investment was urgently needed, and the state's finances were mired in a cycle of increasing debt. The raising of public employee salaries by the UP government, following the Fifth Pay Commission in 1997, created an immediate budgetary crisis.[22] At this time, BJP governments held power in both Lucknow and New Delhi, creating a window for change. Multiple reforms were planned, including reform of the power sector. In 1997, UP's Principal Secretary of Finance, Sushil Chandra Tripathi, personally initiated a dialogue with the World Bank regarding the state's financial situation. Talks between CM Kalyan Singh's government and the World Bank ended with an agreement mandating fiscal and public sector restructuring, a new industrial policy, and the decentralization and reform of panchayats.[23] Power sector reform was seen as particularly crucial, as the UPSEB remained a serious drag on the state's finances.

Reorganization and reform of the electricity sector was initiated in 1999. The agreed programme stipulated an unbundling of the UPSEB over several years, the encouragement of new private generation, the rationalization of tariffs, tariff-setting by an independent regulator, investment in transmission infrastructure, and a timetable for the creation of multiple discoms and their privatization.[24] The Uttar Pradesh Electricity Regulatory Commission (UPERC) had already been established. The UP Electricity Reform Act of 1999 split the UPSEB into three independent corporations: the Uttar Pradesh Power Corporation Limited (UPPCL) for transmission and distribution, the Uttar Pradesh Rajya Vidyut Utapadan Nigam (UPRVUNL) for thermal generation, and the Uttar Pradesh Jal Vidyut Nigam (UPJVNL) for hydro generation. A World Bank loan of US $150 million was then approved, to be matched by government funding targeted towards improving the state's transmission system and metering.[25]

The government pushed ahead with reforms despite significant union resistance. Employee unions were opposed to privatization because it meant the loss of their status as public sector employees and created uncertainty surrounding their pensions, which had been invested by the UPSEB in fixed power sector assets.[26] More than 100,000 employees went on strike, while unions nationwide joined in solidarity. The UP government was strongly supported by the central government throughout these strikes. The strikes finally ended when the government agreed to fund the pensions of the UPSEB workers and reinstate workers who had been sacked for striking.[27]

The process of privatization was started in 1999, when bids were invited to acquire the yet-to-be-created Kanpur Electricity Supply Company Ltd. (KESCO). Four bidders were pre-qualified;[28] however, these bidders were concerned about the government's projections of technical and commercial losses for KESCO's distribution network, difficult targets for loss reduction, estimates of receivable assets, and the lack of detailed asset registers. Risks in terms of uncertain energy input prices, demand for electricity, tariffs, and operating expenses were judged to be too high and the potential benefits not attractive enough.[29] Only one final bid was submitted in 2000, but even it was withdrawn shortly after.

The 1999 reforms offered the most notable window of opportunity in thirty years for transforming the power sector in UP. The hope was that commercially operating discoms would close deficits and reduce AT&C losses, tariffs would be set non-politically by the UERC, and that reforms would promote investment in new generation and transmission capacity. Further, parallel reforms attracting industry to UP, if successful, would have added lucrative industry consumers to the discoms' revenue sheets. The UPPCL was established as an independent company in 2000, with no debts listed on its books. However, the BJP-led government backed away from difficult decisions to support the UPPCL's turnaround, worried about its prospects in upcoming elections due in 2002. The government failed to provide previously promised transition support to the UPPCL and froze tariffs, despite the UPPCL hoping to raise them significantly, arguing that rates could be raised once performance improved.[30] In 2001 and 2002, the UPPCL faced a large deficit and had to borrow new funds.[31] It was unable to improve revenue collection or reduce AT&C losses. To make matters worse, the secession of Uttarakhand from UP in 2000 cost the UPPCL most of its cheap hydro-power generation, resulting in rising power purchase costs.[32,33]

Stalled Reform: 2002–7

The BJP lost power in the 2002 state assembly elections. After a short period of President's Rule, a BSP-led coalition government was formed with the support of the BJP and Rashtriya Lok Dal, headed by Mayawati Prabhu Das. This government fell little more than a year later. It was replaced in 2003 by an SP-led coalition government with Mulayam Singh Yadav as CM, which continued until 2007. The power sector was partially reformed by 2002, but key reforms were still pending, most notably the creation of four new discoms and their privatization. In the contentious political context following 2002, however, reforms largely stalled. The BSP and SP-led coalition governments followed a largely populist approach to the power sector: tariffs were not raised to meet the cost of supply, and levels of electricity theft remained high with no strong action being taken.[34] The core problems of low revenue realization and high AT&C losses had not been dealt with, and the UPPCL continued to accumulate debt.

When Mayawati became CM in 2002, UP's both wider fiscal and narrower power sector reforms were stalled, and the World Bank had begun to withhold further funding in response.[35] Nevertheless, the World Bank was initially optimistic that reforms would resume, and in early meetings with the new government it appeared open towards funding a number of projects that Mayawati was looking to start.[36] However, it subsequently turned down the state's application for funding. In response, Mayawati declared that she would not be held to the World Bank's 'diktats', and that privatization in the power sector would not be advanced.[37] The World Bank responded by suspending loan payments for power sector reform.[38] Shortly after this, nevertheless, the UP government changed course: it created four discoms in July 2003 as independent subsidiaries of the UPPCL, stating that each would be privatized. A second financial restructuring plan involving Rs 1,340 crore was announced for the UPPCL, and the government agreed to acquire Rs 1,337 crore of employee pension fund liabilities.[39] By August, the World Bank had lifted its suspension of funds.[40]

The BSP-led government collapsed in 2003, and was replaced by an SP-led coalition government. The new government immediately adopted a populist approach to the power sector, quickly moving to fulfil its election promise to increase rural electricity supply from 8 to 14 hours. However, the costs of this expansion were not fully covered, leading to the deterioration of the UPPCL's financial position. As a result, the World Bank formally cancelled their involvement with power sector reform.[41] The SP-led government nevertheless stated their intention to continue with reforms. The UP's 2003 Power Policy outlined the government's focus on transmission network upgrades, metering, tariff rationalization, private investment in generation, and private involvement in distribution. In 2004, the UPPCL invited private actors to bid for the state's five discoms,[42] and in 2005, the government shortlisted Torrent, Reliance, and TATA as approved bidders.[43] However, opposition from the power unions, and evidence at the time that privatization in Odisha was not going smoothly convinced the government to not proceed any further.[44]

The SP again exploited the power sector for populist purposes prior to the 2007 state assembly elections, announcing a lower flat rate tariff structure for power loom weavers in the summer of 2006.[45] As before, the UPPCL did not recuperate these losses through other means.[46] The subsidy most benefitted the east of the state, an electorally crucial region for the SP. The UPERC tried to strike down this subsidy on the basis that the government had not complied with the regulatory requirement to provide advance compensation to the UPPCL for the cost of the subsidy. However, instead of providing the subsidy by adjusting the pre-existing tariff for weavers, which would violate regulations, the UPPCL provided the subsidy via an electricity bill rebate, thus bypassing this requirement.[47]

The structural conditions of the power sector did not see any improvement between 2002 and 2007. Industry electricity consumption continued to stagnate while large numbers of new domestic consumers, paying tariffs well below the cost of supply, gained connections. Neither would privatization likely have solved the state's problems; it is doubtful that it would have been any more politically tenable for governments to allow large tariff increases to be made by private discoms in order to close the gap between revenue and costs. During the years of BSP and SP-led coalition governments, there were strong political incentives to pursue aggressive electrification, and increase hours of supply to rural constituencies, rather than focus on reforming the system to achieve solvency.[48] The 2003 UP Power Policy renewed key elements of the 1999 reform programme, raising the prospect that further reforms might be implemented, but it also emphasized populist measures, including extending hours of supply, rural electrification, and the provision of subsidized electricity to key constituencies.

Stable Government, Populist Policies, and Central Government Bail-outs: 2007–17

Since 2007, UP has been ruled by stable, single-party governments: first by the BSP, then the SP, and now the BJP. Over this period, a significant amount of private generation capacity has been built in UP, and the UPPCL has signed a number of long-term power purchase agreements (PPA), committing themselves to purchasing large amounts of relatively expensive power from private companies. There has been investment in strengthening and extending the grid, taking advantage of Accelerated Power Development and Reform Programme (APDRP) and Restructured Accelerated Power Development and Reforms Programme (R-APDRP) funding. Electrification and extending the hours of supply have continued to be political priorities. Nevertheless, electrification rates in UP remain low, standing at 37 per cent in 2011.[49] Average industrial load and revenue from industry have remained flat, as Figure 13.1 shows, and industry consumers have continued to significantly cross-subsidize domestic and agricultural consumers.

The state's discoms continue to report poor operational and financial performance, as highlighted in Figure 13.2. As a result, the UPPCL built up large debts in the years following 2007. Between 2006–7 and 2010–11, while the BSP was in power, the accumulated losses of the UPPCL increased from Rs 16,700 to Rs 42,745 crore.[50] By 2016, following four years of the SP government, the UPPCL's debt levels had risen to Rs 53,211 crore despite central government financial support.[51]

The main interventions the BSP government made in the power sector were to promote private investment in generation and seek the privatization of distribution. There was little interest from the private sector to take over entire discoms, therefore, in 2009 an announcement was made that distribution would be privatized in cities where losses were high. Agra and Kanpur were the initial selectees, and following a bidding process, Torrent was awarded franchises for both cities. In 2010, the company took over distribution in Agra, with a contract to be supplied electricity at a fixed rate from Dakshinanchal Vidyut Vitran Nigam Ltd. (DVVNL), Agra's regional discom.[52] As a result of union resistance, on the other hand, Torrent was unable to take over distribution in Kanpur. Union coordination played a decisive role: while resistance was not well-organized in Agra,[53] effective protests were organized in Kanpur. When privatization was proposed for KESCO, revenue recovery at the discom had been falling for several years, and AT&C losses were high. Yet after privatization was announced, revenue recovery went up significantly within several months.[54] The unions then argued that privatization of KESCO would be a case of privatized profits and socialized losses.[55]

When the SP took power in 2012, the UPPCL faced an acute financial crisis and was unable to pay its suppliers. In July 2013, and again in February 2014, private generators in the state reduced production because of outstanding debts.[56] In December 2012, the UPPCL could not pay dues of Rs 2,574.66 crore for power it had drawn from the Northern Grid.[57] Banks were refusing to lend to the UPPCL.[58] The SP regime, then, had little choice but to sign up for the central UPA government's power sector financial repackaging programme (FRP). The scheme was made available to states on the condition they would hike tariffs, and draw up plans for remaining public discoms to be privatized. In 2013, a 35 per cent tariff hike for domestic users and 45 per cent for the rural sector was proposed.[59] It was further agreed upon that the UPPCL would submit tariff hike requests to the state government for the next eight years.[60] However, once the FRP had been agreed to, planned tariff hikes were not implemented without any apparent punitive response from the central government: in early 2013, a loan of Rs 1,558 crore was made by the Power Finance Corporation to help the UPPCL.[61]

In 2012, the SP government set out with plans to privatize distribution in Meerut, Ghaziabad, Kanpur, and Varanasi. There was still a memorandum of understanding (MOU) in place for Torrent to take over KESCO, and the government let it be known that they intended for this to happen.[62] Proposals for privatization were again met with resistance from employee unions, who planned strikes and threatened a work boycott.[63] The SP did not have a strong commitment to privatization,[64] and so these latest proposals experienced little progress. Furthermore, in 2015 the government cancelled the Torrent KESCO MOU.[65] By 2016, the finances of the UPPCL were again dire.[66] The arrival of the central government Ujwal DISCOM Assurance Yojana (UDAY) was therefore opportune, freeing the state government from the need to develop a state-level political solution for loss making discoms. In 2016, the SP government signed up for UDAY, allowing for yet another financial restructuring of the state's discoms. It is notable that under UP's UDAY agreement there are no stipulations for privatization; instead the focus is on investment and bringing down AT&C losses.

Both the more recent BSP and SP governments avoided large-scale reform of the power sector. Their focus on privatization, moreover was unlikely to solve the state's power sector problems in the first place: privatization itself does nothing to deal with high AT&C losses, the political context of tariffs and subsidies, high power purchasing costs, and low industrial demand. The Torrent franchisee in Agra, furthermore, does not provide a flattering example of privatization. Currently, DVVNL is contracted to supply power to Torrent at a rate lower than its marginal cost. Over the first two years of the arrangement, the DVVNL incurred a loss of Rs 490 crore from the arrangement. Further losses are projected to be Rs 5,348 crore for the remaining 18 years of the contract. There is also evidence that collusion and improper practice occurred during the bidding process for the Agra franchise.[67] In a state with a competitive multiparty political environment, neither the BSP nor the SP government was willing to raise tariffs for domestic and rural consumers to meet the cost of supply. Before the state assembly elections in 2007, 2012, and 2017, all four main parties made promises to increase hours of supply, reduce the cost of electricity, or provide free power to certain groups despite the need for the UPPCL to recover more revenue.[68,69]

The BSP and SP governments also both failed to concertedly crack down on theft. Over recent years, so-called 'VIP areas' have received longer hours of supply and seen higher levels of theft. For example, during the SP government's time in office, theft was higher in the politically important western districts of the state. In Etawah and Mainpuri, line losses were over 50 per cent in 2015.[70,71] VIP districts received 24 hours electricity supply, even though such unbalanced provision is illegal.[72] There is anecdotal evidence that local politicians protect power thieves, and that politicians routinely interfere in the operation of discoms, influencing employee transfers and the distribution of power cuts.[73] In recent years, the UPPCL has exempted hundreds of feeders from power cuts in response to demands from local politicians.[74] Investigative articles and the documentary *Katiyabaaz* have detailed the often dangerous situations power engineers find themselves in when trying to crack down on theft, and the interference of local politicians in drives to tackle illegal connections,[75,76] accounts that match the anecdotes of officers at the UPPCL.

On paper, UP has five discoms which operate independently and in a commercial manner. In practice, the state's discoms have never been allowed to operate independently, and there has been no political will to make this happen. A single, politically appointed chairman oversees the UPPCL and the discoms. All the discoms buy their power from the UPPCL, cannot arrange their own long-term PPAs, and charge their customers the same tariffs regardless of their unique customer mix. Anecdotally, the creation of multiple discoms in UP has led to little change: promotions at the discoms are still overseen by the UPPCL, and discoms still share the same rules and regulations.

While the UPERC should be playing the central role of impartially setting tariffs and enforcing regulations, it has faced headwinds against doing so. Tariffs have been raised considerably over the last two decades, but only during the financial repackaging of discom debts, and never in the run-up to elections. Cross-subsidization has not been reduced significantly. The UPERC has pushed for improvements in metering, revenue collection, and billing, and set customer registration targets for the discoms in an attempt to bring free-riders into the system. Tariff increases to recoup losses that are above target levels have been disallowed; however, revenue requirement submissions are regularly filed late,[77] and orders for 100 per cent metering have been ignored.

Open Access (OA) regulations have been in place since 2004. However, in practice the UPPLC has only approved OA for a very small number of instances because of the importance of industry revenue for the state's discoms. There have been Renewable Purchasing Obligation (RPO) regulations in UP since 2010. Again, however, these are not often adhered to, and the UPERC has been unable to enforce them.[78]

***

This chapter illustrates how the failure to improve the operational and financial performance of UP's discoms can be attributed to the populist approaches of successive governments, and their fear of reforms potentially hazardous to re-election chances. It additionally highlights how UP's large base of subsidized domestic and agricultural consumers, small base of cross-subsidizing industrial consumers, and expensive power purchasing costs make any reversal of financial fortune very difficult to engineer.

Further research is needed on the failure to reduce AT&C losses in UP. There is a shortage of evidence on the relative importance of political interference versus administrative incapacity in explaining persistently high levels of theft. Politicians are more likely to be re-elected when theft in their constituencies has risen,[79] but there is little empirical evidence of how and to what degree this theft is enabled.

When looking forward to the future, several issues stand out. All political parties in UP remain committed to rural electrification and increasing hours of supply. Further electrification, while socially laudable, will worsen the finances of the state's discoms unless governments are willing to fully finance subsidized tariffs, reduce power purchase costs, or an industrial base can be fostered. It may be the case that in future years UP can rely upon additional central government-led bail-outs of its power sector. If not, then difficult political and financial decisions will be necessary. Thanks to the growing political commitment to renewables in India, renewables will constitute a greater portion of UP's energy mix in the coming years. Uttar Pradesh now has rooftop solar power and micro-grid policies. If rooftop solar power generation amongst industrial consumers grows, this will pose a clear threat to the discoms, who rely heavily upon industry revenue. In contrast, if rural communities install a large number of solar micro-grids and this results in a reduction of their grid reliance, then discoms may financially benefit.

Privatization has fallen off of the UP government's agenda over the past three years. If this results in a focus on enacting policies that might allow the discoms to reduce their AT&C losses and reduce theft, or efforts to break the historical pattern of populist tariffs and subsidies being enacted for politically and numerically powerful groups, carried out to build electoral support, then it would be a positive shift. Steps towards greater reliance on automated meters and closer monitoring of where losses are occurring do appear to offer the promise of loss reductions. Yet, as long as theft is informally sanctioned, it is unlikely that technology will provide a panacea for UP.

Notes and References

1. Navroz Dubash and Sudhir Chella Rajan, 'Power Politics: Process of Power Sector Reform in India', *Economic and Political Weekly* 36(35), 2001: 3367–90.
2. Lucia Michelutti, *The Vernacularisation of Democracy: Politics, Caste and Religion in India* (New Delhi: Routledge, 2008).
3. Sudha Pai, 'Populism and Economic Reforms: The BJP Experiment in Uttar Pradesh', in J. Mooij (ed.), *The Politics of Economic Reforms in India*, (London: SAGE Publications, 2005): 98–129; Sudha Pai, Pradeep Sharma, Pralay Kanungo, and Rahul Mukherji, 'Uttar Pradesh in the 1990s: Critical Perspectives on Society, Polity and Economy', *Economic and Political Weekly* 40(22), 2005: 2144–7; Kanchan Chandra, 'Post-Congress Politics in Uttar Pradesh: The Ethnification of the Party System and Its Consequences', in R. Roy and P. Wallace (eds), *Indian Politics and the 1998 Election* (New York: Cambridge University Press, 1999), 55–104.
4. Miriam Golden and Brian Min, 'Theft and Loss of Electricity in an Indian State', *Working Paper* (London School of Economics and Political Science: International Growth Centre, 2012); Brian Min and Miriam Golden, 'Electoral Cycles in Electricity Losses in India', *Energy Policy* 65, 2014: 619–25.
5. Interviews with current and former regulators and power officers. Lucknow. July 2016.
6. Golden and Min, 'Theft and Loss of Electricity in an Indian State'; Min and Golden, 'Electoral Cycles in Electricity Losses', 619–25.
7. Government of India, 'Open Government Data Platform India', available https://data.gov.in. (accessed 20 August 2017).
8. Jean Dréze and Amartya Sen, *An Uncertain Glory: India and Its Contradictions* (London: Penguin, 2013): 296, 297.
9. Noida Power Company, 'About Us', available http://www.noidapower.com/AboutUs/CompanyProfile.aspx (accessed 20 August 2017).
10. Planning Commission, *Annual Report (2013–14): On the Working of State Power Utilities & Electricity Departments* (New Delhi: Planning Commission, 2014): 18.
11. CEA, 'Monthly Generation Reports', available http://www.cea.nic.in/monthlyreports.html. (accessed 20 August 2017).

12. Census of India, *2011 Census* (New Delhi: Government of India, 2011).

13. Brian Min, *Electrifying the Poor: Distributing Power in India* (Ann Arbor: University of Michigan, 2011), 2.

14. UPPCL, *Petition before the Uttar Pradesh Electricity Regulatory Commission* (Lucknow: Uttar Pradesh Power Corporation Limited, 2000), 6, 7.

15. UPPCL, *Petition before the Uttar Pradesh Electricity Regulatory Commission*.

16. A 'captive power plant' refers to an electricity generation facility managed by an energy user for their own energy consumption.

17. GoUP, *Power Policy 2003* (Lucknow: Government of Uttar Pradesh, 2003).

18. Anjula Gurtoo and Rahul Pandey, 'Power Sector in Uttar Pradesh: Past Problems and Initial Phase of Reforms', *Economic and Political Weekly* 36(31), 2001: 2943–53; World Bank, *India—Uttar Pradesh Power Sector Restructuring Project* (Washington, DC: World Bank, 2000).

19. World Bank, *Staff Appraisal Report India Uttar Pradesh Power Project* (Washington, DC: World Bank, 1988); World Bank, *India—Uttar Pradesh Power Sector Restructuring Project*.

20. Michelutti, *The Vernacularisation of Democracy*.

21. Pai, 'Populism and Economic Reforms', 98–129; Pai et al., 'Uttar Pradesh in the 1990s', 2144–7.

22. Jason Kirk, *India and the World Bank: The Politics of Aid and Influence* (New York: Anthem Press, 2010); Pai et al., 'Uttar Pradesh in the 1990s', 2144–7.

23. Kirk, *India and the World Bank*.

24. GoUP, *The Uttar Pradesh Electricity Reforms Act, 1999* (Lucknow: Government of Uttar Pradesh, 1999).

25. World Bank, *India—Uttar Pradesh Power Sector Restructuring Project*.

26. Gurtoo and Pandey, 'Power Sector in Uttar Pradesh', 2943–53.

27. Gurtoo and Pandey, 'Power Sector in Uttar Pradesh'.

28. Srikumar Tadimalla, *Privatisation of Kanpur Electricity Supply Company (KESCO) a Case Study* (Mumbai: Infrastructure Development Finance Company Limited, 2000).

29. Tadimalla, *Privatisation of Kanpur Electricity Supply Company*; Saugata Bhattacharya and Urjit Patel, 'Markets, Regulatory Institutions, Competitiveness and Reforms', in *Workshop on Understanding Reform Global Development Network* (Cairo: Infrastructure Development Finance Company Limited, 2003).

30. Kirk, *India and the World Bank*.

31. World Bank, *India—Uttar Pradesh Power Sector Restructuring Project*.

32. For a good analysis of this reform period, and why reforms failed to bring about an improvement in financial performance at the UPPCL, see Gurtoo and Pandey, 'Power Sector in Uttar Pradesh', 2943–53.

33. World Bank, *India—Uttar Pradesh Power Sector Restructuring Project*, 43.

34. Golden and Min, 'Theft and Loss of Electricity in an Indian State.'
35. Arvind Singh Bisht, 'WB Refuses Loan Instalment to UP', *The Times of India*, 16 December 2001, available http://timesofindia.indiatimes.com/india/WB-refuses-loan-instalment-to-UP/articleshow/1661329691.cms (accessed 1 September 2017).
36. Kirk, *India and the World Bank*.
37. Archana Srivastava, 'No "New Privatization" in Energy: CM', *Times of India*, 13 May 2002, available http://timesofindia.indiatimes.com/city/lucknow/No-new-privatisation-in-energy-CM/articleshow/9709321.cms (accessed 1 September 2017).
38. World Bank, *India—Uttar Pradesh Power Sector Restructuring Project*.
39. Brajendra Parashar, 'Uday on Horizon, but Past Bailouts Disappointing', *Hindustan Times*, 21 December 2015, available http://www.pressreader.com/india/hindustan-times-lucknow/20151221/281809987854933   9 (accessed 10 September 2017).
40. World Bank, *India—Uttar Pradesh Power Sector Restructuring Project*, 3.
41. World Bank, *India—Uttar Pradesh Power Sector Restructuring Project*.
42. The Hindu, 'Bids Invited for Power Discoms', *The Hindu*, 2 November 2004, available   http://www.thehindu.com/2004/11/02/stories/2004110208 250300.htm (accessed 1 September 2017).
43. Joydeep Ray, 'UP Shortlists Torrent, Rel, Tata', *The Business Standard*, 1 March 2005, available http://www.business-standard.com/article/economy-policy/up-shortlists-torrent-rel-tata-105021401058_1.html (accessed 1 September 2017).
44. Interview with retired official at the UPPCL and former member of the UPERC, Lucknow, July 2016. All interviews were conducted by the author on a not-for-attribution basis.
45. Golden and Min, 'Theft and Loss of Electricity in an Indian State'.
46. Business Standard, 'Powerloom Tariffs Quashed, UP Govt Unfazed', *Business Standard*, 6 February 2006, available http://www.business-standard.com/article/economy-policy/powerloom-tariffs-quashed-up-govt-unfazed-106070801047_1.html (accessed 1 September 2017).
47. *Hindustan Times*, 'Tariff in Powerloom Sector Not Revised: PCL', 7 July 2006, available http://www.hindustantimes.com/india/tariff-in-powerloom-sector-not-revised-pcl/story-2MC44vEmYfDwHtfbG3a4zL.html (accessed 1 September 2017); UPERC, *Revised Tariff Rates for Power Loom Consumers* (Lucknow: UPERC, 2006); UPERC, *Clarification/Corrigendum to Tariff Order for the FY 2008–09* (Lucknow: UPERC, 2008).
48. Pai et al., 'Uttar Pradesh in the 1990s', 2144–7.
49. Census of India, *2011 Census* (New Delhi: Government of India, 2011).

50. Virendra Singh Rawat, 'UP Power Corporation to Cut Losses by Rs 4,300 Cr This Year', *Business Standard*, 20 January 2012, available http://www.business-standard.com/article/companies/up-power-corporation-to-cut-losses-by-rs-4-300-cr-this-year-112042300012_1.html (accessed 10 September 2017).

51. Ministry of Power and Government of India, *Uday (Ujwal Discom Assurance Yojana) Scheme for Operational and Financial Turnaround of Power Distribution Companies (Discoms)* (New Delhi: Ministry of Power and Government of Uttar Pradesh, 2016).

52. Deepa Jainani, 'Now, UP Power Body Dumps Price Waterhouse', *The Financial Express*, 21 January 2009, available http://www.financialexpress.com/archive/now-up-power-body-dumps-price-waterhouse/413202/ (accessed 2 September 2017); *The Indian Express*, 'Maya Govt's Agra Power Contract Led to Colossal Loss', 28 August 2012, available http://indianexpress.com/article/cities/lucknow/maya-govts-agra-power-contract-led-to-colossal-loss/ (accessed 1 September 2017).

53. Interview with union representative, Lucknow, July 2016.

54. Pankaj Shah, 'Torrent to Handle Power Distribution in Kanpur', *The Times of India*, 29 April 2012, available http://timesofindia.indiatimes.com/city/lucknow/Torrent-to-handle-power-distribution-in-Kanpur/articleshow/12916993.cms (accessed 10 September 2017).

55. *Times of India*, 'Employees to Strike over KESCO Privatisation', 26 February 2009, available http://timesofindia.indiatimes.com/city/kanpur/Employees-to-strike-over-Kesco-privatisation/articleshow/4197580.cms (accessed 10 September 2017).

56. Deepa Jainani, 'As Unpaid Bills Mount, UP Can't Buy Enough Power', *The Financial Express*, 17 July 2012, available http://www.financialexpress.com/archive/as-unpaid-bills-mount-up-cant-buy-enough-power/975374/ (accessed 10 September 2017); Deepa Jainani, 'RPower, Lanco Snap Supply to UPPCL on Non-Payment', *The Financial Express*, 16 February 2013 available http://www.financialexpress.com/archive/rpower-lanco-snap-supply-to-uppcl-on-non-payment/1075136/ (accessed 10 September 2017).

57. V.K. Gupta, 'UPPCL Unable to Liquidate Power over Drawl Dues of Rs. 2574 Crore', *Indian Power Sector*, 12 December 2012, available http://indianpowersector.com/home/2012/12/uppcl-unable-to-liquidate-power-over-drawl-dues-of-rs-2574-crore/ (accessed 10 September 2017).

58. Virendra Nath Bhatt, 'Akhilesh Yadav's Power Woes', *Tehelka*, 15 January 2013, available http://www.tehelka.com/2013/01/akhilesh-yadavs-power-woes/ (accessed 10 September 2017).

59. *NDTV*, 'Pay 35 Percent More for Power in Uttar Pradesh from Today', 10 June 2013, available http://www.ndtv.com/india-news/pay-35-percent-more-for-power-in-uttar-pradesh-from-today-524889 (accessed 10 September 2017).

60. Deepa Jainani, 'Consortium of Banks Agrees to Buy Rs 13k-Cr Bonds to Bail out UPPCL', *The Financial Express*, 7 October 2013, available http://www.financialexpress.com/archive/consortium-of-banks-agrees-to-buy-rs-13k-cr-bonds-to-bail-out-uppcl/1179173/ (accessed 10 September 2017).

61. Jainani, 'Consortium of Banks Agrees'; Deepa Jainani, 'PFC Bails out UPPCL with Rs. 1,558-Crore Loan Package', *The Financial Express*, 6 April 2013, available http://www.financialexpress.com/archive/pfc-bails-Out-uppcl-with-rs1558-crore-loan-package/1098436/ (accessed 10 September 2017).

62. Pankaj Shah, 'Torrent to Handle Power Distribution'.

63. Virendra Singh Rawat, 'UP Powermen Warn against Privatisation of Electricity Distribution', *Business Standard*, 21 July 2013, available http://www.business-standard.com/article/economy-policy/up-powermen-warn-against-privatisation-of-electricity-distribution-113072100433_1.html (accessed 10 September 2017); *Times of India*, 'Power Privatisation: Staff Threaten Indefinite Strike', 16 April 2013, available http://timesofindia.indiatimes.com/city/lucknow/Power-privatisation-Staff-threaten-indefinite-strike/articleshow/19570632.cms (accessed 10 September 2017).

64. Interviews with regulators, officials, and journalists, Lucknow, July 2016.

65. Financial Express, 'Uttar Pradesh Cancels Distribution Pact with Torrent Power', *The Financial Express*, 24 June 2015, available http://www.financialexpress.com/economy/uttar-pradesh-cancels-distribution-pact-with-torrent-power/89267/ (accessed 10 September 2017).

66. Ministry of Power and Government of India, *Uday (Ujwal Discom Assurance Yojana) Scheme*.

67. *The Indian Express*, 'Maya Govt's Agra Power Contract Led to Colossal Loss', 28 August 2012, available http://indianexpress.com/article/cities/lucknow/maya-govts-agra-power-contract-led-to-colossal-loss/ (accessed 10 September 2017).

68. Hari Kumar, 'Cows, Laptops and Loan Waivers: Campaign Promises in UP', *New York Times*, 17 February 2012, available https://india.blogs.nytimes.com/2012/02/17/cows-laptops-and-loan-waivers-campaign-promises-in-u-p/?mcubz=1 (accessed 10 September 2017).

69. *BBC*, 'Akhilesh Yadav Emerges as Challenger in Uttar Pradesh', 15 February 2012, available http://www.bbc.com/news/world-asia-india-17023112 (accessed 10 September 2017).

70. Golden and Min, 'Theft and Loss of Electricity in an Indian State'; Min and Golden, 'Electoral Cycles in Electricity Losses', 619–25; *NDTV*, 'Pay 35 Percent More for Power in Uttar Pradesh from Today', 10 June 2013, http://www.ndtv.com/india-news/pay-35-percent-more-for-power-in-uttar-pradesh-from-today-524889 (accessed on 10 September 2017).

71. Pankaj Shah, 'Torrent to Handle Power Distribution'.

72. *The Indian Express*, 'UP: HC Says 24-Hour Power Supply to VVIP Areas Illegal', 6 February 2013, available http://indianexpress.com/article/news-archive/web/up-hc-says-24hour-power-supply-to-vvip-areas-illegal/ (accessed 10 September 2017).

73. Golden and Min, 'Theft and Loss of Electricity in an Indian State'; Min and Golden, 'Electoral Cycles in Electricity Losses', 619–25; Simon Denyer, 'Power Thieves Prosper in India's Patronage-Based Democracy', *The Washington Post*, 4 October 2012, available https://www.washingtonpost.com/world/asia_pacific/power-thieves-prosper-in-indias-patronage-based-democracy/2012/10/03/50d2d7e8-eadf-11e1-a80b-9f898562d010_story.html?utm_term=.2f6d7604ba81 (accessed 10 September 2017).

74. Brajendra Parashar, 'UP Politicians Grab 18% Power for Their Turfs', *Hindustan Times*, 17 September 2012, available http://www.hindustan-times.com/india/up-politicians-grab-18-power-for-their-turfs/story-CUfqKtqx7pKIm0yKnZoUHK.html (accessed 10 September 2017).

75. Simon Denyer, 'Power Thieves Prosper in India's Patronage-Based Democracy', *The Washington Post*, 4 October 2012, available https://www.washingtonpost.com/world/asia_pacific/power-thieves-prosper-in-indias-patronage-based-democracy/2012/10/03/50d2d7e8-eadf-11e1-a80b-9f898562d010_story.html?utm_term=.2f6d7604ba81 (accessed 10 September 2017).

76. *Katiyabaaz*, DVD, Deepti Kakkar and Mustafa Fahad (India: Globalistan Films, ITVS, 2014).

77. GoUP, *Report of the Comptroller and Auditor General of India (Public Sector Undertakings) for the Year Ended 31 March 2013* (Lucknow: Government of Uttar Pradesh, 2014).

78. UERC, *Suo-Moto Proceedings to Review the Regulatory Obligation of Purchase of Quantum of Energy from Renewable Resources Achieved by Obligated Entities Viz Distribution Licensees, Captive Users and Open Access Consumers* (Lucknow: Uttar Pradesh Electricity Regulatory Commission, 2015).

79. Golden and Min, 'Theft and Loss of Electricity in an Indian State'.

14

JONATHAN BALLS

Uttarakhand

The Golden Combination of Cheap Energy and a Large Industrial Base

Uttarakhand enjoys limited power cuts, has some of the lowest electricity tariffs in India, and is close to achieving full electrification. The state's public discom, the Uttarakhand Power Corporation Limited (UPCL), has reported aggregate technical and commercial (AT&C) losses below 20 per cent in recent years, has moderate debts, and does not require government subsidy support. This position reflects a transformation from Uttarakhand's achievement of statehood in 2000: in its first years of operation, the UPCL's AT&C losses were above 50 per cent, and revenue realization was low.

How has Uttarakhand's power sector been transformed since 2000? This chapter shows how the strong position of the state's power sector and the UPCL has been made possible by the state's large base of cheap hydropower capacity, coupled with the development of heavy industry. The chapter highlights two key decisions in 2003 that started the state's transformation. First, the Uttarakhand Electricity Regulatory Commission (UERC) moved to cut the rates that the UPCL paid for hydropower and lowered retail tariffs, reducing the discom's power purchasing costs and shifting the state to a low-tariff environment. Second, the Government of India launched a generous incentives package for industries to set up in Uttarakhand. The ensuing mass arrival of industry delivered a large base of paying customers to the UPCL.

Uttarakhand has a competitive political environment, with power alternating between the Congress Party and Bharatiya Janata Party (BJP). How, then, have successive governments and the political dynamics of the state shaped Uttarakhand's power sector beyond the headline story of transformation? This chapter outlines how no significant reform interventions have been made. Due to the UPCL's favourable financial performance, reform of the power sector has not been a political necessity or a priority. This is not to say that the quality of power supply and tariffs has not been subject to political contestation. However, because tariffs for all classes of consumers are low, it has not been necessary for governments to make targeted populist interventions on tariff or subsidy levels for politically or numerically important groups to boost their electoral chances, as has happened in other states such as Uttar Pradesh (UP). While agricultural tariffs are heavily subsidized, agricultural consumption represents a small overall percentage of electricity consumption, meaning the fiscal impact of this subsidy is relatively insignificant. The main focus of governments when it comes to the power sector has rather been new large hydropower projects.

This chapter, on the other hand, also describes how successive governments have not tackled notable ongoing problems at the UPCL despite the headline story of transformation. Over the last 16 years AT&C losses at the UPCL have remained high amongst all consumer groups besides heavy industry, despite falling rapidly as a percentage of overall sales. This chapter traces the UERC's proactive role in highlighting these problems and pushing for action to be taken.

Uttarakhand's situation shows how when a state benefits from cheap power and a windfall of industrial consumers, considerable fiscal breathing space is won. Losses and theft associated with non-industrial connections are not financially crippling for the sector, and because tariffs can be naturally low, there is a low likelihood of falling into the trap seen in other states where populist measures to keep tariffs low for strategically important groups, enacted to consolidate political support, undermine the finances of the sector. Were it not for its golden combination of cheap hydropower and a large industrial base, Uttarakhand's distribution sector would likely resemble that of its neighbour UP, where discoms are struggling operationally and financially. Uttarakhand further highlights how an independent regulator can play an important role in identifying problems at a discom, but also how the power of regulators in India to enact reforms is limited.

This chapter begins with a section on the historical background of Uttarakhand's statehood and the genesis of its power sector (see Table 14.1 for a timeline of key events in Uttarakhand). Three proceeding sections then look at the three five-year parliamentary terms since 2002. The first of these sections details the unfolding story of transformation resulting from industrialization and the lowering of tariffs. The second and third cover the years since, during which industrialization has continued and the UPCL has been financially solvent, but high AT&C losses beyond industry have persisted. The chapter draws on secondary data and on interviews conducted in August 2016 with 20 individuals, including bureaucrats, regulators, business people, consumer representatives, and journalists. Figure 14.1 shows the financial and physical profile of Uttarakhand's power sector, while Figure 14.2 shows supply-side costs and revenue recovery. Uttarakhand has a population of just over 1 crore,[1] and achieves above the national average on household expenditure, literacy, and on some health indicators.[2] Uttarakhand had an allocated power capacity of 3,719 megawatt (MW) as of November 2016.[3] Per capita consumption of electricity was 1,154 kilowatt hour (kWh in 2015),[4] and electrification reached 97.5 per cent of households in 2015–16.[5]

TABLE 14.1   Timeline of Key Events: Uttarakhand

State Politics		Power Sector Events
• State of Uttarakhand formed on 9 November 2000	2000	
	2001	• Uttarakhand Power Corporation Limited (UPCL) constituted, with responsibility for transmission and distribution • Uttarakhand Jal Vidyut Nigam Limited (UJVNL) constituted, with responsibility for hydropower generation
• Congress Party wins state elections	2002	• Uttarakhand Electricity Regulatory Commission (UERC) constituted

(Cont'd)

TABLE 14.1   *(Cont'd)*

State Politics		Power Sector Events
	2003	• Government of India launches New Industrial Policy and Other Concessions for Uttarakhand and Himachal Pradesh • UERC reduces rate the UPCL pays for hydropower, rationalizes tariffs, and reduces tariffs for most consumer groups
	2004	• Power Transmission Corporation of Uttarakhand Limited (PTCUL) constituted, with responsibility for transmission • Open Access (OA) regulations drawn up, but no procedures for taking OA set out because no demand from industry perceived
	2005	• UERC engages IIT Roorkee to audit the accounts of the UPCL
	2006	• UERC study of accounts of the UPCL
• BJP wins state elections	2007	
	2008	• State policy for harnessing renewable energy sources launched • 2008 Hill Industrial Policy • Seasonal gaps between electricity demand and supply from 2008 onwards
	2010	• Renewable Purchasing Obligation (RPO) targets set out • Procedures set out for OA, following demand from industry
	2011	• Extension of 2008 Hill Industrial Policy
• Congress Party wins state elections	2012	• Government provides Rs 915 crore package to the UPCL
	2013	• New RPO targets set out

(Cont'd)

TABLE 14.1   *(Cont'd)*

State Politics		Power Sector Events
		• Uttarakhand Solar Power Policy released
		• Moratorium on new large hydropower following severe floods
	2015	• New Open Access regulations set-out
		• 24/7 Power for All plan signed
		• Uttarakhand Renewable Energy Development Agency (UREDA) invites bids for on-grid solar power
	2016	• UDAY MOU signed
		• Power Purchase Agreements for power from gas plants signed
• BJP wins state elections	2017	

Source: Author.

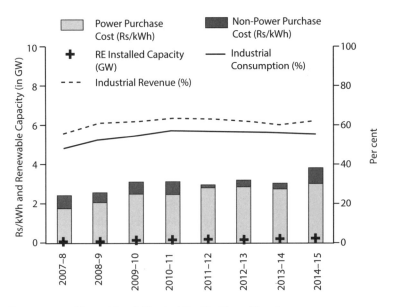

FIGURE 14.1   Financial and Physical Profile: Uttarakhand
Source: CSO, *Energy Statistics* (New Delhi: Central Statistics Office, Ministry of Statistics and Programme Implementation, Government of India, 2010, 2012, 2014, and 2016); PFC, Reports on Performance of State Power Utilities (New Delhi: Power Finance Corporation Limited, 2011, 2013, 2015, and 2016).

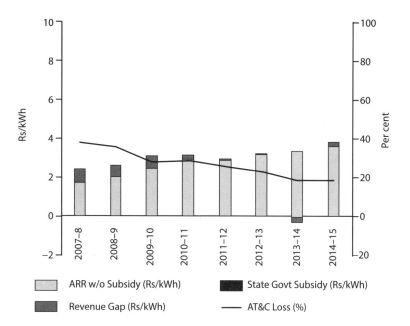

FIGURE 14.2   Supply-side Costs and Revenue Recovery: Uttarakhand
Source: PFC, *Reports on Performance of State Power Utilities* (New Delhi: Power
Finance Corporation Limited, 2011, 2013, 2015, and 2016).

Historical Background

The state of Uttarakhand was formed in November 2000, carved out
of UP following years of popular protests motivated by economic and
political marginalization.[6] While talk of statehood for Uttarakhand
dates back to decades before then, the movement for separation gained
traction in 1994 when the Samajwadi Party (SP) government in UP
introduced a 27 per cent quota on government jobs and education for
Other Backward Castes (OBCs). In the Uttarakhand region, the OBC
population was just 2 per cent of the overall population. With high
unemployment and poor economic development, government jobs,
and education were a key aspiration for people, and many thus felt the
quota policy unfairly deprived them of opportunities.[7]

An interim BJP-led government oversaw Uttarakhand from 2000
until 2002. It adopted the model of one public generation company
and one public transmission and distribution company for the state.
In 2001, the UPCL was constituted and delegated responsibility for

transmission and distribution, while the Uttarakhand Jal Vidyut Nigam Limited (UJVNL) was established to manage the state's hydropower. This model was implemented at the same time that the BJP government in UP was reforming its power sector, and was planning the privatization of distribution.[8] Notably, Uttarakhand did not adopt similar reform plans.

Prior to 2000, the area that would make up Uttarakhand had low levels of industrial electricity consumption and subpar transmission infrastructure. Geographically, Uttarakhand includes a mix of hill and plains districts. Plains districts such as Dehradun and Nainital were more developed: per capita consumption in those areas was 595 and 518 kWh respectively in 1995–6. Hill districts were much less developed: for example, Pithoragarh's per capita consumption in 1995–6 was 72 kWh, and in Garhwal it was 45 kWh.[9] Uttarakhand inherited 370 crore units (MU) of hydropower, however, and enjoyed an overall energy surplus throughout the year. In 2003, the total energy available to Uttarakhand was 5,300 MU, while the state's requirement was 3,900 MU. Industrial consumption made up 21 per cent of overall consumption in 2001–2, and AT&C losses were 55 per cent.[10]

Journey to Industrial Strength: 2002–7

The Congress Party emerged as the largest party from state elections in 2002, and N.D. Tiwari became the chief minister (CM). The government took the reins of power at a time when Uttarakhand had ample surplus power. The tariff structures inherited from UP were still in place, and cross-subsidization by industry consumers was high. The only notable power sector reform the government carried out was the creation of a separate company for transmission in 2004, the Power Transmission Corporation of Uttarakhand Limited (PTCUL). Central and state funding was used to invest in strengthening and extending the state's transmission infrastructure. The focus of the government was primarily on promoting new large hydropower dams, which were seen as crucial for the future economic prosperity of Uttarakhand.[11] However, developing new dams proved to be a slow process, with planned projects facing environmental opposition and corruption allegations.

Two key sets of decisions taken in 2003 laid the foundations for rapid transformation in the power sector. First, in 2003 the UERC issued its first tariff ruling, reducing the purchasing power costs of the UPCL and shifting Uttarakhand to a low-tariff policy. The UERC determined that the prevailing rate being paid to the UJVNL of 60.5 paisa per unit was arbitrarily high, ordering instead a lower rate of 37 paisa. By calculating the costs of the UPCL on the basis of this low rate, the UERC simplified and reduced tariffs for most classes of consumers.[12]

The UERC's tariff changes and broader regulatory role were contested by the UJVNL and UPCL. The UJVNL went to the Appellate Tribunal for Electricity (APTEL) court to challenge the reduction in the amount they were to be paid for hydropower. They were partially successful; the APTEL court overturned several aspects of the UERC's 2003 tariff ruling and ordered changes to what depreciation rates and return on investment the UJVNL could claim.[13] While the UPCL did start to submit annual revenue requirement petitions to the UERC in 2003, each year they did so late, and each time multiple shortcomings were identified by the UERC. Tariff determination was therefore repeatedly delayed while the UERC waited on late tariff submissions and for shortcomings to be rectified. In 2004, the UERC resorted to a suo moto tariff determination after more than a year passed without receipt of an annual revenue requirement.

The UERC's independence was also tested by the state government, which tried to give tariff directions on several occasions.[14] Further, in response to the proactive independence of the UERC's during its first years by the then chairman of the commission, the government changed the commission size from one to three members, providing the opportunity to appoint two further members. The reflection of one former regulator on this period of institutional adjustment is pertinent: 'When we established the commission, the government had not yet realized the full impact of creating regulatory commissions. When we set up, and were making the first regulations, no one bothered about the regulations. However, when they realized that the commission was independent-minded, the government decided to make the commission a three-man commission, bringing in two new members'.[15]

Second, in 2003 the Government of India launched an industrial policy for Uttarakhand and Himachal Pradesh, providing generous tax and central excise benefits to industry investing in the states. Qualifying industries were eligible for a 100 per cent outright excise duty exemption for a period of 10 years, and a 100 per cent income tax exemption for five years with a partial exemption for a further five years. Other benefits and subsidies were also offered.[16] The government in Uttarakhand also acted to attract industry by setting up and promoting industrial parks.[17] Uttarakhand's then-Chief Minister N.D. Tiwari played an important role here. Tiwari had previously been CM of UP on three occasions, where he was known as the 'father of industrialization', and held several positions in Rajiv Gandhi's government including Minister of Industries.

Between 2004–5 and 2014–15, Uttarakhand achieved a compounded annual growth rate (CAGR) of 16.5 per cent for industry and 12.3 per cent in services, putting it well above the national average of close to 7 per cent.[18] Between 2005–6 and 2007–8, the rate of industrial growth was above 30 per cent.[19] Large corporations including Tata Motors, Bajaj Auto, Mahindra and Mahindra, Hero Honda, Ashok Leyland, and Nestle flocked to the state, bringing Rs 30,000 crore in investment.[20] Between 2000–1 and 2010–11, the number of factories in the state more than tripled.[21] Several steel producers were attracted by cheap electricity tariffs. In the five years following 2002, the distribution sector in Uttarakhand was transformed, and a favourable consumer mix was won. By 2007–8, high-tension (HT) industry[22] made up 46 per cent of consumer sales (see Figure 14.3).[23] Consumption by cross-subsidizing consumer groups grew rapidly, outpacing consumption by subsidized groups by 2004–5.[24]

Since its inception, the UERC has been notably proactive in identifying and highlighting problems at the UPCL with billing, revenue realization, and metering. In the UERC's first tariff ruling in 2003, problems with the UPCL's accounts and auditing were identified, and the UPCL was accused of hiding losses by inflating the reported consumption of unmetered agricultural users.[25] In 2005–6, having seen little evidence of improvement, the UERC engaged IIT Roorkee to audit the UPCL's accounts. This study found large numbers of unmetered connections, connections listed as metered that were unmetered, and metered connections that had been listed as defective for many years, where customers were being charged a fixed rate rather than based upon their actual consumption.[26] Seeing that little remedial action had been taken by the UPCL, the UERC carried out a further study between 2006 and 2007. The results showed the same problems as the previous study, but also identified basic errors in bills and suspiciously low recorded load factors for some large industry consumers.[27]

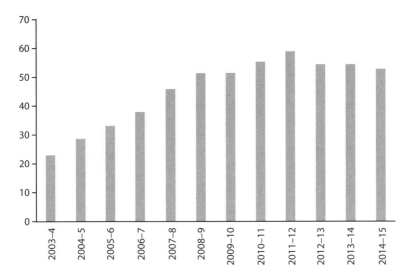

FIGURE 14.3   High-Tension Industry Consumer Sales as a Percentage of
Total Sales

Source: UERC, *Order on Approval of Business Plan and Multi Year Tariff Petition for Uttarakhand Power Corporation Ltd. For Second Control Period* (FY 2016–17 to FY 2018–19) (Dehradun: Uttarakhand Electricity Regulatory Commission, 2016), 275.

Between 2002 and 2007, Uttarakhand's power sector and the fortunes of its discom were transformed by cheap power and the arrival of large paying industrial consumers, rather than politically led reform or a concerted crackdown on losses. With cheap power, tariffs could be kept low, and with growing industry consumption, overall AT&C losses fell rapidly, and cross-subsidization was reduced. However, a secondary story also emerged in these years: the UPCL was making almost no progress in reducing AT&C losses beyond heavy industry consumers. The UERC actively highlighted this, but the UPCL did not take action, and the state government moreover did not push for action to be taken.

Reaping the Windfall, 2007–12

State elections in 2007 saw the BJP emerge as the biggest party in the state assembly. Despite industry having flocked to the state, a strong anti-incumbency mood prevailed, with the BJP painting the Congress government as having failed to bring development beyond a few industrial areas.[28] The years following 2007 featured greater political instability. First, B.C. Khanduri was appointed as CM, but in 2009 he was replaced by Ramesh Pokhriyal, who was the preferred choice of local BJP MPs. Khanduri returned as CM in 2011 amidst scam allegations surrounding the government, allowing the BJP to champion an uncorrupted figurehead during the ensuing state elections campaign.[29]

The BJP took office as seasonal gaps between demand and allocated supply were becoming a problem. Consecutive years of rapidly rising demand for electricity had not been matched with gains in supply capacity. In 2008, a year when hydropower output was reduced because of drought, there was a shortfall of 20–30 lakh units of power.[30] In successive years, large seasonal shortfalls again occurred. To deal with seasonal fluctuations in hydropower generation, Uttarakhand makes arrangements for power banking with other states. During months of surplus generation, they sell power out of the state, and during the deficit months, power is returned. By 2008, however, these power banking arrangements were not adequate to smooth seasonal supply–demand mismatches.

Cross-subsidization had reduced considerably by 2007, and tariffs remained low for all consumer groups. Between 2007 and 2012, supply became increasingly unstable as the UPCL implemented long hours of load shedding. The headline rate of AT&C losses at the UPCL continued to steadily decline, from 38 per cent in 2007–8 to 23 per cent by 2012–13.[31] This decline was largely driven by the UPCL's growing base of industrial consumers. By 2011, industrial consumers were only 1.1 per cent of the UPCL's customers, but contributed 63 per cent of its revenue.[32] Beyond industrial consumers, AT&C losses remained high (see Figure 14.4).

Between 2007 and 2012, reform of the power sector was again not a government priority. Plans were put forward for the privatization of power distribution at Roorkee and Rudrapur in Udham Singh Nagar district, where AT&C losses were very high.[33] However, these plans made little progress. Central government Accelerated Power Development and Reform Programme (APDRP) funds and state funds were utilized to invest in the state's transmission infrastructure and in the UPCL's systems.[34] The government's energy sector focus, much like the previous government, was primarily on promoting new hydropower capacity. However, environmental objections stalled many projects, and the

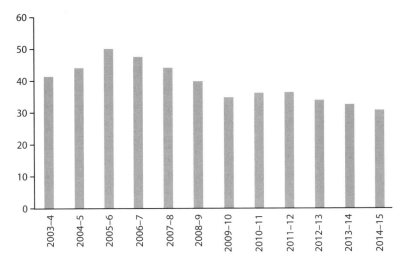

FIGURE 14.4   AT&C Loss for Consumers Excluding HT Industry Consumers
Source: UERC, *Order on Approval of Business Plan and Multi Year Tariff Petition for Uttarakhand Power Corporation Ltd. for Second Control Period* (FY 2016–17 to FY 2018–19) (Dehradun: Uttarakhand Electricity Regulatory Commission, 2016), 276.

CM had to cancel several that became mired in corruption allegations.[35] Notably, the government took steps at the turn of the decade to commission gas-fired power plants to meet projected demand increases.[36] Only limited short-term populist interventions occurred in the power sector, which did not seriously threaten the finances of the UPCL. For example, shortly before state elections in 2012, the UPCL begun to purchase expensive power on the open market in order to reduce load shedding just prior to elections, violating guidelines from the UERC.[37]

Ongoing industrialization continued to strengthen the structural position of the power sector. In 2008 the government launched the Hill Industrial Policy and introduced new development incentives—particularly for industrial projects in hilly areas—and in 2011 extended them through to 2025.[38] While industry electricity demand grew less rapidly during this time, industry tariffs contributed more than 60 per cent of the UPCL's revenue by 2012.

The UPCL's response to the situation of power shortages was to request large increases in tariffs, particularly for heavy industry, putting Uttarakhand's low-tariff status at risk. Tariff increases were approved by the UERC following government direction. However, industry groups successfully challenged the UERC's 2009–10 and 2010–11 tariff orders in the APTEL courts, on the basis that tariff increases had been made according to the policy direction of the government instead of existing regulations.[39] As a result of the ruling, higher tariffs were withdrawn, and the UPCL resorted to longer hours of load shedding.[40] Demand management measures were also implemented to deal with the power crisis, including peak and off-peak tariffs and rebates for customers buying solar-powered water heaters.[41]

The UERC continued to be the main institution actively pushing for improvements at the UPCL. In their 2009 tariff orders, the UERC reported that few improvements had been made, despite multiple 'brainstorming' meetings and the UPCL's hire of 1,100 additional staff to tackle losses.[42] The UERC highlighted problems with 'ghost' consumers, fictitious meter numbers, and suspiciously low load factors for some industry customers.[43] In subsequent years, the same problems were repeatedly identified. In 2011, the UERC reached the damning conclusion that 'it is evident that the three major functions of the licensee, i.e. metering, billing, collection are in total disarray. Lot of efforts are required by the licensee to set them right'.[44] The UERC refused to reduce losses above targets through higher tariffs. However, it had little ability to effectively enforce measures, except to fine individual officers at the UPCL. Notably, the UERC, now a three-member commission, became less assertive compared with its first years of operation, taking a less confrontational stance with the UPCL and generators in the state.[45]

Procedures for industry to make use of Open Access (OA) were proposed in 2010 by the UERC per industry demands in light of seasonal load-shedding.[46,47] The UERC drew up procedures that distinguished between short-term, medium-term, and long-term OA, establishing different charges for each. Transmission, wheeling, and cross-subsidy charges were not given for short-term OA during seasonal deficit periods.[48]

Between 2007 and 2012, Uttarakhand's power sector was benefiting from the windfall of cheap hydropower and a large industrial base. Over this period, the government did not implement power sector reforms, and populist measures on tariffs and subsidies for politically and numerically important groups were not pursued. AT&C losses associated with non-industrial connections remained high at the UPCL, and as was the case with the previous government, there was no concerted drive to tackle this problem.

Reaping the Windfall, and Pushing towards 24×7 Power, 2012–17

State elections in 2012 returned the Congress Party to power, but without an overall majority. Between 2012 and 2016, Uttarakhand continued to experience political instability. Vijay Bahuguna was inaugurated as CM. Following severe flooding and strong criticism of the government's response, however, Harish Rawat replaced Bahuguna in 2014 at the behest of local Congress Party officials.[49] Controversy ensued: over the next two years, President's Rule was imposed twice.

Uttarakhand continued to see seasonal power shortages between 2012 and 2017 as the UPCL repeatedly resorted to load shedding.[50] To meet growing demand, the UPCL increasingly turned to short-term power from the open markets, which was available at cheap rates. In 2016, an average of almost 24 hours of power per day was supplied to urban areas, 22–24 hours to rural areas, and 19–22 hours to industry.[51] The UPCL's financial losses are low, and a net profit of Rs 323 crore was achieved in 2013–14. Accumulated financial losses at the UPCL stood at Rs 1,695 crore.[52] AT&C losses, furthermore, fell below 20 per cent by 2014–15. In 2013–14, industry consumers were 0.6 per cent of the 17.8 lakh consumers in the state, yet accounted for 56 per cent of consumption and 63 per cent of revenue.[53]

Like previous administrations, the Congress government did not carry out significant reforms in the power sector. In 2012, the government relieved the debt level of the UPCL with a Rs 915 crore subsidy package.[54] In 2015, plans were announced to privatize power distribution at Kashipur in Udham Singh Nagar district and Roorkee in Haridwar district, where losses are high.[55] However, employees from Uttarakhand's power companies threatened to strike,[56] and plans were shelved shortly thereafter.[57]

In 2015, the government proposed a 24/7 power plan for Uttarakhand, promising 24-hours-per-day electricity to all classes of consumers by 2018. Plans for new capacity to meet higher demand were drafted, with shortfalls to be met in the short term by power purchased from the open market.[58] The government also announced its intentions to reach 100 per cent electrification of households, with just over one lakh households identified as remaining in need of a connection.[59] In 2016, Uttarakhand also signed up for the central government Ujwal DISCOM Assurance Yojana (UDAY) in order to access financial support for transmission system upgrades.[60] The UPCL, however, ultimately did not require the financial repackaging support of UDAY.[61]

The new Congress government was primarily focused on promoting industrialization in hill districts, recognizing their lack of development.[62] Looking forward, however, uncertainty remains over the extent to which the power sector will continue to benefit from a large industrial base. Industrialization has slowed in recent years, and the central government benefits that initially attracted industry are set to expire soon. It is unclear whether industry will stay in Uttarakhand once these benefits end, especially if electricity becomes unreliable or tariffs rise. Indeed, following tariff rises in 2016, industry associations warned that Uttarakhand was losing its low tariff status, and that unscheduled load shedding was a serious impediment to production.[63] Over the last three years the share of grid consumption attributable to industry has fallen, likely at least partially the result of industrial consumers switching to OA.[64] From 2011–12 to 2013–14 the quantum of power traded through OA increased from 10.34 MU to 281 MU, although in 2014–15 the figure did decrease to 181 MU.[65]

If industry turns in greater numbers to OA in the coming years, the UPCL's financial position will be threatened. At the same time, as Uttarakhand continues to add large numbers of domestic connections and seeks to provide 24 hour electricity to all consumers, the UPCL will likely see its losses grow, as it incurs higher losses amongst domestic consumers. Similarly, providing 24 hour electricity to agricultural consumers will likely lead to increased financial losses at the UPCL. While agricultural users represent a small amount of the UPCL's demand, the UPCL intentionally does not provide 24-hour supply to agricultural feeds in order to reduce the losses they see from those connections.[66]

There is furthermore uncertainty surrounding the ability of Uttarakhand to rely upon cheap power into the future. After major flooding hit Uttarakhand in 2013, the Supreme Court suspended all new large hydro projects, save for one. It is unclear whether this ban will be lifted, but even if it is, building new dams remains a slow and politically contentious undertaking. The Congress government has introduced incentives for micro and small hydropower,[67] however, to date these sources show little sign of producing the large increases in capacity required by projected need.

With new hydropower unlikely to supply growing demand in the short or medium-term, Uttarakhand is investigating alternative sources of electricity provision. The UPCL, for example, has been buying short-term power through e-auctions to meet immediate demand.[68] While this power is currently cheap, continued low rates cannot be guaranteed. In 2014, the government agreed to buy 2.5 MU per day of cheap hydropower from Himachal Pradesh.[69] Significantly, there has also been growth in gas-powered generation: in 2016, the government signed a 25-year agreement to buy electricity from three gas-based power plants.[70] However, gas electricity is significantly more expensive than hydropower. A rate of Rs 4.70/kWh was provisionally approved by the UERC for gas-based power in 2016–17, while the average approved purchase rate of power overall was Rs 2.83.[71]

There has also been a turn towards non-hydropower renewables, reflecting changing central and state government priorities. The 2013 Uttarakhand Solar Power Policy, for example, sets out a solar power generation capacity target of 500 MW by 2017.[72] These renewables likewise remain more expensive than hydropower. In 2016, the government invited applications for 10 MW of grid-connected rooftop PV,[73] with an agreed feed-in-tariff of Rs 9.2 per unit.[74]

Between 2012 and 2017, the headline rate of AT&C losses at the UPCL continued to fall (see Figure 14.2). However, losses beyond heavy industry remain high (see Figure 14.4). In 2012, nearly 40 per cent of reported theft came from three cities: Haridwar, Kashipur, and Rudrapur.[75] The UERC has continued to identify where improvements at the UPCL are needed, and they have prohibited the establishment of higher tariffs in order to cover losses accrued by the UCPL above set targets, or to cover bad debts. The UERC has also set penalties if targets are not met. Yet, the UPCL remains reluctant to follow orders,[76] and the UERC still struggles to enforce compliance.

Between 2002 and 2007, Uttarakhand continued to reap the benefits of cheap hydropower and a large industry base, moving towards 24/7 power and full electrification. The government did not carry out large structural reforms, nor did it push for privatization. Doing so was seen as unnecessary, as the power sector has been largely financially solvent.

Like in previous years, populist intervention on tariffs or subsides for strategically important groups were not seen. Again, however, the government did not materially address persistent high AT&C losses associated with non-industrial consumer connections.

Identifying how electricity theft can be effectively tackled is difficult, and it appears that there is little political will to solve the problem. Regulators and officials frequently express the view that theft in plains areas is politically protected. At the same time, administrative and institutional problems at the UPCL are likely part of the problem. Anecdotally, the plains districts are understood to be 'plum postings' because of their earning potential for UPCL officers, resulting in bureaucratic inefficiency and corruption.[77]

***

The years since statehood in 2000 have been a period of transformation for Uttarakhand's power sector, the result of cheap hydropower and a large industrial base. Notably, few structural reforms have occurred over the last 16 years, and this transformation has taken place separately from any politically led reform of the power sector, or any crackdown on prevailing problems with theft and losses. While populist measures on tariffs and subsidies have not become a key part of political practice in Uttarakhand, because they are naturally low, there has not been proactive political action to tackle high AT&C losses amongst non-industrial connections, which remained high. The performance of the UPCL has improved not as a result of dealing with existing problems, but by revenue from a strong base of industrial consumers.

Looking forward, this status quo appears fragile as Uttarakhand continues to buy more expensive gas and renewable-based electricity, and as industrial incentives expire. Uttarakhand has not yet faced a discom financial crisis as UP has every few years, nor has it had to solve other common dilemmas such as a low base of industrial consumers, blowback from large tariff increases for domestic and agricultural consumers, or the need for a comprehensive crackdown on theft. If power purchasing costs rise significantly, and tariffs increase as a result, unprecedented and difficult political decisions about whether or not to protect powerful consumer groups may soon be faced.

Notes and References

1. Census of India, *2011 Census* (New Delhi: Government of India, 2011).
2. Jean Drèze and Amartya Sen, *An Uncertain Glory: India and Its Contradictions* (London: Penguin, 2013), 298–329.
3. 'Monthly Generation Reports', CEA, available http://www.cea.nic.in/monthlyreports.html (accessed on 20 August 2017).
4. GOI and GOU, *24/7 Power for All Uttarakhand* (New Delhi: Government of India and Government of Uttarakhand, 2015), 5.
5. GOI, *National Family Health Survey-4 2015–16* (Mumbai: International Institute for Population Studies, 2016).
6. Anup Kumar, *The Making of a Small State: Populist Social Mobilisation and the Hindi Press* (New Delhi: Orient Black Swan, 2011); Emma Mawdsley, 'Uttarakhand Agitation and Other Backward Classes', *Economic and Political Weekly* 31(4), 1996: 205–10.
7. Emma Mawdsley, 'After Chipko: From Environment to Region in Uttaranchal', *Journal of Peasant Studies* 25(4), 1998: 36–54.
8. See chapter in this volume on Uttar Pradesh for details of this reform period.
9. UPERC, *Order Dt 01/09/01-Tariff Order of UPPCL for F.Y. 2001–02* (Lucknow: Uttar Pradesh Electricity Regulatory Commission, 2001), 9.
10. UERC, *Order on ARR and Tariff for Financial Year 2003–04* (Dehradun: Uttarakhand Electricity Regulatory Commission, 2003), 3, 14, 15.
11. Interviews with former UPCL officers and journalists, Dehradun, August 2016. All interviews were conducted by the author on a not-for attribution basis.
12. UERC, *Order on ARR and Tariff*, 17, 108.
13. Appellate Tribunal for Electricity. *Appeal No. 189 of 2005* (2005).
14. Interviews with two former regulators at the UERC, Dehradun, August 2016.
15. Interview with former UERC regulator, Dehradun, August 2016.
16. GOI, *New Industrial Policy and Other Concessions for the State of Uttaranchal and the State of Himachal Pradesh* (New Delhi: Department of Industrial Policy & Promotion, Government of India, 2003).
17. Tapas Chakraborty, 'Himalayan Singur, Minus Mamata', *The Telegraph*, 11 August 2008, available https://www.telegraphindia.com/1080811/jsp/frontpage/story_9676358.jsp (accessed 27 August 2017).
18. The Associated Chambers of Commerce & Industry of India, 'U'khand Emerges Numero Uno Clocking Highest Growth in Industry & Services Sectors across India: Assocham Study', 5 August 2016, available http://www.assocham.org/newsdetail.php?id=5847 (accessed 27 August 2017).

19. P. Naithani, 'On Industrial Development of Uttarakhand: Policy Framework and Empirical Evidences', *The Journal of Industrial Statistics* 3(1), 2014: 151.

20. P. Joshi, 'Uttarakhand CM at Centre of Two Scams', *India Today*, 21 November 2010, available http://indiatoday.intoday.in/story/uttarakhand-cm-at-centre-of-two-scams/1/120669.html (accessed 27 August 2017).

21. Naithani, 'On Industrial Development', 151.

22. HT Industry refers to a sub-group of large industry consumers connected with high-tension wires.

23. UERC, *Approval of Business Plan and Multi Year Tariff Petition for Uttarakhand Power Corporation Ltd. For Second Control Period (FY 2016–17 to FY 2018–19)* (Dehradun: Uttarakhand Electricity Regulatory Commission, 2016), 275.

24. UERC (2005), *Transmission & Distribution for FY. 2005–06* (Dehradun: Uttarakhand Electricity Regulatory Commission, 2016), 112.

25. UERC, *Order on ARR and Tariff for Financial Year 2003–04* (Dehradun: Uttarakhand Electricity Regulatory Commission, 2016), 91.

26. UERC, *Order on Retail Tariff for Uttarakhand Power Corporation Ltd. For 2007–08 & 2008–09* (Dehradun: Uttarakhand Electricity Regulatory Commission, 2008), 27, 28.

27. UERC, *Order on Retail Tariff for Uttarakhand Power Corporation.*

28. Mishra, Subhash, 'Right up the Hill', *India Today*, 12 March 2007, available http://indiatoday.intoday.in/story/bjp-wins-assembly-polls-of-uttrakhand/1/156123.html (accessed 27 August 2017).

29. Rakesh Mohan Chaturvedi, 'Uttarakhand Politically Unstable since Formation', *The Economic Times*, 28 March 2016, available http://economictimes.indiatimes.com/news/politics-and-nation/uttarakhand-politically-unstable-since-formation/articleshow/51577198.cms (accessed 27 August 2017).

30. Business Standard, 'Severe Power Crisis May Hit Industry in Uttarakhand', *Business Standard*, 8 January 2008, available http://www.business-standard.com/article/economy-policy/severe-power-crisis-may-hit-industry-in-uttarakhand-108010801092_1.html (accessed 27 August 2017).

31. UERC, *Order on Retail Tariff for Uttarakhand Power Corporation Ltd. for FY 2014–15* (Dehradun: Uttarakhand Electricity Regulatory Commission, 2014), 269.

32. UERC, *Order on Determination of Retail Tariff for FY 2011–12, Re-Determination of Tariff for FY 2009–10 & Truing up of Revenues and Expenses from FY 2005–06 to FY 2009–10 for Uttarakhand Power Corporation Ltd* (Dehradun: Uttarakhand Electricity Regulatory Commission, 2011), 121.

33. S. Prashant, 'Rawat to Privatise Power Distribution in 2 Towns', *Business Standard*, 3 March 2015, available http://www.business-standard.com/article/economy-policy/rawat-to-privatise-power-distribution-in-2-towns-115030301341_1.html (accessed 27 August 2017).

34. UERC, *Application No. 1005 UPCL/C-4 Dated 03.02.2010 Filed by Uttarakhand Power Corporation Limited Seeking Approval of the Commission for the Investment on the Project Covering the Works Covered under Part A of Restructured-Accelerated Power Development & Reform Program of Ministry of Power, Govt. of India Including Non-RAPDRP Areas for the Development of Integrated and Unified Solutions* (Dehradun: Uttarakhand Electricity Regulatory Commission, 2010).

35. Joshi, 'Uttarakhand CM.'

36. The Hindu, 'Gail Plans to Set up Power Plants in Uttarakhand', *The Hindu*, 21 June 2011, available http://www.thehindubusinessline.com/companies/gail-plans-to-set-up-power-plants-in-uttarakhand/article2123182.ece (accessed 27 August 2017).

37. S. Sharma, 'UPCL Violated Guidelines Blatantly in Power Purchase', *The Tribune*, 8 February 2012, available http://www.tribuneindia.com/2012/20120208/dplus.htm (accessed 27 August 2017).

38. *Business Standard*, 'Uttarakhand Seeks to Give Fresh Boost to Industry,' 23 July 2007, available http://www.business-standard.com/article/economy-policy/uttarakhand-seeks-to-give-fresh-boost-to-industry-107072301031_1.html (accessed 27 August 2017); S. Prashant, 'Uttarakhand to Set up 11 New Industrial Hubs', *Business Standard*, 14 November 2011, available http://www.business-standard.com/article/economy-policy/uttarakhand-to-set-up-11-new-industrial-hubs-111111400033_1.html (accessed 27 August 2017).

39. *Appeal No.152 of 2011* (2011). Appellate Tribunal for Electricity.

40. In an interview with a former regulator and official of the UPCL, it was recounted that because the UPCL was unable to raise tariffs to buy expensive short-term power, they resorted to load shedding, Dehradun, August 2016.

41. UERC, *Order on Determination of Retail Tariff for FY 2011–12, Re-Determination of Tariff for FY 2009–10 & Truing up of Revenues and Expenses from FY 2005–06 to FY 2009–10 for Uttarakhand Power Corporation Ltd.* (Dehradun: Uttarakhand Electricity Regulatory Commission, 2009), 98, 233.

42. UERC, *Order on Retail Tariff for Uttarakhand Power Corporation Ltd. For 2009–10* (Dehradun: Uttarakhand Electricity Regulatory Commission, 2009), 96–127.

43. UERC, *Order on Retail Tariff for Uttarakhand Power Corporation Ltd. for 2009–10.*

44. UERC, *Order on Determination*, 134.
45. This account of the UERC becoming less proactive for a number of years was confirmed in multiple interviews with regulators and officers, Dehradun, August 2016.
46. UERC, *UERC Terms & Conditions of Intra-State Open Access Regulations, 2010* (Dehradun: Uttarakhand Electricity Regulatory Commission, 2010).
47. Interviews with regulators and industry associations, Dehradun, August 2016.
48. S. Prashant, 'Uttarakhand Approves Open Access System for Industries', *Business Standard*, 9 November 2010, available http://www.business-standard.com/article/companies/uttarakhand-approves-open-access-system-for-industries-110110900078_1.html (accessed 27 August 2017).
49. Sanjev Singh, 'Uttarakhand: Congress Faces Rout, Can Harish Rawat Stop the Slide?' *FirstPost*, 20 March 2014, available http://www.firstpost.com/politics/uttarakhand-congress-faces-rout-can-harish-rawat-stop-the-slide-1442915.html (accessed 27 August 2017).
50. The Pioneer, 'Power Crisis Deepens in State', *The Pioneer*, 9 August 2014, accessed 27 August 2017: http://www.dailypioneer.com/STATE-EDITIONS/dehradun/power-crisis-deepens-in-state.html; *The Pioneer*, 'UPCL Faces Power Crisis as Output Dips', *The Pioneer*, 22 June 2015, available http://www.tribuneindia.com/news/jammu-kashmir/state-faces-power-crisis-as-generation-dips-to-one-third/186474.html (accessed 27 August 2017); *The Hindu*, 'Uttarakhand Reels under Severe Power Crisis', *The Hindu*, 14 June 2012, available http://www.thehindu.com/news/national/other-states/uttarakhand-reels-under-severe-power-crisis/article3527826.ece (accessed 27 August 2017).
51. GOI and GOU, *24/7 Power for All Uttarakhand*.
52. GOI and GOU, *24/7 Power for All Uttarakhand*.
53. UERC, *Order on Approval of Business Plan and Multi Year Tariff Petition for Uttarakhand Power Corporation Ltd. For Second Control Period (FY 2016–17 to FY 2018–19)* (Dehradun: Uttarakhand Electricity Regulatory Commission, 2010), 252.
54. P. Prashant, 'UPCL Gets Rs 915-Cr Package from Govt', *Business Standard*, 30 August 2012, available http://www.business-standard.com/article/economy-policy/upcl-gets-rs-915-cr-package-from-govt-112083002012_1.html (accessed 27 August 2017).
55. Tribune News Service, 'Power Supply in Roorkee, Kashipur to Be Privatised', *The Tribune*, 5 March 2015, available http://www.tribuneindia.com/news/uttarakhand/power-supply-in-roorkee-kashipur-to-be-privatised/49751.html (accessed 27 August 2017).

56. Shahla Siddiqui, '11k Power Employees Threaten Stir against Govt's Privatization Bid', *Times of India*, 20 May 2015, available http://timesofindia.indiatimes.com/city/dehradun/11k-power-employees-threaten-stir-against-govts-privatization-bid/articleshow/47372226.cms (accessed 27 August 2017).

57. Tribune News Service, 'Govt Fails to Privatise Power Distribution', *The Tribune*, 1 July 2015, available http://www.tribuneindia.com/news/uttarakhand/governance/govt-fails-to-privatise-power-distribution/100709.html (accessed 27 August 2017).

58. GoI and GoU, *24/7 Power for All Uttarakhand*, 5.

59. GoI and GoU, *24/7 Power for All Uttarakhand*, 4.

60. Vineet Upadhyay, 'Uttarakhand Joins Uday Scheme Aiming to Gain Power Surplus Worth Rs 962 Crore', *Times of India*, 2 April 2016, available http://timesofindia.indiatimes.com/india/Uttarakhand-joins-UDAY-scheme-aiming-to-gain-power-surplus-worth-Rs-962-crore/articleshow/51659011.cms (accessed 27 August 2017).

61. Interviews with officers at the UPCL, Dehradun, August 2016.

62. Kautilya Singh, 'Small Is Beautiful: Why Uttarakhand Is Role Model for India', *Times of India*, 2 August 2014, available http://timesofindia.indiatimes.com/city/dehradun/Small-is-Beautiful-Why-Uttarakhand-is-role-model-for-India/articleshow/39494938.cms (accessed 27 August 2017).

63. Tribune News Service, 'PhD Chamber Resents Power Tariff Hike, Unscheduled Cuts', *The Tribune*, 28 April 2016, available http://www.tribuneindia.com/news/uttarakhand/community/phd-chamber-resents-power-tariff-hike-unscheduled-cuts/228510.html (accessed 27 August 2017).

64. UERC, *Order on Approval*, 255.

65. UERC, *Order on Approval*.

66. Interviews with UERC regulators and officers, Dehradun, August, 2016.

67. GoUK, *Policy for Development of Micro & Mini Hydro Power Projects Up to 2 Mw-2015* (Dehradun: Government of Uttarakhand, 2015); Anupam Trivedi, 'U'khand's New Power Policy to Favour Local Communities', *Hindustan Times*, 4 February 2015, available http://www.hindustantimes.com/dehradun/u-khand-s-new-power-policy-to-favour-local-communities/story-YHrwblqXNj0iCUQu0941PM.html (accessed 27 August 2017).

68. Debapriya Mondal, 'Uttarkhand to Be First State to Buy Short-Term Power through E-Auction', *The Economic Times*, 28 April 2016, available http://economictimes.indiatimes.com/industry/energy/power/uttarkhand-to-be-first-state-to-buy-short-term-power-through-e-auction/articleshow/52008898.cms (accessed 27 August 2017).

69. Anupam Trivedi, 'Uttarakhand Buys 2.5 Mn Units of Power from Hp Daily', *Hindustan Times*, 1 August 2014, available http://www.pressreader. com/india/hindustan-times-jalandhar/20140801/282003260564734 (accessed 27 August 2017).

70. D. Kunwar, 'Kashipur Plants to Power State', *The Times of India*, 6 June 2016, available http://timesofindia.indiatimes.com/city/dehradun/Kashipur-plants-to-power-state/articleshow/52625639.cms (accessed 27 August 2017).

71. UERC, *Order on Approval*, 183.

72. GoUK, *Policy for Development*.

73. Tom Kenning, 'India's Uttarakhand Inviting Applications for 10 MW Rooftop and Small-Scale Solar', *PV Tech*, 2 March 2016, available https:// www.pv-tech.org/news/indias-uttarakhand-inviting-applications-for-10mw-rooftop-and-small-scale-s (accessed on 27 August 2017).

74. Shahla Siddiqui, 'Now, Consumers Can Set Up Solar Plant and Sell Surplus to UPCL', *Times of India*, 8 May 2015, available http://timesofindia. indiatimes.com/city/dehradun/Now-consumers-can-set-up-solar-plant-and-sell-surplus-to-UPCL/articleshow/47207725.cms (accessed 27 August 2017).

75. Prashant, 'UPCL Gets Rs 915-Cr.'

76. Interviews with regulators at the UERC, Dehradun, August 2016.

77. This view was expressed commonly in conversations with electricity officials, journalists, and industry representatives; however, there is no empirical evidence on the matter.

15

ELIZABETH CHATTERJEE

Insulated Wires

The Precarious Rise of West Bengal's Power Sector

The trajectory of West Bengal's power sector since 2000 has been one of the most distinctive and periodically encouraging of any Indian state.[1] Dismissing New Delhi's prescriptions for power sector liberalization with the line 'one size does not fit all',[2] in 2005 the coal-rich eastern state embarked upon its own mode of power reforms based on continued but reformed state ownership (Table 15.1). Driven by senior bureaucrats within the energy department and the public utility, this technocratic model focused on improved corporate governance and accountability. Rather than attempting to create an arm's-length relationship between utilities and the government through competition or a grafted-on regulator, the reformers hoped to strengthen the utility internally, thereby providing solid foundations for its autonomy.

Between 2006 and 2011 this model proved strikingly successful. Tariffs were consistently revised, rural electrification accelerated, albeit from a low base, and aggregate technical and commercial (AT&C) losses dropped. Despite relatively low industrial revenue (Figure 15.1), by 2011 West Bengal had become one of only three states with profitable utilities, topping performance indices (Figure 15.2).[3] Yet the sector has subsequently become more troubled. Tariff revisions have failed to

TABLE 15.1 Timeline of Key Events: West Bengal

State Politics		Power Sector Events
• CPI(M) first elected, beginning 34 years of one-party rule (Chief Minister: Jyoti Basu)	1977	
	1999	• West Bengal Electricity Regulatory Commission established
• Buddhadeb Bhattacharjee becomes Chief Minister, accelerating liberalization	2000	• Public sector enterprise reforms initiated
	2001	
	2002	• Anti-power theft law passed
	2003	• CPI(M) calls for amendments to national Electricity Act • Government of West Bengal forms committee on power restructuring
• CPI(M) dominates in Lok Sabha elections	2004	
	2005	• Power reform efforts initiated • Centre's Rajiv Gandhi Grameen Vidyutikaran Yojana for rural electrification launched
• CPI(M) re-elected for seventh consecutive time with enlarged seat share	2006	
• Violence erupts against pro-industry projects in Nandigram and Singur	2007	• Unbundling of WBSEB into WBSETCL (transmission) and WBSEDCL (distribution)
• CPI(M) loses many village-level elections	2008	• Performance-based incentive scheme and audits introduced in utilities
• CPI(M) loses two-thirds of its seats in national elections; Trinamool gains	2009	

(Cont'd)

TABLE 15.1   (Cont'd)

State Politics		Power Sector Events
	2010	
• Trinamool Congress wins state election (Chief Minister: Mamata Banerjee) • Deaths discourage crackdown on power theft	2011	• Banerjee blocks tariff hikes
	2012	• Tariff freeze leads to financial deterioration; government permits hikes • Publication of renewable energy policy
• Trinamool dominates in local elections	2013	
• Trinamool dominates in national elections	2014	• Tariff revisions delayed
	2015	• Domestic tariffs go up sharply with retrospective effect; sporadic protests
• Trinamool decisively re-elected; CPI(M) vote collapses	2016	• Tariff revisions delayed • WBERC debates ending cross-subsidy payments from industry

Source: Author.

keep pace with rising costs,[4] AT&C losses are escalating once more, and the quality and morale of personnel appears to have declined[5]—although West Bengal continues to outperform many other states.

What explains this reform trajectory? First, why were power reforms successfully initiated? While West Bengal did not have to contend with powerful farmer lobbies, it was a densely populated, nominally communist state with a long history of union activism and popular protest, an unusually high government debt burden, and flagging industrial development—hardly an obvious reform pioneer. Second, why did the reforms' initial performance gains start to plateau?

This chapter argues that West Bengal's power reform trajectory is inseparable from the state's wider political scenario, especially the

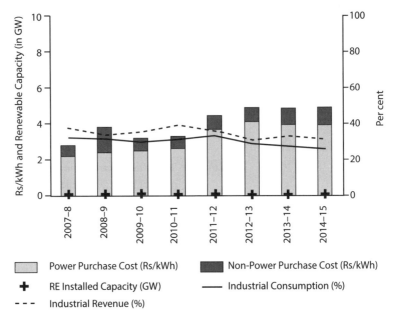

FIGURE **15.1**   Physical and Financial Profile: West Bengal
Sources: CSO, *Energy Statistics* (New Delhi: Central Statistics Office, Ministry of Statistics and Programme Implementation, Government of India, 2010, 2012, 2014, and 2016); PFC, *Reports on Performance of State Power Utilities* (New Delhi: Power Finance Corporation Limited, 2011, 2013, 2015, and 2016).

degree of party–political competition. Under (democratic) one-party dominance, regimes may opt to 'tie their own hands' through insulated power governance as the electoral and financial gains from insulation are greater in the *longer term*, offering sustained performance and helping to attract lucrative industry.[6] The Communist Party of India (Marxist) (CPI[M]) governed West Bengal effectively unopposed between 1977 and 2011 (Table 15.2). This gave it the perceived strength to tilt towards a long-term strategy that sought to insulate utilities against short-term political interference.

Under increased political competition, by contrast, regime time horizons are shorter. Administrations opt for subsidies that temporarily head off popular resistance at the cost of longer-term financial health. While improved electricity supplies were popular, the CPI(M)'s overall prioritization of industry came at the cost of public support. After years

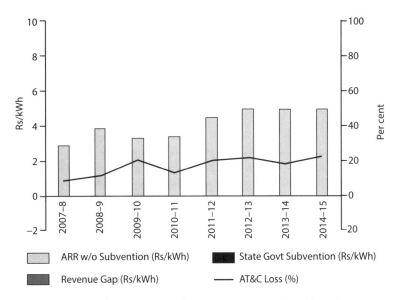

FIGURE 15.2   Supply-side Costs and Revenue Recovery: West Bengal
Source: PFC, *Reports on Performance of State Power Utilities* (New Delhi: Power Finance Corporation Limited, 2011, 2013, 2015, and 2016).

of local unrest and declining CPI(M) electoral performance from 2008, 2011 saw the first change in government in 34 years. Over its first term (2011–16) the new Trinamool Congress regime enacted power policy in the shadow of this increased party-political competition, opting for the short-term gains from accelerated rural electrification, populist subsidies, and tolerance of power theft over long-term governance. Nonetheless, the internally-focused reform path has proven a source of limited but real resilience: the utilities' new culture and accountability mechanisms appear to have survived somewhat intact, and performance remains above pre-reform levels.

West Bengal's power experience thus demonstrates, first, that comparatively weak farmer lobbies can help to facilitate reform. Second, it suggests the promise and limits of public sector reform as an alternative to the model of deregulation and privatization advocated by the World Bank in the 1990s and the central government-endorsed Electricity Act 2003. Third, it illustrates the significance of party-political competition and developments in the wider economy in shaping and undermining power reforms. The following sections explore the prehistory, process,

TABLE 15.2 CPI(M) and Trinamool Seat Share and Vote Share in West Bengal Elections, 2001–16

		Election						
		2001 State	2004 National	2006 State	2009 National	2011 State	2014 National	2016 State
CPI(M)	Seat share (%)	49	62	60	21	14	5	9
	Vote share (%)	37	39	37	33	30	23	20
Trinamool	Seat share (%)	20	2	10	45	63	81	72
	Vote share (%)	31	21	27	31	39	40	45

Source: Author.

key characteristics, and sustainability of this distinctive model of power reform.

Historical Background, 1977–2004

Despite inheriting the largest installed generation capacity of any province at independence, after 1947 West Bengal electrified slowly. Thanks to the state's longstanding reputation for labour militancy, the lucrative industrial consumer base was slow to grow. The West Bengal State Electricity Board (WBSEB) was also structurally deprived of high-paying consumers to bolster its revenues for expansion. Kolkata is served by the private Calcutta Electric Supply Company (CESC), while the industrial belts around Durgapur and Asansol–Raniganj are monopolized by other utilities outside the state government's control. Rural electrification proved especially sluggish, in contrast to western and southern states with wealthy agricultural lobbies.[7] This urban bias was in part geologically determined—the state's wet, fertile climate meant that irrigation was less of a priority than in drier areas—but it was also politically conditioned.

By the mid-1970s West Bengal's power sector was in a state of crisis, mirroring the state's wider power vacuum. Load shedding extended for up to 12 hours even in Kolkata. A new Left Front government, headed by the CPI(M), began a slow stabilization of the sector—though WBSEB's financial performance remained among India's worst until the end of the century. The CPI(M) would hold power for the next 34 years, winning seven consecutive state elections to become India's longest-serving state administration (Table 15.2).

The neglect of rural electrification persisted even under this nominally communist regime, despite its loyal rural voter base and famed land reforms. The 2001 census recorded a rural household electrification rate of only 20.3 per cent, well below the all-India average of 43.5 per cent. This neglect suggests the shallowness of the CPI(M)'s pro-poor reforms in practice. Its leadership was dominated by urban, educated, upper-caste elites conscious of the importance of placating urban constituencies and large industrial houses with adequate electricity, even while offering poor voters only modest redistribution.[8] Its land reforms also helped to prevent the emergence of a wealthy farmer lobby by creating an agrarian class with significantly smaller holdings than their counterparts elsewhere, while its powerful party–state organization in rural areas headed off alternative modes of organization (discussed later). West Bengal thus largely escaped some of the power sector's canonical problems—notably low tariffs for farmers, which elsewhere led to financial debilitation. Agricultural consumption currently remains under 10 per cent of total load, and more recently the government has enforced agricultural tariff hikes unthinkable in many other states.[9] Together the CPI(M)'s one-party dominance and the absence of powerful farmer lobbies would provide the preconditions for West Bengal's successful power reforms of the mid-2000s.

Technocratic Power Reforms, 2005–10

In 1991 the Union government began 'big bang' liberalization reforms, with power generation the first major sector opened to private investment. West Bengal was an unlikely liberalizer: its governing elite retained a publicly anti-market ideology, and the stance of its administrations to New Delhi has traditionally been oppositional.[10] Nonetheless, the CPI(M) was more pragmatic than dogmatic, and West Bengal's dire fiscal situation was becoming increasingly obvious. In the mid-1990s Chief Minister Jyoti Basu (governed 1977–2000) adopted a 'new' liberal industrial policy and began to woo private investment. This was accelerated by his replacement, the reformist Buddhadeb Bhattacharjee (2000–11), although the party's nominally communist ideology favoured public sector reform over outright privatization.

With the need to rein in public expenditure paramount, the crucial precursor to electricity reform arrived through the successful divestment of 'sick' public sector enterprises (PSEs) from 2000. The same personnel—reformist PSE secretary Sunil Mitra and PricewaterhouseCoopers (PwC) consultants—would provide the core personnel for power reforms. Several lessons from this earlier experience would be applied, such as the importance of financial restructuring and the need to win over employee unions.[11]

In these reform efforts the CPI(M) was able to draw on its organizational strength and the resilience of its rural support base. Despite never winning more than half of all votes, its domination was so absolute that West Bengal was labelled a 'party-society'.[12] The CPI(M) was a disciplined, cadre-based organization. This centralized structure concentrated power in the hands of the Chief Minister, and over the years close relations developed between the political apex and senior bureaucrats.[13] At the grassroots the party combined formal decentralization and local patronage to formidable effect, acting as the sole arbiter of local disputes and assimilating social organizations such as unions into the party–state matrix. Its success was founded on its ability to balance this dual character: the 'elevated' domain of centralized policymaking from Kolkata, and the 'embedded' domain of local clientelism and rural corporatism.[14]

This combination of centralized decision-making and embeddedness helped to shape a distinctive reform trajectory. While the party–state gave the Chief Minister the authority to push for major policy change, reformists also argued that it risked hollowing out official institutions; grassroots corruption and high-handedness were becoming major concerns.[15] This pushed the regime towards policies that aimed to distance utility decision-making from everyday political pressures. While these would bring practical gains, the move towards apex-led industrial transformation rather than local responsiveness would later come at the cost of popular support.

First drafted in 2000, the Electricity Act finally passed into law in 2003. While at the national level communist parties criticized its vision, the Act opened a window of opportunity, enabling reformists to depict changes as externally imposed.[16] In 2005, with the reformers' credibility bolstered by the PSE successes, the Chief Minister shifted Sunil Mitra to the power department with a mandate for reform and a strong hand: WBSEB's performance had already begun to improve, bringing with it some fiscal breathing space. Although privatization and major job losses were ruled out, Mitra's team otherwise enjoyed wide latitude.[17]

While rejecting the Act's 'one-size-fits-all' approach thanks to the disasters that had beset other Indian states as a result of the World Bank's 1990s blueprint, West Bengal's reforms similarly sought to insulate utilities from political influence, albeit in the context of state ownership. Indeed, the reforms emerged incrementally from a months-long critique of previous failures in other states by PwC consultants with first-hand experience. If the Act's solutions emphasized the discipline imposed by competition and independent regulation, the core of West Bengal's reform model was to empower the utilities and improve accountability mechanisms. One reformer captured the logic clearly:

The first step was to isolate the utility—to the extent that the political economy allows—from political interference. We never believed the government would be out of the sector entirely: that's too optimistic given that the sector is government-owned and fulfils welfare goals. But we could keep it slightly at arm's length. You can only do this if you assure the government that the sector will be run well, because politicians have two interests in the sector: (1) the quality of service, and (2) the efficiency of the customer interface. If you falter in either of these the political executive takes note.... In any case, both power theft and political interference are often only excuses for inefficiency within the utility itself. So our efforts were driven by internal reforms. All other desirable ends, like good consumer management, follow from this improved accountability system.[18]

Profitability, the guarantor of financial autonomy, was the cornerstone of the reform effort.

Unbundling was merely a means to this end.[19] Informed by other states' difficulties, the West Bengal team determined that multiple distribution companies (discoms) would be problematic in the absence of private competition: it would exacerbate regional asymmetries and the scarcity of managerial talent. Accordingly, in 2007 WBSEB was split into a transmission utility, the West Bengal State Electricity Transmission Company Limited (WBSETCL), and a single discom, the West Bengal State Electricity Distribution Company Limited (WBSEDCL); a separate generation entity had already existed since 1985.

In managerial terms, the reforms centred on the imitation of private sector best practices in corporate governance—in particular, 'shadow listing' and the drafting of Articles of Association in accordance with Clause 49 of the newly published Securities and Exchange Board of India agreement governing listing on the stock exchange. The Articles aimed to institutionalize an arm's-length relationship with the government. Genuinely independent directors were recruited from across India, including private-sector executives. Behind closed doors even divestment was discreetly considered for its promise of further autonomy and additional government revenues.[20]

After these overarching changes to the utility's structure and governance, the reformers turned to examine the wider workforce. Business operations were scrutinized, while detailed job descriptions were developed in order to facilitate performance monitoring. The steep pyramid of the utility bureaucracy was gradually trimmed in favour of high-quality technical staff with increased wages, and the hierarchy somewhat flattened through street-level outsourcing for activities like bill collection.[21] In this process a long campaign to convince mid-level employees of the necessity of reform paid dividends by preventing union activism: 'It was difficult for the bottom level of employees, but we understood the rationale,' explained an engineering union representative; 'there has been a culture change against the earlier phase of resistance'.[22]

WBSEDCL had already adopted information technology more swiftly than most other Indian utilities. This propensity for technological solutions was accelerated in the name of removing—or at least tightly monitoring—'the human element', taking advantage of central funding for automation.[23] Remotely readable meters were installed to monitor urban feeders and bulk consumers, providing real-time data to improve billing and catch theft, though plans for software-aided resource planning fell behind schedule.[24] These measures were designed to slim down the bureaucratic apparatus and increase its transparency—albeit at the cost of discreet privatization.[25]

While the Electricity Act 2003 accorded regulators a crucial position, throughout these reforms the West Bengal Electricity Regulatory Commission (WBERC, established in 1999) took on a supportive but secondary role. While soliciting WBERC's seal of approval, reformers were all too aware of the perils of 'the regulation of government by government'.[26] Nonetheless, in practice WBERC generally protected the utility's interests, at least while both agencies seemed to share the same technocratic priorities. Between 2007 and 2011 it consistently raised tariffs, and opted for light-touch annual balancing of the accounts rather than scrutinizing every utility investment decision upfront. Around 2007 WBERC also ceased public hearings, arguing that these were too frequently anarchic and unproductive, and instead accepted only written submissions.[27] Surprisingly, some consumer groups agreed that public contributions offered little except knee-jerk resistance to even justifiable tariff hikes.[28] Conversely, the utilities continued to enjoy heavy representation on WBERC's advisory committee.

During the reforms' high point between 2007 and 2011, relations with the regulator remained generally close. When the discom temporarily bore the burden of political interference (for example, in postponing tariff petitions) and then later sought financial redress via steep tariff hikes, however, WBERC was reluctant to allow it to pass on the cost of its inefficiencies to consumers—as seen below in the recent case of regulatory assets.

In contrast to the World Bank model, West Bengal's locally developed reforms maintained conspicuous state ownership. Transmission and most generation (68 per cent) remains in public sector hands, as does distribution outside Kolkata and the Asansol–Raniganj belt. Open access to the wires by private generators was allowed in theory, but not in practice: the utilities have so far successfully lobbied the regulator for high wheeling charges to discourage elite consumer exit, a settlement that industrial lobbies generally tolerate.

For its first few years this model appeared an impressive success story. From recorded losses of US$300 million in 2002, by 2011, West Bengal had become one of only three states with (marginally) profitable discoms, with revenues more than covering the cost of supply (Figure 15.2). Thanks to its corporate governance reforms, the World Bank named West Bengal's utilities among India's best governed, an exemplar of arm's-length management despite state ownership.[29] Thanks to automation and improved vigilance, AT&C losses fell from more than 40 per cent in 2001 to 23.2 per cent in 2007–8. In the Government of India's first formal assessment, WBSEDCL accordingly received an 'A' grade.[30]

As the quality of service began to rise, the goalposts shifted in line with increased consumer expectations; a relatively new 24×7 imaginary has swiftly come to dominate in urban areas, in which even brief blackouts are intolerable.[31] Both WBSEDCL and CESC thus devote increasing resources to improving consumer services.[32] This should not be overstated: in many rural areas supply remains uneven, and newly connected households often embrace electricity only warily until they assess its financial impact. In such areas slow connections, aggressive disconnections, and billing problems continue.[33]

Even so, the belated gains in rural electrification were especially significant. Funded through a centrally sponsored scheme, connections doubled from 3.57 million to 8.57 million between the 2001 and 2011 censuses, and the proportion of rural households using electricity as their primary light source doubled from 20.3 to 40.3 per cent. Nonetheless, these achievements could not prevent the popular backlash against the Left Front's pro-business reforms. By 2008 opposition parties had taken control of more than half of the state's villages, and in the 2009 general elections the CPI(M) lost two-thirds of its seats in the national parliament (Table 15.2).

Intensifying Party–Political Competition, 2011–16

The CPI(M)'s strategy relied on the hope that an improved investment climate, with quality electricity its centrepiece, would attract new industry to the state. Its elitist, technocratic governance style may have begun to deliver in the power sector, but the general pro-business tilt came at the cost of the party's socialist credentials. After 34 years in control, it lost the elections of May 2011. A post-poll survey of voters suggested that the CPI(M) was voted out not because of its record on public service delivery, but for betraying its pro-poor ideology—notoriously embodied in the coercive land seizures at Nandigram and Singur in 2007.[34]

In its place, the Trinamool Congress swept to a majority (Table 15.2), adding much of the Left Front's formerly loyal rural support to its existing base among the urban petty bourgeoisie. Yet it had to navigate a much more competitive political space. This and its lower-class voter base helped to shape the new administration's populist stance towards the power sector. For much of its first term it prioritized pro-poor expansion through channels both formal (accelerated rural electrification) and informal (apex-level attempts to reduce tariffs, and the tolerance of theft coordinated by local satraps).

Some elements of this populism were desirable: in the five years following 2011, the number of electricity connections in the state nearly doubled again, to 16.37 million. Thanks to heightened party–political competition, the government nonetheless remained sensitive to popular opinion, especially around elections. Upon taking office new Chief Minister Mamata Banerjee felt she had little choice but to block tariff revisions, and WBSEDCL's finances rapidly began to deteriorate.[35] WBERC similarly delayed releasing the annual tariff order due in April 2016, just before the most recent state elections, when the Trinamool Congress again emerged with the largest number of seats. Pressure was generally indirect: 'I never received a phone call from the chief minister or anything like that', emphasized one former regulator. Instead, both WBSEDCL and CESC moderated their tariff petitions before elections.[36] The hikes that were belatedly permitted could not keep pace with the increasing cost of power procurement, interest payments, or employee salaries, as West Bengal found itself locked into expensive contracts with central generator NTPC Limited. Belated revisions meant tariffs lurched abruptly upwards, antagonizing consumers already facing some of the country's highest tariffs.

After around 2013, when several reformers had formally exited the sector, the decline of governance was exacerbated by a widely perceived deterioration in the quality of senior personnel—viewed as a deliberate strategy to ensure their compliance.[37] WBERC was left without a chairman and with only one member for almost two years, though the remaining member fought to maintain a degree of regulatory independence (discussed later). Several interviewees raised questions about the quality of its new members. The WBSEDCL also struggled to find second-generation champions to take on the less glamorous work of reform sustainability in the face of interference. As a senior bureaucrat declared: 'The utilities are not at all independent. We are poking them at least eight times a day, eight hours a day!'[38]

The new administration also lacked the CPI(M)'s disciplined party machine, flawed as it was, as a substitute for bureaucratic cohesion. United by opposition to the Left Front and the charismatic personality of Mamata Banerjee rather than a coherent programme, the Trinamool Congress is more loosely structured.[39] Beyond populism, as one former official explained, 'there are problems that Mamata cannot control: political will won't stretch downwards to solving problems of disconnections or theft'.[40] AT&C losses had begun to climb as early as 2009 as the CPI(M)'s dominance had begun to wane, and continued to rise under Trinamool (Figure 15.2); recent central reports accordingly criticized WBSEDCL's declining collection efficiency.[41] Many interviewees thus now characterize the power sector's problems as a law-and-order situation.

As a result of these trends, since 2011 WBSEDCL has struggled with spiralling debts, increasingly resorting to short-term borrowing to finance even everyday operations. In 2016 its credit rating was downgraded, the ratings agency citing rising regulatory assets, uncertainties around tariff revisions, and high T&D losses.[42] In place of tough political choices the administration has opted for optimistic technical fixes like rural feeder segregation, though agricultural consumption remains minimal.[43] Technology is still cast as a prophylactic against 'the human element' at the street level, through smart grid pilots and big data analytics to identify theft—no matter that the 'human element' of apex-level political interference may persist.

Yet signs of resilience remain. Not all power bureaucrats have simply bowed to political pressure. While the high-calibre first generation of reformers are no longer formally connected to the sector, they continue to provide a watchful eye and an unofficial source of advice to the struggling second generation.[44] Faced with the tariff freeze of the Trinamool regime's early months, they interceded with the Chief Minister's trusted lieutenants, warning of imminent power cuts.[45] As load shedding began to make itself felt, Banerjee agreed to tariff revisions and renounced political interference.[46] While reformist bureaucrats were relieved, this episode suggests that reform sustainability has depended on the personal networks and commitment of individuals rather than institutional consolidation.

The regulator, WBERC, has also provided a source of modest resistance, in the face of political meddling in personnel appointments. It intervened when WBSEDCL sought to raise tariffs to compensate for regulatory assets, alleging that WBSEDCL's on-paper profits relied on a deliberate misclassification of costs incurred due to its own inefficiency. A respected discom board member similarly resigned over such 'creative accounting'. Even within the beleaguered discom, the effects of corporatization have continued to resonate with utility personnel. New staff appear to have internalized reformed professional norms, and managers still see the utility as 'a professionally managed organization, not a government entity', while acknowledging the negotiated character of their autonomy.[47]

As this suggests, West Bengal's deterioration is only relative. The WBSEDCL still enjoys greater independence than many other state utilities. Tariffs have been revised upwards, if belatedly, and most officials still complete their tenures. It is also easy to exaggerate the contrast with the previous administration: electricity theft was on the rise again from 2010 and still remains well below pre-reform levels (Figure 15.2). 'From the outset we always had doubts about sustainability,' one reformer admitted. His overall verdict was more optimistic, however: 'It's true that the sector is not at the level it rose to, but it is considerably better than the level that we started at.'[48]

Structural changes may eventually encourage the Trinamool administration to take up a more long-term approach. The 2016 elections provided it with an even more emphatic mandate (Table 15.2), supported by mass defections of CPI(M) local cadres. The confirmation of five more years in power and the collapse of CPI(M) support may put a temporary end to the era of intense party-political competition, thus increasing the leadership's perceived room for manoeuvre. At least in theory, the government may have the confidence to abandon populism in favour of a more long-term development agenda.

There are both electoral and fiscal reasons to believe this might occur. First, Bengali voters appear to reward infrastructure provision. A 2016 post-election survey suggested that Trinamool won on the back of its perceived dedication to economic development, with voters particularly emphasizing discernible improvements in electricity and roads.[49] This fits with a body of political science scholarship which suggests that rising consumer expectations may encourage a shift away from short-term clientelism to rewarding more sustained and programmatic 'good governance'—such as '24×7' power over cheap but unreliable supplies.[50] Officials recognize that the priority will shift from ensuring basic access to high-quality supply, and efficiency must rise in tandem.

Second, structural factors may once again override party ideology. As for the CPI(M) in the early 2000s, the pressure to attract industry and private investment is acute, both to provide employment to the Trinamool's young urban voters and to generate revenues in this most debt-ridden of states. Once again, then, the hope is that high-quality electricity will bring in lucrative business and so boost growth. This supports the case for reducing political interference in the sector. There is even discussion of dropping electricity cross-subsidies altogether, although this remains politically unlikely and discom finances continued to deteriorate through 2017.[51]

Electrifying an industrialized Bengal may be a pipe dream, in any case. Despite robust overall economic growth, the declining industrial share of electricity consumption and revenues suggests that improved power supplies have not succeeded in attracting industry. Electricity alone cannot provide a silver bullet for West Bengal's political economy; industrialists and others call instead for wider reforms, especially on land acquisition and other infrastructural bottlenecks.[52] Such policy areas have proved far less amenable to Buddhadeb Bhattacharjee-style apex-led technocratic solutions. Without such lucrative industrial consumers, though, the future of the electricity sector hangs in the balance.

As one donor agency official lamented: 'Can an island of excellence survive where everything else sucks?'[53]

***

West Bengal's power reform experience sheds light upon a number of aspects of electricity reforms in India. First, it provides lessons about the political preconditions necessary both for successful and sustainable institutional change. Comparatively weak farmer lobbies provided the precondition for reform. Changing levels of party–political competition and the ensuing shifts in policy strategies—and, secondarily, the ruling party's organizational characteristics—have proved instrumental in determining the sector's trajectory. One-party dominance facilitated a technocratic mode of reform, while party–political competition shifted the policy onus back towards short-term particularist handouts.[54] Second, West Bengal's power reforms under public ownership provide encouraging signs that public sector reform can provide a viable alternative to liberalization—but also show the limits of such an isolated 'island of excellence' in transforming a state's economic trajectory.

Until 2011 power policy was shaped under the one-party dominance of the CPI(M), unhampered by party-political competition and with opposition from farmers and unions largely contained within the CPI(M)'s powerful machinery. The CPI(M) leadership's bureaucratic centralism and industrial vision combined with its rising mistrust of the lower party-state to produce a pragmatic but statist effort to depoliticize power. The resulting reforms were technocratic and centred on internal governance changes, capacity building, and technology-aided process streamlining. While rejecting outright privatization, they incorporated some elements of private-style management: corporate governance norms, frontline outsourcing, and independent directors and consultants.[55] The goal was to foster improved accountability and financial and operational independence from the government, both at the apex and by 'reducing the human element' in day-to-day operations.

However, improved power performance was inseparable from the state's broader political economy. The 'good governance' gains from the CPI(M)'s technocratic turn could not compensate for the perceived betrayal of its socialist ideology. Upon replacing the CPI(M) in 2011, the Trinamool Congress inherited a far more obviously competitive political scenario. Aiming to retain voters, it therefore shifted power policy in a pro-poor, 'populist' direction, weakening (though not ending) utility independence. In this way, party–political competition and the time horizons of power governance appear inversely related. The technocratic, utility-centred mode of power reforms proved only somewhat resilient under this renewed political pressure, although West Bengal continued to perform better than many of its counterparts. Today the sector's future is precariously balanced. Trinamool's decisive electoral victory in 2016 may eventually herald a return to long-term power policymaking. Yet this study suggests that the electric 'island of excellence' will continue to be buffeted by wider economic and political currents.

Notes and References

1. This chapter uses 'West Bengal' rather than 'Bengal', as at the time of writing the state's name change had not been formally approved. The author is grateful to the 35 individuals who gave so generously of their time and insights in July and August 2016, and to the Confederation of Indian Industry for permission to observe their 2016 Energy Conclave in Kolkata. All the interviews quoted were carried out by the author on a not-for-attribution basis.

2. This phrase recurred both in interviews and contemporary assessments; see PwC, *West Bengal Power Sector Reforms: Lessons Learnt and Unfinished Agenda*, Report 68330 (PricewaterhouseCoopers; AusAID, 2009), 16; World Bank, *India: Organizational Transformation of State-Owned Enterprises: Case of West Bengal Power Sector, Outcomes from Knowledge Sharing Workshops* (Internal Memorandum: World Bank, 2009), 3.

3. Sheoli Pargal and Sudeshna Ghosh Banerjee, *More Power to India: The Challenge of Electricity Distribution* (Washington, DC: World Bank, 2014), 94.

4. While the official data represented in Figure 15.2 appears to show that tariffs are meeting costs, this relies on a disputed classification of some losses as future receivables. See discussion of the dispute between the utility and the regulator over regulatory assets for more information.

5. Interview with former power official, Kolkata, 7 August 2016; interview with regulator, Kolkata, 12 August 2016.

6. On the relationship between political competitiveness and politicians' spending on clientelistic policies (at least until economic growth shifts increasing numbers of voters to prefer good governance instead), see

Steven Wilkinson, 'Explaining Changing Patterns of Party-Voter Linkages in India', in *Patrons, Clients, and Policies: Patterns of Democratic Accountability and Political Competition*, ed. Herbert Kitschelt and Steven Wilkinson (Cambridge: Cambridge University Press, 2007), 110–40.

7. Sunila S. Kale, *Electrifying India: Regional Political Economies of Development* (Stanford, CA: Stanford University Press, 2014).

8. Atul Kohli, *Democracy and Discontent: India's Growing Crisis of Governability* (Cambridge: Cambridge University Press, 1990), 267; Kale, *Electrifying India*, 170–5.

9. Aditi Mukherji, 'Political Ecology of Groundwater: The Contrasting Case of Water-Abundant West Bengal and Water-Scarce Gujarat, India', *Hydrogeology Journal* 14(3), 2006: 392–406.

10. Aseema Sinha, *The Regional Roots of Developmental Politics in India: A Divided Leviathan* (Bloomington, IN: Indiana University Press, 2005).

11. Interview with former senior power sector official, Kolkata, 11 August 2016; interview with former consultant, Kolkata, 12 August 2016; Stephen J. Masty, 'Communication, Coalition-Building and Development: Public Enterprise Reform in West Bengal and Orissa States, India', in Sina Odugbemi and Thomas Jacobson (eds), *Governance Reform under Real-World Conditions: Citizens, Stakeholders, and Voice* (Washington, DC: World Bank, 2008).

12. Dwaipayan Bhattacharyya, *Government as Practice: Democratic Left in a Transforming India* (Delhi: Cambridge University Press, 2016), 123–54.

13. Interview with former senior discom official, Howrah, 5 August 2016; interview with former senior power official, Kolkata, 11 August 2016.

14. Dwaipayan Bhattacharyya, 'Left in the Lurch: The Demise of the World's Longest Elected Regime?' in Sudha Pai (ed.), *Handbook of Politics in Indian States: Regions, Parties, and Economic Reforms* (New Delhi: Oxford University Press, 2013); Bhattacharyya, *Government as Practice*.

15. Surajit C. Mukhopadhyay, 'Left Front Win in West Bengal: Continuity, but Also Change', *Economic and Political Weekly* 36(22), 2001: 1942–4.

16. For example, they claimed that such reforms were an essential condition for the state government's forgiveness of WBSEB's debts; interview with former senior power official, Kolkata, 11 August 2016.

17. It is important not to overstate the depth of support for the power reforms in the CPI(M)'s upper ranks, however. In 2004 Bhattacharjee's own power minister publicly argued that State governments, not regulators, should determine tariffs. Reform bureaucrats describe having to circumvent their own power ministers; interview with former senior power official, Kolkata, 11 August 2016.

18. Interview with former senior utility official, Kolkata, 5 August 2016.

19. Interview with former senior utility official, Kolkata, 5 August 2016.

20. Interview with consultant, Gurgaon, 30 August 2016.

21. Interview with senior discom manager, Kolkata, 18 August 2016.

22. Interview with engineers' union representative, Kolkata, 18 August 2016. Nonetheless, the interviewee raised fears about limited oversight of the newly outsourced lower tiers.

23. On the extent and limits of these innovations within 'Stelcorp' (as WBSEDCL is renamed), see Ritam Sengupta, Richard Heeks, Sumandro Chattapadhyay, and Christopher Foster, 'Exploring Big Data for Development: An Electricity Sector Case Study from India', *Development Informatics Working Paper No. 66*, University of Manchester (2017).

24. Interview with consultant, Gurgaon, 30 August 2016.

25. WBSEDCL engineers have raised concerns about both frontline outsourcing and dependence on Tata Consultancy Services to manage enterprise software; interview, engineers' union representative, 18 August 2016.

26. Phone interview with donor agency official, 3 August 2016; interview with former senior discom official, Howrah, 5 August 2016.

27. Interview with former regulator, Kolkata, 31 July 2016.

28. Interview with consumer group representatives, Kolkata, 3 August 2016.

29. Sheoli Pargal and Kristy Mayer, *Governance of Indian State Power Utilities: An Ongoing Journey* (Washington, DC: World Bank, 2014), 29–33, 82.

30. Ministry of Power, *State Distribution Utilities First Annual Integrated Rating* (New Delhi: Government of India, 2013).

31. Interviews with CESC managers, Kolkata, 30 July and 2 August 2016.

32. Often criticized by Kolkata consumers, CESC's very healthy profits partly stem from its over-performance against WBERC targets set with reference to the state discom. While currently enjoying a monopoly, its senior managers see a competitive scenario as inevitable, and hope to have developed both superior efficiency and a loyal consumer base when it arrives; Interviews with CESC managers, Kolkata, 30 July and 2 August 2016.

33. Interviews with consumer group representatives, Kolkata, 3 August and 9 August 2016.

34. Bhattacharyya, 'Left in the Lurch', 228; *Government as Practice*, 224.

35. Interview with former senior discom official, Howrah, 5 August 2016; interview with former senior power official, Kolkata, 11 August 2016.

36. Interview with former regulator, Kolkata, 31 July 2016; interview with regulator, Kolkata, 12 August 2016.

37. Former power official, personal communication to author, 11 August 2016; interview with regulator, Kolkata, 12 August 2016.

38. Interview, Kolkata, 19 August 2016.

39. Mukulika Banerjee, 'Populist Leadership in West Bengal and Tamil Nadu: Mamata and Jayalalithaa Compared', in *Regional Reflections: Comparing*

Politics across India's States, ed. Rob Jenkins (New Delhi, Oxford: Oxford University Press, 2004); Bhattacharyya, 'Left in the Lurch', 229.

40. Interview with former power official, Kolkata, 11 August 2016.

41. Ministry of Power, *State Distribution Utilities Fourth Annual Integrated Rating* (New Delhi: Government of India, 2016): 32; and *State Distribution Utilities Fifth Annual Integrated Rating* (New Delhi: Government of India, 2017): 33. In 2016 WBSEDCL received an overall 'B+' grade, like the majority of mediocre-performing discoms, falling further to a 'B' in 2017.

42. ICRA, 'WBSEDCL rating', available http://www.icra.in/Files/Reports/Rationale/West%20Bengal%20-R-29032016.pdf (accessed March 2016).

43. Interview with former power minister, Kolkata, 10 August 2016.

44. Interview with former senior discom official, Howrah, 5 August 2016; interview with former senior discom official, Kolkata, 7 August 2016.

45. Interview with former senior discom official, Howrah, 5 August 2016; interview with former senior power official, Kolkata, 11 August 2016.

46. Interview with former senior discom official, Howrah, 5 August 2016; interview with former senior power official, Kolkata, 11 August 2016.

47. Interviews with senior discom manager, Kolkata, 18 August 2016; phone interview with donor agency official, 3 August 2016.

48. Interview with former senior discom official, Howrah, 5 August 2016.

49. Shreyas Sardesai and Suprio Basu, 'Poor Dump Left for Trinamool, Muslims Solidly behind Didi', *Indian Express*, 22 May 2016.

50. Wilkinson, 'Explaining Changing Patterns', 132–40. A study of rural Bengal also found that providing one-time benefits did not succeed in winning voter loyalty, while recurring benefits and broad-based changes did; Pranab Bardhan, Sandip Mitra, Dilip Mookherjee, and Abhirup Sarkar, 'Local Democracy and Clientelism: Implications for Political Stability in Rural West Bengal', *Economic and Political Weekly* 44(9), 2009: 46–58.

51. Interview with regulator, Kolkata, 12 August 2016; interview with former discom manager, Kolkata, 7 August 2016; interview with senior power bureaucrat, Kolkata, 19 August 2016.

52. Now that reliability has improved, industrialists do not consider electricity a primary issue; interview with industry lobbyist, Kolkata, 8 August 2016.

53. Phone interview, 3 August 2016.

54. For a more extended exploration of this argument, see Elizabeth Chatterjee, 'The Politics of Electricity Reform: Evidence from West Bengal, India', *World Development* 104, 2018: 128–39.

55. Such strategies have also been deployed in state-owned enterprises at the national level; see Elizabeth Chatterjee, 'Reinventing State Capitalism in India: A View from the Energy Sector', *Contemporary South Asia* 25(1), 2017: 85–100.

NAVROZ K. DUBASH
SUNILA S. KALE
RANJIT BHARVIRKAR

Conclusion

Mapping Power in Comparative State Context

The central aim of this volume is to understand the relationship of politics to electricity outcomes. The case studies provide convincing information on the need for such an understanding. In state after state, efforts at shifting electricity outcomes have foundered on perceptions or realities of the electoral costs from doing so. Thus, in West Bengal, internal management reforms were partially rolled back by a new government promising subsidies. Tamil Nadu has faced a rising tide of constituencies demanding ever greater subsidies, which require the state to dig ever deeper into its coffers. Efforts to insulate electricity decisions from politics, through the reform prescription of unbundling, regulatory commissions, and privatization have also had an uneven record at best, as in Delhi and Odisha. But, notably, there are also cases where electricity has contributed to productive politics, such as the relatively recent efforts to win votes on the back of rural electricity provision in Bihar, and the gradual linkage of better quality power and electoral prospects in Gujarat.

Moving beyond establishing *that* politics matters, to showing *how* politics matters requires deeper exploration of the rich empirical information in the state-specific chapters in this volume. These help to detail the more specific pathways through which electricity and politics are linked and whether and how these linkages can be shaped over time. Efforts to shape outcomes have included careful political management of key groups, the projection of electricity decisions as arm's length from politics by use of regulatory processes, negotiation with unions, and enhanced transparency and better accounting, among many others. How do we understand and make sense of the range of tactics used, and their relative success and failure?

In this concluding chapter, we refocus the discussion on the key questions that animate this volume: how do politics and electricity outcomes shape each other, through what pathways, and with what implications for the future of the Indian electricity sector? Our approach, as discussed in the introduction, is inductive. In the introductory chapter, we summarized each state case, which were laid out in full in the subsequent chapters. Here, we first draw out the high-level conclusions that emerge from a comparison across states. We then return to our analytic framework to show how four key concepts (demand for access and quality, demand for subsidies, cost of supply, and financial space) provide a useful way to understand the linkage between electricity and politics, and illustrate this discussion with empirical examples from the book. Next, we provide a simple scaffold for categorizing states based on the relationship between politics and electricity outcomes. We suggest that while outcomes are diverse it is also possible to group states into a finite set of categories, and doing so provide insights into the political economy of electricity. Together, these three elements—the state-specific narratives, the key concepts, and the outcome categorization—provide an analytic toolkit that sheds light on state electricity sector politics. We end with a forward-looking reflection on the insights a political economy analysis can provide on key aspects of India's energy future and particularly a transition to renewable energy. We begin, however, by drawing out the high-level conclusions from across the state-specific chapters.

Development, Politics, and Reform: Every Unhappy State Is Unhappy in Its Own Way

The chapters in this volume represent, arguably, the first systematic effort to understand the interaction between politics and electricity outcomes across a broad swathe of Indian states. The cases show that while there are common outcomes across states, the combination of explanatory factors and their intersection with political processes is distinctive in each state. To paraphrase Tolstoy's famous observation about families in *Anna Karenina*, the case studies show that every unhappy state is unhappy in its own way. But the other half of Tolstoy's observation, that 'all happy families are alike', does not apply here. Where states have positively linked politics and electricity outcomes, the pathway typically involves engagement with features that are unique to the state.

Understanding state electricity outcomes, then, requires both multi-causal explanations and attention to path dependence. Thus, in Uttarakhand, the combination of low-cost hydropower, increasing industrial load, and a failure to address loss levels in the plains was critical to understanding the trajectory of the power sector. In Maharashtra, persistent demands for subsidies from key constituencies—farmers who were part of politically important sugar cooperatives—was balanced against the relative wealth of the state, but the ability to move beyond this equilibrium was stymied by persistent supply-side shocks. Both multi-causality and path dependence pose a challenge to electricity sector policy-making. They make it far less likely that abstract reform prescriptions conceived out of global experience, or simple mimicry of policy across states, will have the desired results.

To say that outcomes are diverse is not to say, however, that they are infinite. There are certainly empirical regularities across states, which we draw out in the remainder of this conclusion. Here, we focus on three sets of high-level conclusions, around development, politics, and reform that help provide insight into state specific trajectories.

Development

Continued poverty, low incomes, and a precarious existence for large numbers of Indians, mean that social welfare concerns continue to play a substantial role in shaping Indian electricity debates. Demands for tariff reduction are the most common empirical phenomenon observed across all states. At the same time, the demands for reliable electricity for industrialization are growing. In Maharashtra, for example, the political dominance of the agricultural cooperatives over power sector decisions is being challenged by industrial interests.

Indian electricity is likely to continue to be shaped by this tussle between social and industrial interests. In recent years, stimulated by the Electricity Act, the thrust of electricity policy has been to dis-embed social objectives from within electricity decision-making and focus the sector more directly on commercial and economic principles. Under this vision, social concerns would be addressed separately, perhaps through instruments such as direct benefit transfers.

The core issue is less the availability of instruments for social policy, however, and more the political credibility of promises to address social concerns around the provision of electricity. As demonstrated by the many instances of political mobilization around electricity, including in relatively wealthy states such as Maharashtra and Andhra Pradesh, many Indian citizens remain at economic levels where electricity prices make a material difference to livelihood prospects. In a context where the historical salience of electricity to Indian development outcomes remains powerful,[1] the political credibility of promises to address social concerns in electricity—whether directly or indirectly—has to be won, and not assumed. This is not to argue that the electricity sector should be run entirely as an instrument of social policy, blind to considerations of financial viability; Tamil Nadu's approach of eternally expanding subsidies has definite limits. But we do advocate recovering the idea of the electricity sector as an engine of development and empowerment, even while containing the spiral of growing cross-subsidies, exit from the grid, and declining quality and finances.

Politics

The state experiences suggest that social welfare concerns remain the starting point for Indian electricity politics, despite repeated efforts to bracket them. In India's democratic process, these concerns often take expression as competitive populism, particularly in electricity, which complicates the challenge of governing the sector. For example, the list of states that have experienced competitive tariff reduction at election time is long, and includes Andhra Pradesh, Karnataka, Gujarat, and Uttar Pradesh. Consequently, there is a larger question that pervades this study: in a poor country such as India, with persistent demands for social gains through access and subsidies, can reform occur in a context of competitive populism? Are the pressures to 'buy' votes through electricity sops always going to overcome long-term reform and change?

The cases discussed here suggest a nuanced answer. Sustained improvements in electricity outcomes are dependent on reform efforts that, over time, bring convergence between electoral and political outcomes. Developing this convergence may come with short term costs, which is why effective electricity reform frequently requires significant acts of political entrepreneurship. The electricity sector needs more savvy politics, not de-politicization.

Notably, an absence of competitive populism through single party governments or long incumbency has been no guarantee of successful electricity reform. This is illustrated by Odisha, West Bengal, and Bihar on the one hand, which all had long periods of stable governments but failed to provide electricity access, and on the other, by Delhi and Andhra Pradesh, both with highly popular and long-lived governments that nevertheless carried out politically unsustainable reform. Political stability can be useful, but is not the whole story. In Gujarat, political stability was enabling when mated with a sensible and politically informed reform process backed by some fortuitous fundamentals. In Bihar, constituencies were mobilized around enhanced electricity access through savvy politics enabled by the availability of low-cost power purchased from other states. While incumbency is no guarantor of successful electricity outcomes, it can, however, provide more political space to devise and implement state specific political strategies to bring about changes in electricity outcomes.

The specificity of political strategies is often driven by the particular mix of constituencies in the state. In Tamil Nadu, Andhra Pradesh, Punjab, and Maharashtra, farmers are a key constituency demanding subsidies; yet in Odisha, Jharkhand, and West Bengal, they are far less important because of low agricultural load. Indeed, in the latter set, there has been relatively little mobilization even for rural electricity access. In West Bengal and Andhra Pradesh, managing distribution company labour unions was important to reform.

State electricity politics can also be shaped by political considerations that originate outside the electricity sector. Particularly important is the ability of a state to attract and retain industry, which is salient to the importance of cross-subsidies in electricity sector finances. Attracting industry is only very partially a function of electricity and far more a function of other complex factors. Thus, Gujarat, Maharashtra, and Karnataka benefit from high industrial load, West Bengal and Uttarakhand struggle with attracting industry, and Jharkhand and Rajasthan struggle in its absence. The politics of agriculture—crop support prices, fertilizer and seeds pricing policies, and crop insurance—and the physical context for irrigation are other important contributors to electricity politics.

As we discuss in more detail later, there have been relatively few cases in India of a virtuous circle between electoral and electricity outcomes. Where it has been achieved, however, it has been based on creative and entrepreneurial political action.

Reform

The case studies provide an opportunity to reflect on two decades of state electricity distribution reform. Barring some notable exceptions, reform efforts failed to seriously engage state-specific political contexts but instead sought to carve out zones of depoliticized decision making. Instead, typically formulaic and technocratic reforms have brought about some transparency gains, but have not, by themselves, brought about the desired insulation from political pressures. This is not to say that technical or institutional changes are unimportant; but they are most useful when embedded in an explicit effort to shift the sector towards productive politics.

Odisha and Delhi are the only states to implement the full reform package of corporatization, unbundling, regulation, and privatization. These big bang, privatization-focused reforms have often operated under the assumption of forging political insulation, which has proved to be a fool's errand. In Odisha, the pioneer state, reform has completely unravelled with all four regional discoms having returned to public hands by 2015. With the benefit of hindsight, reform was never likely to be politically sustainable, because it was not tailored to the political conditions of the state. Specifically, the Odisha reforms systematically created disincentives for enhanced rural access, rather than incentivizing rural access, which could have brought political gains, as are being seen in Bihar. Delhi, the other pioneer, fared somewhat better. Reforms did lead to quality improvements with the promise of political gains, arguably briefly realized. But these gains materialized only by pushing the political costs down the road in the form of regulatory assets. The most ambitious, privatization-oriented reforms failed the test of political sustainability.

In another set of states, a subset of reform efforts was more closely tied to state-specific circumstances and internal management reform. In Gujarat, unbundling and creation of the regulatory commission, combined with feeder separation, provided the transparency and institutional structures for a politically backed bureaucracy to work to improve quality, and shift the state into a virtuous cycle. West Bengal provides another example of a tailored reform effort; bureaucrats made a deliberate decision to shift management practices internally rather than privatizing, by, for example, creating incentives for performance, improving data, and, critically, bringing labour on board. The result was to produce slowly improving outcomes. Similarly, in Bihar, introducing new top leaders and removing the risk to them of initiating new contracts enabled more effective management of the sector. In Andhra Pradesh, management reforms aimed at laying the ground-work for privatization proved useful even though privatization was shelved: incentives for operational reform, consumer satisfaction efforts, and decreases in field-corruption were all achieved. These examples illustrate a more general point: internal managerial reforms can frequently be a necessary and important part of reforms, but implementing them also requires sufficient levels of administrative capacity in the state to design and implement these changes.

In a set of reluctant reformer states, the reform prescription was followed but little changed in practice. These include MP, where reform took 12 years; Punjab, where the price of winning acceptance of reform was to change as little as possible; and Tamil Nadu, where reform led to a regulator that substantially coordinated with the executive. These reluctant reformers are overrepresented among states that have drifted into a vicious cycle of growing mismanagement, financial losses, and ever greater political demands.

Perhaps the most important lasting effect of reforms has been the entrenchment of a new institutional actor, the state electricity regulatory agency. Like with reform itself, the experience with regulatory agencies has been diverse. In some states, such as Tamil Nadu and Jharkhand, there were concerns that the regulatory agency was insufficiently independent from the executive, while in Delhi, the regulatory agency was perceived as actively oppositional, particularly in the case of one regulator. In some cases, such as Andhra Pradesh, the regulator was an important component of internal management reforms, particularly early on. The one consistent outcome that emerges across states is that the introduction of the regulatory agency has increased the transparency of the electricity institutional landscape. In addition, the regulatory agency, through information disclosure requirements and regular hearings, has created a space for greater civil society engagement in electricity governance. In particular, Maharashtra represents a case where civil society actors have been deeply engaged and used the regulatory forum to productively find solutions to political demands on the power system. Despite some gains, the results have nonetheless fallen short—Maharashtra's electricity system continues to operate in a relatively modest equilibrium.

Collectively, the key insights from the case studies suggest that reforms have been insufficiently informed by state-specific politics and the resultant compulsions of the sector. The next two sections address two dimensions of a framework for the empirical exploration of state politics and electricity.

Key Explanatory Factors for State Electricity Politics

While electricity outcomes are multi-causal, some of these same factors are important across multiple cases, even while they combine to give different, path-dependent outcomes. In this section, we revisit the framework laid out in the introductory chapter to highlight what we have learned about these key variables from the case studies. Our objective is to unpack the ways in which these factors have proved to be salient in specific empirical contexts, so as to inform their use in future policy analysis and studies.

Demands for Access and / or Quality of Service

Mobilizing rural constituencies to demand electricity access or, where access is already available, service quality, and then meeting those expectations, can provide a powerful source of political gain. Where an active demand for electrification emerged, as in Bihar (2012–17), West Bengal (2011–16), and in many of the already electrified states in earlier historical eras (as in Maharashtra and Tamil Nadu), savvy political actors capitalized on this potential by building a constituency on the basis of public goods provision. Bihar under Nitish Kumar's government exemplified this possibility: with lower caste constituencies mobilized to demand services after Lalu Prasad's government, Nitish Kumar's government was able to explicitly build political support by working to fulfil this promise.

The relationship between political gains and electrification takes a predictable form that has implications for state governments. Political gains are initially high because the benefits of electricity access are immediate and obvious to voters, while the costs are relatively low, both because up-front costs are often subsidized by the centre and because subsidy needs are low in the context of limited demand. However, as expectations increase for quality and quantity of supply and if a pattern of expectations is created around unsustainable subsidies, the political benefits become harder to reap. The lesson is that while low access states have low hanging political fruit available to them, there is a risk that, badly managed, electrification can sow the seeds of future political liabilities.

Given the considerable initial political gains, it is surprising that potential demand for access is often not politically expressed. In many states with low levels of electrification, such as Odisha, Jharkhand, Bihar (1990–2004), West Bengal, and Madhya Pradesh, political mobilization around the issue of access did not occur. One reason is that typically poor and un-electrified communities face challenges in politically mobilizing around electricity; Bihar, where explicit mobilization of low-caste communities occurred prior to the demand for electrification, is the exception that proves the rule. Another is that state governments may prioritize other objectives over political gains from enabling access, such as rent extraction in Jharkhand under an extremely unstable political regime, and revenue generation through electricity sales in Odisha. In some cases, electrification may progress without an explicitly mobilized constituency, such as when it is driven by central funds for rural grid extension, as has happened relatively recently in Odisha. Without a political commitment at the state level, though, there is a risk of de-electrification—where infrastructural investments fall into disuse and once-live wires go dark, as in the case of Bihar (1990–2004) and Madhya Pradesh.

In states with high levels of electrification, public demand is focused on better quality supply rather than access. In some states, there was active mobilization in favour of better quality, as in Gujarat (2002–16) and Delhi (2006–13), providing a political opportunity to generate a virtuous cycle. Winning political support by ensuring better quality is often a hard road to hoe, as it involves untangling historically entrenched interlocking patterns of poor quality, declining scope for cross-subsidies, declining finances, and lower investment. Delhi (2014–17) illustrates the continued political lure of subsidizing power and Andhra Pradesh's (2014–17) stealthy approach illustrates how concerns about the political risk of placing the upfront cost of transition on the consumer weigh heavily on decision makers. Further—as consumers are unable to assess the exact improvement in quality of supply beyond their personal experience, develop a resigned sense about not-perfect quality, or undertake their own measures to improve their own quality (for example, batteries, diesel gensets, and so on)—the political salience of quality of supply can fade over time. In other states, such as Karnataka (1999–2017), Gujarat (1990–2001), and Uttarakhand, a lack of mobilization for better quality supply confines the sector to a moderate equilibrium.

Demand for Explicit or Implicit Subsidies

The demand for subsidies is a central and arguably unavoidable aspect of electricity politics in India, as it has been in many countries undertaking rural grid expansion, and even more so in the context of low-income countries. Demand for *explicit* subsidies include mobilization by various groups for subsidized tariffs. Most of the public attention over the last several decades has been on subsidies for Indian farmers. But as the case studies show, subsidy demands have been made by a wide range of groups. Demand for *implicit* subsidies can take the form of direct theft and opportunities for graft where efforts to restrain these actions risk political costs.

In recent years, electricity policy debates have tended to gravitate to a view that all subsidies, particularly cross-subsidies, are problematic. Furthermore, when they lead to a cycle of distorted accounting as in the cases of flat rate tariffs and de-metering, or turning a blind eye to theft, they can undermine management of distribution utilities. But as the discussion below illustrates, appropriately managed, subsidies may also play a role in political transitions. Given their centrality to electricity politics in India it is important to understand the varied patterns of their use, rather than to dismiss them wholesale.

The empirical record on states' use of subsidies falls into three broad patterns: use of subsidies as part of a transition arrangement (Gujarat); a long-term accommodation (Karnataka, Andhra Pradesh, and Maharashtra) and a vicious cycle where rampant subsidies affect finances and quality (Uttar Pradesh, Rajasthan, Punjab, Tamil Nadu, and Madhya Pradesh). We discuss each in turn.

A key element in Gujarat's turn towards better quality power was an accommodation with key consumer groups, notably farmers, to shift towards a more restricted but higher quality, and predictable supply (that is, eight hours guaranteed supply during specific periods of the day) in exchange for lower costs. Over time, a virtuous cycle emerged in which citizens recognized superior quality and became more willing to pay higher costs. Continuing with subsidies while ensuring supply at a promised level of quality was a key part of the bargain.

In many other states, particularly those with a long track record of providing access, specific forms of long-term accommodation have been reached, shaped by state characteristics. In Karnataka, the accommodation is regional, with wealthier discoms subsidizing less wealthy discoms, plus support from a hefty government subvention. In Maharashtra, by contrast, public utilities have maintained subsidies but at the cost of quality of supply (through measures like predictable load-shedding), locking the state into a moderate equilibrium.

In a third set of states, the effect of subsidies has been consistently pernicious. In Rajasthan, Uttar Pradesh, and Madhya Pradesh, a vicious cycle has emerged in which demands for subsidies exert a heavy cost on discom functioning, producing unpredictable load-shedding, worsening financial and technical performance, and increasing debt. In Punjab the heavy cost of subsidies for farmers has been partially offset by increasing electricity duties and cess on other consumer categories in a cycle that is unlikely to be sustained. Tamil Nadu is a particularly extreme example, where demands for subsidies have extended to ever more disparate constituencies extending from farmers to fisheries. The exact form and ability to accommodate these demands is heavily informed by a particular state's financial space as well as constraints.

In addition to demands for explicit subsidies, demands for implicit subsidies—turning a blind eye to high theft levels (also limited metering, under-bill-recovery, and, to some extent flat-rate tariffs that make accounting easier and thereby enable theft)—have been a persistent pattern in many states. While this is normally prevalent in high access states, where patterns of theft have become entrenched, they can also occur in low-access states like Jharkhand, where an extractive rentier economy based on procurement processes has grown up around the electricity sector.

Among the explanatory factors described in this section, the political demand for subsidies is the most widely prevalent across states, and perhaps the most closely associated with mal-governance in policy discourse. The discussion here reinforces how widespread subsidy demand is, but also suggests a cautionary note: subsidies cannot be done away overnight, because they are deeply entrenched within state political economies, often shaped by state-specific political configurations or even geographic factors. Engaging politically sustainable reform of the electricity sector will likely require management of subsidies rather than their outright abolition.

Power Supply Costs

The risk of locking a state into purchase of high cost of power supply has periodically been a major concern, and one that shrinks the financial space available to discoms. In recent years, there has been a growing pattern of overinvestment in power generation, and a tendency towards a lock-in to high-cost power. Conversely having access to low-cost power provides considerable flexibility to states in dealing with political demands. However, as with the other factors, the ways in which low- versus high-cost power acts to constrain states can operate in very state-specific ways.

In one set of states, Uttarakhand, Karnataka, and Odisha, a transition from a legacy of low-cost hydropower to higher cost power de-stabilized an existing pattern of accommodation. In Uttarakhand, the inheritance of low-cost hydropower enabled the state to attract industry, but required subsequent investment in higher cost as the overall demand in the state outgrew the available low-cost supply. Other states have battled a legacy of high-cost power over the decades, often in response to overestimates of demand. Maharashtra, for example, has repeatedly been locked into high-cost power—the Enron episode in the mid-1990s and again from 2010 to 2015—that shrunk its room for accommodating pressures. In Delhi, contracts for high-cost power signed in anticipation of the Commonwealth Games in 2010 created upward pressure on tariffs, while in Rajasthan, high-cost power contracts were signed under allegations of crony capitalist relations. In Andhra Pradesh, by contrast, deliberate investment in new generation was a reaction to a decade of politically costly shortages in the mid-2000s. In yet other states, such as Odisha, investment in new generation capacity was intended as an explicit effort to forging an industrial strategy based on selling surplus power, even though electrification rates in the state remained low. Bihar provides the opposite example—growing electricity access has partially been enabled by purchasing low cost surplus power from other states, which remains a winning strategy as long as this surplus power is available at low costs.

This pattern of locking into high-cost power is not inevitable; accurate demand estimation is a necessary step for managing these pressures more effectively. Yet issues of power purchase costs often have roots beyond technical ones, extending to crony capitalist relations and industrial development strategies. Also, it is worth noting that locking into high-cost power severely ties a state's hands; benefits of fully exploring flexible demand response goes beyond economic gains, to also provide flexibility in managing demand politics.

Financial Space

If demands for access and subsidy constitute the political demands on the state, there is another set of factors, in addition to the cost of supply, that constitute the ability to manage those demands, particularly financially. This amalgam of factors we refer to as the 'financial space' available to the state—or metaphorically what we refer to as 'the breathing room' each state has with which to manage pressures. A state with greater financial space can better manage political pressures, either through accommodating them in the short term, or, more ideally, formulating a long-term resolution of political demands. These factors are an amalgam of (a) the ability to cross-subsidize which depends on load profile (proportion of industrial users) and the extent of open access utilization and/or captive power use that limits that cross-subsidy; and (b) extent of potential transfers from non-electricity sector fiscal resources, from either the larger state budget (typically possible in wealthier states) or the centre, to buffer the financial costs of electricity subsidies and/or mismanagement.

1. Industrial Load, Open Access, and Captive Power

The ratio of above to below cost consumers plays a large role in determining a state's financial space. Consequently, states with large or growing numbers of industrial and commercial consumers that are served by discoms have greater financial space to use cross-subsidies as a way to manage demands for subsidies from various other consumer groups. The ability to rely on large industrial load is one of the most important ways in which state electricity politics and economics is shaped by factors not directly under the control of the power sector, but rather by aspects of larger state political economy.

Gujarat, Maharashtra, Andhra Pradesh, Tamil Nadu, Karnataka, and Uttarakhand all have large industrial sectors, which has been an important enabler of their ability to cross-subsidize. For some states with low industrial demand, like Punjab, the effort to attract industries has led to lower tariffs for industry and further constraints on cross-subsidy. In some cases like West Bengal, where industrial consumers are directly served by dedicated companies (Jamshedpur Utilities and Services Company [JUSCO] and the Damodar Valley Corporation [DVC] in Jharkhand and Calcutta Electric Supply Corporation [CESC] in West Bengal), states are severely limited in their ability to cross-subsidize.

Even if states are able to attract industry, however, the benefits of doing so are diminished by implementation of open access. The case studies provide ample evidence that open access reduces a state's ability to manage political demands on the electricity sector by shrinking the available pool for cross-subsidy. With few exceptions, therefore, states in India have resisted implementing open access. As the Karnataka and Maharashtra case studies note, discom managers and others in the energy bureaucracy understand that allowing open access will threaten the delicate balance governing the state's distribution sector. Thus, even while there has been considerable frustration in policy circles about limited implementation of open access since the passage of the Electricity

Act in 2003, from a political vantage point, low levels of interest in open access from states are easily understood.

Captive power has similar effects. The steady turn of industrial consumers away from the grid and in favour of in-house generating units characterizes the power sectors of many states. Tamil Nadu and Maharashtra typify this, although the dynamic is present in almost the entirety of the country. Unlike the situation with open access, industrial consumers can decide on captive generation completely on their own without any say of the discom. From the discom's perspective, the load simply vanishes from the grid.

2. Direct Financial Support from State Governments or the Centre

Depending on their financial ability, many states in India provide direct subventions to distribution utilities. Andhra Pradesh, Punjab, Bihar, Karnataka, Delhi, Maharashtra, and Tamil Nadu all give fairly regular subventions, which are key factors in maintaining sectoral stability. In Bihar under Nitish Kumar, for example, the state government has given a subvention to cover the operational costs that are increasing because of rising levels of electrification, the latter underwritten by central funds. Apart from Bihar, though, the majority of states that provide direct government subventions are among India's wealthier states, which contributes to their ability to accommodate political pressures, such as for low tariffs. In the case of Delhi, for example, state government support has enabled discoms to respond to pressures for relatively high quality supply.

The central government has a long track record of providing direct political support, often considered a bail-out, of state power sectors, starting with the Accelerated Power Development Reform Programme and, most recently, UDAY. These efforts at providing financial space are often accompanied by requirements to reduce losses and implement various other reform measures, but have also been critiqued for providing a carrot but not much by way of a stick.

There are precious few instances of states using financial breathing room to change structural conditions so as to alleviate long-term political pressures. Uttarakhand arguably had an opportunity to do so, using its access to low cost hydro-power, but squandered this by failing to reduce loss levels in the plains and by locking itself into high-cost power to service new industrial buyers. Gujarat provides a more positive example, where feeder separation enabled transparency gains and better management of power to farmers. By contrast, states like Tamil Nadu have used successive bailout programmes only as a short term band aid. The uses to which financial space are put by a state are a significant determinant of its long-term prospects.

State Political Economy Outcomes: From Vicious to Virtuous Cycles

In opening this volume, we suggested that efforts to reform the electricity sector to improve outcomes are likely to founder, sooner or later, if they cannot generate political payoffs from change rather than requiring elected governments to bear political costs. Notably, this is not to suggest that these need to be immediate political payoffs, but there needs to be a convincing pathway to political gains. Nor is it to suggest that politics is restricted to electoral politics. Rather, political entrepreneurship that may include engaging with specific consumer groups to reach an accommodation (notably but not only with farmers), unlocking bureaucratic politics, and striking deals with labour unions are all important to the politics of electricity reform. The key point, however, is that seeking non-engagement with politics, or efforts at political insulation, are a chimera.

Based on the state cases, we suggest states can usefully be sorted into six categories, organized around two axes (Figure C.1). The primary axis along which we sort states is the nature of the relationship between political outcomes and electricity outcomes. At the positive end of the spectrum there is a *Virtuous Cycle* between the two: electricity outcomes, based on credible reform efforts, actually enhance political popularity, further incentivizing the political class to improve electricity outcomes. At the other end of the spectrum, states are in a *Vicious Cycle*: electricity and political outcomes negatively reinforce each other leading to seemingly endless deterioration of electricity quality and access. In between are states where the relationship between electricity and politics is partially de-linked, either because electricity consumption is sufficiently small that it does not drive politics, or, in a more significant set of cases, where a temporary accommodation has been reached to enable an equilibrium, even if a fragile one. For these *Accommodation*

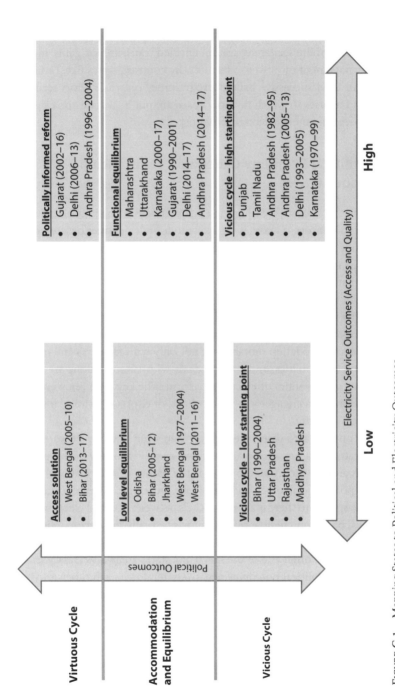

FIGURE C.1   Mapping States to Political and Electricity Outcomes
Source: Authors.

and Equilibrium cases, a key puzzle is to understand the state-specific accommodation that has led to the equilibrium, which may be at a relatively low level, or at a relatively high functioning level.

The second axis maps states on whether they have relatively high or low functioning electricity sectors. Low functioning states have low levels of access and, if higher levels of access, then extremely low service quality, with the inverse true for high functioning states. We separate out these two categories of states because the political challenges tend to be distinct for each.

In Figure C.1 we categorize states according to their location in these categories. Some states are listed in multiple boxes at different time periods, reflecting their movement across categories. Others remain in the same category across long periods. Understanding the reasons for stasis or for change within a state, and exploring why some states shift across categories while others remain stable sheds light on the political economy of electricity in states. The categorization of states across the six resultant boxes provides insight into the many patterns of state electricity politics and, significantly, when combined with the analysis of different drivers above, provides a diagnostic to take to state reform.

First, there is a seemingly obvious, but surprisingly seldom utilized, pathway to a virtuous cycle for low outcome states: promise and deliver on enhanced electricity access (*Access Solution*). In recent years, only Bihar, unambiguously, and West Bengal, more ambiguously, have explored this pathway. Bihar's push to electricity access under Nitish Kumar, and consequent political gains had an important precondition—the political mobilization of lower caste communities to demand services under Lalu Prasad Yadav, and the consequent de-centring of upper castes in Bihar's political firmament. In West Bengal, while the Communist Party of India (Marxist) (CPI[M]) took rural constituencies for granted, it was only after the rise of the Trinamool Congress (TMC) that rural constituencies were explicitly mobilized around access. This explicit dependence on mobilization may explain why this route is under-utilized, but it also points to an important avenue for an aspiring leader. Both cases also point to the challenges of successfully implementing this path. Bihar has wisely taken advantage of low-cost power available in the market, but risks repeating patterns of high loss levels observed in other states, and West Bengal is flirting with populist tariffs in a manner that risks undercutting the ability of the state to deliver on its promises in the long term. For states in this cluster, the key risk is locking into problematic patterns of subsidy demand or high-cost power even as they get diminishing political returns from access over time.

Second, for high energy outcome states, the pathway to a virtuous cycle is more contingent, because it frequently involves designing a politically feasible transition out of entrenched deadlocks (*Politically informed reform*). Of the three states that have shown signs of managing this transition, only one, Gujarat, has done so in a manner that appears politically sustainable. Gujarat's virtuous cycle was enabled by farmer acceptance of short-term curtailment of electricity as part of a larger promise of future improvements in agricultural supply, which it has steadily sought to deliver. Moreover, several conjunctural factors were also critical—an empowered bureaucracy backed by a stable government, high industrial load, and transparency through feeder separation. By contrast, Delhi is arguably the best exemplar of the standard reform model, and while the Dixit government did win some political gains from initial improvements in service quality, the trajectory of tariff gains, public suspicion of some private actors, and a growing estrangement from the regulator all contributed to unwinding the virtuous cycle. In Andhra Pradesh, management-oriented reforms had real effects on outcomes and contributed for a period to a virtuous cycle, only to be undercut by big bang privatization reforms that created politically unsustainable tariff expectations. For this cluster of states, the challenge is identifying risks to perpetuation of a virtuous cycle that undercut the complementarities between political wins and electricity wins.

Third, by far the majority of the states studied are stuck in a pattern of accommodation and equilibrium—whether low level or relatively functional (*Accommodation and Equilibrium*). However, even as they share this characteristic, much like with Tolstoy's families, they each are in a state of stasis in their own way and as an outcome of state specific factors. Odisha and Bihar (2005–11) did not have mobilized constituencies demanding power and continued to have low access levels. Jharkhand, in a climate of rapidly changing governments, treated the electricity sector as a source of procurement based graft, and was further hampered by limited industrial load it could access as a source of cross-subsidy. Higher performing states in the '*Functional Equilibrium*' category are even more complex, as they have developed state-specific and entrenched patterns of accommodation. This includes regional accommodation in Karnataka, and a continuous postponement of reckoning through creation of regulatory assets in Delhi and Tamil Nadu. The challenge for these states is to first identify the state specific accommodation, next create breathing room in the form of enhanced financial space, and then craft a political transition out of the existing entrenched position towards a virtuous cycle.

Fourth, a smaller but still significant number of states are in a pattern of negative reinforcement between politics and electricity outcome (*Vicious Cycle*). Whether starting from low levels or relatively higher levels of access and quality, these states are trapped in a negative spiral. Rajasthan faces growing demands for subsidy fed by competitive populism, which in turn has led to declining finances and subsidy, all exacerbated by investments in high-cost supply. In Punjab, despite a high starting point and growing prosperity, electricity subsidies to farmers have become baked into expectations, and are reinforced by successive parties, even as high-cost power pushes state finances into ever more parlous circumstances. The challenge for these states is to identify the key drivers of a vicious circle and find a way of first halting, and then reversing the cycle.

Taken together, the key explanatory factors in the previous section and the categorization of state political economy outcomes discussed here, are intended to provide a diagnostic with which to approach state electricity politics. The explanatory factors provide a roadmap to key variables for study, which are potential ingredients in knitting together state specific explanations for change. The categorization helps provide a way of making legible the relationship between electricity and political outcomes, and whether they are mutually reinforcing, undercutting, or locked into a stable, if unproductive accommodation. Ultimately, the intent is not to provide a mechanistic toolkit, but rather a framework for dialogue and understanding of how to map power, which is the first step to productively reforming electricity politics.

How Can Mapping Power Help Manage the Future of Indian Electricity?

Indian states are grappling with how to manage problems from the past even as the sector is poised for dramatic changes in the future.

Specifically, the two emerging factors impacting Indian states that are described in the introductory chapter—uncertain patterns of electricity demand growth, and technological changes leading to rapidly decreasing costs of renewable energy and scope for improved energy efficiency—have major implications for the future of the power sector in India. Mapping power is indispensable both to disentangling the past and preparing for the future. Here, we deploy the framework developed in the introduction, and the empirical insights gained from the chapters, to reflect on and pose questions about how Indian electricity will negotiate an increasingly complex future.

As discussed in the Introduction, a shifting demand scenario has led to a paradoxical situation in India today where the country has a power 'surplus' even as more than 40 million households live in the dark, and many more have highly unreliable supply.[2] Viewed from the perspective of sectoral politics, and the way in which they shape the institutions of electricity, the paradox melts away. The discoms, and their respective state governments, in an effort to limit their losses, have an incentive to only provide a minimal quantity and quality of supply to those grid-connected customers whose tariffs are less than the cost of serving them. They also have strong disincentives to connect new citizens to the grid, because almost all would also end up having below-cost tariffs. Simply calling for tariff increases to match costs in the context of poor service quality and low credibility of discoms to deliver improvements is unlikely to win voters consent. Resolving this situation requires delivering a credible pathway that appropriately sequences politically credible quality improvements and tariff increases. This in turn, requires financial space to design and implement reforms.

However, applying the analytical framework used for this volume suggests that the conjunction of continued slow industrial demand growth, which would limit the amount of cross-subsidies available, and a continued central government push for expanding access and providing reliable supply to all citizens (that is, the 2017 announcement of a newly restructured 'Saubhagya' scheme to achieve this end), could lead to a further financial squeeze on the distribution companies.[3] The growing tendency across many states towards lock-in to high-cost conventional power contracts increases the challenge of delivering on this pledge.

Periodic bailouts, the most recent of which is UDAY, are intended to ameliorate this squeeze, by increasing the financial space available to discoms and enable them to implement various reform measures: reducing losses, enhancing energy efficiency, reducing fuel costs, and so on. Such programmes can, indeed, be useful, by creating the conditions under which state governments can undertake more systematic reforms aimed at generating a virtuous cycle between political and electricity outcomes. However, this potential is only realized if the breathing room generated by bailout programmes is explicitly and intentionally used to bring about long-term changes that fundamentally alter key factors—political demands for access and subsidies, or factors that enable demand pressures to be addressed, such as supply costs and fiscal space. Instead, the case studies suggest that at the state level, UDAY has been used as a limited effort to bring about technical changes at best, or at worst, to postpone the day of reckoning. There is only limited evidence that UDAY is tied to specific efforts to change either the political demand pressures of tariffs or to deal with foreboding new developments such as the lock-in to high-cost power in some states.

The second factor described above, decreasing costs of renewable energy (RE) power, has the potential to complicate the political economy of India's power in multiple ways. First, because of the modular and scalable nature of renewable energy, it has the potential to exacerbate the problem created by uncertain demand. As described in the 'Introduction', deployment of small-scale renewable energy is already cost-effective and is growing among industrial and commercial users.[4] If these customers reduce their consumption from the grid, it would leave a shrinking cross-subsidy base, much as was feared in the early 2000s with the introduction of open access. If utilities are forced to raise costs on an ever-declining cross-subsidy base, thereby encouraging more exit, a particularly Indian form of the 'utility death spiral' will result.

Moreover, lost-cost RE, in the short run, could amplify the negative effects of a surfeit of relatively higher-cost conventional electricity supply described above. Even as RE enables flight from the grid, a growing requirement of cross-subsidy to cover the costs of surplus capacity would accelerate that flight. There is even a risk that conventional power interests could lobby for systematic disincentives to promote renewable energy despite its falling costs and environmental benefits. Indeed, discoms across the country are already resisting the implementation of net-metering policies—allowing consumers to sell self-generated electricity back to the grid—because of this fear.[5]

However, viewed differently and backed by the right policies, low-cost RE could be turned into a political opportunity to address the challenge of access. To do would require enabling states to proactively address the problem of high-cost long-term contracts in order to take advantage of increasingly cheap RE. While the financial costs of this measure cannot be ignored, the history of electrification globally provides evidence that there are considerable positive economic spillovers to enhanced access. If these economic gains can be unlocked, it opens the door to a new perspective, one that focuses on bridging a short term financing gap to yield long-term structural changes in the sector thereby delivering political and economic payoffs. This requires foregrounding the understanding of electricity as a development engine that can generate long-standing social and political gains, as discussed earlier, rather than only as a sector to be bent to short-term commercial principles. While the solution is not easy or trivial, framing the question around the political gains that come from development enhancing electrification rather than narrow short term accounting is the first step.

Notably, if accomplished, a transition to lower cost RE would bring about a long-term decrease in a key variable affecting the political economy of power—the cost of supply—creating a structural situation of more financial space to address political demands. In particular, it would reduce the pressure to raise retail tariffs or to depend on cross-subsidies, thereby lowering the incentives for industrial and commercial users to turn to behind-the-meter RE. Alternatively, RE provides a distinct option with which to engage key constituencies, for example by providing farmers the up-front costs to adopt behind-the-meter RE, thereby reducing their long-term political claims on the electricity system.

Another technology driven change—energy efficiency measures enabled by information technology—provide an uncertain effect on electricity politics. By enabling more useful energy services per unit of electricity, energy efficiency could decrease political demand for subsidies if targeted at customers that are being subsidized, expanding the breathing room to design and plan transitions. However, if energy efficiency programmes are targeted to the commercial and industrial consumers—their cross-subsidy potential will reduce thereby worsening the financial space for discoms.

The grid retains its central importance in this version of the future energy world, not just in a technical sense—for balancing load and ensuring stability of RE and expanding the scope for energy efficiency—but in a political sense. If, as seems likely, better-off consumers are best placed to take advantage of new technologies, each casting off from the grid as an island of electricity affluence, the challenges of keeping the lights on for the rest will only grow. Latecomer states with low levels of grid expansion will be even further disadvantaged as there will be diminishing incentives to build a grid to serve only poor customers. In the near future, it will be important to pay attention to how the grid spreads or constrains the spread of economic and political power along with electrical power. Accurately mapping power now is necessary if Indian states are to ensure a reasonable electricity future for all, not just some, of its citizens.

Notes and References

1. Sunila S. Kale, *Electrifying India: Regional Political Economies of Development* (Stanford: Stanford University Press, 2014).

2. Government of India, 'Shri R.K. Singh launches "Saubhagya" Web-Portal—a Platform for Monitoring Universal Household Electrification', *Press Information Bureau*, Ministry of Power, available http://pib.nic.in/newsite/PrintRelease.aspx?relid=173548 (accessed on 17 April 2018).

3. Government of India, 'PM Launches Pradhan Mantri Sahaj Bijli Har Ghar Yojana "Saubhagya"', *Press Information Bureau*, 25 September 2017, available http://pib.nic.in/newsite/PrintRelease.aspx?relid=171101 (accessed on 17 April 2018).

4. Nikita Das et al, 'India's Journey towards 175 GW Renewables by 2022: A July 2017 Update', July 2017, Prayas (Energy Group), available http://www.prayaspune.org/peg/publications/item/356-india-s-journey-towards-175-gw-renewables-by-2022-version-2-0.html (accessed on 17 April 2018).

5. Bloomberg New Energy Finance, 'Accelerating India's Clean Energy Transition', November 2017, available https://about.bnef.com/blog/accelerating-indias-clean-energy-transition/ (accessed on 17 April 2018).

Index

Editors and Contributors

Editors

Navroz K. Dubash is professor at the Centre for Policy Research in New Delhi, India, where he coordinates the Initiative on Climate, Energy, and Environment. His research and writing include energy politics and governance in South Asia, global and comparative national climate politics and policy, and the governance of water in South Asia. He has edited the *Handbook of Climate Change and India* (2012), among other works. Dubash is an active participant in the Intergovernmental Panel on Climate Change and has served on advisory committees to the Government of India on energy, water, and climate change.

Sunila S. Kale is a faculty member at the Henry M. Jackson School of International Studies at the University of Washington, Seattle, USA, where she also serves as chair and director of the South Asia Studies Center and Program. Her teaching and research focus on the politics and political economy of India and South Asia, history and politics of energy and electricity, and development studies. She is the author of *Electrifying India: Regional Political Economies of Development* (2014), and is at work on two new books: the first on development and displacement in eastern India's mining economies, and the second (with Christian Lee Novetzke) on yoga as a political idea.

Ranjit Bharvirkar is a Principal at the Regulatory Assistance Project where he directs the India programme. He has more than 16 years of experience in conducting electricity policy analysis and providing technical assistance to state- and national-level policymakers in the US and India. He recently contributed to India's Renewable Electricity Roadmap Initiative undertaken by the Government of India. He has worked as a researcher at Lawrence Berkeley National Laboratory and Resources for the Future, California, USA, on various topics such as energy efficiency, impacts of environmental policies on the power sector, and others. He has co-authored several journal articles, conference papers, discussion papers, and book chapters. He holds a bachelor's degree in civil engineering from the Indian Institute of Technology Bombay, India, a master's in environmental engineering from North Carolina State University, USA, and a master's in public policy from the University of California at Berkeley, USA.

Contributors

Jonathan Balls works on economic, energy, and development geography. His research has focused on the off-grid solar power market in the northern Indian state of Uttar Pradesh, bottom of the pyramid capitalism, frugal innovation and entrepreneurship, and electricity market governance. He completed his DPhil at the School of Geography and the Environment, at the University of Oxford, England, and holds a BA in Geography from the University of Cambridge, England. Jonathan started a three-year 'New Generation Network' post-doctoral position at the Australia India Institute, University of Melbourne, Australia, in November 2016. In this position, he is doing research on mapping ecosystems for frugal innovation in India, and on the governance of micro-grids.

Rohit Chandra is a doctoral student at the Harvard Kennedy School, Massachusetts, USA, studying energy policy and economic history. He is currently writing a political and economic history of the Indian coal industry from 1960–2015. In the past, he has worked with the Centre for Policy Research, New Delhi, Center for Advanced Study of India in Philadelphia, and Brookings India.

Elizabeth Chatterjee is a postdoctoral scholar in the Department of Political Science at the University of Chicago, USA. She holds a doctorate in international development from the University of Oxford, England, where she was a fellow of All Souls College. Her work has appeared in *World Development*, *Contemporary South Asia*, and the *Journal of the Royal Asiatic Society*, among other venues. Her research interests include the transformations of the contemporary state, environmental and energy governance, and the politics of quantification. She has also held visiting fellowships at the University of California, Berkeley, and the University of California, Irvine, USA.

Mrigakshi Das is a doctoral scholar at the School of Business Management at Xavier Institute of Management, Odisha, India. He has done his B.Com and M.Com from Gauhati University, Assam, India. His research interests are power sector issues mainly focusing on managerial and financial issues.

Kalpana Dixit teaches political science at the Tata Institute of Social Sciences, Tuljapur campus, Maharashtra, India. Her doctoral research focuses on politics of regulatory reforms in electricity sector in Maharashtra. Earlier, she was associated with Prayas, a public advocacy organization in Pune, and was involved in policy research and advocacy on issues of public concern. She is a recipient of the Indian Council of Social Science Research (ICSSR) Doctoral Fellowship and was selected for the Graduate Fellowship programme of the Watson Institute for International Studies, Brown University, USA. Her research interests include politics of policy, role of civil society in shaping public policy, state and society relationship, and political economy of infrastructure development.

Megha Kaladharan is a lawyer and works at Trilegal, an Indian law firm, in its energy and infrastructure practice. She focuses on regulatory and policy challenges in the Indian renewable energy sector and has experience in working with the private sector, government agencies, and think tanks. She has also advised multilateral agencies and governments on the development of public private partnership projects in the South Asian infrastructure sector, most recently on an energy efficient street lighting project. She holds a BA LLB (Honours) degree from the National Law School of India University, Bengaluru, India.

Mahaprajna Nayak has worked as an editor (with publishing and now newspaper), research scholar, and teacher. He has dabbled with different disciplines to develop an interdisciplinary understanding of contemporary social and political issues. He has been observing developments in data-centric urban governance for a few years now. However, his deeper engagements have been with language and pedagogy, among students learning English as third language.

Hema Ramakrishnan is a faculty member at the Madras School of Economics, Tamil Nadu, India, since 2001. Her research over the last three decades has mostly been on various issues relating to the electricity sector—optimal pricing, financial performance, restructuring, and regulatory approaches in different countries and their implications. Currently her research agenda is to address the challenges faced by rural consumers in having adequate access to electricity. She is engaged in understanding the institutional and political economy aspects of the sector and suggesting an institutional way forward to promote improved and affordable access to energy for rural consumers, while addressing environmental sustainability and financial viability.

Siddharth Sareen is a postdoctoral research fellow at the Centre for Climate and Energy Transformation and the Department of Geography, University of Bergen, Norway. He leads a project on solar energy governance (2017–2020), which focuses on sustainability transformations in Portugal through attention to changes in institutions, accountability relations, and infrastructure. He has worked on the political economy of energy transitions, on resource politics in conflict regions, and on integrated development approaches, in multiple regions of India, and sees these as enduring interests. Following an Integrated MA in Development Studies at the Indian Institute of Technology Madras and a Double PhD in Development Studies and Forest and Nature Management from the University of Copenhagen, Denmark, and Padova University, Italy, Siddharth has previously completed postdoctoral appointments at the Institute of Economic Growth in India and Erfurt University in Germany, and held visiting researcher positions at Aarhus University, Denmark and the Nordic Institute for Asian Studies, Denmark.

Md Zakaria Siddiqui is research fellow at Sydney based Institute of Economics and Peace. He is applied social scientist with quantitative focus. Curretly his work is focused on developing quntitative measures and correlates of positive peace. He has consistently contributed on contemporary debates on Indian social and economic development such as energy, health, employment, minorities, and scientific diaspora.

Meera Sudhakar is a PhD student, currently working in the broad area of electricity policy at National Institute of Advanced Studies (NIAS). Her research interests are broadly in interdisciplinary enquiries that lead to better empirical and theoretical understanding of development policies. Her PhD work is attempting to understand a technology policy through a historical and sociological lens. In the past, she has worked at the Center for Study of Science Technology and Policy (CSTEP), Bengaluru, India, and is also an enthusiastic birder.

Ashwini K. Swain is executive director at Centre for Energy, Environment & Resources, New Delhi and a visiting fellow at Centre for Policy Research, New Delhi. Earlier, he has worked for CUTS Institute for Regulation & Competition, Agence Françaisede Développement, University of York, UK, University of Wisconsin-Madison, USA, and National Institute of Public Finance and Policy, New Delhi. His research interests include political economy of electricity, interface between energy service needs and climate mitigation goals, and water-energy-food nexus, especially in Indian context. He has also worked on public participation in service delivery, and has a keen interest in political economy of India and political analysis. In addition, he has been actively engaging with civil society organizations and public agencies at national and subnational level on these issues. He holds a PhD in Politics from University of York, UK and MPhil and MA degrees in Political Studies from Jawaharlal Nehru University, New Delhi, India.